James Still in Interviews, Oral Histories and Memoirs

Contributions to Southern Appalachian Studies

1. *Memoirs of Grassy Creek: Growing Up in the Mountains on the Virginia–North Carolina Line.* Zetta Barker Hamby. 1998

2. *The Pond Mountain Chronicle: Self-Portrait of a Southern Appalachian Community.* Leland R. Cooper and Mary Lee Cooper. 1998

3. *Traditional Musicians of the Central Blue Ridge: Old Time, Early Country, Folk and Bluegrass Label Recording Artists, with Discographies.* Marty McGee. 2000

4. *W.R. Trivett, Appalachian Pictureman: Photographs of a Bygone Time.* Ralph E. Lentz, II. 2001

5. *The People of the New River: Oral Histories from the Ashe, Alleghany and Watauga Counties of North Carolina.* Leland R. Cooper and Mary Lee Cooper. 2001

6. *John Fox, Jr., Appalachian Author.* Bill York. 2003

7. *The Thistle and the Brier: Historical Links and Cultural Parallels Between Scotland and Appalachia.* Richard Blaustein. 2003

8. *Tales from Sacred Wind: Coming of Age in Appalachia. The Cratis Williams Chronicles.* Cratis D. Williams. Edited by David Cratis Williams and Patricia D. Beaver. 2003

9. *Willard Gayheart, Appalachian Artist.* Willard Gayheart and Donia S. Eley. 2003

10. *The Forest City Lynching of 1900: Populism, Racism, and White Supremacy in Rutherford County, North Carolina.* J. Timothy Cole. 2003

11. *The Brevard Rosenwald School: Black Education and Community Building in a Southern Appalachian Town, 1920–1966.* Betty Jamerson Reed. 2004

12. *The Bristol Sessions: Writings About the Big Bang of Country Music.* Edited by Charles K. Wolfe and Ted Olson. 2005

13. *Community and Change in the North Carolina Mountains: Oral Histories and Profiles of People from Western Watauga County.* Compiled by Nannie Greene and Catherine Stokes Sheppard. 2006

14. *Ashe County: A History.* Arthur Lloyd Fletcher (1963). New edition, 2006

15. *The New River Controversy.* Thomas J. Schoenbaum (1979). New edition, 2007

16. *The Blue Ridge Parkway by Foot: A Park Ranger's Memoir.* Tim Pegram. 2007

17. *James Still: Critical Essays on the Dean of Appalachian Literature.* Edited by Ted Olson and Kathy H. Olson. 2008

18. *Owsley County, Kentucky, and the Perpetuation of Poverty.* John R. Burch, Jr. 2007

19. *Asheville: A History.* Nan K. Chase. 2007

20. *Southern Appalachian Poetry: An Anthology of Works by 37 Poets.* Edited by Marita Garin. 2008

21. *Ball, Bat and Bitumen: A History of Coalfield Baseball in the Appalachian South.* L.M. Sutter. 2009

22. *The Frontier Nursing Service: America's First Rural Nurse-Midwife Service and School.* Marie Bartlett. 2009

23. *James Still in Interviews, Oral Histories and Memoirs.* Edited by Ted olson. 2009

James Still in Interviews, Oral Histories and Memoirs

Edited by TED OLSON

CONTRIBUTIONS TO SOUTHERN APPALACHIAN STUDIES, 23

McFarland & Company, Inc., Publishers
Jefferson, North Carolina, and London

ALSO OF INTEREST

James Still: Critical Essays on the Dean of Appalachian Literature, edited by Ted Olson and Kathy H. Olson (McFarland, 2008)

LIBRARY OF CONGRESS CATALOGUING-IN-PUBLICATION DATA

Still, James, 1906–2001.
James Still in interviews, oral histories and memoirs / edited by Ted Olson.
    p. cm. — (Contributions to Southern Appalachian studies ; 23)
    Includes bibliographical references and index.

    ISBN 978-0-7864-3698-9
    softcover : 50# alkaline paper ∞

    1. Still, James, 1906–2001—Interviews. 2. American literature—Appalachian Region—Biography. 3. Appalachian Region—Intellectual life. I. Olson, Ted. II. Title. III. Series.
PS3537.T5377Z46   2009
811'.54—dc22 [B]   2008047784

British Library cataloguing data are available

©2009 Ted Olson. All rights reserved

No part of this book may be reproduced or transmitted in any form or by any means, electronic or mechanical, including photocopying or recording, or by any information storage and retrieval system, without permission in writing from the publisher.

On the cover: inset James Still (courtesy Hindman Settlement School—used with permission); focal James Still 1955

Manufactured in the United States of America

McFarland & Company, Inc., Publishers
  Box 611, Jefferson, North Carolina 28640
    www.mcfarlandpub.com

Table of Contents

Preface 1

Introduction: The Source of the River:
  James Still's Literary Legacy • TED OLSON 3

I. Still in His Own Words: Interviews and Oral Histories

James Still: Portrait of the Artist as a Boy
  in Alabama • WADE HALL................................. 13

An Interview with James Still • J. W. WILLIAMSON 23

"Daring to Look in the Well": A Conversation • JAMES STILL
  and JIM WAYNE MILLER...................................... 44

An Interview with James Still • TOM and CAROL FRENCH-CORBETT
  and LOIS KLEFFMAN 58

An Interview with James Still • LAURA LEE and FOXFIRE STUDENTS..... 73

Pattern of a Writer: Attitudes of James Still • DEAN CADLE........... 98

James Still on His Life and Work: An Interview • JUDITH JENNINGS... 133

James Still: Conversation with a
  Kentucky Writer • L. ELISABETH BEATTIE 155

Conversations with James Still • FRANK EDWARD BOURNE 176

II. Still on Other People's Minds: Memoirs

Obscurity Begins Back Home for Kentucky's
  James Still • RENA NILES 185

"I Write Because I'm Unhappy When Not Writing"—
  James Still • GURNEY NORMAN.............................. 192

"...Some things a man does just for himself": In Regard
  to Writing, That's the Philosophy of Gifted Kentucky
  Author-Poet James Still • JOE CREASON 195

Before Saying Yes: Discovering James Still's
  "First Sweetheart" • ANN W. OLSON......................... 201
James "Lucky" Still: A Fortunate Man • CAROL BOGGESS............ 205
Sgt. James Still's Gold Castings • JACK D. ELLIS.................... 216
Both Ends of a Walnut Log: The Correspondence of James Still
  and Jesse Stuart • JAMES M. GIFFORD *and* ERIN KAZEE.......... 219
Why Does Knott County Send the Largest Ratio of
  Graduates to College? • JESSE STUART....................... 233
Personal Memories of James Still and Jesse Stuart:
  These Noted Writers Had a Great Effect on a
  Young Knott Countian • WILLIAM HENRY YOUNG 236
Green Peppers and a Straw Hat • JAN WALTERS COOK 240
Travels with Mr. Still: In Search of
  Richard Jefferies • JUDITH JENNINGS 242
Still Writing After All these Years: An Author Who Began
  His Career Nearly a Half Century Ago in Hindman, Kentucky,
  Is Being Rediscovered and Honored • SHIRLEY WILLIAMS............ 248
Writing About James Still: "Be ye in the world, but not
  of the world" • HERB E. SMITH............................... 257
A Memoir of James Still • JONATHAN GREENE...................... 261
In Remembrance of James Still • LINC. FISCH 265
Terrain of the Heart • LEE SMITH................................ 276
Remembering James Still • SILAS HOUSE......................... 279
Remarks at James Still's Funeral (May 1, 2001) • LOYAL JONES 283
His Side of the Mountains: The Enduring Legacy
  of Southern Poet James Still; An Interview
  with Editor Ted Olson • JEFF BIGGERS 285
Reflections on Pappy Still • TERESA L. PERRY REYNOLDS............. 292
On the Occasion of James Still's 100th Birthday • HAL CROWTHER ... 298

Index 303

Preface

TED OLSON

Few authors from the Appalachian region have received more critical acclaim than James Still, a native of Alabama and adopted son of the Kentucky hills where he spent all his adult life, from 1932 until his death in 2001. Dean Cadle, in the short preface originally published with his essay "Pattern of a Writer: Attitudes of James Still" (*Appalachian Journal* 15.2 [Winter 1988]), noted:

> Philosopher Irwin Edman considered Still "a lyric talent of the first order." Peter Wilson (*San Francisco Chronicle*) wrote that "with no pretensions to being a prophet, he has unmistakingly the qualities of an artist," and Percy Hutchinson (*New York Times Book Review*) ... wrote: "His language is the homespun of his ancestors, the warp from Chaucer, the woof out of the English Bible."

Still's works were the subject of *James Still: Critical Essays on the Dean of Appalachian Literature* (McFarland, 2007), the first book-length collection of scholarly essays to explore his literary legacy. This new book, *James Still in Interviews, Oral Histories and Memoirs*, is intended to help readers more fully understand and appreciate the many facets of Still's literary voice and vision.

The first section of this book features written transcriptions of virtually all of the formal interviews in which Still participated and oral histories that he offered. Most of these interviews have been difficult to locate since their initial publication, having originally been published in periodicals with limited distribution. It is hoped that through this compilation of all such interviews in one continuous document that is chronologically organized, the reader may detect changes in Still's attitudes toward his life, his work, and his increasingly central role in Appalachian literature and in the field of Appalachian Studies. In essence, the republication of such interviews collectively will serve as an important vehicle for illuminating the development of Still's literary persona.

The second section of the book presents a collection of non-academic essays that explore Still's work not from critical or scholarly perspectives (the approach found in the essays in *James Still: Critical Essays on the Dean of Appalachian Literature*), but rather from personal perspectives—not critical essays but memoirs. Including previously published though hard-to-find pieces as well as never-before-published pieces, the memoirs—written by people who knew Still the person as well as Still the author—serve to enhance Still scholarship by providing significant information on and analysis of one of the Appalachian region's most important cultural figures. This section of the book provides a forum for a wide range of people—all of whom have been inspired in some way by James Still's life and work—to reflect upon the author's influence on their own individual lives, or to comment upon the nature of Still's community and regional roles. Taken together, these memoirs—some of which were written by such widely known figures in Appalachian literature and Appalachian Studies as Loyal Jones, Gurney Norman, Jonathan Greene, Lee Smith, Hal Crowther, Silas House, and Herb E. Smith—serve as testimonials to a life well lived. Like the interviews in the first section, these memoirs about James Still will be valuable to future students of Still's work in that they will provide keen insights into the author's mind and soul.

Still's literary legacy has received additional attention recently because of the appearance of other scholarly books. In late 2007, Kentucky-based Wind Publications published Claude Lafie Crum's book-length study, *River of Words*, which illuminated Still's literary persona and traced his influence upon younger Appalachian writers. Soon to appear will be Carol Boggess' long-awaited literary biography of Still.

In *River of Words*, Crum asserted that Still's literary legacy is most evident in the work of certain authors associated with Appalachian literature. Naming a range of authors as having been deeply influenced by Still, Crum eloquently illustrated that Still was a central figure in Appalachian literature, and such an argument certainly upholds the validity of the sobriquet applied to Still for some years now: "the Dean of Appalachian Literature." Yet, my hope is that future scholars of Still's work will follow the lead of earlier champions of Still (such as Dean Cadle, Jim Wayne Miller, and Cleanth Brooks, among others), whose analyses of Still's work acknowledged his central role in Appalachian cultural studies but who also underscored the universality of his work. As Robert West observes in his essay on Still's poetry (included in *James Still: Critical Essays on the Dean of Appalachian Literature*), Still's work has not yet reclaimed the national prominence in which it was once esteemed. The collections of Still's papers now held at the University of Kentucky and Morehead State University will play a leading role in Still scholarship, and a happy outcome of such scholarship would be the drawing of increased national and international attention to Still's work. It is my hope that both books from McFarland—*James Still: Critical Essays on the Dean of Appalachian Literature* and *James Still in Interviews, Oral Histories and Memoirs*—will combine to make the case that James Still, while remaining a central "Appalachian author," is also an author whose work is worthy of a much broader audience.

Introduction: The Source of the River: James Still's Literary Legacy

TED OLSON

In the last decades of the nineteenth century and the early decades of the twentieth century, a number of authors wrote novels, short stories, and poems that assessed Appalachia and Appalachian culture, and most of those authors were not born or raised in the Appalachian locales of which they wrote. Some of those literary works—particularly those written by authors Mary Noailles Murfree and John Fox Jr.—were widely popular across the U.S. Since the emergence of the interdisciplinary academic field known as Appalachian Studies during the late 1960s and early 1970s, scholars have observed that such late nineteenth and early twentieth century literary works borrowed from and catered to nationally held stereotypes about the region's people and culture. Murfree and Fox and their contemporaries produced stereotype-laden accounts of Appalachia in part because stereotypes sold magazines and books and in part because the authors' own impressions of the region were heavily influenced by stereotypes circulated in American popular culture and transmitted principally by the media. Had their knowledge of Appalachia been primarily based on personal connections, those "local color" writers surely would have rejected the stereotypes, and would have recognized that such stereotypes compromised the veracity of their work. Unfortunately, many outsiders (including writers and journalists), throughout the twentieth century and into the new millennium, continued the pattern of exploitation begun by the local color writers by making money through manipulating the images of Appalachian people.

James Still was born outside the eastern Kentucky locality in which he lived most of his 94 years, but he was no "outsider." His purpose for settling in Knott County, Kentucky, during the Great Depression was not to exploit his new neighbors, as many local color writers and industrialists had done, or to "reform" his neighbors, as many missionaries and social workers had done. To be sure, Still came to Knott County because he wanted and needed work—he accepted a librarian job at the Hindman Settlement School. But Still stayed there because he found the place beautiful and its people fascinating. He would soon begin to write about that place and those people, and he subsequently became known as one of the leading writers of the "Appalachian literary renaissance," a literary movement conterminous with the Great Depression which was comprised of a new generation of literary figures whose writings about Appalachian subjects were based less on stereotypes and more on personal experience in the region.

While born outside of the community about which he wrote, Still avoided the pitfalls of local color writing—stereotyping and imprecise representation of Appalachian dialect—because he wrote out of his own direct contact with the region and its people, as he conveyed in his essay "A Man Singing to Himself":

> "How did you avoid 'hillbilly' writing?" is another question I frequently hear. Those who ask that question have in mind the stereotypical mountaineer and his dialectical speech as rendered by several authors of fiction in the past. My answer is, I was hardly aware of those authors, didn't have access to their books. My experience was with the folk themselves. As for handling dialect in my writings, in the effort to represent the way folk actually talk: well, dialect of any sort on a printed page has always bothered me. Peculiar spellings can't account for the tone of voice, the body language, or the intent behind the statement. My aim is to invoke speech, to try to get the true sound of it to happen in the reader's head. Aberrant spelling rarely accomplishes it. I try to preserve the "voice" of the speaker.

The people of Knott County came to view Mr. Still as a valued member of their community. The writing he generated in eastern Kentucky neither sensationalized nor sentimentalized his neighbors' regionally distinct way of life, and thus Mr. Still did not break the trust he had forged between himself and those neighbors. He wrote empathetically about Appalachian people because he was their colleague at the Hindman Settlement School, he was their neighbor, and he was their good friend. His writings—within all the genres in which he worked—reflect how well he knew those people. Mr. Still resisted preconceived notions; he wished simply to observe the people and places around him and to reflect upon the subtleties of their lives and of their culture. He generally avoided public recognition for his literary output, as that would have imposed artificial barriers between himself and his neighbors. Although he happened to live in and to write about eastern Kentucky, Still's literary evocations of the Cumberland Plateau and of the folklife he witnessed therein constitute some of the finest writing about any region in the U.S.A. Given his innate sensitivity to the nuances of regional culture, it might be surmised that, had Still chosen to reside elsewhere—say, in Texas, where he once speculated that he might move—he would have written well about that place.

During the latter half of the twentieth century, Still was known outside Knott County primarily as the author of the novel *River of Earth* (1940), which generations of readers have enjoyed and which many scholars and students have identified as a classic literary response to the economic and social realities of the Great Depression as it was manifested in Appalachia. Still, however, was far from a single-work author, having produced another novel, numerous short stories, several children's books, a folklore study, and many poems. Indeed, Still displayed remarkable skill in all of the literary genres in which he worked. His fiction continues to attract critical attention; his poetry, which was arguably the foundation for all his literary output in other genres, continues to attract new readers today; his folkloric writing is respected for its keen insight into pre-industrial Appalachian life; and his children's literature is widely loved.

Born July 16, 1906, and living into the next century, James Still lived longer than virtually all of the others among his acclaimed generation of American literary figures. Author Hal Crowther maintained that "James Still was the last — and least known — of America's 'Greatest Generation' of writers." While not read nationally, Still attracted considerable attention during his later years within Appalachia and across Kentucky for his stylistically distinctive literary works, virtually all of which were set in eastern Kentucky yet which explored universal themes.

Integrally associated with eastern Kentucky and eventually receiving the sobriquet "the Dean of Appalachian Literature," Still was born and reared in east-central Alabama (Chambers County). Attending college at Lincoln Memorial University (in Harrogate, Tennessee), Vanderbilt University (in Nashville, Tennessee), and the University of Illinois (in Champaign-Urbana, Illinois), Still subsequently moved, in his mid–20s, to Kentucky during the early years of the Great Depression. Calling the Cumberland Plateau home until his death on April 28, 2001, Still lived primarily in Knott County (either at the Hindman Settlement School in Hindman, or 11 miles from that town in a century-old log house on Wolfpen Creek). Despite the public's longstanding perception of him as a hermitic figure, Still was always a citizen of the world. He served three years in Africa and the Middle East for the U.S. military during World War II; he taught in the 1960s at Morehead State University in Morehead, Kentucky; and, later, while based in Knott County, he gave frequent readings and talks across Kentucky and Appalachia and often traveled to other states and other nations both to conduct research and to experience other places and other cultures. As much as he loved his adopted home in Knott County, Still was always curious about the rest of the world.

Best known as the author of the acclaimed novel *River of Earth*, published by Viking Press in February 1940, Still also wrote numerous short stories, many of which initially appeared in such prestigious periodicals as *The Atlantic*, *The Saturday Evening Post*, and *Virginia Quarterly Review*. Still's short stories were eventually incorporated into several book collections, including *On Troublesome Creek* (1941), *Pattern of a Man and Other Stories* (1976), and *The Run for the Elbertas* (1980). He received numerous honors for his fiction: *River of Earth* was co-recipient (along with Thomas Wolfe's *You Can't Go Home Again*) of the Southern Authors' Award in 1940, while several of Still's short stories were included in the anthologies *O. Henry Memorial Prize Stories* and *Best American Short Stories*.

An equally vital component of Still's literary productivity was his poetry. Still published poems in many of the most respected periodicals in the U.S., including *The Atlantic*, *Esquire*, *The New Republic*, and *Poetry*, and his poetic output would be compiled in four books: *Hounds on the Mountain* (1937), *River of Earth: The Poem and Other Poems* (1982), *The Wolfpen Poems* (1986), and *From the Mountain, From the Valley: New and Collected Poems* (2001). Poetry was certainly Still's longest-lasting literary interest. One of his earliest poems, "Dreams," saw print in April 1931, more than four years before the publication of any of his fictional works. Indeed, Still developed his unique literary voice — today associated mainly with his fiction — through the writing of poetry. Approximately one-third of the poems in Still's final collected poems volume (*From the Mountain, From the Valley*) had already been written — and many of those poems had already been published — when, in 1936, Still's first significant work of fiction (the short story "All Their Ways Are Dark") was accepted for publication by a literary periodical (*The Atlantic*). While his productivity in the writing of fiction slowed after the 1950s, Still continued to place new poems in respected literary periodicals into the 1990s. One of the Still poems most beloved by contemporary readers, "Those I Want in Heaven with Me Should There Be Such a Place," was written and published in the early 1990s.

Upon their publication, Still's first three books — *Hounds on the Mountain*, *River of Earth*, and *On Troublesome Creek* — were reviewed (favorably, more often than not) in a wide range of periodicals, from *Time* magazine and *The Saturday Review of Literature* to *The Southern Literary Messenger* and *The Boston Evening Transcript*. Additionally, his early work garnered praise from some of the nation's most celebrated authors. In *The Saturday Review of Literature*, William Rose Benét reviewed Still's first book, *Hounds on the Mountain*, asserting that Still's poetry "is all very simple and direct, but also natural and authentic. But that is not to be taken as meaning that it is not the language of poetry as distinguished from the language of prose. It is, in fact, the sure speech of poetry." While other critical responses to Still's poetry were less favorable, authors and critics uniformly lauded *River of Earth*. Marjorie Kinnan Rawlings described that novel as "vital, beautiful, heart-breaking and heart-warmingly funny," while Delmore Schwartz called it "a symphony." Robert Frost enjoyed *River of Earth* so much that he later invited Still to attend the dedication of Amherst College's Robert Frost Room.

Stephen Vincent Benét's review of *River of Earth*, which appeared in the periodical *Books*, was particularly insightful in that Benét articulated a central issue which, then as now, requires addressing in any interpretation of Still's work, the question of whether that work is of strictly regional interest or whether it possesses universal merit. Benét commented that Still's novel was "rich ... with salty and earthy speech, the soil of ballad and legend and tall story.... [Y]ou can call it regional writing if you like — but to say so is merely to say that all America is not cut off the same piece."

The critical reaction to *On Troublesome Creek* was less glowing, and most critics saw the short stories in that collection as essentially miniaturized restatements of plot-lines and character types previously explored in *River of Earth*. For example, William Jay Gold, in a 1941 review published in the *New York Herald Tribune*, asserted that *On Troublesome Creek* was essentially an extension of *River of Earth*, calling the short story collection "a footnote to the author's one novel *River of Earth*.... [T]he locale is the same, there is evident the same feeling for effective and vivid detail, together with the sureness in handling dialect that help to make the novel an outstanding contribution to our regional literature." Gold may not have interpreted Still's short stories as independent artistic statements, but his response to *On Troublesome Creek* identified Still as a leading figure in American regional literature. Another critic, who signed a 1941 *Christian Science Monitor* review of *On Troublesome Creek* with the initials M.W.S., was less supportive of Still's short stories, claiming, "The first group [of stories in *On Troublesome Creek*] ... make up the bulk of the book, and they could indeed serve as the framework for a novel of considerable stature, if Mr. Still were ever to feel inclined to expand his work beyond the excellent, but undeniably repetitive, tales which have occupied him hitherto."

Had Still read such reviews, he might well have been discouraged that his work was not being examined on its own aesthetic terms or valued as work worthy of the widest possible audience. At this time in his career, though, another concern was occupying his thoughts: World War II.

For his literary endeavors during the period of his greatest literary productivity, Still received two Guggenheim Fellowships and was invited to participate in the Bread Loaf Writers' Conference (located in Ripton, Vermont), the MacDowell Colony (Peterborough, New Hampshire), and Yaddo (Saratoga Springs, New York). While staying at these literary retreats, he met a number of the leading American writers of that era, including Robert Frost, Katherine Anne Porter, Carson McCullers, Paul Green, John Gould Fletcher, and Robert Francis; several of these writers became lifelong friends and supporters.

Still's initial burst of literary activity was curtailed by his involvement in World War II. His actual time in service lasted from 1942 to 1945, but that experience continued to affect him for years — so much so that, after his return to eastern Kentucky, he wrote comparatively little for an extended period. Through the 1970s, Still farmed at Wolfpen Creek, worked as a librarian at the

Hindman Settlement School, and taught at Morehead State University. While not writing as prolifically as he had in the 1930s, Still continued his lifelong practice of reading voraciously, devoting hours each day to perusing a range of books on such diverse subjects as Mayan culture, mountaineering, and the history of warfare, as well as to investigating countless books of literary interest.

Renewed attention to Still's work resulted from the confluence of several events, including the appearance of Dean Cadle's influential article on Still in *The Yale Review* in December 1967, a 1968 paperback reprinting of the 1940 edition of *River of Earth*, and the emergence of the interdisciplinary academic field of Appalachian Studies during the late 1960s and early 1970s. During the mid– to late–1970s, his short stories and *River of Earth* were republished in new editions by Frankfort-based Gnomon Press (*Pattern of a Man and Other Stories*) and the Lexington-based University Press of Kentucky (*The Run for the Elbertas*). Thereafter, Still's literary reputation expanded across Kentucky and Appalachia. Newfound interest in his work rekindled Still's enthusiasm for publishing his work. His most popular books from this period containing new material—as opposed to his collections of older work incorporated into his Gnomon Press and University Press of Kentucky collections—were primarily intended for young readers: *Sporty Creek: A Novel about an Appalachian Boyhood* (1977), which Still compiled from revised, previously written short stories; *Jack and the Wonder Beans* (1977); and *An Appalachian Mother Goose* (1998). Other books from this phase of Still's career included three collections of folklore that he had gathered from the people he had met in eastern Kentucky—*Way Down Yonder on Troublesome Creek: Appalachian Riddles and Rusties* (1974), *The Wolfpen Rusties: Appalachian Riddles and Gee-Haw Whimmy-Diddles* (1975), and *The Wolfpen Notebooks: A Record of Appalachian Life* (1991). During this period, Still received several literary awards, including the Marjorie Peabody Award of the American Academy and Institute of Arts and Letters, the Kentucky Arts Council's Milner Award, the Southern Fiction Writer Award from the South Atlantic Modern Language Association, and the Appalachian Book of the Year Award from the Appalachian Writers Association. Additionally, several writing scholarships were named after Still in recognition of his pioneering role in Appalachian literature. In 1995, he was named the State of Kentucky's first official poet laureate.

It is hardly surprising, given the unique trajectory of Still's literary career (characterized by a sudden, brilliant emergence and then a long period of relative silence), that only two scholarly studies of his works—Dayton Kohler's 1942 comparative study of Still and Jesse Stuart, and the aforementioned *Yale Review* essay by Dean Cadle—were published before the "rediscovery" of Still in the 1970s. Since the 1970s, the author's work has been widely valued for its aesthetic integrity as well as for its representation of a world and a way of life that new generations of readers have perceived as being endangered if not extinct.

In addition to being aesthetic masterpieces and important historical documents, James Still's writings may serve as an excellent vehicle by which to correct the widespread national (and, indeed, international) stereotype of Appalachian people — an image largely manufactured by the media via local color novels, print and broadcast journalism, "hillbilly" recordings, Hollywood movies, syndicated television programs, and comic strips. The teaching of Still's works to a more broad-based audience would not only promote underappreciated works to a wider readership, but would also expose diverse readers to a poignant yet unsentimental depiction of the Appalachian region and its people.

I

STILL IN HIS OWN WORDS: INTERVIEWS AND ORAL HISTORIES

James Still: Portrait of the Artist as a Boy in Alabama

WADE HALL

Preface

When I moved to Kentucky in 1962 from Gainesville, where I was teaching at the University of Florida, I was familiar with a number of Kentucky-based authors—Robert Penn Warren, Jesse Stuart, Harriette Simpson Arnow, Elizabeth Madox Roberts, and James Still, as well as earlier writers like John Fox, Jr., and James Lane Allen—all of whom I assumed were native Kentuckians. I was correct, except for one, James Still, who had been born almost a generation before me three counties northeast of where I was born in Alabama. To readers of Still's poems and fiction, it seemed that they were surely written by a native of the Kentucky mountains.

Nevertheless, James Still brought his birth and his upbringing with him from Alabama when he arrived in Knott County, Kentucky, in the Summer of 1932. Indeed, writers carry their birth places around with them all their lives. A character in a story by Elizabeth Madox Roberts, "In the Mountains," says it very well. A young boy leaving his native mountains to find freedom and fortune in the flatlands meets an old man coming back to the mountains after a lifetime away, and the old man says to the boy: "Hit don't matter how far you go and how long you stay, hits what you done as a youngun that makes you what you are." Or as James Still has said, "Who we are, where we came from, what our ancestors did before us, and where we lived and how we lived has much to do with what we might compose in verse and story."

Or as Mr. Still said to me at my kitchen table in Louisville some six years ago, "After you're about six years old, you've picked up just about everything that makes you what you are—your speech patterns and attitudes. Even now I can see my parents physically present in me. I have my father's hands and my mother's fingernails. At family reunions I look about and I can see little pieces

Wade Hall. *James Still: Portrait of the Artist as a Boy in Alabama*. The King Library Press, 1998. Reprinted with permission.

of myself all around me. After my father died, I came to my home in Kentucky and realized I was my father." Even more to the point, he said, "Although I've written almost nothing specifically about my native state, I nonetheless consider myself an Alabama writer because—for better or worse—I brought Alabama with me when I came to Kentucky. Furthermore, people are about the same deep down once you get to know them and get beyond their external differences. Maybe one reason I felt so immediately at home in the Kentucky mountains was the fact that my mother was from the mountains of north Georgia. Maybe a reason I've never written fiction about Alabama is that I felt too close to it, and I was pained by it. I don't think I would have become a writer if I had stayed in Chambers County, Alabama. Yet I had what I would call a happy childhood, surrounded by caring parents and other relatives."

The portrait which follows shows James Still as a young writer-in-the-making while getting born and growing up in the rolling fields and creeks, the timberlands, the schools and churches, the courthouse and the stores of Chambers County between July 16, 1906, when he was born at home in his mother's bed, attended by a relative, a Dr. Gaines, and the fall of 1924, when he headed north to Harrogate, Tennessee, and enrolled as a freshman at Lincoln Memorial University. I have based it on many hours of taped interviews and conversations with Mr. Still in various places, ranging from a classroom at Bellarmine College in Louisville to the front seat of my car as we drove some 450 miles down Interstate 65 to his old home-place in Alabama in 1993. Because I have grown fond of oral biographies, I have shaped his own words into a self-portrait.

James Still: A Self-Portrait

>Those, those were my days,
>My thought and my ways.
>How did I stand the times?
>Read my tales, spin my rhymes.

Let's start out with some ancestry and vital statistics. My mother was Lonie Lindsey, and my father was James Alexander Still. He always signed himself J. Alex Still. His parents were William Watson Still and Annie McLendon. Her parents were James Benjamin Lindsey and Carrie Jackson. My ancestors were of English and Scotch-Irish stock and settled in Virginia, the Lindseys at Berryville and the Stills near Cumberland Gap. I believe that both sets of ancestors fought for the Revolution and were given land as a reward, the Lindseys settling in north Georgia and the Stills in east Alabama. When my mother was a girl their kitchen floor was packed earth. Her family lived in the gold country, and her father mined just enough gold to fill his teeth. Later, when a tornado destroyed their home, they moved to Alabama. My mother was 16.

My parents married in 1893 and homesteaded in Texas, where my first two sisters were born. Then they moved back to Alabama and Papa ran a drugstore for a while and boarded the schoolmaster in order to learn the Latin required for a druggist. He planned to return to Texas, but one of my sisters died of scarlet fever and Mama refused to leave. Papa never got over his Texas fever and liked to dress in Western boots and hat, and we often ate sourdough bread.

When I was a boy I heard a lot of talk about Texas, and I always thought of Texas as our once and future home. But about the closest I ever came was when I was stationed for a while at San Antonio during the Second World War. My parents' old farm is now a part of the Fort Hood military reservation.

Papa's main profession was veterinary medicine, though a more appropriate term would be horse doctor. He had little formal training for his profession, except for a few short courses he took at what is now Auburn University, which is nearby. He was also a farmer and a horse trader. He once told me, "Son, I've never cheated anybody in my life, except in a horse trade. And that doesn't count because it's a game."

Papa seemed to know all the horses in Chambers County. I think that was because he was either present at their birth or doctored them when they were sick — or both. Every time he passed a horse, he spoke and raised his hat, as if he were addressing a friend — as indeed he was. Papa was also the rabies officer for the county and gave shots to dogs. In those days, that would be a life-threatening job. After he was bitten three times, he would never dare to catch one. Luckily, he usually had veterinary students from Auburn doing their internships under him, and they would hold the dogs while Papa stuck the needles in.

Papa was fair-complexioned, red-headed, and kept his full head of hair until his death. His eyes were as blue as a wren's egg. And he was a handsome man. One of my aunts kept reminding me, "Too bad you're not good-looking like your daddy." Papa also had a wonderful voice. I don't remember him singing in church, but I heard him many a time singing off by himself an old Baptist hymn called "Walking in the King's Highway." Except for his little bit of veterinary training, Papa didn't have much formal education. He used to say I had a long childhood because I went to school so much. He only got as far as "baker" in his blueback speller.

When I was born on July 16, 1906, my parents were living on Double Branch Farm near Lafayette in Chambers County in east central Alabama, which has on its eastern border the Chattahoochee River, and across it the state of Georgia. My name was James Alexander Still, like my father, so I was a junior, but I started signing myself James Still to avoid confusion with Papa and to keep him from opening my mail.

Before me, my mother had had five girls. I was the first boy. After me, she never had another girl. Before it was over, the count was five girls and five boys. This is the full list: Lois, Elloree, Nixie, Lonie, Inez, James, William Comer, Tom Watson, Alfred, and Don. Nixie was the one who died of scarlet fever when she was about seven. William Comer was named after an Alabama governor, and Tom Watson was named after a local politician who became a congressman and a senator. Don was my half-brother, who was born to my father's second wife after my mother died. Except for Elloree, who moved to Florida, and Inez, who moved to New Orleans, all my brothers and sisters lived out their lives in Chambers County.

Aunt Fanny was our black wet nurse, and she helped Mama tend to us. We loved her completely. When I got big enough, I'd slip off to her house and she would let me sop syrup out of a bucket lid. When mama sent somebody after me, Aunt Fanny would pretend to hide me under her bed. Her common law husband was named Porter, and he was white for his race. He had been struck by lightning twice, which we believed was the cause.

One of my first memories is of picking cotton at the age of four in a sack my mother made for me. Papa had said I could go with him on the wagon to the cotton gin if we finished a bale that day, so I kept urging my sisters to pick faster. We made it. I did go to the gin with my father and lost my cap up the suction tube.

When I was five my Grandma Still died and we moved in with Grandpa and my maiden Aunt Enore. The farm was near Marcoot between Pigeon Roost Creek and Hootlocka Creek. That was about the time I fell and stuck a rusty nail in my stomach, from which I finally recovered, though I had to learn to walk a second time. With so many children coming along, in our family once you learned to stand alone, you were treated like an adult.

I was a quiet but independent child, so I'm told, and didn't like to be fondled. I wouldn't allow my aunts or other kissing relatives to smack me. I was known as the one you didn't kiss. Despite my standoffishness, they generally liked me. I was the one who was always welcome to go and stay long periods with my aunts and uncles. My brothers and sisters preferred to stay at home.

Grandpa Still's house was a typical planter's house built before the Civil War — gray, with sand mixed in the paint, large rooms, high ceilings, an attic filled with the past, and a kitchen and dining room set back and away from the living quarters as a precaution against fire. I remember very well the boxwoods around the front steps and bordering Grandma's flower beds. I can still smell the cape jasmines that were brought to fragrance with buckets of water thrown over them on summer nights.

A year later, when I was six, we moved to the Carlisle Place two miles out of Lafayette on the Buffalo Road. Within a year we were living in a house newly built and mortgaged on forty acres of land. It was a typical middle-class house of the time — roomy, with a hall down the middle, veranda halfway around. From a low hill on the place we could see the Talladega Mountains to the north and to the south, though we couldn't see them, were the Buckelew Mountains, where Joe Louis (Barrow) was born in 1914. In time, after moving north and acquiring the surname of his stepfather he became a famed boxer.

On the Carlisle Place we all worked in the fields, including Papa, when he was not out tending to a sick horse or cow, and Mama, when she was not cooking or doing house work. We usually had a black man come and help with the plowing in the spring, but then it was up to us children to do most of the field work. Cotton was our main crop, but we also raised sugar cane, sorghum, and corn. On long, hot days the rows seemed to stretch to infinity. To protect themselves from freckles and suntan, my sisters greased their faces and necks with cream, wore stockings on their hands and arms and wide-brimmed straw hats on their heads. Only fieldhands were suntanned and freckled. My sisters did not work within sight of the road.

When the boll weevil came to our cotton fields, we walked the rows and picked them off and dropped them to their death in cups of kerosene. We also picked potato bugs and dug chufas, a nut grass with a bulb we ate because it tasted like cocoanut. We ate the enemy.

We took our seasonal work in the fields as something we expected to do. My younger brothers never worked in the fields, and my sisters and I only after school and on Saturdays during peak seasons—chopping and picking cotton, May and September. One day my sister Inez, who was hoeing cotton in the row next to mine, began to tell a story which lasted for hours. It sounded like a true story, and I thought it was. It made the long hours and hot sun bearable. When I learned it was a story she made up as she went along, I was amazed. At that moment in my life, my horizon expanded beyond what I could see and experience and into the enchanted kingdom of my imagination. By her example, Inez had showed me that I could make up my own stories. And I did.

One day one of my sisters brought home a book from school about a boy and his dog and his sled. They read it over and over to me until I knew every word in the book. Finally, I started to school when I was seven at the "college" two miles down the road in Lafayette. In years gone by, it had actually been a sort of college, but in my time it only took us through the fifth grade and was greatly in need of repair. One night the roof of the gymnasium fell in. Three of my sisters and I walked to school everyday carrying our lunch of two biscuits and bacon. My first teacher was Miss Porterfield, who wrote my name on my desk with chalk, handed me an ear of corn, and told me to outline it with the grains. By the end of the day, I could write my own name. For the first time, I knew what my name looked like.

One of my classmates in the first grade was a city boy named Clyde McLendon. One day he told us little country boys that at his house he had two spigots. You could turn one and it would run cold water, and you could turn the other and it would run hot water. None of us had ever seen such a marvel, and we didn't believe him. So he took a bunch of us over to his house to the back porch where the spigots were. Lo and behold! He turned one on and cold water came out. He turned the other on and hot water came out. It was a great mystery to us all.

I was a small boy for my age and was the only one who had to stand on a box to reach the blackboard. Nevertheless, on Class Day I stood up in chapel and recited Robert Louis Stevenson's "Birdie with a Yellow Bill" and brought down the house, though I later discovered it had little to do with my oratorical skills. My knee pants were unbuttoned. On Field Day I ran in the sack race, and Inez won the fifty-yard dash and received a glorious box of chocolates. Some thirty years later, Miss Porterfield told me she remembered my class and the names of every child in it. Then she looked at me and added, "I never thought *you* would be the one!"

Chambers County is not exactly a crossroads of history, but it has been connected to some distinguished families. Woodrow Wilson's grandfather taught school in the old Presbyterian church, and Stonewall Jackson's father-in-law was pastor there for a while. Indeed, I felt very much a part of our most important historical event, the Civil War — the War Between the States, as it was commonly called. Grandpa Still had lost a finger to a Yankee bullet. Grandma Lindsey's first husband was named Green, and he was fatally wounded in the North Georgia campaign against Sherman. Before he died, someone brought him home in a wagon. I heard Grandma tell that he looked so bad she didn't even know him when he got home. She saw him leaning over the fence, and she went over and picked him up and carried him inside the house. But he didn't live long. After he died, she married my grandfather who was three years younger than she was. He was an orphan and had never seen his father and therefore, according to their belief, he could cure thrush, which was a mouth fungus. He was raised by an uncle, who one time got angry with him and whipped him severely on his legs with a lash, which he also used on his slaves. When Grandpa Lindsey was an old man in his eighties, the scar tissue on his legs broke down and he began to bleed.

I remember vividly the war stories told and retold by the Confederate veterans who reminisced on Grandpa Still's veranda. On Confederate Memorial Day in school, we would have several veterans talk in chapel about their war experiences, and we would sing Confederate songs like "Rose of Alabama," "Lorena," and "The Bonny Blue Flag." Then we students marched with "bonny blue flags" to the cemetery to decorate the graves of our dead heroes. Of course, we didn't understand what the war was all about, but we were sure we would win the next time. Years later I began to visit the war's battlefields, preparing myself to write my own Civil War novel. It was to be based on the prison at Andersonville, Georgia, which was only about a hundred miles southeast of Lafayette as the crow flies, but alas MacKinlay Kantor got there first.

At home we had four books: the Bible, *The Anatomy of the Horse*, *The Palaces of Sin, or the Devil in Society*, and a large book with its back cover missing, called *The Cyclopedia of Universal Knowledge*. *The Palaces of Sin* was an inventory of sins to be avoided at all cost, including drinking and playing cards. From *The Cyclopedia of Universal Knowledge* I got my first liberal education, for it contained information on subjects ranging from philosophy and history to the pruning of fruit trees and rules for letter writing. It also included poems, and from its pages I memorized "Ozymandias" and Cleopatra's swan song, "I am dying, Egypt, dying." The horse book and the Bible did not engage my attention nearly as much.

Occasionally, I saw a silent picture show, like *Damon and Pythias* and *The Kaiser, the Beast of Berlin*. When World War I ended, a truck load of revelers drove through town shouting "The war is over! The war is over!" One day a teacher gave me a ticket to a Chautauqua program that included a classical guitar performance and the popular lecture, "Acres of Diamonds," which is about mining the treasures in your own back yard. When a circus came to town, our class learned to spell *elephant*, *lion*, and *tiger*. Sometimes Lafayette was a stopping place for famous people like novelist Jean Webster, author of *Daddy Long Legs*, the politician William Jennings Bryan, and the warden of Sing Sing, whose name I have forgotten. Once Papa had me shake hands with Alabama's Governor Comer. The big event of the year was Christmas, when Santa Claus left us children perhaps an apple, an orange, a few peppermint sticks, and a handful of nuts. Once I was lucky and got a toy pistol.

Two events I witnessed as a boy helped make me a lifelong liberal. Early one morning I attended a gruesome hanging in front of the county jail, and it turned me against capital punishment. Later, in my teens, I saw a Ku Klux Klan initiation, which turned me against prejudice in any form.

Blacks were the permanent underclass, but the county allowed two black men to vote. One was "Old Black Joe," our school janitor, and the other was Green Appleby, a barber who served only whites. I remember two other blacks with great fondness: "Puss" Irwin, the court house janitor, and his assistant, Joe Barrow, the father of Joe Louis. In those days ice water was very uncommon, but in the court house there was a water fountain into which blocks of ice were placed. On especially hot days our teacher would march us over and Puss Irwin would hold each of us up to the fountain to get a drink of ice water. I doubt if he ever drank any of the cold water because it was a fountain that he could not drink from legally. I'm sure there was no ice in the fountain marked "Colored." When my father died, the wake was held in my sister's home in nearby Fairfax. There I met one of Joe Louis's daughters, who was my sister's cook.

For a couple of years we lived in town in the Judge Norman house, owned by a family to whom we were distantly kin. It was a huge house with many rooms, surrounded by a spacious lawn with flaming crepe myrtles and sweet magnolias. We could also smell the cotton seed oil being processed in a nearby plant, and we could hear the laughter and singing coming from the black quarters, where we were told the people were carefree and content. Another neighbor was "Cotton Tom" Heflin, the politician after whom one of my brothers was named.

When the First World War ended, cotton prices fell disastrously. We were living then on the Carlisle Place when our farm mortgage was foreclosed, and we moved about twenty-five miles east to Shawmut, a mill town on the Chattahoochee River where most of the people worked in the textile mills, doing mindless work spinning and weaving for slave wages. We lived on Lanier Avenue, or "Boss Row" as it was called, and my father served as veterinarian for the townspeople who kept cows and horses in their backyards.

In junior high school I played basketball. I also read Balzac's *Father Goriot*, against the librarian's advice, and it was sensory revelation. Until then, about the only fiction of value that I had read was *Treasure Island*. Inspired by Balzac, I began to write my first novel about boats and sailors and whales—about which, of course, I knew nothing. I'd never even seen a boat larger than a bateau, and I'd never seen a sailor or whale or the sea. The novel was not a success. It wasn't even completed. I was more successful with my essay on insect control, which won second prize in a *Birmingham News* contest. The first prize winner recommended insecticides. I suggested birds. When I was eight or nine, I wrote a story on a school tablet with a pencil. Recently, I found it and read it again and decided the author showed some promise. When I was in the ninth grade, we moved on down the Chattahoochee Valley to Jarrett Station, and I attended Fairfax High School. I also published my first poem in *Boys' Life*, "A Burned Tree Speaks."

Chambers County didn't have much of a literary tradition. I never knew anybody who ever did any serious writing. It was not until graduate school that I became acquainted with our most important author, Johnson Jones Hooper, a journalist and humorist of the Old Southwest who created a realistic rascal named Simon Suggs. A lot of critics have called Suggs the literary father of my character, Uncle Jolly, in *River of Earth* and *Sporty Creek*. But the two characters are not kin — at least not blood kin. Uncle Jolly is, however, distantly related to one of my great grandpas and one of my numerous cousins. Like many of my characters he is unlettered but not ignorant, and like all of them, he is largely a creation of my imagination.

When I was a boy we never traveled much and seldom left the county. One time I went with my scout troop to Atlanta, and I've since been to Birmingham and Mobile once or twice. To this day, I've never been to Tuscaloosa. But as a boy I read about distant places and I heard the trains blowing in the night, and I yearned to go where they were going. My chance finally came when I finished high school. I applied to go to the Berry school in Rome, Georgia, where I could work and support myself and study at the same time; but they turned me down. Then one day near the end of my senior year, one of my teachers who was the son of a dean at Lincoln Memorial University showed me a catalogue of that school, where a boy like me could work his way through. It was located near Cumberland Gap at Harrogate, Tennessee, and had been founded after the Civil War as a tribute to an area that had remained loyal to the Union and was named in honor of the Kentucky-born President who had saved the Union.

In the fall of 1924, therefore, when I was eighteen, I left home with sixty dollars in my pocket that I had earned as an office boy at the textile mill and as a paper boy for the Atlanta *Constitution*. When I arrived at the college, I was but a few miles from where my Still ancestors had settled several generations before. I did not know it, of course, but I was also headed in the direction of Knott County, Kentucky, little more than a hundred miles across the Cumberland Mountains to the northeast. Later, I would find there a home where I could live and write from 1932 to the present. Knott County was even more backward than the Chambers County that I had left. It was almost inaccessible, with no trains and almost no roads. There were only three cars in town when I arrived, so the bad roads didn't affect many of us. Papa had taught me to drive when I was a boy, but I was never to own a car until I was fifty years old. Despite the primitive conditions I found in Hindman and Knott County, I immediately knew that I had found my final and literary home.

During all the years that have passed since I left Chambers County, I have kept in close touch with my family. Until a few years ago we had a family reunion each year on the first Saturday after the 4th of July at White Plains just north of Lafayette. But now the Alabama I knew doesn't exist any more. Chambers County has more people and more highways. Most of the land is in tree farms. There are few row crops to be seen. I can hardly find a parking place on the court house square. Most of all, I have no brothers and sisters to visit. They're all gone now. My brother Alfred was the last. When he died, I wrote this poem I call "On the Passing of My Brother Alfred":

> After this death it will
> be easier
> To pass beyond, to go
> where he went,
> Out of this light into
> a greater light.

I can never forget those people who made me, who shaped me toward the man and writer I was to become. Now I want to pay tribute to some of them who meant so much to me when I was but a boy in Alabama. I tried to say my love for them — and for two of my special pets— in this poem:

Those I Want in Heaven with Me Should There Be Such a Place
First, I want my dog Jack,
Granted that Mama and Papa are there,
And my nine brothers and sisters,
And "Aunt" Fanny who diapered me, comforted me, shielded me,
Aunt Enore who was too good for this world,
And the grandpa who used to bite my ears,
And the other one who couldn't remember my name —

There were so many of us;
And Uncle Edd—"Eddie Boozer" they called him-
Who had devils dancing in his eyes,
And Uncle Luther who laughed so loud in the churchyard
He had to apologize to the congregation,
And Uncle Joe who saved the first dollar he ever earned,
And the last one, and all those in between;
And Aunt Carrie who kept me informed:
"Too bad you're not good-looking like your daddy";
And my first sweetheart, who died at sixteen,
Before she got around to saying "Yes";

I want my dog Jack nipping at my heels,
Who was my boon companion,
Suddenly gone when I was six;
And I want Rusty, my ginger pony,
Who took me on my first journey—
Not far, yet far enough for the time;

I want the playfellows of my youth
Who gathered bumblebees in bottles,
Erected flutter mills by streams,
Flew kites nearly to heaven,
And who before me saw God.

Be with me there.

An Interview with James Still

J. W. WILLIAMSON

The following conversation is based on a taped interview that took place in D. Hiden Ramsey Library at the University of North Carolina at Asheville on July 12, 1978.

Williamson: You have said about the way you have lived and written and avoided publicity that you have "remained intact." What exactly did you mean by that?

Still: Well, if I ever made such a statement, which I doubt, I would like to retract it. Consider my geographical location in Knott County, Kentucky. There has been a road past my home a car can pass over for only a dozen years. During nearly four decades of living there, only two journalists ever made their way to my door. They were welcomed. (My brother once asked, "Why do you live in such a hell of a place?" A Letcher County editor said, "This place is heaven!") Until recently no newspaper in the region ever mentioned me; my books were not for sale in any store. I was not news. It's true I failed to go to New York to accept the award of the American Academy of Arts and Letters and I did not accept the invitation to the Phi Beta Kappa poet at Columbia University in the early 1940s because I didn't have bus fare and, as I thought, suitable clothes to wear at such functions. Faded denims were not the all-purpose garments they are nowadays. And I might spike another rumor while I have the floor: I'm not a hermit. (I do spend more time alone than most. I'm a pretty good fellow when nobody is around. It's when I'm with people that my bad qualities surface.) A great part of my adult life has been spent in schoolhouses, and you'll agree it's a fraction difficult to practice hermitry in a classroom packed with students. And how could I remain intact in the face of great economic and social changes in my neighborhood and in the world? I have many and varied interests: I'm something of a botanist, experiment with wild plants. I've carried on semi-scientific studies of the leaf miner for years. (I say semi- as I don't have the basic training to give my studies authority.) I read, study, travel. The

[Williamson, J. W.] "An Interview with James Still." *Appalachian Journal* 6.2 (Winter 1979): 121–41. Copyright *Appalachian Journal* and Appalachian State University. Reprinted with permission.

past seven winters I have spent in part in Central America — Mexico, Honduras, Guatemala, Belize, El Salvador — studying Mayan civilization. And hope to return in February. The enigma of the Mayan collapse fascinates me and I would like to correlate it with the Appalachian cultural collapse of a considerably different nature which began visibly after World War II and was in the making long before.

How do you feel about writers who seek publicity?

If you equate publicity with puffery, I would say what a waste of time and energy! But I wouldn't blame an author for doing anything reasonable to bring his writings to the attention of the public. Agreed I haven't done much in this line myself. Frankly, I wouldn't know what to do. I especially applaud authors being invited to give "readings" on campuses. This is recognition of a living contemporary literature — alive and breathing authors not yet embalmed in textbooks.

I was starting off to ask you about other Appalachian writers —

At one time or another I've had the privilege of meeting about everybody who writes in Appalachia. Those of my day. I read their poetry and non-fiction.

You don't read their fiction?

I've read Wilma Dykeman's novels with admiration. The only fiction I've passed up is that about my area of southeastern Kentucky. The reason: overlapping material. I can't long hold back from Harriette Arnow's much-praised *The Dollmaker*. I'm already familiar with her non-fiction.

Writers outside of Appalachia, though. What writers do you admire?

Oh, a great many. The Scandinavian authors. The great Russian novelists and short story writers — Chekhov, Gogol, and Turgenev, particularly. Here at home, no use to start. Too many of them. I might leave out somebody. But I wouldn't forget Mark Twain. I read mainly non-fiction — history, biography, science. Last year I read the whole Francis Parkman *corpus* in American history, plus a biography and scholarly studies of his work. A great reading experience. I've been reading for fifty years, several hours a day.

One of the reviewers of *River of Earth* in 1940 suggested you were of the school of Elizabeth Madox Roberts. Do you recall that?

I don't recall, or never knew. Was there a *school* of Elizabeth Madox Roberts and who were the pupils?

"School" may not have been the word used.

I was a friend of Elizabeth Roberts. I treasure the letters from her — the few. I think *The Time of Man* an exceptional and unduly neglected work. She was a genius of sorts and her books could only have been written by a woman — a woman of great literary and intuitive powers. As for "school," I reject the assumption that I belong to anybody's school. Too independent for that. I am my own man, literary and otherwise. Or so I view myself.

James Still signing copies of *Sporty Creek* at Joseph-Beth Booksellers, Lexington Green, Lexington, Kentucky. Photograph taken October 9, 1999, by Linc. Fisch. Used with permission.

You weren't influenced by her?

I can't imagine being influenced by anybody. What we had in common was the same publisher and the same editor: Marshall Best at Viking Press. (Best once located a typographical error in Joyce's *Finnegans Wake*.) And *River of Earth* was the only book for which she ever volunteered to write a blurb. If you don't have your own view, your own material, your own approach, then your talent would be considerably flawed. As I would not be a protégé, I have no protégés. I intend to be Jim Still all the way home. As for material, ye gods! I can't live long enough to touch what is in my head and happening before my eyes from day to day. For some thirty-five years I have kept daybooks in which I have recorded things I hear, ideas that occur to me. Every facet of my community's life is recorded. Nothing is there I did not personally hear, witness, or was told about by somebody I knew. Or popped into my head from God knows where.

Are the notebooks a kind of stewpot for your own fiction?

No, not consciously. I rarely take them up except to enter another item. The act of writing something down impresses it in memory. A time may come when these daybooks may be considered a valuable contribution to studies of folklife. Nobody could do this again here as that era has largely disappeared. For whatever they may be worth, they're irreplaceable.

What will become of the notebooks?
  I haven't figured that out.

These are private notebooks. You don't show them to anybody?
  I never have. Many of the entries are too cryptic, written for my own eyes. Many need fleshing out. And I have another collection: hands. I have an outline of the hands of many an oldtimer. A hand can say almost as much as a photograph. I owned no camera, so I "took" their hands.

I would like to ask, is there an Appalachian literature, distinct from, say, Southern literature?
  I'd say that would be fairly restrictive. Southern literature is good enough for me.

Why?
  Long ago I read a sentence somewhere which caused me to consider or reconsider a good many things: "The king of England is a myth." I was led to consider the myths we live by, legal myths such as county lines, state lines, and so on. Appalachia is that sort of myth, an imaginary place. Or is made a legal myth by the Appalachian Regional Commission. Where does it start? Where are the boundaries? The ARC includes the county in which I was born in Alabama. My mother was born in Heard County, Georgia, another Appalachian county according to the ARC.

Would you refer to yourself as an Appalachian author?
  I doubt it would occur to me to do so. In fact, I don't refer to myself as anything. When I've filled out forms that ask occupation I usually write *farmer*, which comes as close as need be. If I had income tax to pay I would say *retired* and that would also be a myth. I'm about as un-retired as at any period of my life.

You have also written books for children?
  As I don't write "Appalachian" stories, I don't write for children—children alone. My so-called "children's" books are for all ages, and I have knowledge adults are reading them. If children find books of mine they can and will read, I could not be more pleased. I'm not writing for any particular age group. But I'll say this from my heart, I'd rather light up a child's eyes than earn a grunt of approval from a dozen of their elders. Take my re-telling of Jack and the Beanstalk as it could only have been told back in Knott County, *Jack and the Wonder Beans*. It's for grandpa and grandma as well as grandson and granddaughter. It may be that this book has a chance of greater longevity than any of my other works. All my powers and my gifts, such as they are, came together in those few pages. The news that some children are sleeping with this book and that their elders are reading it with some delight tickles me in a spot that is hard to get to, to scratch—as the saying goes.

What do you think of the movement at the moment to establish, to say there is an Appalachian literature?

Is it far enough along to be called a movement? I haven't thought about it but would say on the spur of the moment all power to 'em. This seems to contradict what I've said before, but not so. Call it paradoxical.

Have you met Gurney Norman?

On several occasions. He's a good conversationalist, a splendid oral storyteller. He throws away better stories than some of us can write. His magnanimity toward other writers is admirable. You have said somewhere that he is "a healer of wounds" and I would agree to that without questioning what wounds. It's my guess—I'll not say theory—that creative people, due to their hypersensitivity, incur a good many psychic wounds during the course of a lifetime. Even born with a few. Perhaps.

He has said himself in an interview that he owes a good deal to you in learning how to become a tale-teller.

Actually?

Yes. I wonder if you see him as developing into a writer to be reckoned with?

He has to be reckoned with at this moment.

You are represented in the Higgs and Manning anthology of Appalachian literature.

With a short story.

That whole phenomenon of getting together an anthology and putting you in it as an Appalachian writer: does it bother you at all to see that?

On the contrary. Dr. Higgs and Dr. Manning did me the honor of choosing the narrative I would have picked for the anthology myself, and I regret only they did not include a couple or three of my poems, to have me whole, unsplintered. Their poetry selections were the least satisfactory elements of the book. Yet, anthologies of this sort by their very nature can only be chips and whets. So far as I know, and curiously enough, it's still the only anthology of Appalachian writing available.

Let us change the direction a bit. I was surprised to find that in 1940 when *River of Earth* first came out it was reviewed in *Social Forces,* the journal for sociologists. It was not what one would call an adequate review. What was interesting to me was that it was taken note of in the academic world by sociologists as an important thing to know about.

It surprises me as well. And may I throw in here that I was surprised when Archer Taylor, dean of folklorists, wrote about my use of language, and my short story "Mrs. Razor" was included in two medical textbooks *[The World of Psychoanalysis* and *The World Within: The Creative Mind Dealing with Psychiatric Materials]*.

With that review in *Social Forces* in mind: you certainly weren't writing a sociological treatise on the lives of hill people during the Depression.

Not at all. I did have an early awareness that at least in my area something was there that would not last much longer. The poems in *Hounds on the Mountain* [1937] will verify the recognition at that period. We were living in the nineteenth century, so to speak, and the twentieth would not long be denied. The American chestnut was beginning to die on the mountains from a blight that could not be detected with the naked eye, and a blight equally as invisible was at work on folk culture as it then existed.

About the writing of *River of Earth*—

I remember beginning it in the old Hindman School building on a Saturday afternoon. I don't know what I thought I was up to, but I haven't forgotten the moment when the characters began to live and talk to me. I finished the manuscript in 1939 in the log house on Dead Mare Branch where I still live. Not having a suitable table, I perched the typewriter on two steamer trunks, one atop the other. I had expected to write an additional chapter, had it clearly in mind, so clearly that I could produce it today, but when I wrote the last sentence of the book as it now stands I realized I had ended the journey. In my relief I jumped to my feet and ran around the stacked trunks a couple of times. Viking Press had already contracted to publish it on the basis of several sections they had read. Later, when I asked my editor if he could suggest changes he replied, "We trust your instincts." The original manuscript and those of several other of my books are in the archives of the University of Kentucky.

You worked at the Hindman Settlement School for several years?

Six years the first hitch, and I came back after thirteen years' absence in the army and on Little Carr Creek, Dead Mare, and Wolfpen—these streams boxed me in—and put in seven more. Thirteen years altogether. During the first six years the school had little money to pay the staff—the Depression years. I worked three years without pay, as did others, and glad of the employment. We were fed, sheltered. The time came when I was in need of razor blades, socks, and breeches, and about that time I began to write verses and short stories, and a bit of money came in, not much, two dollars, five dollars, such amounts. The fourth year the school managed to pay me fifteen dollars a month, and increased it a mite the next two. Over the six-year period I averaged six cents a day. And why did I stay on? No amount of money could have substituted for the joy I felt from 1932 to 1939. The literary juices were flowing. I was beginning to publish in *The Atlantic, The Yale Review, The Sewanee Review, The Virginia Quarterly Review, Poetry, The New Republic, The Nation,* and others. I was assigned Box 13 at the Hindman post office. The postmaster said nobody else would have it. So much for luck. And I might comment that Hindman was surely the only place you could cash a check at four A.M. and call for your mail at midnight. The cashier was an early riser, the postmaster an insomniac. Well, there was a three-year period, I believe, when I was never out of a current periodical. Everything I wrote was accepted somewhere. And this is not to crow. There are six thousand periodicals currently being published, and probably a like number then, and anything literate could find a niche somewhere. Then I began *River of Earth*.

You moved to your present home to complete the novel?

Partly. But there was something else. I wanted to dig in the ground, to grow things. I'm a peasant at heart. It's not merely a sustained interest with me — it's a passion. I'm overtaken by it annually when the birds begin to hallo in the spring. Well, I moved over to a farm beside Dead Mare Branch and into a log house which records in Letcher County say was standing in 1840 — now a part of Knott County — myth in action. As I tell it, after six years of coolie wages I was so rich I retired. The house is not a cabin, mind you. A two-story log house. A cabin by my definition is a temporary structure, pitched together, probably of unskinned poles. This house — the Jethro House as some refer to it — is now designated a pioneer landmark structure by the Kentucky Historical Commission. The farm was nine miles over a wagon-rutted road from the county seat, some stretches of it in the creekbed. One neighbor said of me at the time, "He's left a good teaching job and come over in here and just sot down." I did sit down — to a typewriter and completed the novel. Jethro Amburgey, the dulcimer maker of wide fame, built a proper table for me to work on. When he died years later he left the farm to my care as a lifetime inheritance. By now the grounds around the house are a cross between a botanical garden and an experiment station. I tell visitors, "Don't let the grass and weeds give you an idea I'm lazy." (My mother never ironed my shirttails because superstition had it I would grow up indolent. It didn't help. My laziness consists of not doing what other people think I should be doing.) If green grow the rushes-O, they serve a purpose. Where else would the rabbits, blacksnakes, ground squirrels, and terrapins live as my neighbors, much less the fowls of the air? Thoreau says, "Shall I not rejoice at the abundance of the weeds whose seeds are the granary of the birds." And speaking of movements, have you heard about the unclipped lawn movement recently promulgated in *Horticulture?* And the toads? The common toady-frog is becoming rare. Well, sir, I am working, along with various projects, with the wild strawberry and the wild violet. With trillium and Adam-and-Eve. I respect the ancient Chinese proverb: "All the seeds of all the flowers of tomorrow are in the flowers of today." And coming back to the toads: Why, one of my toady-frogs might turn into a princess — myth become fact. A while ago I mentioned a sentence I'd read somewhere that deeply influenced my thinking. Well, I came across another once that was equally as enlightening and thought-provoking: "An apple is a modified leaf." This was my lead into plant genetics.

What do you remember of writing *River of Earth*?

Not much. That was far too long ago. It's like this tape: when you record over it, it erases. There may be behind it a wish to forget, to move on to other things. I feel completely objective about it now. This novel, to me, is as a child that was cherished in its composition and youth, a child that grew up and went away and now has a life of its own, and is not now accountable to me, or I to it. Affection remains. I remember when the first green-jacketed copy arrived I broke it out of its wrapper and spoke aloud, "I did this!" And could not believe it. Twenty years ago I would not have discussed the book. I would have said, or indicated, "There it is. It speaks for itself." But, as you can see, I am only speaking of surfaces, not of depths. My guiding thought is: Do not look too closely into the springs of creativity.

When was the novel started? Can you say what year?
It was published in 1940. I must have begun it in 1935 or 1936.

Was it written out of a political consciousness?
Unavoidable, I'd say. I was pretty much up on what was happening in America, and, to a lesser extent, in the world — a constant reader of *The Nation, The New Republic, The New York Times,* and such publications. A great influence on the book was my serving as a home visitor for the FERA [Federal Emergency Relief Administration] for three months during a summer in the mid-1930s. I was a replacement for an absent worker. My territory was lower Knott County — the creeks of Montgomery, Ball, Mill, Lower Troublesome, and Lower Quicksand.

Would that be equivalent to today's social worker?
I suppose. I visited homes over this wide area on foot, and sometimes to the more distant places on a hired plowhorse. (That devil of a horse has a story of her own.) I visited homes by invitation only. Families were required to make a formal request. At their houseseats I counted chickens and livestock, estimated the number of eggs laid a day, the measure of milk the cow gave. I inspected meal barrels, flour, and lard gourd or buckets, tallied mason jars of canned fruit and vegetables, the kitchen garden's promise, the acres of corn in cultivation. I glanced inside houses, noted the clothes on their owners' backs and on their clotheslines. I learned that utter poverty has an odor. Soap seems to be the first sacrifice of the needy. I penciled notes on the spot in a school copybook. These copybooks — raw data — are now at Morehead State University [James Still Room]. They furnished some of the background for the novel. I count it a loss to all of us that other observers were not writing in southeastern Kentucky in those days. They could have brought other viewpoints, and possibly more maturity and a surer talent to the subject.

So you were a government employee essentially?
For a single summer. (Several years ago I walked into a country store and a customer there took the opportunity to deride me offhandedly by saying,

"Come a feller in here, and he's been writing about us. Damn! He don't know how we live." I replied as ungrammatically, "The hell he don't!")

So you were a government employee?

Briefly, at a critical time.

Did that give you a political sense of what was happening that you hadn't had before?

To live in that time and place as I think I've said earlier was to be politically aware. What at first could be taken care of by an occasional truckload of Red Cross flour grew worse as the Depression ran its course. And even that had its comic moments. There is something in my nature that welcomes the incongruous. Say, the arrival of the first shipment of grapefruit. Having never seen grapefruit, and finding them sour, many threw them away — some whose very faces bespoke malnutrition. One man told me, "Somebody did tell us to put sugar on them and they'd be good eating, but we didn't have sugar. My younguns used the grapefruits for baseballs till they busted." I learned there was a general — of course not total — prejudice against *yellow* cornmeal. Even the color of beans made a difference. Cheese was uncommon, so the five-pound loaves were often made into soap or fed to hogs. So went the powdered milk and powdered eggs at a later date. Bureaucrats in the Department of Agriculture didn't bother to investigate local dietary habits. A neighbor said, "What they know up there in Washington wouldn't cover a gnat's ass." A salient fact came clear to me: Even the grossly undernourished will not eat just anything. There's your independent mountaineer at his most independent. Pride is involved as well as custom and habit. Directors of the Hindman Settlement School at the forks of Troublesome Creek could give a full accounting of this matter in their seventy-five years of "feeding" children. To a fellow I happened to know limited himself to a small range of foods I chided, "You don't eat anything your mother didn't poke into your mouth before you were five years old, do you?" and he replied, "That's right." There was at the time a sewing project at Hindman making clothes for the needy. On occasion I'd take a bunch of baby dresses — the kind that stretch two feet below the infant's toes — take them to the meeting point, a post office or storehouse. When I'd announce they were available for both the born and the unborn, there'd be no immediate claimants for the unborn. Presently, as surreptitiously as possible, a prospective parent would admit the need of such a garment. Well, the Depression was a traumatic time and we were all marked by it.

River of Earth **itself as a novel, it isn't a political novel by any means.**

No.

But it has political consciousness, possibly?

Without doubt. Bear with me, for I've never read it through as a book. Just in spots, when a textbook or anthology wanted to reprint a section. It's been dismembered many a time, some sections over and over. What surprises me, the parts I've read, is its starkness. For me to reread anything is to want to rewrite it. I begin tinkering. As for the sections dealing with the mines—the early thirties saw the mine wars in Harlan County, and in the organizing days of the United Mine Workers the conflicts and strikes spread into Perry County, Knott County, and crossed state lines into Tennessee. While a student at Vanderbilt University in 1930 I went to Wilder, Tennessee, to help distribute clothing and food collected in Nashville. In Wilder the scabs lived on one side of town, the strikers on the other. I had never witnessed or imagined people actually starving, but there they were, in the United States of America. There has been a movement lately to give a more "balanced" view, as they say, to state the side of the mine owners, to stress the fact of their limited profits in those years. I equate the mine owners' side with the gun thugs they hired. They killed Barney Graham at Wilder, and many another miner elsewhere. So you see there's a mote in my eye, difficult to remove. The scales remain unbalanced. Yes, I was aware that destiny rode with these people. Their destiny and mine. We were one, then as now.

Have you done any overtly political writing?
Not a whet.

Why not?
For the reason I'm not overtly political. My job is to report life, not to pass judgment. I've never had anything to sell in the way of propaganda. I only want people to have the chance to live the best life possible, to be their own best selves. You could call me a liberal in the old-fashioned sense.

I thought you've said *River of Earth* comes out of a political consciousness.
It comes out of the Depression years, which generated the great social gains which are now taken for granted.

It's not political itself?
We've wandered into a subject, an area where I feel some tension. These things are still going in Harlan County at the moment, and at this moment in Whitley County. How I feel about these matters is self-evident, and I can't go back to a book I've virtually forgotten writing and declare motives that did not exist. All in the world I was saying, and with as much felicity as I could muster, this was how it was with these people at that time. One thing I have never had questioned is the facts of this book. I might say I've rarely let myself get messed up in local politics. They're mostly conflicts of personalities and not of issues, of who's going to control what. However, the interplay interests me immensely. Local politics are like the creek past my house, the same water never comes by twice, yet it looks the same. Ever new, ever changing. Only the cast of characters shifts.

I guess the political consciousness I'm talking about seems to come out simply as an acknowledgment, or a belief that Appalachia is a colony for the rest of the country. Do you react to that phrase at all? Appalachia as *colony*.

I reject the idea. But my rejection doesn't deny that we are often viewed as a sort of colony to be drained of our resources (coal, gas, oil, timber) for the profit of absentee owners.

You don't like the theory?

Theory, hypothesis, supposition, whatever anybody wants to call it.

Would it surprise you to know that a very eminent scholar in Appalachia, someone I think you know, has said that your story "The Run for the Elbertas" could be a sort of parable of Appalachian politics? Do you think of it as a political story?

I haven't thought of it as such.

That it's a kind of parable — the *trashing,* one might call it, of the pretentious. Can you see that use of your story?

It can be looked at in that sense. I sort of like it as a parable now that it has been pointed out to me. I know several Godey Spurlock types, and the prototype for Riar Thomas is a neighbor of mine. I once made a "run" for a truckload of peaches to South Carolina and from that experience came the story. Well, I don't write about real people. The ones walking around in my head serve my purpose.

This story ["The Run for the Elbertas"], like most of your stories, seems worked over. How much polishing do you do?

The fiddling goes on in my head, the main part of it, before I sit down to compose. Then I "play" with the narrative, more play than work. I don't think a poem or story or novel can be "revised" or "polished" into excellence. Not mine, anyhow.

You don't do any polishing?

This is about as close as I can come to it. Or want to come to it. You can understand that?

Yes.

Creation of a poem or story is still something of a mystery to me and I choose not to trouble the muses by idle speculation.

May I talk a bit about point of view in your writing? I was interested in what Mr. [Dean] Cadle said in his article about you [*Yale Review,* December 1967], that you had essentially eliminated the author as a presence in your work. In reading *River of Earth* last weekend, I think I have to disagree with that, and I wonder what you would have to say. It seems to me that there is an author there and he's an ironic author.

Ideally, I do not intend to show my hand. I never step in and say, in effect, here I am, and here's what I think of the situation. Yet the reader knows that the author can't disappear altogether. Every word, every phrase, every act comes out of the central consciousness that is the author. In that sense I am there indeed, all-seeing, all-knowing, and Dean Cadle was not denying this. But such a statement seems to imply that everything is written with cold-blooded calculation. Not so. I don't write anything until the wish to do it overtakes me and the emotion connected with it boils over. When I have done a thing it often seems that it pre-existed and had only to be discovered. The creative act involves a person wholly. More even than he knows about himself, or could guess. The work of the great mental computer that has registered every mini-second of being from the moment of birth. Creativity involves the total experience, inherited characteristics, learning. The joys, the sorrows, the horrors. (Three nights ago I stood by a boy prostrate on a truck seat with crushed lungs and tried to keep up his will to live by giving a running account of what the rescue squad was doing with the other bloodied victims of the wreck. Once I was following a man who was shot dead in my face. I've witnessed several people killed. At age 13 I was in a house that was lifted by a tornado and the top floor blown away. March 28, 1977, I was trapped on a street in San Salvador [El Salvador] during an uprising for hours during which more than one hundred people were killed, hundreds wounded, and no escape from the scene possible. I was in World War II in Africa. I've had many a traumatic experience. How does the creative mind assimilate such data?)

Is the author ironic in *River of Earth*?

I can't say. These remarks are being made from a great distance—forty years.

The narrator of *River of Earth* was not really a seven-year-old boy.

If I remember aright, he was recalling this period in his life at a later time. Elizabeth Madox Roberts said to me after reading the book that I had accomplished the two most difficult things in writing fiction. One, writing a novel in the first person; second, writing from the point of view of a child. They were limitations indeed and you can see how I tried to manage. I didn't know any better in those days.

The manipulation of narrative and point of view and tone in *River of Earth* seems to me its great, its real artistry.

Well, thank you. But the word "manipulation," as I see it, doesn't go with my indulgence in the creative act. Instinct led me, I suppose. Recollect I write poetry as well as fiction and it represents a sense of essence and discipline and structure. I play tennis with the net *up*—to let Robert Frost say it for me. An editor once accused me of trying to eliminate all the words. Said he, "You'll never make it. You have to leave a few."

This business of learning to write, how did you learn?
   The need was there, and, I judge, the aptitude. But I have the feeling I've never learned and I'm sure some critics will go along with that. Writing in itself is the act of becoming. I just started doing it, and that was it, and rather suddenly. I wrote "The Scrape." An examination of that story will show the tools I had to work with in the beginning. A folksy piece of writing that I moved away from later. Or it moved away from me. I don't know how people actually learn to write. Scientific information on how a child learns to read is pretty scrappy, too. It's a turn you have — born with, acquired, probably both. When people ask me how they should start a writing career I tell them, not entirely facetiously, to learn to touch type. Usually takes six months, or you can learn in ten days as I did if the motivation is there. One informed me that Shakespeare didn't use a typewriter, wrote with a turkey feather. What might Shakespeare not have additionally accomplished with a Coronamatic 2200 with a pop-out ribbon! And that's about as far as you can go with practical advice. I haven't found anybody yet who thinks it's relevant. Oh, I suppose it would be well if the budding writer recognized a cliché when he bumped into one, reacted to redundancy as to fingernails scratching a windowpane, was aware of static words in composition — words registering little change. Someone has calculated that Zane Grey's work is ninety-five percent static while James Joyce's is only five percent. *But there is something else.* I understand a cat's purr comes not from its throat but from its arteries throbbing. You write with your heartbeat as much as with your head — rhythm built in. Iambic pentameter.

You have said that you thought a writer was something like a surgeon, probing for a nerve. Here I am quoting you again.
   Well, yes, I said that some time or place. Don't recall. I don't like to be stuck with something I said yesterday, for today I might have a different opinion. But I'll stay with that. I might have an idea for a story and may not get around to writing it until it begins to bother me, dominate my attention. I might set to trying, but until I touch the "quick" with my scapel I haven't actually started. Until that point I'm pranking, fiddling.

So it's your own nerve as much as the reader's nerve?
   Right. At that point the curtain raises, the drama begins — live, in my mind's eye.

Can I get at the process? You have an idea that bothers you, that pinches or something, but when you turn it into fiction you control that emotion so beautifully, you keep it — you don't ever let it out of control. There's some process by which you take a strong emotion and make it tame in art. I don't know if I'm saying that well —
   But is it a "process"? That sounds mechanical. And "tame" is certainly not the right word. When the "process" of creative writing is unraveled, well, we can turn the job over to the computers.

I wonder if choosing an apparent seven-year-old narrator in *River of Earth* was a way of taming the emotion, of keeping sentimentality somewhat out of it, because a seven-year-old narrator — or a man remembering when he was seven — is a way of becoming naive again, of remaining unschooled. An adult might get sentimental about what a seven-year-old would see in very straightforward terms.

I hope sentimentality was not only *somewhat* out of it, as you say, but wholly. I did not consciously choose the narrator. He grabbed the reins from the start. If this is not the way it happened, it is nevertheless the way I want to tell it. (I should have warned you in the beginning that I am the possessor of a solid gold liar's license. I won it — the Rush Strong Medal — as a college senior for an essay whose assigned subject was "The Value of Truth." Uncle Jolly is at work here.)

You taught for a while in academic situations.

Many years. For many years. A couple too many.

You winced. Why did you wince?

You touched a nerve.

What goes on from your viewpoint in colleges? Let's just say in Appalachia? Are they doing what they ought to be doing?

On the whole, I believe, but I deplore the low state of the Humanities at the moment. You can graduate from many an institution here as in the rest of the country without even saying hey-o to Shakespeare, the greatest genius of the English-speaking race. In my opinion there should be some inviolate standards for a college degree, literacy being one of them. The establishment of Appalachian studies courses is a progressive move. Helping students to realize and value their heritage of history, folklore, literature, art, crafts, and music. Appalachia has the resources, the master teachers — Cratis Williams and Harry Caudill and Loyal Jones being the first to come to mind. There are others. No importation necessary.

Well, just take writers; you've said writers shouldn't have to be trained.

Here we go again — stuck with something I may or may not have said, and certainly out of context. Granted that I'm worth bothering with in the first place, how would you have trained me in my youth? What I needed and was available to me were basic courses in history, literature, science, sociology, psychology, languages. I took it from there. Harry Harrison Kroll once said in my presence, "James Still is one fellow who was *not* destroyed by a college education." (You are welcome to your own interpretation.) You're talking to a literary outlaw, so the usual standards don't work in my case. If a student believes he can profit from creative writing classes, I'm for them. From some of the theses and dissertations I've perused, I'd say many of their authors might well have elected a writing class.

But you have taught writing, haven't you?
    No. A myth I'll never live down. The fact I was called Writer-in-Residence at one of the colleges is beside the point. They kept me too busy teaching standard courses to do any writing of my own: British and American Literature, Literature of the South, the Modern Short Story, Advanced Composition. Advanced Composition was supposed to be my specialty. I never advanced it to the stage of creative writing. The former president of the college has recently written to say, "I believe we worked you too hard." Not too hard. I liked college teaching on the whole. My life seemed a preparation for it.

When you're involved in writers' conferences or writers' workshops, where would-be writers are coming to be in your presence, what do you tell them, if you can't teach them, if you can't train them?
    I have served generally as a manuscript consultant. I read manuscripts and discuss them with their authors, much as I might a student's composition. I don't believe I've ever been of much use to anybody, except in the one case when I found a manuscript so excellent that I told its author never to show his work to anybody except editors. I even declined to discuss the manuscript with him. It was none of my business. Just as nobody except editors ever sees unpublished work of mine.

And this author is now published?
    Some seven or eight books. He has made a considerable reputation in fiction, non-fiction, and in poetry. With more to come. I didn't discover him. He discovered himself.

Then you do feel dubious about being in a writing workshop situation?
    Extremely. I want to be of help but don't know how. Is there a *how?* 'Tis said that writing is a lonely business, and would-be writers profit by communion with those who have made some progress in the profession. Maybe writers' workshops are for people who have other needs than mine. In writing fiction I have my characters as company enough. And I have neighbors and acquaintances and a friend or two for all the communion that is good for me.

You've said that you thought a writer ought to stay "wild," which I like.
    Yes. Hard to round up. About his own affairs. He shouldn't be doing what I'm up to now: talking about himself. But what I'm saying is fairly superficial. That way I can sleep tonight, forget it tomorrow.

I think of you — and I think of Wendell Berry — also of Kentucky — who has now, I believe, resigned from the University of Kentucky and is farming.
    I understand he's a contributing editor of *Organic Farming* and has been appointed one of the editors of the forthcoming *New Farm*. When I heard this news I promptly subscribed to both because I have great respect and great hopes for Wendell and want to keep up with whatever he might be doing.

You were at Harrogate [Lincoln Memorial University] when Jesse Stuart was there.
We graduated in the same class.

And Don West.
Don West was a classmate.

Do you have memories about that time that you would like to discuss?
A plenty of memories. I'd want to sort them out, and this is not the occasion. Lincoln Memorial furnished the only opportunity I had to attend college, and I guess the same was true for Jesse and Don. They let us work out the entire cost of four years of schooling, and I am wholly grateful. A book has already been written about that period which you would do well to read if the subject interests you.

By Jesse?
Yes, but the title escapes me. My memories of the time are quite different. The facts are the same but I had different eyes and ears for them. I had my first sweetheart there and the memory of that enchantment has colored all those years into a golden haze.

Were you — did you apprentice yourself to Harry Harrison Kroll?
No. I never apprenticed myself to anybody at any time. I didn't know Kroll in those days except formally, in a classroom situation. I didn't begin to write until several years later. Oh, I scribbled a little, but he didn't know about it. I doubt he had any idea I was interested in writing.

But you were writing.
I did publish several small pieces in Sunday School papers along about then or soon after. I do recall publishing two articles in the scholarly journal *American Speech,* which H. L. Mencken quoted later in *American Language.* I was maybe twenty-five years old, and at Hindman, when I began to write. My first short story was chosen for the O. Henry Prize annual collection, but before they had completed choosing the stories, I published one they liked better and they used it instead. The introduction to the volume mentions this swap. The story then called "On Defeated Creek" (I think) was changed to "The Scrape" and appears in *Pattern of a Man.* I mentioned this earlier.

Don West was a friend of yours during the time at Lincoln Memorial?
I didn't know him well there, but when I was over at Vanderbilt in graduate school he turned up as a student in the School of Religion. Sometimes on Sunday we walked around Nashville. We were country boys and a city interested us. Don was a gifted man, he writes well, and if the day ever comes that he writes his autobiography we'll have a volume to reckon with. I last saw him in 1937.

The three of you — Jesse Stuart, Don West, James Still — interestingly enough were in the same place at the same time, and developed such different careers.

We have been referred to as "the barefoot boys." Yes, we have different careers. We chose the "path less traveled by." Don is the poet of the disinherited. And Jess wrote most of the books, some seventy-five of them, that came out of the Class of 1929. Julia Yenni, author of *House of the Sparrow* and other works, was one of us. Why the Class of 1929 spawned us I don't know. Stuart, I understand, has given credit to Kroll. Kroll had no connection with me or, I believe, with Don West.

Kroll's fiction is certainly different from yours.

In the 1960s I was responsible for Harry Harrison Kroll being asked to join the staff of the Writers' Workshop at Morehead State. I got to know him there personally for the first time, and I liked him immensely. A rare personality. Once Kroll sat in on my reading of a short story, "A Ride on the Short Dog," and when I had finished and invited comments Kroll spoke up and said, "I like the story, but there's no moral to it."

He wasn't, I take it, being ironic himself?

I supposed at the time that he thought there had to be some sort of preachment. He might have meant to say "premise." However, it doesn't show up in his own later work.

"A Ride on the Short Dog" is a good story to talk about, because it may be in essence what I think of as your ironic viewpoint. Your fiction so often seems to teeter between comedy of the highest sort and tragedy. It never quite goes either way.

That's a pure definition of irony.

Is that basically the way you see your work?

It may be the way I see the world. It is not done with purpose aforethought. Isn't that the way life is? My life anyhow.

The opening chapter of *River of Earth*, with the mother burning down the house, is on the one hand wildly comic and yet terrifically poignant.

The necessity was such she had to take this step. A force put, as we say. I miss the humor in this particular act. I don't see it as humor.

But the act is framed by humor. That chapter, I understand, was first published in *The Atlantic*.

As non-fiction.

Do you think they saw it essentially as a comic story?

As they published it as non-fiction they must have thought it a true account. We never discussed it. I recall only once when Edward Weeks, the editor, offered advice. It was to the effect that I should use dialect selectively. Wise words. Dialect has always bothered me in reading fiction, my fiction included. I hope a collection of Edward Weeks' letters to authors is published eventually. Those letters are splendid. As for the dialect — idiom — did you have problems in reading *River of Earth*?

Well, the context usually supplied the definition.
Yes, that is my hope, my opinion.

The language is delightful. Lots of words I don't know, but the context usually took care of that and I was never stopped so that I wouldn't go on.
There are no footnotes or glossary in *River of Earth*. Not needed, as you say. However, *Pattern of a Man* has a glossary. *Way Down Yonder on Troublesome Creek* and *The Wolfpen Rusties* and *Sporty Creek* have footnotes. My editors told me these books would be read in city schools and some of the words are not in dictionaries. I recall Mark Twain's *Life on the Mississippi* has footnotes for those not familiar with steamboating and other arcane matters.

About having a glossary: Why don't books that are published out of, say, New York ghetto life have glossaries? Why a glossary for a book about Appalachia? Is there a necessity for such a thing? Does it strike you as unfortunate?
No. If you don't like the glossary, you can ignore it. And *River of Earth* might do well with one. I'm the one who over the years has had to reply to letters from students, teachers, and the curious inquiring what was meant by certain words and phrases.

I guess what I'm getting at is maybe, well, *Foxfire*—that phenomenon — caused it — the way people look at things Appalachian, as something quaint and totally foreign that has to be interpreted for them, almost as though it were ancient history or alien. What do you think about the *Foxfire* phenomenon?
I hadn't imagined there was so much interest. I'm pleasantly astonished at its enormous success. To my knowledge, no other books about Appalachia have had such widespread attention and universal approval.

May I ask about a specific passage of idiomatic speech — Preacher Mobberly's sermon — how it came into being? Did you hear snatches of that sermon and manage to recall them, or is that a sermon you wrote?
I wrote it. Naturally, I've heard many an Old Regular Baptist sermon. I imagine I could sit down and write any number of sermons of this nature that would be true to the doctrine and spirit of this church. Yet, I'd bet the fact we used to memorize Psalms in school was a stimulus.

Your stories have a way of ending abruptly.
When to end a story is equally important as when to begin one. When a thing as been accomplished, there's no reason to drag it out. Anticlimax is the enemy. The resolution must be earned, however.

I think your stories end with such abruptness sometimes that it makes the reader go back and say, what was the narrative really about?

I don't agree. It is all there, I see to that. I don't do much beating around the bush — may I use the cliché? — and I don't wallow about verbally. The static rating of my fiction is rather low, and I press for absolute clarity. I demand of a reader his whole attention, his eyes and ears and his understanding. He must meet me halfway, not expect me to do the whole job. Look again and you'll find many of my stories do not end abruptly.

Those boys in "The Run for the Elbertas" and "A Ride on the Short Dog" are very interesting, to me, partially because I have heard them referred to as kinds of modern political heroes, or at least embodiments of a kind of Appalachian folk hero.

They are the product of their community, the people around them, the mores. Now that folk here are getting around to reading some of my works I am asked occasionally if Godey Spurlock was not in fact certain young fellows who live in the area. Godey is fictional, as are all my characters. Godey is a bit under size, with a dwarf complex, a banty rooster, cocky as they come, knows the clever replies to anything you might say — and with scars. I know his parents, his home, what he eats, what he does with himself all day long. I know several actual Godeys. He's a number of them rolled into one, and none of them.

Is he important to you as an embodiment of something?

Godey was my vehicle for telling this story. The story is a great deal more than the actions of Godey Spurlock. He is of course the thorn in the flesh of anybody who has anything to do with him. Take Riar Thomas, the man who took Godey and Mal on the peach trip — people say to me, "Well, why didn't Riar dump the boys along the way. Drive off and leave them?" My reply is that they're missing something important. These boys came from his community, he hauled them off, and he must bring them home, no matter what. He had a duty to their parents.

They're bound together in a community sense.

Yes. No matter what the boys do.

You seem to have Godey in just two stories, or are there more?

Just two.

Do you have other characters that reappear?

I can't think of any. Now, *Sporty Creek* is something of a sequel to *River of Earth*. It starts with one of the same episodes. But the characters bear different names, except Uncle Jolly.

I'm sort of circling a lot of things.

So am I.

In 1940, at least a lot of the reviews that I have read of *River of Earth* emphasized or mentioned its episodic quality. It's obviously the novel of someone who feels more at home writing short stories, possibly, than writing novels.

The opposite is true. The short story form is tight, unrelenting. The novel lets me ramble, poke my elbows out a bit. Any novel in which there is lapsed time between sections might appear episodic. This family moved a lot. I think I skipped the actual moving, set them up in their new homes before proceeding. I trust you are not lumping together "reviewers" and "critics." Their functions and responsibilities are at variance.

Well, it seems as though you — each incident in *River of Earth* is a kind of episode.

Does the lapsed time explain it?

But it seems to me that the tribe of literary critics are bothered by it.

Never ask a parent to low-rate his own child. What I've read of the book, I've found sad. It didn't seem so years ago. It's their denial of self-pity that strikes me, raises them up.

Sad is not the first word that would come to mind.

It's the first word that comes to me. There are synonyms, of course.

There's a kind of cosmic sadness, I think.

It's because of their future. I know the bleakness, the hopelessness.

Uncle Jolly — the Father called him a "fool." Does he do that with a smile on his face?

With a grin.

He's more of a jester, a clown, but not unintelligent.

Right.

Did you see Uncle Jolly's function in the novel — I don't know if that's a word you would like, the *function* of a character —

Say that again.

I've tried to put my finger on it. He is in some ways a center for the whole novel.

A major character, not the center.

An emotional center, almost like a chorus.

I doubt I thought of him in those terms.

In some ways I guess I see him as the most — outside the narrative voice itself — the most intelligent, the character who perceives most, who understands most. Do you see him that way?

I see him as free of the petty concerns that control the others. He has a solid base, a home. He'll live there to the day of his death, without apparent change.

The mother is defending one thing, the father defending something else, and Uncle Jolly seems almost to be able to cross all kinds of boundaries. He's not defending any one thing.

Nobody can hem up Uncle Jolly because he never gets himself into a corner. His life has a roundness, a wholeness. He's one of the rare people who can't cry for laughing.

He's his mother's last bulwark, the last child that takes care of her.

We've all had the experience of childhood. It may be that the artist remembers more of it, his reactions to events, his fears and joys. Perhaps he cherishes memory more and wants to preserve it, and in so doing relives it.

Do you project another novel?

Don't you think they've cut down enough trees to make the paper to print my writings? On the other hand, I had a letter a while back that inquired, "Are you still alive?" I'm alive. Don't count me out.

"Daring to Look in the Well": A Conversation

JAMES STILL *and* JIM WAYNE MILLER

JWM: During the month of August 1983 at Yaddo I had the opportunity to converse with James Still on a daily basis, so what I'm doing here this evening is a continuation of that conversation. I recently came across an interesting statement by Saul Bellow, Jim. He said that "a writer is a reader who has been moved to emulation." How did you begin writing?

JS: I wish I remembered and could tell you. I don't think I began exactly. I never had any thought of being a writer. I didn't know what it meant, to tell the truth. I do recall writing a little poem once, which, honestly, is not too bad. I was fourteen. I pitched a little tent — you know you have to have romantic associations with the poem — I pitched a little tent in the yard, and I went into that tent and wrote this little verse. I still know the poem now — I won't say it, I assure you. But I'm still astonished when I see this little verse. I do intend to publish it some day to show how far you can come from something of that sort.

Well, that Bellow statement suggests that there's some kind of connection between reading and writing. What sort of things did you read?

We had no books in our home. Well, there was the Bible, of course, which nobody was reading. I tried to read it once, but I got stopped in the "begats." My father was a veterinarian; that is, a horse doctor, a man with no formal training at all. We had one volume called *The Anatomy of the Horse*, which wasn't very entertaining. And we had another one which was called *The Palaces of Sin, or The Devil in Society* and which had to do with a man inheriting a million dollars and going to Washington, D.C., where he observed the wicked life that was being led by the congressmen and senators. It seemed that these people played cards and they also drank gin. Now I didn't know what gin was. I knew all about liquor, but I thought gin must be pretty bad. Then there was one more book. It was called *The Cyclopedia of Universal Knowledge*. It was a very large

Still, James, and Miller, Jim Wayne. "'Daring to Look in the Well': A Conversation." *Iron Mountain Review* 2.1 (Summer 1984): 3–10. Reprinted with permission.

James Still drawing water from the well. Photograph by Earl Palmer. Courtesy the Hindman Settlement School. Used with permission.

book. I remember that one of the backs was torn off. But it had a great many things in it, including how to play all kinds of games, even the game of hoyle.* There were about twenty poems—great poems by Keats, Shelley, and so on. I memorized those. And I knew I was surely the only person in my area who knew twenty words of Arabic when I was eight years old. I also knew maybe twenty-five words from various languages, how to say hello, good morning, and so on. I learned from that book how to prune fruit trees, how to write business letters. And there was a little bit on physics and on the chemistry of that day.

Did you get any urgings or guidance from your parents as to what you ought to be?

None. Well, my father wanted me to be a lawyer. I'm sure he did, though he never said it, because he dragged me around to every lawyer in the county and anywhere else. I was always being introduced to lawyers and judges. And when the governor came to town, he pushed me through the crowd to shake hands with him. But I never thought of being a lawyer. That was nothing I wanted to do. My father never urged me toward anything. In fact, I don't recall my parents ever asking me if my homework was done. I don't think we did homework in those days. I carried my books home every night and then carried them back to school, but I don't think I ever opened them. I don't recall that I did. Anyway, they were sort of dull. However, in time I came across other books—Tom Swift books and Tom Slade books. I didn't care for them really. We subscribed to the *Country Gentleman*, and Zane Grey had serialized novels in it. But I didn't like them. I don't know how I learned so early, but anyway I didn't care for them at all. But one day we moved at last to a little town called Shawmut, and in one corner of a building there was a small library. There was an elderly lady who took care of the library, but she would never let you touch the books; she would go bring you one. And one day she kept bringing books and I didn't want to read them—I didn't like them—so she told me to go look for myself. So I went back, and I found a book called *Father Goriot* by Balzac—I'd never heard of him. It had no pictures in it and had very small print and looked very unpromising, but I took it home. And that night I read this book. I don't know that I read all night, but I read a long time. That was my first approach to literature. And I never turned back. After then I read adult books when I could get them. I think the only other book I read about that time was *Treasure Island*, which was a children's book and an adult book as well. I looked at it again not long ago, and I think it is still a classic, a very fine book.

---

*Probably Mr. Still was referring to the well-known rule books associated with the 18th century Englishman Edmond Hoyle (books that gave rise to the phrase "according to Hoyle," meaning "in accordance with the rules"). The interviewer may have misunderstood or mistranscribed Mr. Still's words here.

Now this town you mentioned, Shawmut, where you encountered the library and the works of Balzac, was in Alabama?
Yes, it was.

From there you came up to Lincoln Memorial University in Tennessee?
Well, not from there. We moved again.

But from the state of Alabama you came to LMU?
I did. I graduated from high school there in Fairfax, Alabama, and then I went up to Lincoln Memorial. The way I happened to get there was we had a substitute teacher, or rather, one of the teachers left school and they hired a man through a teachers' agency. All my teachers were women — well, I recall one who wasn't — all the way through school until this man. And one day he said his father was dean of a school in Tennessee, and he left some catalogues on his desk if anybody wanted one. I seemed to be the only person who wanted one. So I saw in reading it that they had work programs. And when I graduated, I went there. I didn't have any money, but I went. They didn't know what to do with me, but they kept me. I was very small — you wouldn't believe it. So they signed me up in the Academy; they couldn't imagine I was college age.

Now, we're sitting here at a literary event. There's a writer here to be interviewed. What kind of literary events or literary influences did you encounter at Lincoln Memorial?
None.

Well, you had access to a library there, I'm sure.
Oh, yes, that was the main thing about that school, and it's the main thing about any school as far as I'm concerned. If you've got a good library, that's about all you need. Oh, it's good to have a few teachers to lead you and to direct you to the library where the information is. I think a teacher should just crack the door open. That's all you can hope to do. That's all I ever hoped to do when I tried to teach. I did work in the rock quarry in the afternoons and then in the evenings as a janitor in the library. I was always too tired to study. I didn't have time to study. I don't suppose I did very much. But I did have that library. As soon as it closed at nine o'clock, I locked the door, swept the floors, emptied the wastebaskets quickly. And then I had this marvelous library all to myself. Some nights I never left. I slept in the magazine room. Anyway, I was like a child in a candy store: I didn't know where to start eating. It was frustrating.

That was not your only college campus experience. What about the situation as you found it at Vanderbilt or later at Illinois?
I think I should mention, before I go on, Harry Harrison Kroll, who was there at LMU as a teacher. I did have a couple of classes under him. I sat in his classes anyway. One was called the teaching of composition. We just wrote compositions: that's all we did, one a day. And I had a Shakespeare class. We would

read the parts in class. I usually would sit back with my book and another book inside of it. Anyway, I tried to make up for that later.

There were some connections, of course, between Harry Harrison Kroll and some of those teachers at Vanderbilt. Did you encounter any different kind of literary scene at Vanderbilt when you were there?

Oh, yes, it was quite different. Well, I don't want to give the wrong idea about Lincoln Memorial. I'm sure it's greatly improved since my day: they had nowhere else to go. I think it's a standard school nowadays, like any other. And I appreciated the chance to be there. I went with nothing and came away with a little bit more than that. But anyway, I went to Vanderbilt to graduate school. I don't know why they let me in, because I didn't know anything except what I'd read. I had read madly for four years. As I look back, they were pretty good books. Even there, I wanted to write. I thought, then, I wanted to write things, and I did. There used to be Sunday School magazines—many of them that they gave out in church for children on Sundays. Many denominations. And so I wrote and, as we say, sold—for a dollar, two dollars, three dollars—little articles on various subjects. I don't know what they were about, but I do remember that I did it.

So you were already at that time behaving very much like a writer. How do you work now?

I could say now that I don't. I will do anything to keep out of writing. I want to with all my heart, really, but it's very difficult to go to that desk, except when I get to working on something, say, a long piece. Some nights I can hardly wait for day so I can go back to work. But once it's finished, that's it. I'm through with it.

You just wait until you're struck again?

Well, until some idea comes along and I want to do it. I want to write to get rid of it, partly. You know, some idea bothers me. I've written many stories because they bothered me. I kept thinking about a little dialogue, the characters came to life in my head and they begin to talk a little bit and finally I'm putting it down. Somebody said to me once, you make it sound so easy. Well, it wasn't, I don't think. But I didn't have any large ambitions. I just wanted to write one poem, and then, of course, in a little while I had to write another one, and pretty soon another one. It's sort of a disease, I think: once you get it, there's no cure. The same way with stories. I'll have to say I've known a good many unhappy writers. I read about them and hear about their great unhappiness. I think they had unrealistic goals, maybe. And I don't think I was ever unrealistic about it. In fact, for the most part, this has been the happy part of my life. I enjoy doing it. Even if nobody else reads it, that's okay. I like for everything to be published, and I intend for it to be published. That doesn't mean that the first magazine I send a story to is going to take it. But I don't worry about that. Maybe they're not buying turnips today. So I send it to the next best place. And I didn't know any better than to send them to the *Atlantic Monthly*. The *Atlantic*, I believe, published my first story. Is that right?

Yes, and then some twelve or thirteen pieces beyond that.

But they kept changing until whatever it is today. I don't know. I subscribe to it, but I just look at it nowadays.

Well, after Lincoln Memorial University, Vanderbilt, and the University of Illinois, you went over into Knott County in east Kentucky and joined the Hindman Settlement School staff. Can you describe that situation — the way it was at that time?

The situation was that after I got out of school with three little degrees I still didn't have a job and couldn't get one. I was very frustrated and unhappy about that. I went everywhere trying to find a job. I went out to pick cotton in Texas. I was twenty then; in fact, I'd been there before. I went to Atlanta and signed up, I remember, with an employment agency and paid them three bucks. But I couldn't get a job, even pumping gas — no kind of job. I even went to a foundry in Rome, Georgia. I hitchhiked around, all over, but I never found anything. Then I ran across a man you may know of, Don West, who had been a classmate of mine at Vanderbilt, and at Lincoln Memorial too, and he wanted me to work in Knott County for the summer. This was for a Vacation Bible School for the Congregational Church. Well, I was having nothing to do with that. He wanted me to organize the Boy Scouts and the baseball teams. I worked with his brother-in-law there all summer. We had the Boy Scouts and we played baseball and camped all summer long. It was very pleasant. And they asked me then to stay and work with him, which I did. They had no money to pay us, but they did feed us and house us and furnished soap. So I worked six years, three years with no salary. I would have been very happy to have had one, I assure you. At that time, I liked the place. But when I was going to have to leave — you run out of socks, eventually, and razor blades — they found somebody who would send $15 a month to keep me there, so I stayed on. Times got better and they paid a little, and at the end of six years I figured up one day I had worked six years for an average of six cents a day. I felt so rich, I retired. I went nine miles away back in the country — backwoods in those days, and some say backwoods now. By this time I was publishing a few stories and poems. And my publisher at Viking asked me to take a year off and they would put me on a salary. But I was kind of proud: I wouldn't accept their salary. But I did go back to this big log house, where I still live, and I raised a garden and finished writing the novel *River of Earth* there. Then I had the luck to have *The Saturday Evening Post* take a story. That wasn't such great luck except in terms of money: they paid very well indeed — actually, fabulous prices for those days. So after then I just wrote one story a year for them. That was all.

You could sustain yourself on one story a year?
Not only that, I could go to Florida for February.

Robert Penn Warren said that he quit writing stories because they robbed him of poems. Have you ever been in doubt about the way an idea ought to go, which way it should be developed, either as a story or a poem?
Well, they're two different things, so different. I think that when I'm writing prose I don't write poems. I do recall once writing a story, and while I was working on it this idea for a verse, I call it, came in my mind. It kept bothering me, so finally I quit and wrote it. It wasn't a very good one. But I remember *The Saturday Evening Post* published both the poem and the story.

I wanted to get a response from you about the way you saw it, because I developed this notion in a critical piece on your work that there are many, many connections between the themes in the prose fiction and in the poems: similar images, similar thematic developments. I quoted from Katherine Anne Porter, who had commented on your *River of Earth* and on *Hounds on the Mountain*. She said something like this: the novel is an extension of the experience that gave rise to the poems. She saw a connection there, too. So I've got a lot riding on this thesis, and that's why I was asking about it.
The same person was writing both of them. I think they all come from the same place. The poems are just a little shorter. I've written two this past year. I think I don't have another one in me. Last winter I was driving one night in the fog, and a fox flared up in front of me, and I ran over it and killed it. I felt pretty bad about that, and I kept thinking about it. In fact, I wrote a letter to you on some other subject and mentioned this, but when I mentioned it I had to write the poem, which I did the next day.

People are interested in the lives of writers maybe more than they ought to be, because after all it's the work that matters, it's what gets written that matters. And yet there's this persistent interest in the way it gets written. You think about all those *Paris Review* volumes, interviews with writers called *Writers at Work*, and so forth. I think this is probably a legitimate interest, after all. One of the things that interests me particularly in your work is that it is so beautifully focused on this one particular part of the world, really eastern Kentucky, and one particular phase of its history and its culture, and yet I know you have a longstanding interest in Central America. Is there any connection between these two things, or are they just two things you happen to be interested in?
I've had a longstanding interest in a number of things. I used to go off on jags reading in a certain area. For example, I was a Civil War buff for many years. I read every book on it I could get hold of. And then one day I got through, and I didn't read another one and may never read another one. Well, I might. I was interested in Tibet once. I'm interested in mountain climbing.

I have quite a library on mountain climbing in the Himalayas. But I've always been interested in primitive peoples. Now I'm not saying that the people where I live are primitives, but they're more so than they are in Lexington or Louisville. I would read anything about, say, the aborigines in Australia. Once I got interested in the South Sea islands, and I read everything I could possibly find. I just had to go there, but I couldn't. And I haven't got there yet. But that doesn't mean I'm not going. Oh, yes, Central America. Well, I don't know how to start it, really. In the winter of 1971, I decided to go to Yucatan. I was hired to teach a little winter semester, and they paid me $1000, and I decided I would spend it on a trip to Yucatan, which I did, and I was hooked when I went down. So since then I've been there five times, and to Guatemala five times and to Honduras a couple times and very briefly to El Salvador and southern Mexico—to Chiapas and Tabasco.

I'm interested in Mayan civilization. That's the main thing. And I believe the thing that holds me is the great mystery of the disappearance of the Mayan people—the virtual disappearance within 50 to 150 years. There seems to be no logical explanation for it. And the usual ones don't apply, apparently—the ones you would think of right off—disease, earthquakes, and so on. After all, these people lived in several different conditions. A great many scholars are working on this, and I have been reading after them. I don't do any digging, I assure you, in that 140 degrees temperature. I just want to go down and see again. And then when I learn more I want to go and look again. I didn't go the past winter, but winter before last I was in Belize—that is, British Honduras—and Guatemala again. I may go this year.

I believe you got in a little trouble down there one year, didn't you?
Yes, a little more than that, I think.

I'm referring to 1977.
Yes, I was in El Salvador on the streets when there was an uprising. It was the beginning, at least for me—I didn't know anything about it—it was the beginning of the civil war that has been going on ever since. I flew down to Mexico City. Of course, they never tell you these things before you get there. Somebody should have warned me. And I flew into El Salvador. When I hired a taxi to take me to the hotel, he took me only part way, because the barbed-wire was across the street. I had to walk the rest of the way. But I didn't see anybody. I didn't know there had been a curfew for a week. Anyway, I went to the hotel. I usually stay in a good hotel when I go to a country I haven't been in before, so I'll be okay. Then maybe I'll move the next day. But there were no guests in the hotel, as far as I could see. And in the dining room that night, which was beautiful place, a marvelous place, there were only two people. That afternoon I walked around. I went to a church, which was filled with people, and I am fairly certain I heard a sermon by the cabinet official who was later assassinated during Mass. That was the church, I'm almost certain. I walked

around, and soldiers came out and looked at me. They saw I was Americano, and, you know, Americanos don't have much sense from their point of view. As my hotel had no tourist office, I was told that there was one in another hotel nearby. When I got there, there was a sign saying that we should call a certain number, which I did. A lady answered, and I told her where I wanted to go. I wanted to go to Santa Ana to see the Mayan ruins there, and she said that she had a trip the next day and maybe she could talk the others into going. But she said, "It will be a very long day." Talk about prophecy.

The next day the curfew was over, the streets were crowded, and I thought I would walk up to the tourist office again. I remember there were so many people on the main avenue there that I walked in the gutter. But then the stores did not open; the great metal covers were all fastened down. It's a very beautiful city, incidentally, and very modern — this part of it anyway. This was the main avenue going up to the government buildings. At a little distance I saw a group of marching people. I thought they had swords, but they actually had iron bars, as it turned out. I watched them. They marched up to a bus. Everybody jumped off. They threw a bottle of gasoline in and started burning it. Then they started turning over cars and pulling people out. There were no police, no soldiers anywhere that I could see. And I wondered about that. Then all of a sudden people began to run every which way, like turkeys in a thunderstorm. There was the sound of running feet. I didn't know, of course, what had happened. What had happened was that the army had blocked us in with tanks. There was no escape. Pretty soon they began to fire into the crowds. There were over 200 killed that day, according to the report in *Newsweek*. I was right there among them, trying to stay out of groups. I got up against the wall. Two little groups came to me and begged me to join them. You know, it would have been real nice to have an American assassinated that day for publicity. I kept saying, "No Español." I knew what they were saying, but I didn't go.

When the first rush came I was out in the street and I was swept off my feet, but I never did touch the sidewalk. I was just pushed and I managed to get to my feet again. I had a straw hat on, and it went sailing somewhere. You won't believe this, but somebody brought that hat back and pulled it down way over my ears. Sometime that morning a little boy rushed up to me — maybe he was ten — and he spoke in English and he said in anguish, "What do you think of my country now?"

Well, I kept trying to stay out of groups. It looked like they were firing wherever a little group came together. And riot guns sound like firecrackers: they don't sound dangerous. To me they didn't. I saw a big cathedral, and I decided to go toward it, but when I got there the iron gates were chained. So I started going toward what I thought were government buildings, and they were. I got in front of the census bureau — about the size of this room, very small. I was across the street from it. A big gentleman was standing there. He didn't look like a native; he was too tall. He didn't speak to me. I decided that this was his post. As we stood there, here came a truck with soldiers firing bursts once in a while, left and right. And there was nowhere to go. But the man turned to me — he had a big key — and he opened a door and said, "Come into the American house." That was the name of this little pension, this little boarding house, which had eleven boarders, I remember. He went in and told me to sit down, and I did, and he went away.

Eventually the boarders, who were in their rooms, came out. I stayed there all day, and the firing went on all day. It went on until 3:30 the next morning. They shared their food. They had had no deliveries of food for a week. I think we had fried bananas and plantains or something. We had very little to eat. Anyway, the next day the water came on, the radio came on, lights came on. It was all over. I went back to my hotel and asked them if they could get a taxi to take me to the airport. They did. I felt so good when I got out of the main street.

But when I got to the airport, of course the army was there. A plane was going to Costa Rica within 30 minutes. I was booked on it — I had an open ticket already. But when I started to board the plane, they wouldn't let me get on. They took me back into the station and detained me for five hours. They asked for a picture. Well, I had one on the passport, but I had no other picture. I once wanted to go to the restroom, and there was a soldier there with a big gun with a bayonet on the end of it. He wouldn't let me in. Somebody finally let me in, and he noticed and went right up behind me and stood there.

When that sort of thing happens, do you ever keep notes or keep a journal? Did you ever think of making a piece of writing out of anything like that?

No, but I wrote a letter the next day to Mr. Perrin at Berea, which you might read someday. No, I never did.

Well, have you kept anything like a journal, or have you made notes either on these travels or on just day-to-day living in Knott County?

Yes, I have day-books. I've kept them for 35 years about every facet of life in this area where I live, Knott County mainly, but all around — Pike County and Harlan County — and I think it's a valuable record because it can never be done again. After all these little writings of mine have faded away, which may not be too long, these day-books will probably be a valuable collection for folklorists, sociologists, and so on.

I think I'm beginning to see the connection, then, between your interest in that passing way of life there and the passing way of life that you've been studying down in Central America. Is that the connection, do you think?

It's partly, yes, I think so. I don't know that I study. I just let it happen. I just read for fun, and if the information sticks in my head, that's fine.

I mentioned a moment ago Saul Bellow. I mentioned Robert Penn Warren. I mentioned Katherine Anne Porter. Who are some of the writers that you have known, maybe some of these among them?

I really haven't known any of them, to tell the truth. I did know Robert Frost somewhat over the many years. I used to see him occasionally at one place or another. And as you said, Katherine Anne Porter and Elizabeth Bishop and Eleanor Clark. When I say I know these people, I mean I've met them and talked with them.

Well, you must have had some impression of them.
Well, yes, those I met at Yaddo I did, because I was with them a great deal, especially in the winter of 1951 when we were frozen in. This was our company for many hours a day.

There's a biography, published recently, of Katherine Anne Porter, and a lot of people have been going back over that long life. She was born, I believe, in 1890 and lived to be 90 some years old. Was she there in '51?
She was always there when I was. Let's see. She was there in '40, '41, and '51. I knew her best, though, that winter, as I told you. We'd sit at breakfast for hours. After all, the snow was very deep and it never melted. We just had some more snow. We lived within a very small perimeter there. So we used to talk. And that's pretty good company — Elizabeth Madox Roberts, Elizabeth Bishop, and Eleanor Clark. I remember for a long time it was just we four. And Yaddo being what it is, we had four people and four cooks, so we ate most of the time. And played ping-pong. Katherine Anne was a very poor loser.

I got to thinking recently again about how much you have dealt in both your fiction and poetry with horses. And now I learn that there was this early book in your home, *The Anatomy of the Horse.* Your father was a veterinarian, who went out and treated horses. You have some special affinity for horses, obviously.
I like them all right. I never owned one. I might be able to buy one, but I can't feed him. A horse eats more than you do.

You've even written a poem about "Man o' War," that great all-time champion.
Well, an epitaph.

I heard you read that on National Public Radio, which is, by the way, another phase of your writing that you've taken on the last few years. For the benefit of people who haven't been listening to NPR, tell what it is you do there.
Well, I do three-minute spots. I do a whole bunch of them at one time. I don't read them, though the last bunch I did write out a little bit and then looked at them. But up until now I haven't read them. I go over to the Appalshop film studios and do a dozen at a time. They're sent up to Washington and occasionally they put one on. I hardly ever hear them. If I'm at home, they call me, and I might listen. But I usually pick them up on the car radio when I'm on the road somewhere.

Well, you usually work a poem into those comments, don't you?
　　I do sometimes, yes.

I remember you did the one about the bad-man, "Are You Up There, Bad Jack?" recently. I'll bet there's someone in this audience who is interested in writing. Do you have any advice for anyone seriously interested in taking up the craft or the art or the trade?
　　Not long ago I read somewhere about an actress. I'd never heard of her, but she was quite famous. She was ninety-two. And they asked her, "Do you have some advice for an actor or an actress who's already here in New York trying to get ahead?" She said, "Yes. Go home."

That's not very encouraging.
　　Well, I think if you need to do it — I suppose I did — you do it. I wouldn't have done it if I hadn't had this need to do it. I've never written a story with just the idea of publishing it, except one, and it was very bad. It's been called my best by a few people. That's inevitable. However, I don't know what to advise them. I certainly would get a good all around education — I think I would do that — and if you can't help it, well all right. Good luck to you.

We talked about the schools you went to and the composition classes you attended. This was pretty much expository writing, wasn't it? But what about courses devoted exclusively to imaginative writing — novels, short stories, poems, and plays? Are they helpful, do you think? Would you advise people to take them?
　　I think writing, as everybody knows, is a pretty lonely profession, if you can call it a profession. A vocation, or whatever it is. The chances of making a living at it are very slim. When you get into commercial writing, that's another field. I'm not talking about that. I don't know anything about that; it's another world altogether. I think you've got to be willing to live the life of a writer. That is, it's got to be one of your priorities and maybe your main one. You've got to make a living somehow. In my case, I taught school. I'm not sure that's the best place to be. However, it's about the only shelter writers have had in the last quarter of a century, I suppose — a place where you can be certain of making a living and be near your own subject. I think it's a different matter for every person who wants to go into it. People speak about ambition. I never thought for a moment that I'd write as many stories or poems as I have or that anybody would pay any attention to them. I'll tell you how I learned, if anybody can ever say. When I was in Lincoln Memorial, people used to send to the library old magazines and other things they didn't want. Among the magazines that would come to the library was *The Atlantic Monthly*. I began to read it, and I liked it and I decided I wanted to write something for it. I just wanted to write one piece for the magazine. I was supposed to save one copy and then burn the others in the furnace. But I would save one for the library and one for myself.

That summer I sent home maybe as many as 50 copies of *The Atlantic*. I wasn't in school that summer. I went home — it was during the Depression, and there was no work — and read and studied those magazines. I read everything in them. I think that's where I learned, if I did. *The Atlantic* was a magazine of some prestige in those days — less so now.

Well, you've done some teaching in colleges and universities and taken part in writers' workshops, and people have submitted to you poems and stories. What quality in a poem or a story would suggest to you that there may be some promise?

I never taught creative writing. However, I have read manuscripts, and I'll be perfectly frank. Only once have I read a manuscript that I knew was the real thing. I never had any doubt about it. In fact, this person, who was a senior in the University of Kentucky, came up to Morehead, and he submitted three short stories. I read them and had him in for an interview. But what I said to him was, "I'm not going to talk about these stories. This is professional work. And I want to advise you, for one thing, to stay away from writers' conferences because you have nothing to learn from them. You're already a professional. Frankly, I don't like any of these stories. They don't interest me, but it's professional writing, and I think all three can be published." So what we talked about instead of the manuscripts was how he could go about being a writer, living the life of a writer. Several years ago at the University of Kentucky he was present at a little seminar I was giving there, and he came up to me and said he wanted to thank me for what I did for him. This man by now has published many books; he's famous all over the country. But I began to feel very proud that I had recognized his talent. Now, I didn't discover him; he discovered himself. Well, I said, "I didn't do anything for you. I just told you that you have already arrived, in a sense." He said, "No, that wasn't it." He said, "What you did for me was that you were the first person who ever showed any confidence in my work and that was the thing that meant something to me." I believe those were the words.

Would you care to say whom you're talking about?
Wendell Berry.

Well, this business of managing life. Is that what you were doing all that time even though it looked as though you might not be getting on in the conventional sense — working six years for an average of six cents a day? You were getting on as a writer, weren't you?

Not in Kentucky. And not anywhere in the South. Although I was publishing all over, really — in *Esquire, The Saturday Evening Post, The Atlantic Monthly, The Yale Review, The Nation, The New Republic,* and *The Sewanee Review* — still I do not recall anybody in that area ever telling me they had read a book of mine. Not once. So apparently I can work without very much encouragement. I wasn't doing it for anybody anyway — just for myself.

Well, you know all that has changed now.

Oh, yes, there are a few school teachers.

It took people a while to find out about you. They're reading you now.

I recall that a professor at the University of Kentucky thought that students in the high schools and colleges in the state did not know about its poets, and should know. So he brought together a collection of eighty-seven Kentucky poets. At that time I was publishing in all these magazines, but I was not one of them. I didn't make it.

What should I have asked you that I didn't?

It seems to me you've covered a lot of ground. I don't know. I've heard people talk about the craft of writing in the *Paris Review* volumes, but you'll notice that they're never talking about the art. They always talk about the craft. And I'm a little superstitious about it. When I was a child, we never dared look in the well. It was said if you were going to die that year you would see yourself in your casket. So we would draw our water without looking. I'm a little fearful of looking into, shall we say, the wellsprings of creativity. I don't know what I would find there. I'm not sure why I do these things. I'm not sure. I don't know. I just do it.

An Interview with James Still

TOM *and* CAROL FRENCH-CORBETT
and LOIS KLEFFMAN

Preface

On November 15, 1985, Tom and Carol French-Corbett, along with Lois Kleffman, editor of the Jackson County *Sun*, had lunch with writer James Still at the Hindman Settlement School in Hindman, Kentucky. Afterwards they drove to Still's log cabin and recorded a remarkable conversation with this 80-year-old writer. The interview was published the next year, in the first volume of the periodical *Limestone, A Literary Journal*, long edited at the University of Kentucky. Said Still, "I've always been skittish of interviews. Some who would do one have never read a word of my scribbling. There are at the moment two interviews awaiting publication. I have in all honesty all my life been pursuing my version of happiness and fulfillment without much regard for the opinion of others. And the selfishness in this activity should not be overlooked. However, what little attention I am getting now has come late, and it will pass. A recent issue of *Newsweek* dealt with the up and coming writers in the South. I'm not mentioned. These are the literary gents and ladies who are going to bury me. That's as it should be. In twenty-five years I'll be relegated to a footnote. Yet the sun broke through for a moment in my life. It was ... is enough."

The Interview

Limestone: Tell us a little of your family background.

Still: My father's people came in pioneer days down here in Jonesville, Virginia, which isn't far away. In a sense I've come home. You'll see a sign where Alfred Taylor Still was born. That was one of my forebearers. He is the father of osteopathy. From there they went to Missouri, and then settled all over.

*Tom and Carol French-Corbett and Lois Kleffman, "An Interview with James Still," *Limestone, A Literary Journal*, vol. 1 (1986), pp. 53–75. Reprinted with permission.

How did they turn up in Alabama?

The reason my grandpa went to the hills in Alabama is because his forebears fought in the Revolutionary War. And there was a kind of sweepstakes. They gave land to the veterans, and that's the land he drew.

Now my mother's people were Scotch-Irish, near Frederick County, Virginia, Foxfire county. There again they fought in the Revolutionary War and were given land there. My grandfather, when my mother was about eight or so, went over into Alabama and swapped land with somebody. So that put my two grandpas within three or four miles of each other. These are two families that wouldn't think of having anything to do with each other socially somehow.

What was your mother's name?

Lindsey. Her mother was Jackson. My father's mother was McClendon.

So the dedication of *River of Earth* to Lonnie Lindsey Still is to your mother?

Yea. Her name was Barcelona.

So it came to be Lonnie?

It's usually spelled "Lona."

You were born in Alabama?

I was born in the same county as Joe Louis. I never saw him. My father was a veterinarian, and he took me with him to the Barrows—you know his name was really Barrow—to see some sick horse. And he introduced me to some of Joe Louis' uncles and aunts and cousins. When my father died in 1957, Joe Louis' daughter was the cook in my sister's home. And she said her father Joe was married two or three times. Apparently he sent her home. She never saw a dime of his money. See, these people were originally slaves, and they took the name of their master—Barrow.

Now when I was a little boy—first two or three grades—they had a high school in the courthouse. There was a black man—he was kinda yellow looking, really. He was a skinny fellow who was a janitor. Very popular with everybody. We'd go in there and he'd let us drink ice-water. You see we couldn't reach. He'd hold us up to drink. I remember he got an assistant there. His name was Joe Barrow. That's Joe Louis' father. If we didn't see the little black man, Puss Irwin (everyone called him Puss), if we didn't see Puss, we were afraid of this man Barrow. I can see him now, sitting on the steps. Well, this man Barrow died, and his mother took the children and went to Detroit and married a Louis.

Was your home in Alabama?

Uh-huh. We moved down into the Chattahoochee Valley by the time I was in 8th grade. See, I was born about twenty-five miles from where Carson McCullers was born in Georgia. I knew Carson. In fact, she gave me a book once, autobiographical. She bawled me out one time, too.

Anyhow, I met her family up at Bread Loaf, at the writer's conference there. I had a fellowship, and she did too, along with Eudora Welty, Robert Francis, and two or three others.

When was this?

About 1937. *The Heart Is a Lonely Hunter*— an extraordinary book for a girl that age to write. I hate to say it, but I don't think I ever saw her completely sober. One day I read she was staying over in Brooklyn in some house — a lot of writers got together and were living in this huge house. Everybody there was famous. I told here she ought to go home. She asked me to recommend her for a Guggenheim to write *A Member of the Wedding*. I had to return the papers to the Guggenheim Foundation, but I made a copy. She couldn't spell very well. One day she told me her brother just got married and moved out, leaving an empty room. So she asked me to come down to stay a while. I did try to look her up, but couldn't find the house. There's one book here, a biography of Carson McCullers. It's a terrible book. I suppose you couldn't deny any of the facts, but there's a line you've got to draw somewhere. You just don't destroy a person. It tells all.

Now this is a girl [taking another book], Katherine Anne Porter, I have a lot of admiration for, because I knew her in Yaddo. I've been there seven times. Someone told me I shouldn't tell people I was friends with Katherine Anne Porter.

Why not?

She admits to thirty-seven lovers. Well, I said I was not one of them. I was very much aware she was at least 20 years older than I. Although she was ageless. Her second husband was 26. The day they married he found out she was 50. She said their marriage lasted one day. Toward the end of her life she was getting paranoid. See, Katherine Anne, when I knew her, had nothing. She lived out of a suitcase all of her life. She had nothing. But she lived the grandest life. Last summer I was privileged to read 87 of her letters nobody had ever read. But anyway.... See, Katherine Anne invented a childhood. She actually was born in a log house. Not a very bad circumstance. But she wasn't proud of her family at all. And so she made up a very beautiful youth, you know, Southern mansions, magnolias, and stuff. And eventually people knew better.

How did you come to meet Don West? Did you meet him in college?

He was there, and I have to admit I didn't know him very well there. He was a friend of Jesse Stuart. They were close friends. But when I went over to Vanderbilt, Don was there in the school of religion. And then I got to know him better. We didn't know anybody else, so we used to go to places together.

Did you do your undergraduate work at Vanderbilt also?

No. Lincoln Memorial, down there in Tennessee. Very unusual school. In my day it was then Berea. Everybody worked. And it was the kind of school I needed at the time. You got personal attention.

You went to the University of Illinois at Champaign/Urbana?
Yes. The only thing open to me.... Jim Wayne Miller, for example, the reason he had to go to Vanderbilt. He applied, and had to have a scholarship. But there were no scholarships available except in German. So he took German. He got a doctorate in German. So the only scholarship available to me was library school at the University of Illinois. So I went there and got a degree in library science.

So I had a scholarship from Benjamin Duke [tobacco merchant], on his deathbed, it turned out. The Dukes gave Lincoln Memorial a building. It's called the Hall of Citizenship. It's still there. It was dedicated the year I graduated. I swiped up all the essay contests I entered except one. I won them all. He read about it. He offered me all expense for graduate school and Duke University. More than that he sent me $200.00 — that was a lot of money then — to bring me over to Duke to get acquainted and make arrangements.

What was your bachelor's degree?
I had a double major — history and literature.

So it was Lincoln Memorial to Duke?
No. I didn't go to Duke, because there was a man named Guy Loomis who gave money for scholarships to Lincoln Memorial. He was a man up in his eighties. Gave money to a lot of schools, and this was one of them. I wanted to write him a little note of thanks, you know. And the person who handled this said he didn't want contact. So I said, well, I can just write him a note. I didn't have to know his name. So I did. And he appreciated it. He had never had contact with anybody else — Berea and a lot of other places. So eventually he came down and had a lot of us out to dinner to get acquainted. And then when I graduated I was the only person who ever invited him to graduation. And he came in his big custom-built Cadillac and he spent a whole week. And I remember his chauffeur. He was very bored. He said, "All this grass! It drives me crazy." Big lawns. He wasn't used to that. He lived in Brooklyn. So Mr. Loomis attended class day and everything. And when I won all these awards, he came out of the auditorium and said, "Wouldn't you like to go to graduate school?" And I said, "Where?" And he said, "Anywhere in the South." Then he also said, "Do you know another student?" And I said, "Yeah, my roommate." So sight unseen, he also gave him a scholarship. But he wanted us to go to the same place. But the other fellow didn't want to go. I decided not to go to Duke. I left Duke when I went to visit there, and came by the University of North Carolina. And so I went to Vanderbilt.

How did you come to Kentucky?
I came back from the University of Illinois, and stopped in Nashville to see Don West. He said he was going to Hindman Settlement. He was going to a vocational Bible school for the Congregational Church, and he wanted me

and his brother-in-law to run a recreational program. And we did. Boy Scouts. We had three Boy Scout troops, three baseball teams, and we camped and did things, and played ball all summer.

What year was it when you came to Hindman Settlement School to stay?
I came in '31, and then in '32 they needed a librarian. I didn't have any job. Nobody was working. They couldn't pay anybody, so they just fed us and housed us. I worked three years with no pay. I got a little bit in the fourth year. At the end of six years I averaged six cents a day for six years. I'd begun to write to make a few bucks.

You had been writing in college?
No, not really. I did write this thing for *American Speech*—two articles which they published, and which H. L. Mencken put in his book which is still around. I'll give him credit for apparently one sentence, but the articles are there, both of them.

So you began to do your writing. Was the first thing you published *River of Earth*?
Well, of course, I was in the magazines—*Atlantic Monthly, Yale Review, Virginia Quarterly Review, The Nation,* eventually even the *Saturday Evening Post*. They kept me up for several years. When I started I sent the *Saturday Evening Post* one story a year. They give you $500 for the first story and then you're paid according to reader response. I can live a year on one story. So I started going to Florida in the winter, just based on one story.

During the war I went away to the Army. When I got back I sent them a story. And the editor wrote me and said it didn't suit the *Post*, and more than that they didn't think there was any magazine in America that would publish it. So I sent it to the *Yale Review* and they published it. So I never sent the *Post* another story. But they did do several poems.

So this was work over and above what you were doing at the school?
Right. Oh, there were little things. You wouldn't call it writing. On some Sunday I'd write a poem or something like that. Everything I wrote is published to this day. I have two or three things I haven't sent out. And I don't always get things where I want them.

Did you ever submit to the *New Yorker*? Did you ever want to be published there?
I wouldn't mind being in there. I subscribed to the *New Yorker* for many years. It comes every week! It's a career! They have a stable. And not many of them can read. The prose is dry, obscure. Private world.

You're obviously an established writer, and you look upon yourself as a poet...
Oh, I do?

Yea, I'd say...

I've never called myself a poet. Never have and never will. I don't call myself a writer either. I don't call myself anything. If somebody said, "What do you do?" I used to say, "A farmer." But I'm not a lot of things. I'll tell you what I like. Not long ago, Al Smith (you know, on "Kentucky Comment" KET, and editor of the *London Sentinel Echo*) introduced me up here in Morehead in July. He called me a philosopher, a rural philosopher. I kinda like that.

You don't feel that you have to produce so many words a week, or...

Naw. I don't write anything like that. I'd be overwhelmed by it.

So what prompts you to write?

I don't know. It's like one time a man spent the day with me. He said, "How did you learn to cook?" "Well," I said, "I got hungry!" which is the way to do anything. I just saw the need. You ever feel like you want to write a letter to somebody? You know what I mean? Not just write a letter. I mean, you know, you want to communicate. And I don't ever write for a lot of people. I just write for one person. Sometimes I have a person in mind I'm writing for.

Sometimes I'm introduced to somebody, and they'll say, "He's a writer." And I don't like that. Immediately a curtain comes down. There's no more rapport. It's destroyed. You don't introduce somebody and say he's a janitor or a plumber. Why should you call me a writer? I just also write some things. And writers write all kinds of things—newspapers. All kinds of people are writers. Anybody composing a note to the milkman is a writer, I suppose.

Do you compose at the typewriter?

Of course, most things are done at the typewriter. That's what that old gentleman gave me was a typewriter. He gave several of us typewriters. I took typing instructions at odd moments when I could. So in two weeks I was typing. It's true it took a lot of practice, but I still already had the keyboard. See, it's a matter of motivation. If you want to do something, if you really want to do it, you can do it. You don't fool around.

I've had the impression you were more of a recluse, but now as we've talked, you're bringing the whole world into this room.

I know people in Central America. I know someone in practically every college and university in the United States. I see people. I go. I go everywhere, all over, up and down.

You are obviously not a recluse.

And I couldn't bear it either. I do require—and I think everyone does—a time alone. I couldn't bear to spend my days in a house with a lot of people. I don't care who they are, my folks or yours or anybody else's. I like weekends. I like Sundays, when I don't see anybody. What I do is prop up in bed over there and read all day. I try to do it on Sundays, but I don't manage it very often.

But, well, I do. I wake up at four or five in the morning, and I may be there at one o'clock in the afternoon. Get up, make some coffee, eat some cereal, eat a banana, you know.

How do you deal with the notoriety which accompanies your work?
I think too much, in some sense, is made of writers. I think I've had far too much attention in the last two years. It's not even good for me. You've got to maintain that serenity of soul. You start believing what people say about you. You've seen it often. Many actors it happens to—many people who are suddenly thrust out into the public eye.

Doesn't it make you feel good to get that recognition though?
I don't know. It's like I told them about Isaac Bashevis Singer. Someone said to him, "Mr. Singer, you have sixteen honorary doctoral degrees, don't you?" He thought a minute and he said "Sixty." Then his wife spoke up, "He said ninety." Then Singer said, "The degrees were cheap but the frames were high." I appreciate all these things. I have five of these doctorates. I appreciate them all. But I don't want anyone calling me doctor. And I tell them, "It's good for just one day, the only day you can call me doctor, if you want to." I don't like titles. I have a hard time calling people Reverend. I wonder especially in the religious world how anybody could be called the Very Right Reverend, how anybody could stand that.

How can you take that day after day, being called that knowing that you're just who you are?
John Stephenson related this to me once. He said, "You remember the first time I talked to you?" I said, "No, I don't." He said, "I've always remembered what you said. I said something about your being humble, and you told me you didn't have a humble bone in your body." I'm that way. I think real humble people are sick. They've got a bad image of themselves. And I don't have. I don't. One of the reasons I get along very well is that I don't go around with a sense of guilt. If I do something I really shouldn't do, the recognition that moment that I've done it is enough. That takes care of it. I forgive myself easily.

That's wonderful. How did you learn to do that?
It came natural. I'm too lazy to worry. I just can't bother about worrying. If there's something I can do about it, I'll do it. But if I can't do anything about it, it's over and done with and out of my mind by next morning. Another day.

When you write, is it blood, sweat and tears, or is it like water flowing from a duck's back?
If I didn't enjoy it, I wouldn't do it. I always call it a painful joy. But I get excited when I'm really into it. It's very difficult sometimes when you stop. Once it's finished, I want to keep on rolling. I'm very alert. I want to turn the

subject loose. But if you're working on something long, you don't want to leave it. When that happens, I'm just not living in this world.

When I finished reading *River of Earth* I wanted to know what happened to that boy. Did he have to be a coal miner or did he get to be a horse doctor?
That's what you have to decide.

I wonder why you didn't write more about that.
There's another book that follows that, and it's called *Sporty Creek*. It really takes up with another family, one of their cousins. Uncle Jolly's in it.
People always ask me about my style. I say, "I don't know what you're talking about." Your style is you, ain't it? I have no more style of writing than I have style of talking. It just comes out.

I'm surprised with your compression of language. You're economical. It's like poetic prose—short images and metaphors which convey a lot. I frequently find myself rereading, just like I do a poem.
Because you didn't understand it?

It goes fast. The images are like a kaleidoscope. Sometimes they are tacked on to each other...
You see an outdoor movie—you're drawing up here, you see, you pass, you see how fast those scenes change? You see, it's the same method. I'm expecting you to keep up with it.

And it's not always easy.
I require a little concentration.

I'm not complaining.
I don't know what it's like. You see, I can read and it doesn't mean anything. Well, these later things, the books of stories, you'll notice a change—like "The Run for the Elbertas"—that's a long story there. *Yale Review* said some years ago in an article on me this story had more things happening in it than any short story ever written in America.

I believe it.
Here's what I think. There are two kinds of fiction stories. One is to hear someone telling a story. You're very much aware all the time that somebody's telling you this story. Then there's another story, the kind I want to write, in which I take you into it, and you're not aware. This is the thing itself.

The story takes over.
And it couldn't be done any other way. That is, this sentence could not have been any other way. What this man said could not have been said any other way. Whereas, sometimes I'm reading along in somebody's works, and I think, I wouldn't have done that. I'd have left this out ... I can correct it.

Have you ever thought of doing any criticism?

No, no, no. I'm not going to fool with that. You get off into a different world there. It requires a different language. Anyway, I don't want to sit in judgment of anyone.

Is there a big distinction between poetry and prose in your mind?

[*With a laugh*] One's prose and the other's poetry. I will say in writing prose, though, what I'm writing here is a paragraph. I don't do a lot of revising. I write a paragraph. I just play with it until it's there. It's like stirring concrete. After a while you can't stir it anymore. I play with it a while until it seems to be right. And then I go on to the next one. And I'm not concerned — I don't think about writing. I don't think about those things. I'm just telling a story.

Frequently the narrative voice in your stories is an older man looking back as young boy in the early part of this century — which seems to approximate your own age and your own youth. Is there a personal connection there?

No. Every character — you're every one of them, and you make instantaneous changes from one character to the next as you write about them. You're every one of them. You have to have that ability. You know an actor — their art depends on how many people they can be. John Wayne was just John Wayne. Never anything else. And there are writers who just write about themselves.

Do you prefer to write of the distant past?

Everything's done in the past. Everything is either yesterday or ... see what I mean? No, I'm not stuck back there, by any means. No. The peach story was much forward of that. These stories came up in the sixties. I'm reaching for a timelessness. I read things today. Take Bobbie Ann Mason. However cleverly she writes nowadays, oh, ten years from now, how outdated that's going to be.

What do you think of Bobbie Ann Mason?

Oh, she's fun to read, anything like that. She's overrated right now. She's popular. Like Joyce Carol Oates. Kinda developed into her own genre — those little gothic things. I can't read her novels at all. Some people thought she was the greatest thing since sliced bread. But not anymore.

Anne Rice, I reckon, writes well. But not for me. I read her story. I liked it. I enjoyed it. But when I got through reading, that was all there was to it. I couldn't go back and pick out something. It's one-dimensional — well, maybe one and a half. Rather sort of caricatures. They don't have any life beyond what we've seen and been told.

Your work bears up well on rereading. I've read several of your things often. They're better each time.

Really?

Really!

The only book I've ever read of mine is *Sporty Creek*.

Is there a conscious reason for that?
I start them and I get going to change them.

Do you sweat over the proofs from the publisher?
It's just cold blood. Oh no. I just look at it like I would somebody else's.

Just like you're proofreading, say, for punctuation?
Well, these books here. I can find typographical errors in other people's books. They're hard to find in my own.

If I write a story nowadays, I do everything on the typewriter. But before I turn it loose, I would sit down and write it out by hand, slowly, copy it by hand slowly. Then if I want to proofread it, really proofread it, I read it backwards — I can see the spelling, punctuation.

But in writing I will say this. Here's a paragraph and there's something wrong with it. I don't know what. Somehow it doesn't go right. So I put it in the typewriter and I copy it just like it was a poem. Each sentence is a line, you know. Then I can check the flow. Presumably, every sentence anybody writes has never been written before. And sometimes I get into a sentence. I'll tell you the truth — I don't know whether it's grammatical or not. I can't tell. I've made a sentence I've never seen before, of course. I'll get out my grammars. I'll run all up and down everything, and still can't decide — then I'll just take it out. If it bothers me it'll bother somebody else.

You'll notice the vocabulary, too, of mine. Ideally in a short story, certainly if the story is in the first person, ideally I would not tell my character to use a word — there would not be a word in that story, rather, that is not in their vocabulary. Now it's true you can't do that absolutely, but that is an ideal.

Your stories are just full of flora and fauna.
Oh, really?

Yea.
Oh, I hope so. I thought there wasn't enough in them. Really?

Yea.
I'm glad. I thought there weren't enough.

That, of course, reflects your own interest.
Yeah. Everything does.

I wonder if the characters would have that much knowledge of nature.
Well, the writer does ... well, now here again. There's two fellows here yesterday. They can't read and write, either one of them. I was coming over here and I picked them up. I see them maybe once in six months. One's exactly my age, or a year older, and one's still older. I used to run around with them a lot of years ago. They notice the plants. I know every weed that grows in the yard. There isn't any dirt here that hasn't passed through my hands around this place.

Do you take notes with any kind of regularity?

Well, I have kept notebooks for 35 to 40 years in which every facet of life has been recorded — things people said and all. Here's the diary — let me show you. I don't like the "diary." Did I bring it in? No. Well, no matter. I wanted to show you the sort of things I put down. Twenty-two or twenty-three volumes in there have been copied now. They're down at the University of Kentucky. Nobody can look at them. They're mine. They're in safe keeping down there, I think. They've made an extra copy. I sometimes have in the past read out of them. There are some wonderful things in there though.

You have an ear for the language of the people in your stories. Do you rely on your own ear for that?

Well, of course, I just write. I don't even think about it until after I finish the story. I don't write *Appalachian* stories. I don't write dialect. I just write what I hear, you know. I just write as I know it. And sometimes I wonder later if I overdo it. You know, I'm very careful about that. There seems to be a great deal of that.

I wrote a poem called "High Field." It just shows my old neighbor when he was 86 years old. His wife had died and he had all these children. I don't know how many of them. He came up this holler with his boys, one of them big enough to work, the others weren't. And went up there in the mountains and was hoeing corn. And he said, "You came up there one day and you grabbed a hoe. You told us who you were, but you didn't tell us why you were there. And you got the hoe." And he said, "I needed help, but you wouldn't accept pay." Well, anyway, he went on to tell me that. And I just wrote it down. And there's the poem, virtually as he said it. See, people are speaking poems, you know, when you can hear them.

Have you decided where you're going to leave your papers?

Oh, Morehead has a room down there full of them. Beautiful room. All books and magazines there. The University of Kentucky has most of this stuff. The last few years, Berea College, some.

See, I have these letters from all kinds of people, like James T. Farrell, at one time or another. I just happened to keep them. I seem to be a collector, but I'm not. Things just accumulate. Oh, the notes! I noticed some I'm doing now — papers, folders, and things. I have this short story I've never written. About 20, 30, years ago I thought of a short story and wanted to write. It kept on. I know the title of it. But every once in a while I'd think of something to go into it. It's never been written. But the file is *that* thick. I wouldn't possibly use all the stuff that I've already thought. The characters would say something to me ... see I know the characters, and they'll say something to me in that story. Yeah, they'll talk to me. I don't talk for them. I don't say they would have said this ... it's just like I'm talking now. I don't think ahead of time what I'm going to say.... But then you go back to your writing and cut it out.

Your writing seems devoid of sentimentality and romance.

Well, I hope so. See, I'm looking for timelessness. That stuff dates the devil. If I knew how to do it in a decent way, I think I would. I can't stand to read that crap myself so why should I write it? Other people are doing that.

You told us coming up here that you really wanted reading to be a happy experience. But a lot of your writing is about sad things.

Life is full of sadness. And, you know, there's such a thing as catharsis. You know about that. And I think the only way you can be happy is to be realistic and face reality.

In reading the opening chapters of *River of Earth*, I was practically in tears.

You were?

Yeah. It was heart-rending. So sad, I wasn't sure I wanted to go on. There is a lean, stark, tough quality it seems to me, in a lot of your writing, like in "Heritage," for example. Is this poem a kind of personal testimonial?

It was at that moment in time. But, you know, the next moment ... I don't even remember writing it. I have no remembrance of writing it.

You don't?

I don't remember writing much of *River of Earth*. I remember writing the beginning of it. And I remember writing the end of it. I was sitting right there with that open door right over there. I remember writing the end of it. I thought I was going to write another chapter. I had in mind another chapter. But when I wrote the last sentence I realized that was it finished.

A man one time was up at a Whitesburg bookstore — a fellow who was in the State Senate. I was introduced to him by this woman as James Still, the author. He said, "I thought you were dead." "Well," I said, "I may be." He said, "You know, when I read that book, when I finished reading that book, I felt funny." I said, "What do you mean?" He said, "I wanted to cry." That's what he said.

There was a man. He was a young priest. He called me and said, "I got a man here who wants to talk to you, if you'll come down to the office." He's a wealthy man. I've noticed his name on Kentucky Educational Television. But anyhow, when I got there, he said, "I wanted to meet you. I read *River of Earth*, and you don't know me, and I never saw you before, and I want to know how you could possibly write the story or my life, my childhood," he said. "You have written it. It's true my mother didn't burn the house down, but everything else in that book is true. That is the life I lived as a child." That's what he said. Well, I'm through with a piece of writing when it becomes true. I believe it when it seems true.

There are things in that book that no matter who reads it, they'll find a truth in there that's part of them.

I hope so, because our lives are pretty much alike — experiences meaning the same thing. A retired school teacher, a librarian, said to me once, "Well, I read the book. Didn't expect much." But she said, "Lived here all my life. But I never saw this country. I never saw it until I read *River of Earth*. I saw the hills and how the people lived, but took it all for granted. Never even thought about it." I thought that was a fine statement. I liked it.

In your stories the mountain woman, the mother, is like a mythic figure of stability.

Yea, yea, yea. She runs all the homes. The women run this country — the houses are families. She didn't have a vote. She was already voting. Although there might have been some of them against voting. As children go off to school, she's the one who sees they go. A woman said to me one day (she had a number of children), "You know, after you've been a'married a while, your husband just becomes one of the children."

Like the man who wasn't very well off, but saw to it his children went to college, especially his daughter. Someone said to him. "How can you make that sacrifice for your daughter? After all, she's just going to get married." He said, "When I educate my son, it's just one person; when I educate my daughter, it's a whole family."

That's exactly right.

To what extent do you consider yourself a regional writer?

Well, I think my writing for the most part, for now (not necessarily in the future), has dealt with, let's say, a region. And I trust I'm not a local colorist. I think about all writers are regional. Faulkner is definitely regional. Doesn't he write about a region? And really, in a sense, Thomas Wolfe does. Even when he went to New York, he took it with him. And Carson McCullers left home. But all of her work except one play is about Georgia. Isn't that a region? Just name anybody. Marjorie Kinnan Rawlings. Hemingway, well, of course, when he wrote the north woods thing, that's a region. He just had several regions, that's all. They're all regional. So in that sense, I'm regional.

Which book of yours was the best commercial success?

None of them. Well, let's put it this way. *River of Earth* was published nearly forty-six years ago. And it's been from three different publishing houses. And it has been a trickle over the years. It sold well the first year. And then, you know, any book, usually every book, is dead in six months. But it sold in hardcover for years, then went into paperback. Then it was on lease to the Popular Library. And then when the lease was up, the University Press of Kentucky brought it out, and they have now published and sold nearly ten thousand. Last year the University of Tennessee bought 700 copies.

Do you have any work that's given you greater satisfaction than others?

I write them and forget about them. But I think if you had to just pick out one in each category, I would say there's a short story. "Mrs. Razor." It's been around a long time. It's been reprinted now over forty times in books. And I would say as a book, a novel, *River of Earth*. As a poem, I wouldn't choose it myself, but apparently the public has chosen it — "Heritage." I've read it so many times. I don't know what's there.

That's the amazing statement. I have a hard time believing that.
Believing what?

That it doesn't mean anything to you anymore.
That's not fair to say it doesn't mean anything. When I say it doesn't mean anything, I don't think about it. I have no feelings of ownership. I'm being very objective about it. I wouldn't be objective about something I'm writing now.

It's so far in the past that it's not part of you anymore?
The minute you write something, it wears off. I used to have students. They wrote poems and things. I noticed the poems people were writing were about fate and destiny. Deep subjects. I said, "Well, while you are doing that, Robert Frost would probably write a poem about a cow eating an apple. But I just thought about it. I thought all of sudden of all the apples I've eaten. And I wrote a poem about a cow eating an apple. But, you see, it went back to the apple that started the Swiss Independence, Adam and Eve, and the apple that conked Newton on the head. But then I came down to a specific case. I said I knew a man who was inventing a perpetual motion machine.... There's a lot of philosophy in this, and, I think, as they say, food for thought. So it's there in the desk. I saw it this morning, and I'll play with it again someday. I'm just playing. I'm not trying to write. But, generally, they're all written in a few minutes, and that's it. Fifteen minutes. I may change a word or something.

When will your new volume of poetry come out?
I think that date's in July. The 16th. I want you all to come to Hindman. They're going to celebrate my birthday! It's going to be a big shindig!

Your eightieth birthday!
They'll all be here from Berea, the University of Kentucky and all over. They're going to have speakers.

Tell us some of your interests above and beyond the literary. I know you have a keen interest in the Mayan culture.
All primitive people, wherever they are. The Prego, the aborigines in Australia. I'm reading constantly about them. Another thing I'm interested in is mountain climbing in the Himalayas. I have a pretty good collection of books on mountain climbing. I'm interested in Tibet. The Civil War — I've gone back to it recently. Of course, I read anything to do with psychology. I'm interested in medicine. I read *Science News* weekly. I have a lot of interests. I'm especially

interested in plant genetics. In my early days of biology, you see, it was known so little. I'm sort of a generalist.

Do you pursue your other interests as much as you do the Mayan civilization?

It's almost minor. I'll start right in pretty soon now. I'll go back to Central America to some places I haven't seen. I'll go back to some of the old places. I got some more books now, and I'll refresh and learn. I know more now. You see I have a particular thing in mind. I was up at the University of Cincinnati — invited up there — I was sponsored by the English department. The chairman had a way of taking you around to meet people — you know, the president and so on. He said, "Here's the provost. He's the man that runs this place." (He's now the president incidentally). "We'll just bounce in and bounce out." That's what he said. So we went in, shook hands with him. He stood up. He said, "I've been reading about you. You've been down to Central America. You're interested in the Mayans. What is your interest down there?" I said, "That's a long story." He said "Well, I want to hear it." He came out from behind the desk, went over to the other end of the office, and here were some comfortable seats. He sent out for coffee. And we sat there. I was there for two hours. The man just pelted me. The chairman wanted to go. He couldn't believe it. He was just going to bounce in and bounce out.

My interests chiefly boil down to this: Why did the Mayans of all the intellectuals among the Indian peoples, why did they virtually disappear from the face of the earth within one hundred and fifty years? Whereas all the others seemed to thrive. Well, that's a great question and is still unanswered. I have a book here on the Mayan collapse. There are various theories about it, and I have my own, which I'm not ready to express yet.

We could almost call you a Renaissance man.

Well, I tell you. I'm nearly eighty. If I couldn't read and didn't have an interest in the world, and didn't want to create things, I don't know what I'd do. I really don't know what I would do.

An Interview with James Still

LAURA LEE *and* FOXFIRE STUDENTS

A group of high school students from Rabun County, Georgia, conducted two interviews with James Still, one in our classroom and one in Hindman, Kentucky, where Still lives. Still looks closer to being sixty years young than eighty years old. Although he moves carefully, all his actions are sharp and enthusiastic. He is very expressive in using his hands and changing his facial features to emphasize a point he is making. His face is plump and cheerful, the forehead creased with years stretching back into a smooth, bald head ringed by short white hair. His ears are those of an elf, slightly pointed on the ends. The eyes sometimes seem sad, but they are active, flitting from face to face and giving us each bright, keen glances as he answered our questions. His eyebrows, arched and thickened on the outer edges, give the impression that he is constantly surprised or questioning.

There is nothing artificial about Still. At the outset of the classroom interview, he appeared slightly nervous but answered our questions in a very earnest, straightforward manner. His hands were constantly moving — as if he were telling a story each time he spoke. At one point he described how he created and developed the short story "The Nest." In the tale, a young girl is sent to spend the night with her aunt who lives on the other side of a ridge. It is very cold, and by nightfall the girl is hopelessly lost. The simple plot belies the magnitude of emotion that went into the writing of the tale; although all the elements of the story — plot, theme, vocabulary — are unembellished and straightforward, Still manages to impart a profound sense of sorrow. As he told us how he felt while he was writing "The Nest," his voice became softer, his eyes began to mist, and the eloquent motions of his hands ceased. It was a far better and more lasting example of the strength and meaning of literature than any textbook explanation.

After we completed the interview and Still returned to Kentucky, we discovered that more questions arose from the material we had gathered. We sched-

Lee, Laura, and Foxfire Students. "An Interview with James Still." *Foxfire* [Magazine] 22.3 (Fall 1988): 123–49. Reprinted with permission.

The Amburgey-Still log house on Dead Mare Branch, Knott County, Kentucky. The house was constructed in 1937 by Jethro Amburgey from half of the logs from the Amburgey homestead which had been built about 100 yards down the slope from the present site. Photograph taken October 1980 by Linc. Fisch. Used with permission.

uled a second interview to be conducted at the Hindman Settlement School, where Still was employed as the librarian during the Depression. His house is a few miles away and he remains closely associated with the school.

Eight of us decided to make the trip. Our journey to Hindman was not a smooth one by any means. Riding around and over the mountains there was like riding a roller coaster. We drove into Hindman late on a dreary afternoon. Winter mists clung to the sides and floors of hollows, and a light drizzle was just beginning. The mountains around Hindman are steep and bunched tightly together, leaving little space in the winding valleys for any centralized town. There is so little room in the valley that to fit in the creek, highway, and string of houses, rock had been cut away from the mountain. "Cutting away that mountainside made this town twice its size," Still told us later.

We stayed overnight at the Hindman Settlement School. After breakfast in the morning, James Still joined us in the kitchen while we were cleaning up the dishes we had used. We began the interview in the school's dining room. This second interview was much more detailed than the first; not only did he answer some in-depth questions concerning his writing but he also shared with us his views on education and politics. He had brought with him some of the twenty-three spiral notebooks in which he had recorded expressions and phrases people used that caught his attention and seemed worth writing down.

Sometimes it would be an exchange of only a few words between two people; other times he would hear reminiscences of past events or full-fledged accounts of local history. These were tidbits that came about through the natural course of conversation; he heard statements that might never have been shared in a tape-recorded interview. Still would make a mental note of these conversational excerpts or jot them down immediately on any available scrap of paper, and later record them in one of the spiral-bound notebooks he used especially for this purpose. On occasion, he would have the opportunity to use some of these excerpts in his writing, since the characters and locations that make up his stories are of the same region from which he collected the contents of the notebooks.

After the interview, Foxfire director Eliot Wigginton visited with Mike Mullins, the director of the school, and the rest of us dispersed into little groups to walk around until it was time for lunch. Still asked if we would like him to give us a ride into town. Suzie Nixon, Darren Volk, and I piled into his Chrysler Le Baron and he drove us into Hindman. He was full of stories and jokes. "See that sign over there?" he asked, pointing to the sign at the entrance to the school, commemorating its founding. "That's the most enduring of my writings."

While Still went into the post office, we waited in his car. In the front seat, a wilting red carnation reposed on top of a pile of multicolored, woven floor mats and assorted sales papers. In the back seat, we noticed tapes of Schubert, Kenny Rogers, and Gregorian chants. From the variety in his musical taste, we ascertained that he must be a person with complex interests. This was not in keeping with our view of his simple writing method or the overall uncomplicated image he portrayed, however. We decided there was really no way we could slide his character into a single, neatly analyzed slot. Later, though, he unconsciously helped us solve some of the mystery of his personality. "There are two different types of people," he told us. "Primary people don't think about *not* saying hello to you and secondary people wait till you say hello first — a type of inverted ego, you know." It appeared to us that Still belonged to the "primary" category.

We returned to the school for lunch. Many members of the staff were there, and several toddlers were seated at a table next to us. At one point, a small boy who had been standing on his chair — much to the chagrin of his mother — toppled to the floor. Silence enveloped the dining room for a tense moment until the child, unabashed, resumed his chair to finish eating. When we expressed our concern, Still smiled. "Oh, he does that every day! I was waiting for him to do that. Now I can relax and eat my meal in peace!"

Although Still now lives inside the city limits of Hindman, he also owns a log house between Dead Mare Branch and Wolfpen Creek on Little Carr Creek. It was willed to him by Jethro Amburgey, a well-known woodcraftsman and dulcimer maker, while Still was a librarian at Hindman. It was during one summer while he was living in the log house that he composed his first novel. *River of Earth* was published in 1940 and is still in print today. It is his most enduring work.

When James Still wants to get away to a quiet place to write, he goes to the two-room house on Little Carr Creek. It is constructed of gray, hewed logs and has two windows on the bottom floor. As we got out of the van and walked toward the house, we noticed two small plank buildings on the right of the path, both weathered gray. The first was an outdoor toilet and the second was a storage building. We were curious so we looked inside the outhouse. Hanging on the left were several corncobs in a glass case. Below the case was a sign that read, "In case of emergency, break glass." Scattered through the trees from the gate to the log house were aluminum pot pie pans with the bottoms up. Stuck through the bottoms were Christmas lights. At night these lighted a walkway from the gate to his house. About forty-five feet from the front door was a water well. Jim Amburgey once said, "I've been coming to this house since I was a child. I come here for a good drink of water. This is the best well in the country." Hanging on the side of the log house at the back door was a beat-up washpan. Still said the washpan had been used in the movie *Coal Miner's Daughter* and was left behind. Below the washpan was a sign made of tin with Still's name on it. Above the door was a horseshoe.

The air smelled like cut grass, and everything was wet from an earlier rain. We could hear the birds singing and the water dripping from the trees. "In spring," Still commented, contemplating the barren flowerbeds, "there are some fifty varieties of daffodils in bloom here."

He led us through the back door into a small kitchen where two cats were asleep on the weathered tile floor. From there we entered the main room of the house. In one corner was a bed with a nightstand by its head. On the table was a modern telephone, and hanging on the wall above it was an old crank phone. In the opposite corner stood a bureau and mirror with old photographs and other memorabilia, and next to that, positioned in front of an unused fireplace, was a gas heater that Still turned on to take the chill out of the damp air when we entered the house. At the far end of the room, a bookcase containing old magazines and novels, such as *The Grapes of Wrath*, occupied one corner; in the other was a ladder attached to the wall, leading to the attic room. In the wall between these two corners was the front door, directly facing the door to the kitchen. In the center of the room, a rocking chair had been pulled up to a table strewn with papers and books.

Still would bring our attention to an object in the room, tell us what it was, where and when it had come into his possession, and what was special about it. Then he would ask us to take notice of something else, keeping us so busy with anecdotes that we hardly needed to ask questions. After we had satisfied our curiosity about his house and were settling comfortably into chairs or on the bed, Still searched through the papers on the center table until his hands closed around an aged issue of *Esquire*. Standing with his back to the heater, he extracted a pair of reading glasses from his breast pocket and proceeded to read aloud "Dance on Pushback Mountain," a poem of his that appeared in the October 1936 issue. He spoke in a very straightforward and natural manner, as if he were remembering a conversation he had heard recently rather than reading print. His voice added a new dimension to the words that we would have missed had we been reading them silently to ourselves.

One thing Still was worried about when he first considered allowing us to print quotations from his notebooks was that spoken words lose a certain value when written. The tone of the narrator's voice, his inflections, his hands and facial expressions all combine to give greater meaning and substance to words. Just by changing inflections, two totally different tales can be made. Still pointed out, for example, how one tale could be told, changing inflections on only one syllable to give it two radically different endings: "The two towns of Sassafras and Vicco were growing so rapidly that their edges nearly touched. The town councils met together to decide if the two towns should merge or not. After the decision had been made, a citizen of Vicco stood up to deliver his opinion. 'Goodbye, God. We're moving to Sassafras!' Whereas the real story ended: 'Good, by God. We're moving to Sassafras!'"

A second reservation came from his concern that the majority of the notebook excerpts are not flashy or sensational but are rather homespun, quiet images of his community. He realized the value of the material, but was it material that needed to be published? In addition, he was concerned that many of the excerpts depended on the mood of the moment or the context of the conversation to be appreciated thoroughly.

In the end, however, he decided that this material deserved to be in print. After we returned home, he began the selection process, and every few weeks a manila envelope would arrive in Georgia containing another collection of pages filled with the sayings, typed and double-spaced, for us to divide up into categories, retype, and arrange. The process lasted for months.

To the very last, we could only guess at the reason Still decided, finally, to allow this material to be published. On one of the last pages he sent us, he provided the answer himself: "The first notebook entry was recorded some forty-five years ago. Most of the participants are dead. Save for their gravestones, this is the only record for some that they lived and laughed and wept and had opinions like the rest of us. I have long tried to speak for them. Here they are speaking for themselves." This book [*The Wolfpen Notebooks: A Record of Appalachian Life*] is the result of Still's decision to publish.

Interview of James Still by Laura Lee

"*This fellow has come over in here from Troublesome Creek and settled in the Old Wiley Amburgey house on Dead Mare Branch and we hain't learnt*

his name yet, or what's in his head. We call him the man in the bushes.'"
[1939]

My paternal grandparents were William Watson Still and Annie McLendon Still, and my mother's parents were James Benjamin Franklin Lindsey and Carrie Jackson Lindsey. My forebears from both sides first settled in Virginia during pioneer days. The Lindseys set down near Berryville, and the Stills in what is now Lee County near Jonesville. There's a roadside marker at Jonesville noting the birthplace of Alfred Taylor Still, the man who conceived the medical system of osteopathy. Jonesville is up the road from Cumberland Gap where I came to attend college in 1924. I didn't know then I was completing a genealogical circle. We've figured that my ancestors fought in the American Revolution and that frontier land was allotted them as reward for their services. The Lindseys in Georgia, the Stills in Alabama. And not many miles apart.

My mother, Lonie Lindsey Still, grew up on a farm near Franklin, Georgia. Her mother, my grandma, had been married before to a Civil War soldier who lost his life in the struggle to head off Sherman in the march toward Atlanta. Grandpa was an orphan, three years younger than Grandma, and having never seen his father could cure thrush in children. Uncle Edd told me that during my mother's childhood the floor of their Georgia home where the cookstove was beaten earth. The move to Alabama, some three miles from the Stills, may have been spurred by the destruction of the home by a cyclone. Beforehand, Grandpa mined enough gold on his land to fill his teeth.

Grandpa Still fought in the Civil War and suffered a wound to the body and had a finger shot off by a Yankee bullet. I recall his discussing with a comrade the mining of the Confederate trenches by the North at Petersburg toward the end of the conflict. He regularly attended Old Soldiers' conventions in Richmond, Montgomery, New Orleans, or wherever held.

There were ten of us children, five girls and five boys. The sisters came first. I am the eldest son and the only surviving member of the family. When my parents first married, they homesteaded in Texas in 1893, and two children were born there. I would have been born in Texas had my parents not come to Alabama on a visit and one of my little sisters died of scarlet fever. Just before she died she asked my mother not to leave her, and so Mama never would go back to Texas and leave her grave. The cotton farm Papa cultivated is now a part of the Fort Hood reservation and I suppose is regularly plowed by tanks and heavy artillery.

I was born in 1906 on Double Branch farm just outside of Lafayette. Sometimes I tell people I was born in a cotton patch. Anyhow, I came to consciousness there. One of my first memories is of running about with a small sack on my back Mama had sewed up for me. I'd pick a boll here and yonder and everywhere. Along about the time I was eight I took on the job of milking the cow. I recollect going out barefoot on cold mornings and the cow stepping on my foot. Before starting to milk into the bucket I'd scoot a stream into my mouth, and a couple into the cat's mouth.

My mother was a worker. She had to be in order to raise ten children, to cook, to make most of our clothes, to do the laundry and ironing, the canning and preserving and keeping house. Besides this, she quilted and crocheted and embroidered and tatted. When she could find a free hour she joined us in the fields. She believed in children working as well, and could always find something for us to do. Except when we were doing our studying. She never weighed over one hundred and ten pounds.

My father was a "horse doctor"—a veterinarian without formal training. A farmer as well. He managed both by hiring a workhand to plow and lay-by, and with the family's help. Cotton was the main crop. Some corn and sugar cane and sorghum and soybeans. And there was Mama's garden. Papa would plow it and afterward she wouldn't let anybody else in it to work. A garden was her pleasure. She had a good one. A picture one. Some of that attitude rubbed off on me. Few people were ever able to suit me plumb in my own.

We children worked alongside our parents, hoeing and chopping and picking and pulling. Fodder is not thought much of now as stock feed, but back then we pulled every blade. Tied it in bundles and hung it on the stripped stalks. My sisters wouldn't work within sight of the road. And to keep from getting a suntan and freckles they rubbed their faces with cream and wore stockings on their arms and wide-brimmed hats on their heads. By the age of twelve I could pick a hundred pounds of cotton a day.

Before I was old enough to be enrolled in school, I'd sometimes go with my sisters. It was a two-mile walk and they often had to carry me part of the way, usually on the way back. I was small for my age. The only child who had to stand on a box to reach the blackboard. The teacher once asked me why I didn't come to school more often, and they tell me I replied, "I would wust Mama would let me."

I had a wonderful teacher in the first grade, a Miss Porterfield. The first day of school she wrote my name in chalk on my desk and handed me an ear of corn and told me to shell the kernels and make an outline of my name. We did this many times over and by the end of the day I had learned its shape and could write it on paper.

Those were stirring and changing times. We soon had a T-model Ford. A telephone. Screen doors. Subscriptions to the *Georgia Tri-Weekly Constitution*, *Farm and Fireside*, and the *Southern Cultivator*. The boll weevil arrived, and nutgrass. World War I was being fought. Schoolchildren gathered newsprint to take to school where it was rolled into tight bundles, dipped in hot paraffin, and sent to France as trench candles. My sister Inez won the fifty-yard dash on Field Day and the prize of a box of chocolate candy. After we had gobbled up the first layer, we found a second beneath and it was like discovering gold at Sutter's Mill.

Aside from the Holy Bible, in our house were three books: *The Anatomy of the Horse*; *The Palaces of Sin, or the Devil in Society*; and a heavy volume with a missing back, *Cyclopedia of Universal Knowledge*.

The *Cyclopedia* opened my eyes to the world. Many a subject was covered such as you'll find in a modern reference work. And more still. How to prune a fruit tree. The language of flowers. Rules for games. The art of social correspondence. Good manners. Twenty-five sample words in several languages. A collection of classic poems. I got the poems by heart.

I wrote my first story when I was eight or nine. I still have it. I titled it "The Golden Nugget," and it was written with a lead pencil on a school tablet. Hard to read now, after seventy years. I found it recently and I'll declare that I saw my future in the piece. A foreshadowing, you might say, of all the scribbling to come. You might not catch it, but I did. It was not going to be the last. The itch to write was there. Along about that time my teacher was reading poems and stories to the class from the *Youth's Companion*, and I had read my first classic, Robert Louis Stevenson's *Treasure Island*. Both undoubtedly caused me to want to tell stories and write poems of my own.

I started a little magazine when I was ten. I had one subscriber — my sister Elloree, who was married and lived nearby. She had a box of folded stationery, and I used enough sheets to make an eight-page issue. I made up stories, which had to be pretty short, and I wrote poems for it. I wrote everything in it. I did a number of them, I don't remember how many. When I was eleven, I made a tent out of croker sacks and pitched it in the yard and wrote a poem in it. I still can recite it except for one line. It is stilted and formal. I used the word "dawn" instead of "morning." Yet, considering my age, it wasn't too bad a beginning. I was trying.

When I was in high school, I started a novel. It was about the sea. I had never seen the ocean, but that didn't stop me. I remember I wrote a while every night. I don't know what became of the manuscript. One summer I kept a notebook — a diary of sorts. It's not what is there that interests me now; it's what I *didn't* mention, what I failed to put in. It tells an awful lot about me. I left out all the things I think are important nowadays. I never mentioned my parents, and hardly my brothers and sisters. I seemed not to be doing anything that summer except picking blackberries and going in "washing," as we called it. Swimming. And I was regularly playing baseball — the things boys do.

And I'd got to see a few movies and I began to write plays. With croker sacks I made a curtain and hung it between two pillars under the house. The rear end of our house was high off the ground. We had moved to Shawmut by then. With the neighbor children as actors and audience I put on plays. One of my plays required a volcano, and I constructed the likes of one, one with smoke coming out. I don't know how we didn't burn the house down. And I was experimenting that summer. I made "gunpowder" to make firecrackers. I took charcoal, beat it to powder, soaked it in kerosene and dried it and packed it into a snuff box, and put a fuse in it. It didn't blow up but it popped. I was always into something. As now.

The boys I ran with claimed they wanted to be either cowboys or railroad engineers. I don't think I made a choice that early. It wouldn't have been either. None of them followed through. The ones I know about became weavers or mechanics in a cotton duck mill in the town, except one who became a textile superintendent. He had us all skinned in the schoolroom.

I became an author without expecting to be. I don't recall the slightest encouragement from childhood all the way through my school years. I didn't know about writing as a profession, something I'd be doing now and then all of my life. Nobody else in my family ever wrote or published anything. There was no precedent for me. I just wanted to write things down, to play with words. At first I had in mind writing a single poem. No thought of composing a second. Then, within a couple of weeks, another idea would pop into my head. The same with short stories. I'd compose one, and was satisfied for a while, and along would come another, and another.

All that was in Alabama. I had started high school in Shawmut and attended two years. Then we moved to Jarrett Station, a short distance from Fairfax, a textile factory town. I attended Fairfax High School and graduated in 1924. But I never got to read the great books until I attended Lincoln Memorial University, which was over the ridge from Cumberland Gap, Tennessee. I arrived with sixty dollars in my pocket, and I was starved for reading material. Every student earned his keep at LMU, and after morning classes I worked afternoons in the rock quarry feeding a rock crusher, and was the library janitor. When the library closed at night I swept the floors and emptied the wastebaskets and rubbed up the tables, and then with the door locked, the several thousand books and collection of magazines were mine until daylight. Many times I stayed the night, too drowsy to make it to the dormitory, and slept on newspapers in the storage room. I was like a child in a candy store. I hardly knew where to start. Somehow I found Thomas Hardy and Joseph Conrad and Hawthorne and Walt Whitman. The library was what Lincoln Memorial meant to me. I was saved by it.

At the library I happened on *The Atlantic*, about the most prestigious publication in those days. The library received gift subscriptions of several copies of each issue and after one was filed I had instructions to put the others in the furnace. What I did was save copies for myself. From donors would sometimes come issues for as many as ten years back. Or more. I kept scores of them and at the end of the term shipped them home. Those were the times of the Great Depression, and I had no employment, so I spent the summer reading. All of them. Every article, every poem, every word. I practically ate the paper. I learned from them more than I can state. Even the art of composition, if it can be said I ever attained it. I decided to write for *The Atlantic*. First and foremost. The odds were great, however.

I began sending verses to them (poems in their pages were listed then as "verse"). I kept getting rejection slips, but I didn't let them bother me. Mind you, I didn't submit anything I thought unworthy of their standards. Eventually, I got a more personal rejection, which read, "We at *The Atlantic* have enjoyed reading your manuscript but regret we cannot use it." And written in ink, "Try us again." Finally, they accepted a poem called "Child in the Hills." My first serious publication. Sort of started at the top, you might say. A man wrote me several years ago to claim, "I'm the person who picked your poem out of the slush pile at *The Atlantic* and insisted that Mr. Weeks, the editor, read it." Since then they have published three poems and ten short stories.

During those years Lincoln Memorial was having serious financial difficulties, which accounted for our Spartan diet. We students ate all the food off the table every meal. The university had an apple orchard and there were plenty of walnut trees on the ridges. We ate pecks of apples and racked a lot of walnuts.

One year, what would have been my junior year, I didn't have train fare to go back to school, or the money to buy the clothes needed. That year I hunted work in several states over the South. The unemployed were everywhere. I walked. I thumbed on the highway. I sometimes rode the rails. One box car I crawled into was occupied by war veterans heading for D.C. to join the bonus army.

I rode out to Texas with some fellows and picked cotton for a while. We were in the fields at daylight and until dark. We baked in one hundred degree sun. My bed was a cotton sack on the floor. The drinking water was alkaline. It was too much. I hitchhiked and rode freights to Georgia. At College Park we rail-riders jumped off the moving train when news reached us railroad dicks were waiting ahead. In Atlanta, I tried Sears, Roebuck for a job. Other places, too. I signed up at an employment agency and nothing came of it. Up in Rome, I applied at a stove foundry. When I asked for work, the boss laughed. I was one of hundreds on the move believing there was a job somewhere. This sounds like hard luck but it wasn't for me in the long run. It was experience I couldn't have had otherwise, and seeing the country from a perspective I couldn't have imagined. I was able to get back in school in the fall when a professor heard of my plight and sent train fare and signed me up for a scholarship. All my university years, six of them, came through the generosity of others.

The class of 1929, my class at Lincoln Memorial, was unique. Some ferment was at work. Nearly a hundred books have been published by its members, which included Jesse Stuart, who was to publish many a book of fiction and poetry, and Don West, who was to earn fame as a labor organizer and activist. I'll talk more about Don in a minute.

At Lincoln I was holding a work scholarship provided by a benefactor. As did most of the others. When I was to graduate I found out his name and address and invited him to the ceremony. Although he had assisted many a student, this was his first invitation. He actually drove down from New York in his chauffeured Cadillac. His name was Guy Loomis, heir to a sash and blind fortune, a gentleman in his eighties. At the ceremony I swiped up all the literary prizes except one I hadn't entered. One award was the Rush Strong gold medal for an essay on the value of truth. Afterwards, Mr. Loomis offered to pay my way to a graduate school of my choice in the South. He also said, "I'll make it possible, not easy." That proved to be the case. I chose Vanderbilt University.

When I entered graduate school at Vanderbilt, Don West was there in the School of Religion. I hadn't known him well at LMU but in Nashville we became better acquainted. Both of us being farm boys, a city was a curiosity to us. On Sundays we'd go to town and wander about, and listen to the street-corner preachers. One claimed to be Jesus. A strike which lasted three years was going on at a coal mine at Wilder, up near the Kentucky border, and Don recruited me to go with him to distribute food and clothes and medicine that the students had got together. This was the strike where Barney Graham was machine-gunned to death. It was my first sight of people starving in America. In America!

When I graduated in June, my benefactor offered one more term of schooling, and in September I was off to the University of Illinois. A year later I was back home with three diplomas, no job, and no prospects. One of my professors, whom I had in some way displeased, had predicted that I would end up driving a team of mules hitched to a wagon. The prophecy began to seem not too farfetched.

I would have gone into the woods and cut trees for the CCC — Civilian Conservation Corps — had they not turned down my application. I applied to the Library of Congress for a position in the reference department. I was catching at straws.

Then, I came to Knott County, Kentucky, to help Don West and his wife, Connie, with a vacation Bible school and a recreational program. Along with Don's son-in-law, Jack Adams, I organized three Boy Scout troops and three baseball teams. We camped and played ball all summer. Jack was to lose his life in the trenches in Spain in the late thirties. While in Knott County, I stayed a week at the Hindman Settlement School, and when I returned home they sent a letter offering a job as a volunteer worker. They would shelter and feed me but couldn't pay me. I was willing, having no other prospects. The school was located at the county seat at the forks of Troublesome Creek. The hardtop road stopped dead in town, and a rutted wagon road took over. The bridge had washed out. You walked a plank, waded, or used a jumping pole. Or rode a highwater horse. I had come to the jumping-off place.

Hindman Settlement had no money to pay its staff. They could offer only room and board and laundry. Any shelter in a storm. The teachers were mostly women. Graduates of Wellesley, Vassar, Smith — mostly Wellesley. And a few men equally qualified. They taught during the day and tutored in the evening. Many had means of their own and had come for a limited stint. Say, two years.

My assignment was the library. Yet with one hundred students confined to a fairly small campus, it meant round-the-clock supervision by all hands.

The library was rich in good books and once a week — my own enterprise — I delivered a box of them on foot to some eight schools. I usually got to all every two weeks. A common cry from the schoolhouse door was, "Here comes the book boy."

I worked three years without pay. With the times improving, the fourth year I was awarded fifteen dollars a month. Slightly more the fifth year, and the sixth. For six years' labor I had earned an average of six cents a day. The publication of a few poems and short stories had kept me in razor blades and socks. And I'd published my first book, a collection of poems reviewers were uncommonly kind to. As I tell it, I was so rich I retired. On a day in June 1939, I moved to an old log house between Dead Mare Branch and Wolfpen Creek, facing Little Carr Creek. To reach it from the county seat you traveled eight miles over a rutted wagon road, and then more than a mile up a creekbed.

The log house I moved into was built in 1827, or as the state historical association claims, 1840. I went there to finish writing the novel, *River of Earth*, for which the Viking Press had offered a contract.

I had found a home. I don't have to depend on memory to describe that spring day in 1939, for I wrote it down: "A pair of black and white warblers teetered along the banks of Dead Mare Branch and minnows riffled the summer pools. Partridges called in the water meadow before the house, and from the cove behind came an occasional *e-olee* of a woodthrush. A pair of rabbits flashed tails among the bluing weeds."

I knew why I had come there, but some of the neighbors were less sure. One said to me, "He's quit a good job and come over in here and sot down." And another who was asked who it was that had moved into the old Amburgey place, said, "We don't know yet. We just call him the man in the bushes." I did sit down and finish the novel. Except for the wife of a widower who had been ordered through a Lonely Hearts Club from Arkansas, I was the first outsider to make my home thereabout. The thirty-one acre farm belonged to Jethro Amburgey, who taught woodworking at the Hindman Settlement School. This house was his birthplace. He was the best known of the dulcimer makers and had learned the craft firsthand from Ed'ud Thomas. We used to think Ed'ud invented them.

When I first moved in I didn't know anybody. Getting acquainted didn't take long for I began to attend the community happenings. Depending on the season, bean stringings and corn shuckings and molasses making and hog killings. In the fall the pie suppers at the Wolfpen school and the school up Big Doubles. Both one-room schools. In June, when sap was at its highest in the birch trees, we went sapping. In time there were four of us who ran together. Sam and John M. Stamper and "Shorty" Smith were my cronies. Sundays we'd ramble the hills searching for ginseng, or pawpaws, or cane patches for fishing poles, or just looking. We visited old graveyards and half-forgotten homeseats, and I listened to their tales. The fourth Sundays in the month I attended the Old Regular Baptist meetings at Littcarr* at the foot of the creek. The church house, and Bern Smith's store, which also housed the post office, was all there was to Littcarr. As I arrived in early summer, it was late to start a garden but I did anyhow, and as the frosts held off until mid–October, I had a garden full of sass—sweet corn, beans, squash, okra, cushaw, tomatoes, cucumbers, and cabbage. There were plum trees and apple trees and walnut trees on the place. Come March I had my own cornstalks to burn when everybody else set fire to theirs the same evening and children danced about the flames. A rite of spring. At Bern Smith's store, and at Mal Gibson's a mile above me, I hung around a lot and helped the other loungers settle the affairs of the world.

Jethro Amburgey's five brothers were neighbors and I was soon acquainted. Melvin, the one living around the bend, came out the first day and asked, "Who's going to do your washing?" and "Who's to do your cooking?" He said, "I want you to eat with us." I agreed to take supper with them five days a week. When I asked about the charge he said, "I just want you to talk to my children." Of course, I wouldn't go without paying, and I did pay. When the cow went dry we sometimes had homemade "beer seed beer," a non-alcoholic drink. When the dried apples came up short we ate vinegar pie.

In those Depression Days, the people on Wolfpen and Little Carr lived almost without money. There was no welfare. No food stamps. Virtually no health services. Although whiskey would always bring in a few dollars, few resorted to moonshining. Honestly, to this day I don't know how many survived. They did grow big gardens and potato patches and a lot of corn, and they had pigs usually, and most had a cow. Not all. Still you need a little more, don't you? With children in school how did they keep shoes on their feet?

I also recall Jim Amburgey visiting. A distant relative of Jethro's. He sat in the door and hung his feet over the steps. I recollect he said, "I've been coming to this place since I was a child. I come here for a good drink of water. This is the best water well in the country."

Later, I got to know the coal camps, and I used to spend weekends once in a while at McRoberts. McRoberts was one of several coal towns practically linked together in the upper reaches of the Kentucky River. The Woodrow Amburgey family were among my best friends. Woodrow was a blacksmith at Consol, and a twin brother of Jethro's. I've never worked in a mine, or expected to. Can't be at ease underground in so small a space. Yet I've visited them a lot of times. The last one I entered I thought I'd smother before I could get out. You can't pay a coal miner enough to face the risk of death. And of black lung.

Actually, I don't see how the miners made it either. They lived out of the

---

*Littcarr," "Litt Car," and "Little Carr" all refer to Little Carr Creek, variously spelled by different interviewers trying to capture Mr. Still's speech patterns.

company store. The coal companies paid them mostly in scrip — their own money, so to speak. They printed little tokens with "Knott Coal Company" or some other operation on them. Pewter coins representing a dollar, or a fraction of one. And if someone wanted to draw money on their salary ahead of time, they'd loan it to them in scrip. They couldn't use the scrip except in the company store, and the prices were usually jacked up. They received little in cash. At the end of the two-week period they often owed the store all or nearly everything they had earned.

"You talk smart but you've got hillbilly wrote all over you."

There are a lot of natural born storytellers and I've encountered them here and there. In Wash Vance's store at KayZee, where he operated a grocery. Seated on lard cans and feed sacks at Bluestone in Rowan County. At Millstone, Mayking, and Mousie, and Hazard. In churchyards. On courthouse steps. Oral storytellers.

I can't name the exact year I started jotting down things they said in notebooks. I did it only for my own eyes. You might say they were written to inform stories and poems to come, yet I never thumbed through looking for an idea or a quotation. To write it fixed it in memory. The purpose of the notebooks was to cover every facet of life in my community as well as all of the county and the counties adjoining. Not just oral comment altogether. Not all the notes got into the notebooks. I keep coming across scraps of paper with notations that might have been included. I recall deciding the material in the earlier notebooks was too scrappy and in some cases I could hardly read my own writing. I reworked the first couple and pitched out a lot. I used ink at first and later ballpoint pens or both, and I began to write in what used to be called library hand. Every letter clear. The period covered is roughly 1931 to 1965. The setting-down, I mean. What has been added since usually harks back to this span — the time we were living mostly in the nineteenth century, so to speak. Nobody else saw the notebooks until Foxfire asked to examine them. Before then I'd never considered publication. I did come to believe they might in the future be of interest to folklorists and social historians.

After a time nothing was put into the notebooks directly. I'd write on a scrap of paper, whatever was handy, most often the backs of envelopes. I'd let them cool off a bit, a week or so, maybe a month, and then decide whether they were worth including. A tape recorder wouldn't have served my purpose even if I'd had one. I wanted only the meaningful, telling statement. I might extract a single sentence from a long conversation. In my limited experience with a tape recorder, I've found the speaker is usually guarded in what is said. Confidentiality is lost. For my type of note-taking, this is important. As for a collection of oral statements such as I did record in writing, while many may not seem much in themselves, taken as a whole I believe they offer a picture of the region not otherwise provided. Another aspect.

I didn't own a camera either. Nobody in my community had one. What I did was to trace the hands of the old timers, about a dozen of them. Next to the photograph of a face, I think the hand speaks volumes. Form dictates function, it is said. These are the hands of men who used them as tools to make a living on the land and under it. In the fields and in the coal mines. Missing are tracings of women's hands. At that time it was not what you would ask a woman to allow you to do.

As I began nearly fifty years ago writing down what people were saying, we can know something of how they spoke and what they talked about. The most we'll know about many, for most are now dead, is what they said, and what I recorded. Anything anybody said, young or old, which seemed unique to the region. An example that comes to mind concerns a four-year-old child who died in front of my house one winter's night, along the creek-bed road in the cab of a truck, of a burst appendix. She was being taken to a doctor. I had earlier written down statements by this child who had a quick imagination. She lives today only on a page or two in my notebooks.

Now and then I still hear remnants of the language spoken by Chaucer and the Elizabethans, such as "sass" for vegetables, "hit" for it, or "fit" for fight. People here are more likely to express themselves in an original manner than any place I know. I think it is something to celebrate. I don't want or expect Appalachian speech to be like any other. It has its own individuality, its own syntax. To be unlettered is not necessarily to be unintelligent. It's a rare day when I'm out and about that I fail to hear something linguistically interesting. I go to the post office and I'll hear somebody say something that's of interest to me. That has a lot to do with why I live here. Of course, there are other reasons. I've traveled a bit, yet I keep coming back like iron filings to a magnet. Here we are more conscious of the individual. Everybody is somebody.

Some of the people who come into the area expect to meet up with barefoot men packing hog-rifles and wearing black hats plugged with bullet holes. The "hillbilly" stereotype. Not too many lately, as roads are beginning to open up the area and some are learning better. Naturally, if a visitor lingers a while he'll notice regional differences in speech and attitudes. Yet he'll find that human nature operates here pretty much as elsewhere. If you want to see what's left of the Appalachia I've written stories and poems about in the past, you'll have to leave the new roads and take up hollows and climb hills. Don't expect to find stereotyped characters in my fiction. Few fit the mold in reality.

But outsiders persist in believing that the woods are still full of barefoot men. Not so long ago the Settlement School was receiving occasional donations that reflect this view. Used Christmas cards, bundles of clippings from newspapers and magazines, and clothes of a type and condition the needy wouldn't be caught dead wearing. Once a truckload of books arrived, and I had the job of sorting them. Only three of the hundreds were suitable for the library. We saved the boxes for the kindergarten children to play in. And I remember a man called me outside to look over discarded volumes he had brought as gifts piled in the backseat of an Oldsmobile. After he had seen the Settlement's collection, he climbed into his machine and drove off, taking his books with him. He had misjudged.

In those days the Settlement School had a hundred or so students. The staff taught by day and tutored in the evening. The first graduate went on to earn a doctor's degree at the Sorbonne in France, and others attended Harvard and like institutions. Two or three years ago, a man came to the Settlement School from a college in Wisconsin, and he said, "I'd hate to tell you what I expected when I came down here. I've met more educated people and college professors in this place than I have in my own state in years." He happened to have come at a time when a residential conference was in session.

So, personally, I've never been bothered about being called a "hillbilly" or "briar." They're synonymous—the "samelike," as we say. I count it an honor except when used as a slur. I was pleased when talking to a "gear-grinder" in a restaurant in Jackson who thought I drove a coal truck. After he had learned otherwise, and we had conversed a spell, he said, "You talk smart but you've got hillbilly wrote all over you."

It's understandable local people have a distrust of anything written about the area. Even if the characters are imaginary as mine are and the situations created. They fear ridicule. Once in Joe King's store in Nickles Town a customer came in and seeing me there caught his opportunity. He spoke up for my benefit, "Come a fellow in here and he's writing about us. He don't know how we live." To which I was quick to reply, "The hell he doesn't." I could have told him what he had for breakfast. From whom he had bought his likker. And something else I don't even want to hint at.

People hereabout have long known I scribble, yet it's easy to see it hasn't been profitable. Several years back I was walking down the street in Hindman and met a prominent citizen who greeted me, "Have you written any big lies about us lately?" I stopped and said, "Yeah, Dock. I wrote one yesterday. It was about you, and it only sounds like a lie." It might be a comfort to some to learn that of the eleven books published, every one cost me in time and travail more than I ever earned in royalties.

What my part of Appalachia had in common with other parts for a long time was isolation from the mainstream of American life and neglect by both our state and national governments. The neglect has only partly been addressed. Yet things are changing. Almost from day to day. My nearest neighbor is spending the winter in Florida. There was a time when the road to his door was the creek bed. Many saw service in the three wars of our day. They've had a glimpse of the world. Especially during World War II, a lot of folk hereabout dug potatoes in Maine, threshed peas in Wisconsin, or picked tomatoes in Indiana. They went up to the factories in Detroit and Chicago and Cincinnati and remained. In recent years the downturn in the economy and homesickness have caused some to move back. Their children speak "buckeye."

Roads, telephones, shopping malls. This would appear to be all good. It's opened up the world and broken down barriers. Most families have a car or truck and move about on roads slick as a ribbon. Jasper Mullins told me a while back he failed to make a garden because he had bought a television set and didn't have time to tend one. There are losses. A sense of community is lost. Around me natural gas wells have done away with the fireplace that represents the cement holding family and neighbor together. Between me and even the middle-aged there is mostly a "Howdy," or a "Hey-o." That's partly due to the generation gap. I'm considered an old-timer. There's only one other alive on my creek. We're survivors. Yesterday's people.

Actually, I don't think I was aware of the word "Appalachia" until a few years ago. I'm reminded of a stranger who stopped at a filling station near Hindman for gas, and who said to the attendant, "I'm from out of state. I'm down here looking around, looking for Appalachia. Where do you think Appalachia is?" The attendant answered, "Appalachia is over in Virginia. It's a town." And the stranger said, "No, no. I mean the area they call Appalachia." To this the attendant said, "I don't know myself, but if you'll go on down the road to the next station there's a fellow who'll tell you. He don't know either but he'll tell you something."

I don't know where Appalachia begins, or where it ends. It's like a fellow once told me, "When I was in the eighth grade, my geography teacher kept mentioning Appalachia, and I couldn't find it in the textbook anywhere. I asked my Pap, 'Pap, where is Appalachia?' And he said, 'Son, you're sitting square in the middle of it.'" That's where I have a feeling I am and have been all these years.

"I hope that by the second paragraph I've got you hooked."

I've never thought to write a story "about Appalachia." The background of my fiction to date is Appalachia, what I know best, and naturally my tales have a regional flavor. I've been asked, "After all these years, haven't you about run out of material?" I can't live long enough to handle all the stuff already in my head. Another question, "Are you still writing?" My answer is, "Am I still breathing?"

While I've had a number of adventures, both physical and mental, the greatest one has been the act of becoming a creative writer. It has been a way of life. Not a hobby. Not a sometimes thing. While I'm about all sorts of other activities, my center has been making words work for me. Many people come tell me they're interested in writing, but when I talk to them a bit, I learn they're thinking most of the ends of the business—publishing and possible income. Any writer of merit I know is constantly trying to find the time and a place to sit at his typewriter and indulge himself. It can be smothered down for a while, but if the urge is genuine, it will find some sort of out. It has broken up many a personal relationship. Don't expect anybody to understand. They won't. I've never found anybody who did.

Rather than thinking of myself as a writer, though, I think of myself more as a storyteller. I would be a storyteller even if I couldn't write. Anybody who stays around me long will hear a lot of them. Maybe more than he wants. There seems to be an endless supply. The old ones come back, new ones occur.

I've always written poems and have published a couple of books of poetry. But I only write one when it overwhelms me. I don't sit down and say, "I am now going to write a poem." My poems happen in my head. A first line occurs, almost unbidden, and I'm on my way. Once written, they seem to have preexisted. Like fishing for a loose pail and finally hooking it, and pulling it up.

Once I intended to write a personal letter I had put off for a long time. A reply was overdue. I sat down to type it, but, no. Of a sudden the first line of a poem popped into my head. "If the legs of the bird be broken...." It had apparently been in the making unbeknownst to me since I saw my nephew wound an egret in flight in Florida. I had chided him for unnecessary cruelty. However, the poem came to be titled "The Broken Ibis," for I had seen a picture in a newspaper of a wood ibis downed by weather in Kentucky. It was as tall as a man, and personified man. I empathized with the lost and bewildered bird. The empathy shaped itself into an idea that would not rest until it found expression.

This speaks of how one poem came into being. It doesn't necessarily apply to others. A recent verse of mine involved two events. The cleaning out of a water well, which is a dangerous undertaking, particularly an old well like my own. A boy did the job, for only he had shoulders narrow enough to squeeze through the top. His father managed the bucket. I stood by anxiously. He drowned at last at another time, in another year, in a flooded creek. "Apples in the Well" melded these events into one and I trust lent them significance.

After a poem is on paper I may play around with it, may change a word or two. Put in a comma, take one out. Punctuation is important. I call it "mental breathing." After all, you've got to get your breath as you read a poem, so you put a period. Give your reader a chance to collect his wits for the next sentence.

A poem needs to flow like a stream, distinguishing it from prose. You might say the banks control the direction. Emily Dickinson's "stairway of surprise" says it aright. It expands. Grows like a crystal in a chemical bath. It used to be thought music and the dance had some relationship with poetry. Modern poetry has clouded the kinship. It has lost much of its tonality. Explaining the footwork doesn't necessarily explain how poems actually get realized. The mystery of a poem is a part of the pleasure of bringing one into being. I never rationally expect to write another one, and then ... and then....

You may write one in five minutes. Or ten. Perhaps fifteen. Allen Tate pranked with his "Ode" for a quarter of a century. Coleridge composed "Kubla

Khan" in a dream, a dream disturbed. A recent anthology of verse is titled *The Made Thing*. Are poems made by hands? We do know that in the writing there are a host of things to do at once. All that you are and can know and can be comes together and is concentrated on a single point, like a glass drawing fire from the sun. For all the honor heaped upon its name, poetry comes a cropper on the market. Do you know anybody who has bought a book of current poetry this year? When Ezra Pound challenged a fellow poet to a duel, his adversary suggested that they stand at twenty paces and fire their unsold volumes of verse at each other.

In writing a novel there is more freedom. You are in charge. You can play God, be omnipotent. Be everywhere, or nowhere. You can know unspoken thoughts and motives. You can ramble up to a point. Stick out your elbows verbally. The writing of one goes on a long time. Every morning there's something to look forward to. A trip of discovery. You are many people, in succession. Words at work. That's the true reward. I never knew a writer whose efforts I respected who was not in love with the dictionary. They're not satisfied with just one. They're all over the place. My problem of looking up a word is that I may find myself at play there an hour later.

I might mention here that nearly all my stories and poems come out of something somebody said or I read in the newspaper — maybe an anecdote I heard that sticks in the mind like a burr and doesn't go away. First thing I know, a character invents himself and becomes a real person, and every once in a while I'm thinking about him. Until my character starts talking to me, though, I'm not making progress. He'll speak his own words. He'll get my attention, and the first thing I know, he'll be talking to me and I'll start making notes. My characters name themselves. Until that happens, I'll call him "John" or "Mary" until he or she tells me their name. There's a lot of name symbolism in my stories— Godey Spurlock, for example.

And I think a story should not only sound like truth but in a sense it has to come true. Also be logical. I hope that my readers will think it's honest. And it has to be psychologically sound as well. Take the story, "The Nest." I remember the act of writing it. A painful experience. I would never have thought about writing it except that at Hindman, a senior left school before he was to graduate to marry a young widow with a child — a daughter. They lived on lower Troublesome Creek in one of the hollows. The child was about five or six. The father and mother went on a visit for the weekend and sent her to stay with grandparents, just around the curve. She knew the way, had been there many times, yet she became lost and spent two nights on the mountain in subzero weather. She somehow survived. I've been told that her cheeks froze and burst. She's alive today, though I've never met her.

Somehow she learned about the story, and she tells people it is hers. In a way it is. The happening bothered me. It stayed with me, preyed on me. By itself it wasn't a story. An incident. In the beginning it was no more than I've told you here. That's all I had to go on. Then eventually it evolved into "The Nest."

I don't usually remember much about writing a story, but I remember this one. It's written as a series of flashbacks. As the child climbed the mountain, I kept giving the reader a varied narrative. No repetition. In a short story, every sentence should build. It needs to go forward. It should, as quickly as possible, touch a nerve and start a response in the reader — have the reader identify with the character or characters, and then with every sentence there must be additional revelations. A story growing.

Actually I used words of one syllable as often as I could. Well, it wasn't possible altogether, but you'll find it simply written, and dealing with a problem in child psychology.

When she comes up against the rock wall ... I don't know how a reader would respond. I felt terrible myself. It was as if it were true. I got the child down to the fence on her way home, and I couldn't go on writing. It was torment. I don't think I ever lived a story like I did this one.

About three weeks later, I took the child to the end. When she got down to a bench of the mountain it began to snow, she was numb and cold. And do you remember the line, "The bench had the width of the world"? I remember wondering if it was too broad a statement, but I let it stand. At a book autographing in Hazard last year, the mayor's wife told me she wished I had never written the story, and I asked, "Why not?"

She said, "It bothers me. I still think about it."

I said, "That's the reason I wrote it. It was bothering me, and I got rid of it."

So generally I don't know that I'm going to write a story. Something will have been cooking in my mind, and I'll really want to get rid of it, so let's say I want to have the pleasure of writing it too. I have, on occasion, just dashed off the first paragraph, knowing it already. Then I write the last paragraph because I have to know where I'm heading. In fact, I know the end before I know anything else. It comes in a flash, usually. When I've written that, I know where I'm going and what's to come of it all; then I start back at the first paragraph and head toward the last. Yet nothing exactly happens the same way twice. I don't claim to have a method.

The place to begin a short story is as near the end as possible. My view of it. If I get stuck, which I often do, I go back to the last paragraph and tinker with it. I don't know how other people write, but it's a game — it's a playground — for me. I don't exactly work — I don't think I work — I gambol hard all the way through.

Many times when I'm having trouble with a paragraph, I set it on the page as if it were a poem and I can usually learn what the problem is — the glitch in the way.

The short story called "The Run for the Elbertas" took longer than any I ever wrote. I got stuck a number of times. It's longer than most magazines or periodicals choose to publish. I remember writing it. I knew what I wanted to do, but not how. When I bogged down I'd go to the last paragraph and fiddle with it a while. Pretty soon it's like stirring concrete. It sets and hardens. I could work almost anywhere in the story I wanted to, and did.

But generally, when I've created the first paragraph, it will stand. That's about how it's going to be. And somehow the characters lead me on. I want a story moving from the first sentence. No request to the reader to hold still while I indulge in description. And I hope that by the second paragraph, I've got you hooked. That's what a writer wishes for. A short story has to be very compressed. A writer has to do so much so quickly: introduce characters, set some sort of premise, all that sort of thing. But while I'm writing, I'm not consciously thinking about technique or verbs or adjectives. It's just as if I were telling a tale, and I'm not thinking about anything except enjoying telling it. That's all.

Later I go back and take care of the more technical details. I don't let my concern about them get in the way while I'm first writing the story. I take out certain words. Change them.

There are words I personally dislike and don't use. Dislike them in any context. There are words I would never think of using. I want to keep the language fresh, to enliven, and to communicate.

Using dialect is truly one of the great problems in writing folk literature. Once dialect is written down, it becomes something else. It's rendered by misspellings, isn't it? Even to the person who has just spoken, it would look puzzling. And yet, to be true to local speech it can't be overlooked altogether. And to have a chance of publication, you'd better be careful in employing it. You'll find some dialect in my fiction, enough to give the flavor of the region. What I hope to do is to evoke speech. I see no particular reason, as a simple example, in dropping the letter *g* from the word *going*. Even if spelled correctly it will sound in the reader's head as they are used to hearing it. In one of my early short stories I used a lot of apostrophes. When I sent it to Edward Weeks, editor of *The Atlantic*, he wrote back, "Dialect is out of fashion." That's not to say a character can't speak idiomatically. Two novels I can name off-hand that handle dialect expertly are Mary Webb's *Precious Bane* and Kentucky's Elizabeth Madox Roberts's *The Time of Man*. While it doesn't happen in these works, dialect can break the concentration of the reader. It calls attention to the writing instead of the story. I don't want my hand to show. I don't want the reader to know I'm even there.

I've had pretty good luck. Manuscripts have been turned back to me, of course, but I kept sending them out. If an editor returns a manuscript, I don't feel upset about it. They're not buying turnips today. Maybe next year or some other time.

My first book was a collection of poems called *Hounds on the Mountain*. It was published in 1937 by Viking Press in a limited edition of 750 copies, and then reprinted. It stayed in print for years. Once I asked my editor if it was out of print, and he said, "Well, no. However, nowadays we are just selling it to the people who deserve it." Eventually it had another printing in a limited edition by another press, and now this book is a collector's item. Wish I had a few copies.

An editor at Viking Press had read some of my stories before then, and when I signed the contract for *Hounds on the Mountain*, I agreed to two other books. The first of those was *River of Earth*. Don't think I had any specific purpose for writing *River of Earth* except to tell the story. I didn't know I was beginning a novel. I wrote the first section and sent it to *The Atlantic*, and they accepted it and published it as an article. They didn't call it a short story. I didn't like that at the time, but, of course, the beginning section doesn't exactly fulfill the short story rules and regulations, even loosely. It became the first section of a novel.

When the editor at Viking asked if I was writing a novel, I said yes I am. He wanted to see some of it, and I sent the first section and the last of *River of Earth*. They sent a contract. Later, I asked him if he didn't feel a bit concerned sending a contract with so little of the book finished. "Well," he said, "we held our breath."

And then I asked him if there were changes he thought I ought to make, and he replied, "We trust your instincts." The only thing they did question in the galleys were certain spellings of words. They follow a certain style manual, so they changed words like "britches" to "breeches"—words like that.

River of Earth came out in 1940. It's been around a long time. There are a lot of good novels that somehow didn't survive. I can think of some that moved me, and I wonder why they are not still in print.

When you ask if *River of Earth* is based on true events, I can say what Mark Twain said about *Huckleberry Finn*. He said there was not an incident in *Huckleberry Finn* that he didn't know about happening to somebody or that had not come to him from some reliable source. I'm pretty sure all the events in *River of Earth* happened somewhere and they came to my mind. In a sense, almost any novel is autobiographical. However, *River of Earth* is not an autobiography, I assure you, although my childhood informs this book.

"I read an average of three hours a day."

I think serious writing should be introduced in kindergarten. Children should have good books read to them early. While I was school librarian at Hindman and all of the grades had a period to visit once a week, we had a children's room with small chairs and a good selection of juvenile works. I would tell stories to the first three grades, telling them rather than reading them, and holding up the book so they could see the pictures. I might read such a story as "The Three Little Pigs," and then have them act it out. I'd find it necessary to caution the child playing the wolf not to actually bite the pigs. For the other grades I was the readers' adviser, introducing them to books such as *Robinson Crusoe, Treasure Island, Little Women,* and *Tom Sawyer.*

Everything is new and wonderful to a child, and that is why I like to deal with children. I wanted them to gain a familiarity with the library even before they could read. I would try not to do too much pointing out but rather let them wander about. I have always listened to children and have them tell me their ideas and feelings. All too often in school a child is not encouraged to speak up. This was my experience. The attention span is very short for first and second graders and needs to be kept in mind. They shouldn't be expected to remain seated for hours at a time. At the library during story hour period I'd asked them to stand up, up on tiptoes, and pick the imaginary apples hanging overhead. Once a child, the son of a doctor, looked up and said, "I don't see no apples." Shouldn't I have guessed that he was going to be a lawyer?

When the grade school was moved to a new location and I no longer had a chance to work with them, I moved on to another job.

For some fifty years I have read an average of three hours a day. A professor of mine in Tennessee years ago told the class that if we expected to get anywhere and be anybody in particular in life, we would have to do the work of ten men. Well, I decided I would at least read more books than ten average men. Most of it in nonfiction. I would read more novels if I could find works of interest. I roughly divide all fictional works into two. One is illustration, the other is art. There are great works in both categories but I'm looking for the ones, the all too rare ones, I personally call art. I'm just curious. I was born curious about the world. I want to know more and more. And anything I can learn informs my writings. Isn't thinking the act of processing information?

Since I can remember I've always had an interest in primitive people, and I believe it began with the first book read to me before I could read myself. A simple book with drawings about the Eskimo, loaned by a teacher. There were dogsleds, Eskimo boys, ice houses. I brought it home time and time again, and my sisters would read it to me. I knew it by heart, but I still liked to hear it.

In the years following, my interest grew to include the Indians of America, sparked by Parkman's *The Oregon Trail,* and the aborigines of Australia and of Tierra del Fuego and Polynesia. Not until 1971 did I begin to concentrate on the Mayans of Central America and make a first trip to the Yucatan. Since then I have spent fourteen winters in part in various countries of the region — Mexico, Honduras, Belize, Guatemala, and El Salvador and Costa Rica. I've visited the major Mayan ruins, some several times over. Besides giving myself a chance to step back in time, I work at why the Mayans, the intellectuals of the Indian people, have virtually disappeared from the face of the earth.

People have asked, "Are you writing, or planning to, about all this?" No. I'm still a tourist, but an informed one as I've made it one of my studies and built up a collection of books on the subject.

It was Maurice Herzog's *Annapurna* that got me interested in mountain climbing, and that was reinforced by a visit in 1940 to the Grand Tetons in Wyoming. I yearned to climb the shining peaks beyond Jenny Lake. I never did. Anyhow, could I not climb the Matterhorn? It was not to be. At least I could read about the subject and vicariously experience the adventure. Thus my collection of books on mountaineering, particularly those dealing with Mount Everest. Mountain climbers, more frequently than most adventurers, reach the end of their tether. It's often life or death. What do they do then? What are their thoughts? How do they react to the challenge? Once, during World War II, I was a passenger on a flight from Cairo to Khartoum in the Anglo-Egyptian Sudan when our C-46 lost one engine and the other was sputtering, threatening to conk out. A possibility we'd go down in the Sahara. I recollect my response and have been buoyed up by it ever since. The pilot managed a crash landing. As a spin-off from Himalayan mountaineering, I took up reading about the primitive people of the Tibetan plateau. One thing leads to another. My reading and interests have always been eclectic.

I'm often asked what advice I have for aspiring writers. I prefer the perspiring writer. Those already at it, no matter the age. Those not waiting for the magic wand. It's not the green thumb that produces the fine sass patch, it's the dirty thumb. Hands in the dirt, scratching. Certainly a good liberal education would be a gain. Your teachers are all at hand — the best authors of the past and present. And a mundane item — learning to touch type, unless you can afford a secretary. Editors don't bother to read handwriting. What I'm saying is you get ready. In all aspects.

For a number of years my aim was to be published in magazines I respected. And when I visited a college library where there were a great many publications, I'd pick up a promising one and the first thing to pop into my head was "What can I do for this periodical?" Yet I didn't wander too far beyond the range of publications I admired enough to become a subscriber. You should have a firsthand familiarity with any publication you hope to appear in. Just the other day, a woman came up to me and said, "I've written some stories and I don't know where to send them." How would you *not* know? You wouldn't raise a hundred acres of cabbages without some knowledge of where you were going to market them.

Beyond that, if my answers to such questions don't fully cover the subject, it's because a working creative artist has his own cave. Who knows what goes on in there?

And having said that, I might move on to say I will talk all around the outer rim of the subject of creativity, yet won't attempt to explain the creative art. Even if I could, which is doubtful. It's my one remaining superstition. When I was a child, we were told that if we looked into a water-well we might see ourselves in our coffins. Thus I dare not peer too closely into the well of creativity. The true how and why. It might desert me. The best I can offer is a personal observation. I write best when I've achieved a state of free association. How does it come about? I don't know. It happens now and again.

If you begin to publish, reporters will find the path to your door. No matter where. I was early described as a hermit. The label stuck. A recent article describes me as having lived for fifty years in a log cabin back in the hills with no plumbing. That hardly tells the story. Once a former classmate was dispatched by a school we'd attended to bring me back to "civilization." I had to explain that the past week had been spent in the Library of Congress in Washington researching for a historical novel. One I never wrote. And the month before I had spent in the woods of New Hampshire at the MacDowell Colony. I didn't have time to be *saved*. To be recollected is that I've spent a good number of years in classrooms. How do you practice hermiting in a classroom? Most of the three years I spent in the U.S. Army I couldn't have thrown out my arms without hitting somebody. One wise reporter commented, "Being a hermit is a state of mind."

I've always viewed myself as running toward the world, not away from it. I need people. They're my stock in trade. And I want a few of them to need me. William Peden in *The American Short Story* reported that my life span was 1906–1954. Could this be an error? As a neighbor once said, "Dead folks don't know they're dead." I think I'm still alive and kicking. Don't give me out.

Pattern of a Writer: Attitudes of James Still

DEAN CADLE

December 16–17, 1958

I reached Hindman in the afternoon and had dinner with Still in the Settlement School dining room. Later in the school library he said, *You've come at just the right time. I've been needing someone to talk with.*

For over three hours we talked. Still said: *I couldn't write any more each day than I do now. I need to be with people. And I need my work here with books. I enjoy bringing people and books together. Writing is hard work. And I've got a jillion stories to write. I'll never get them all written. But I can write only so much each day. Most of the time I write steadily two, three, sometimes four hours at a time. But all the time I'm dropping notes into folders I have for other stories. Whenever I hear or see something that appeals to me, I jot it down and drop it in the appropriate folder. Later it may fit in another story. Yet, it may never be used. I will work for years on some ideas without anything happening; then one day I'll see or hear something that will trigger one of the ideas. Then I take out the folder and begin putting the slips together. Probably I can use only a few of them. The others I sort out and drop into other folders.*

Usually when that happens the whole story is there. It happened that way last Sunday afternoon. I hadn't planned to do any writing, but for over two hours I wrote as fast as I could move my hand. I didn't even lay the pencil down. My hand was cramping but I was afraid to stop. When I finished I was tired all over. You can't do that kind of writing for long periods.

I had known since I met Still in 1946 that he was reluctant about publicizing himself either as a person or as a writer. Anyone who reads the Kentucky journals and newspapers must be aware of the scarcity of publicity about him,

---

Cadle, Dean. "Pattern of a Writer: Attitudes of James Still." *Appalachian Journal* 15.2 (Winter 1988): 104–43. Copyright *Appalachian Journal* and Appalachian State University. Reprinted with permission.

for periodically there are articles about other state writers: giving an after-dinner talk, receiving an award, appearing on television, dedicating something, holding something, giving advice, and peeping over a barricade of their books at an autograph party.

Still explained his attitude that evening, somewhat fiercely I thought, while taking me on a long cold ride before I left for Lexington, because he said he hadn't run his car in several days and it needed warming up. It ran but never warmed up.

I don't think a writer should allow himself to be used to promote his writing, he said. *My writing speaks for itself. What I wear or have for breakfast or even my opinions have nothing to do with my writing. Such things don't get writing done, and they don't make writing any better. They just get in the way. And I don't like to make explanations of my writing. Most explanations are afterthoughts anyway.*

He said the *Atlantic* had accepted another of his stories ["The Run for the Elbertas"]. This is his thirteenth acceptance by them: ten stories and three poems. He said, *This is the only time I've had a character who wouldn't stop talking.* The story is 8,000 words, longer than the *Atlantic* usually uses, so the editor asked him to cut it. But he couldn't, so the editor asked his permission to let *him* do some cutting. *I don't see how they can do it,* Still said, *except maybe a few sentences in one place.*

February 7–8, 1959

The telephone rang about 6 pm. His voice is especially quiet over the phone. *This is Still. I saw your name in the directory and thought I'd call.*

I went to the Lafayette Hotel and brought him back to the apartment, where he stayed until 11:00, talking and looking at books and smoking a Roi-Tan cigar. After unwrapping the cigar he slipped the wrapper ring on his little finger and kept it there all evening.

He was obviously happy and in a talkative mood. And that night I believe Jo Lee and I saw the complete James Still: writer, reader, librarian, man, humane being. Since he was smiling most of the evening, I kept seeing a tiny dash of light bounce from a gold spot in one tooth. And it may also have been the lighting rather than his short body, large ears, and bald head that created for me the impression that this is what a happy Buddha with a Roi-Tan ring and a mouth touched with gold must look like.

He told about a cat he once owned. He found it nearly frozen one morning, unable to move and with patches of tar on its fur. *I couldn't leave it there, so I took it home and placed it on the hearth. It could barely move its head and was too weak to drink milk.*

He awoke during the night and found it gone from the hearth. It had

James Still at the rear entrance of the Amburgey-Still log house on Dead Mare Branch, Knott County, Kentucky. Photograph taken October 1980 by Linc. Fisch. Used with permission.

dragged itself a short distance and was making playful movements. But he discovered most of its body was paralyzed.

Every day for a month he gave it a warm bath and massaged its body. But it did no good. When spring came he carried it nearly everywhere he went, with it clinging to his shoulder or stretched out on his arm.

I had to, for every time I went out the door it began crying. It was awful looking, but I became attached to it. Often I was ashamed to be seen carrying it around, and then I was ashamed of being ashamed.

The first short story Still wrote and the first one he published, "On Defeated Creek"/"The Scrape," was praised while still in manuscript by Edwin Granberry, professor at Rollins College who won an O. Henry Award in 1932 for "Trip to Czardis." (Although "All Their Ways Are Dark" received previous publication, Still wrote it as part of *River of Earth* and the *Atlantic* used it as non-fiction.)

Hounds on the Mountain had been accepted for publication while Still was visiting in Winter Park, Florida, in 1936. One afternoon a friend, Edwin Grover, said, I'll bet you're writing prose, too. A little, Still said. I'll bet you've finished some stories. Still said he had written one. I'll bet you've got it with you, too.

Still said he had finished it a few days before and was carrying it with him in case ideas for changes came. He agreed to let Grover read it providing he would make no comment. Grover made no comment, but he phoned Granberry to ask if he would read it. This was going further than Still desired, but he agreed to go with Grover to Granberry's.

Granberry explained that he preferred not to read the story then, but would read it later if Still would leave it. He said it might be a good story, but more likely was not. You're a guest in my house, he said, and I can see that you're serious about writing, so I would not like having to tell you if I think it is bad.

Still learned later that Granberry read the story about midnight and phoned Grover to tell him he thought the story was good enough to win an O. Henry Award.

The story was printed in *Frontier and Midland* as "On Defeated Creek" but was reprinted as the last story in *On Troublesome Creek* under the title of "The Scrape." And it *was* selected for the O. Henry collection. However, before the book went to press, Still's second story, "Job's Tears," was published in the *Atlantic* and the O. Henry editor used it instead.

Carl Sandburg was visiting in Winter Park at the same time, and Still met him at Grover's. Grover invited Still to come back the following night when there would be fewer people, but Still had a dinner engagement. Just as Still finished his dessert he received a call from Grover: Sandburg says for you to come over. I'm sending a cab for you.

The talk at Grover's went on for hours, with time out for Sandburg to strum his guitar and sing. Late in the evening Still and Sandburg got onto subjects on which they differed, and neither was hesitant in expressing his opinions.

Still has an inquisitive mind and a wide range of interests. He talked about two of them: mushrooms and mountain climbing.

He became interested in mushrooms last year when he found one that resembled the human brain. He began reading about them and identifying those he found. He also talked with his neighbors until he found a man and his wife who had collected mushrooms for years. The three of them plan a hunting trip this spring.

Still has read every book on mountain climbing he could find, some of them over fifty years old. He thinks *Annapurna* the most interesting. He talked of the attempts to scale some of the mountains, and referring to one mountain as My Own he said he was disappointed when he read it had been scaled.

When I said I was surprised by this interest and that I had always felt mountain climbing involved a needless waste of effort and life, he said he was not so much interested in the physical feat of conquering mountains as he was in what the human being can accomplish after it has reached the point of seeming able to endure no longer. *It doesn't have to be mountain climbing*, he said. *It can be war, plague, flood. The only difference is that the individual chooses to climb the mountain. It's the final test of the will I'm interested in. Then you see what amazing things the human being is capable of.*

Throughout the evening his talk returned to people and incidents in Knott County. He told of the boy who was in love with a girl whose father wouldn't let him come to the house. *Desperate to see her, the boy would stand in a clearing* below the house. But the house was hidden by trees, and he could see the house above the tree tops only by jumping. So he would stay there for hours jumping up and down.

A man named Daud (which most people pronounce as "Dog") was on the "Short Dog" bus one day with his daughter who was doing a lot of loud talking. Everyone on the bus could hear her. But the father said nothing to quieten her until she said something close to scandalous about someone; then he said, "Folks with good sense don't hear such things."

One day a teen-age boy became angry with Daud and said, "If you wasn't so old I'd bust you twixt the eyes with a rock." Daud said, "Don't let a few gray hairs make a coward outa you."

On a sweltering afternoon while Still was sitting under his apple tree, a boy from upper Dead Mare Branch whose log house was not so well chinked as Still's stopped and looked from Still to Still's house and back at Still and said, "Your house ain't got no air holes, is it?"

Still has a pair of cut-off denim pants without a zipper he calls his "wateralls" that he wears to wade Little Carr Creek when flash floods wash out the footbridge and the water is too deep for his car. The day after one such flood he was carrying a bag of cement across the creek. *When I got to the center of the creek,* he said, *I felt the button pop and the pants fall to my knees. While I was making the momentous decision of whether to save the cement or save the pants or try to save both, this woman's voice behind me boomed out: "Save the cement!" I didn't think there was a person within a mile, but there were these two women I know who had stopped their car to watch the outcome. I managed to crawdad to the bank.*

Two days later a boy came to the house carrying a pair of sawed-off pants like mine. Before he opened his mouth I knew the story. His mother is a friend of the two women who saw me. He shoved the pants at me and said, "My Momma said you might be needing these."

I don't ask myself if I can find time to write, Still said. *I ask myself if I can find time to do the other things. I build my day around writing, and work in the other things as best I can. If anything goes undone, it's the other things.*

But when I'm away from writing for a few days I have to ease back into it. I don't go straight back to a story. I work around the edges, transcribing notes, thinking about the characters, making revisions. Sometimes I'll sit and look for a long time at what I've written. But once I'm back at writing I find it just as hard to let go. So, you can see why I don't spend much time writing letters, entertaining visitors, serving on committees, giving talks.

In writing, I think I'm like a surgeon. I'm always probing. I keep probing till I touch a nerve. I've got to make the reader feel something deeply. Unless I touch a nerve I don't have a story.

My intention is to tell a story. I cut out everything that interferes with the story line. It hurts me to have to take out some things. But everything that hinders the story sort of takes care of itself. The form of the story is something that just comes.

The flaw in most writing is that the writers have constructed barriers between the story and the reader. The reader has enough trouble without the author muddying the water. Even the simplest arrangement of words is still a screen between the story and the reader. The perfect story would be like a copper wire stretched from a generator to a light bulb.

During the evening Still took half a dozen books from the case near him and examined and talked about them. He would slip on his glasses and look at a book, then hold the glasses poised in his hand and talk, then put the glasses back on. When he was ready to leave he borrowed three of the books, *The Saturday Review Treasury, The Art Spirit* by Robert Henri, and *The Writer's Book* edited by Helen Hull, and phonograph recordings of Faulkner, Saroyan, Steinbeck, and Katherine Anne Porter reading from their works.

It was windy and spitting snow when I took him back to the hotel. We hoped the snow wouldn't stick, for Jo Lee and I planned to go home with him next morning; but it looked heavy whirling to meet the car, and in the light from the hotel windows high above the street we saw it beating against the face of the building.

However, next morning was clear and the sun was shining. We left at 8:00 with Still following. He apparently wanted us to go in front because he would be stopping along the way to take notes, for he had said he got some of his best ideas while driving.

While we had lunch in Jackson Still talked about some of the people he knows there. One of them is Mrs. Marie Turner, Superintendent of the Breathitt County Board of Education. *But we don't get along,* he said; *she thinks I'm one of the mountains' worst enemies.*

The misunderstanding developed — during publication week of *River of Earth* — as a result of Still's being a witness to a murder near the Jackson railroad depot. An account of it that Mrs. Turner disapproved of, saying it was harmful for the area, appeared in *Time* magazine. Convinced that Still supplied the facts, she wrote him that she thought he cared more about the mountain people than to write such adverse publicity.

Still said that he did not understand how a person in Mrs. Turner's position, concerned with knowledge, facts, truth, and justice, would view the murder of a human being on the level of publicity and would imply that the fewer people who hear about a murder the less evil the act is.

In Hindman we stopped at the school library for Still to pick up a red wagon filled with new books, which he took as a birthday present to James, a namesake, the son of "Tubb." From "Tubb's" place, which is about six miles up a valley, we circled back to Still's house. His home is reached more directly by going eight miles beyond Hindman on Highway 160 to Littcarr and one mile up Highway 1410. This was the first time I had been to his house since June of 1946.

(I first learned about Still in the Spring of 1941 when I proofread his story "The Stir-Off" for the Berea College Press, which was to publish it in *Mountain Life and Work*. The story was so refreshing and natural, more convincing than any other fiction I had read about the Appalachian region, that I wrote Still asking if we could visit. But because of the war we did not meet until 1946. When my roommate, Willard Arnett, and I arrived, Still was sitting in the doorway, and I don't recall that he left his chair during the hour we were there; but when we left he walked us to the creek. He told me later that during the better part of the year after his discharge from the service he was unable to write and spent his time staring out the window or sitting in the doorway.)

His house is a two-story almost squarish log building, over a hundred years old, located between Dead Mare Branch and Wolfpen Creek.

Bookcases extend left from the entrance door around the corner to a window in the center of the adjoining wall. Under the window is a cedar chest in which Still keeps copies of books and magazines which have some special significance for him. In the adjoining corner is his bed, and at the foot is the doorway to the kitchen, which is a room that runs the length of the rear of the house. On the other side of the door is a fireplace that has been sealed up, and in front of it is a gas stove.

Various objects hang on the walls. On each is a Van Gogh print, and arranged between the prints are two dulcimers, a bunch of ginseng, a string of red peppers, a straw mat, and hats and caps.

In the corner to the right of the entrance is his writing table. On the wall above it is a long vine that has grown through a crack in the wall from the mass of vines that covers the chimney and much of the end of the house. It clings to the wall above the table and remains green the year round.

Above the writing table is a trap door to the upper room, which is the same size as the lower one. Along two sides are shelves filled with books and magazines. On the floor are boxes filled with correspondence and copies of magazines in which his stories have appeared and a trunk filled with manuscripts he has never submitted for publication.

In the kitchen, which was likely added after the house was built, are a gas stove, a table, a shelf for water buckets, shelves for dishes and food — one filled with books — and a refrigerator, the first he has owned, which he got this summer from a friend.

The house and garden area belong to Jethro Amburgey, who has let Still use them since the late 1930s. (It was also from Jethro that Still bought the 1948 Ford he owns. *Jethro wanted to give it to me, but I couldn't do that. So I paid him $50.*) Jethro taught manual training at Hindman Settlement School for thirty years and gained recognition as a skilled dulcimer maker. He now serves as county health officer.

Until recently Still used a fireplace and kerosene lamps, but he now has a gas heater and electricity.

On the floor near the heater are cardboard boxes filled with jars of fruits and vegetables he has canned. Each year he has a garden, and because he can't eat all he grows he cans it. But he gives away much of what he cans.

He said that until a month ago he had been thinking of not lending books from the school library to first-graders because most of them do not know how to care for them. But the decision had been made for him: A month ago a first-grade girl had bled to death after having a tooth pulled. *If I had not let her have books, think how awful it would be.*

He said he is working on a story he has been trying to write for several years. *I've got several like that. If I live long enough I'll be able to write them. But I don't want to push them. Pushing a story is apt to ruin it for me. Or writing one with a long lapse between sections can also harm it.*

An example is the story the *Atlantic* is holding ("The Run for the Elbertas"). The first and second halves were written at two different periods. He felt the sections differed in "tone," but was uncertain whether the difference was harmful. He asked one of the better students at Hindman to read the story. *She said, The last part is not like the first part. So, I knew I had to rewrite it.*

He said that Appalachian writers have not presented enough of the barbarism. He tried it in his first story, "The Scrape," but said he had not tried it often enough or realistically enough.

I asked if he felt there is any contradiction between his work as a writer (whose duty is to present mountain people as they are, with their folk-customs and often primitive attitudes) and his sense of dedication as an educator and librarian (to teach them to read, to improve their living conditions, and to bring them closer to culture and so-called modern thinking and living). He said, *No. None at all. For I would still write about them as they would be under changed conditions. For it's the people rather than the conditions I'm writing about.*

March 5–7, 1959

Earlier in the week Still sent me a note that he would be in Lexington Thursday night (the 5th), go to Frankfort on Friday, and to Louisville in the afternoon to attend a meeting of librarians.

At the apartment he lit a cigar and slipped the band on his little finger, and immediately began to tell of a knife-swapping incident. On the way home two Saturdays previously he had stopped at Dalton's Restaurant in Stanton where a group of men were drinking coffee and discussing knives. There were a couple of Russell Barlows in the group, but the man who obviously was the envy of the others owned both a Barlow and a "Big Daddy."

I learned a lot about knives, Still said. But because he didn't have a knife he was an outsider. They talked with him, of course. But he simply did not have a knife. Neither did he seem to know a great deal about them.

But Still fixed that when he got home by borrowing an old one-bladed Barlow from Jethro Amburgey. Although about 30 years old, it was a sturdy, sharp, well-kept specimen. And tonight on his way to Lexington he stopped at Dalton's and hung around until four knife-owners came in and settled down to business. Still drew up a chair and pulled out his Barlow.

I tried to be casual about it so they wouldn't know I was a greenhorn. I had to redeem myself for not having a knife the previous time. You'd have thought a miracle happened. Their eyes got big and they all began reaching at once. They all wanted to buy it, especially the owner of the "Big Daddy." He needed a one-bladed knife to give him a set. But it really wasn't worth much, he said; why, in his time he had given away many a one-bladed Barlow.

Still talked about writing, saying that for him a lot of time is not nearly so important as the certainty of writing every day. It is the discipline of doing a certain amount every day that is important, the continual act day after day for years that makes writing almost as natural as the required functions of the body.

A writer in one of the books you let me have says something like this: It's difficult to write a book; once it's written it's difficult to get it printed; and once it's printed it most likely won't be well-reviewed, or won't be reviewed at all; and even if it is well-read, it most likely will be forgotten within a few months. But he says that has nothing whatever to do with writing. And he's right. The writing itself is the only important thing.

He continued with the idea on our way to Frankfort next morning, while we were having breakfast at the Blue Ox Restaurant. He said that many writers confuse salesmanship with writing. Publicity appearances such as lecture tours and autograph parties are actually enemies of writing. Some writers spend so much time telling us how great they are that it is difficult for readers to know how good their writing is. The writer has only one duty: to write. He may have to do many things to make a living in order to be able to write, but if he does those other things in order to sell his writings or to publicize himself as a writer he is then that much less the writer.

He said that most of the people who work at the Settlement and a few townspeople know that he writes, but that most of them who know it know it only because they have been told; very few of them have read his work. Knowing that he writes, he said, is not nearly so important as hearing, for instance, that some woman has had a baby or that a neighbor is doing a little bootlegging on the side.

(I went to Hindman in October 1957, hoping to see Still, but he was in Alabama to attend a funeral. At about 10:00 in the evening I went to Jennie's cafe for coffee. Two attractive women of about 45, both well-dressed, came in. We had coffee and talked. Both worked as waitresses; both had teen-age children; their husbands had been killed during the War. I asked if they knew Still. One knew him only to recognize him; she said that "he works out at the school" and that occasionally he came in the restaurant where she worked. Both had spent their lives in and near Hindman, except for two years in Michigan during the War, yet neither knew that Still writes.)

Still spent the morning at the Louisville Public Library listening to recordings of lectures on Shakespeare's plays. In the evening we went to the Readmore Book Store where I bought a copy of Ward Miner's *The World of William Faulkner*, and then we went to the Blue Boar Cafeteria for supper.

I had known since I saw Still at Morehead in 1952 that he does not care much for Faulkner. He said he had tried to read *The Hamlet* but couldn't get through it. He thinks Faulkner puts too much emphasis on being complex. *A writer should be clear,* he said. *His story may be complex, but his telling of it should be simple.*

We drove slowly back to Lexington. It was a dark-blue night with a bright moon. Still smoked a cigar and talked most of the way. He started and seemed full of talk. It was the longest I have known him to talk without inserting long periods of silence or making remarks that call for answers.

He told of attending the Southern Authors' Award ceremonies in New York in 1940 when he shared the award with Thomas Wolfe — he for *River of Earth* and Wolfe for *You Can't Go Home Again*.

Wolfe's sister, Mrs. Mabel Wheaton (Helen of *Look Homeward, Angel*), accepted the award for the Wolfe estate and read a section from the novel, which was the form of acceptance speech established by the awards committee. However, Still had notified the judges earlier that he did not wish to read from his book.

Reporters wanted to interview both him and Mrs. Wheaton, but Still had already announced that he did not wish to be interviewed. After the ceremony a reporter for the *New York Times* said he had one question: "Are you actually shy?" No, Still said; it's for protection.

Later, Still and Mrs. Wheaton went to a party given primarily in his honor by a group of radio people in a palatial home outside the city. Their host drove them there in his Cadillac, and when they were halfway across the city a taxicab swung in close, and the host slammed on the brakes and jumped out and began yelling at the cab driver.

I thought the cab driver was going to eat him up. Then the host pulled out his wallet and announced he was an FBI man. I was disappointed; the cab driver wilted and began apologizing. I had gotten out, but when our driver paraded his authority Mabel yelled, "James Still! You get back in here!" And when Mabel gave a command you obeyed. She was angry, for she said our host was wanting to show off, to let us know he also was important.

But it was different at the party. There were large rooms filled with expensive furniture and walls lined with books. And the most brilliant conversation I have ever heard. Poured on the floor, drinks would have been ankle deep. And in my honor as a Kentuckian they had mint juleps. I was ashamed to say I had never drunk one.

They wanted me to read from Hounds on the Mountain. *When I said, No, some man volunteered. He had a beautiful, dramatic voice but he did nothing for the poems. I had finished a mint julep, so I felt that if I couldn't read them better I couldn't make them worse. So I got up and read them. The only time I've ever done that.*

(I recall that at Morehead in the summer of 1952 several people at the home of the college president one evening urged him to read some of his poems. He declined. So a woman poet read some of them, and when someone asked Still to comment on them he said, I don't believe I can add anything.)

While we were having coffee in Frankfort Still spoke again of how a seemingly minor incident can trigger a story. The one the *Atlantic* has accepted was motivated by "something" he glimpsed on the roadside while riding in a truck cab. He didn't say what it was, but the "something" was to be the high point of the story; yet when he reached the point where the "something" was to be included it wouldn't fit. It just didn't belong. So now he is working on another story in which the "something" is to be the high point.

But I may not be able to use it this time, either. I have written the first part and am now working on a section later in the story. What I saw on the roadside falls between the two sections — if it will go in.

I asked how he decided when to use prose poems in his stories. He said he includes them to help move characters from one place to another, or to bridge sections of a story, and that they can be used to echo the theme of a story. But always they must fit the tone of the story.

It is irritating that I can't always recall how our conversations on writing begin. We just seem to slip into them, and afterwards I do not recall the sparking word. But this time it seems that his feeling that Faulkner's repetition and often inexactness of word choice led him to talking about the need for precision. After we reached the apartment in Lexington and had eaten, he said:

Exactness pays off. There must be an exactness of language, for both fact and emotion. A major flaw of even the best writers is that they write around the subject, like a cat playing with a mouse. They try to say everything in words instead of suggesting it. English is the most denotative language known to man. So it is time writers — and readers, too; they're as much to blame as writers — stop pretending that English is a pictographic language. One word is worth a thousand pictures. But they will write pages to tell how the object looks instead of working — and waiting — for the one phrase that will suggest it for the reader. The result usually is fuzzy writing. Many readers and most writers demand exactness of facts yet are not bothered by emotional sloppiness. A writer has no choice between being exact or sloppy, with either facts or emotions.

The writer tries to give the shadow of fiction to something as cold as the truth. And if he does it well, the shadow will be here long after the truth has disappeared or become something else. Can a jillion facts about the Trojan War outshine the Iliad?

He said that although an occasional story will burst out in full bloom after it is triggered, more often he works slowly and in pieces. He develops the story in short units: a scene, a paragraph, a sentence. *It is like a movie camera moving in for a single scene,* he explained, *and then cutting.* He will write a scene over and over, like a camera shooting several takes, until it is the way he wants it. Then he will tear off the section and number it and move on to another scene or paragraph, which will not necessarily be the succeeding one. On and on he goes, typing numbered slips of individual units, and after he has collected enough for a page or has come to a logical pause in the story he will put the slips in numerical order and type them on a clean sheet.

He works this way because he needs to see each unit by itself, isolated from the rest of the story, like a single frame projected onto a screen and held there.

But being published is not total joy, he said, *as I learned when* Hounds on the Mountain *came out. I got the package of ten free copies from the post office, and on my way home I sat down on a stump and opened them. I recall how naked I felt.*

A week later I met a friend on the street. I had known him for several years; in fact, he and I used to double date a little. But I never could feel close to him, never had that feeling of trust a person should have for a friend. But it took that little book of poems to expose the real person. He said, "I got a copy of your book this week. And you know what: Every page in it is blank." I thought he was serious, for sometimes that happens. I told him to return it and they would mail him a good one. He said, "I like it better this way."

After one of my stories came out several years ago, I met another friend and he said, "I read your story. Now why don't you cut loose and write a real story?"

There used to be a doctor in Hindman who for years had the habit of asking me as a form of greeting, "Written any lies lately, Still?" I was always tempted to ask, "You killed anyone lately?" But I couldn't, for it would have been too close to the truth.

I feel repaid, he concluded, *in knowing that my handful of stories and poems is the only writing that has come out of that section in over twenty years. And I had to write them.*

March 21–22, 1959

Still, Monroe Amburgey (a brother of Jethro's), and I went to the stock market at Isom in the afternoon. While we were having coffee Still said he had not written enough that week. *It bothers me very much. It's dangerous.*

Talk turned to Bernard Malamud (*I'm getting curious about him*) and Robert Penn Warren (*he has too many curlicues for me*).

We drove to the IGA store in Vicco, and on the way I told him about the mynah bird I had seen in Jennie's restaurant which could imitate a bob white and a gray squirrel and could say, "Hello, Honey," and especially enjoyed screaming, "Let's go to Vicco!"

Still said that recently the Knott County Grand Jury had tried to confirm reports that whiskey was being sold at the restaurant. One woman they questioned took the Fifth Amendment.

When you're out driving with Still he'll wave to people he knows and occasionally will stop the car to speak to someone he hasn't seen for a while. And he'll point out people and places. *The woman living there shot her husband.... That fellow has been in the pen three times.... This is the Red Fox post office. During the past twenty years it has moved all over the county.... The second stone from the right—* nodding toward a cemetery and speaking to Monroe —*is John's grave. He dropped dead, you know...*

On the way back from Vicco he said, *Right over there something happened that changed my life. It was long before I came here, and I don't know any of the people involved. It's something I'm writing on now. Perhaps some day I'll tell you.*

When we got to Littcarr, Still took a small red wagon from the trunk of the car and gave it to Monroe to take to his grandson James, another namesake of Still's. *I've got namesakes all over the country.* The previous week when the grandson saw Still, he looked down at his heavy shoes, then up at Still and said, "Big Man, you're wearing grandpa's shoes."

That evening I was in the hotel lobby in Hindman reading a newspaper when the landlady brought in the current *Saturday Evening Post* and asked if I had read an article in it by Jesse Stuart. She said, "We may be more interested in him than you are, you know, because we live closer to him."

I asked if she had read anything by Still. She said, "No, I haven't. But I hear he does some writing."

Next morning Still and I drank coffee and talked at his house until noon, and during part of the time he washed dishes and cooked a chicken dinner. He would put on something to cook and then sit down and talk.

Although he feels that Katherine Anne Porter has written some of the best short stories in America, he is puzzled that she has remained well known, especially since she has published little during the past several years and since other good story writers who have continued to publish have hardly made a dent. He said it is a comforting indication that a writer of serious short fiction does have a chance in the United States. However, we agreed that the indication is less comforting when we considered that for the past fifteen years or more Miss Porter has traveled throughout the country lecturing at writers' conferences and serving as writer-in-residence at numerous colleges. Furthermore, *Mademoiselle* magazine has published several articles by her, usually illustrating them with a photo of her. Remove the combined influence of her campus and *Mademoiselle* audiences and one wonders what her reputation would be.

Still knew Katherine Anne long before I met her in November 1947, when she spent a week at Stanford University (and she spent the spring quarter of 1949 there teaching). When I was introduced as being from Kentucky, the first thing she said was, "Do you know James Still?"

I repeated to Still a bit of advice she gave to a class in writing: Stop worrying about publishing. There's too much concern about it and not enough about writing. If what you write is worth anything, somebody is going to publish it.

Still replied: *I have never understood why there is so much concern about "undiscovered talent." There is plenty of talent. You can find it most anywhere. And I think it will be used as long as there is a need for the person to use it. I think many talented people never write, or quit writing, because they don't feel the need to — don't have to. The need to do other things becomes stronger. And I feel that much of the writing being done comes more from some need than from talent. It may be a need to make money or to become "known" or to "prove" oneself. But you get good writing only when there is real talent combined with an artistic drive to create.*

I genuinely sympathize with anyone beginning a writing career. Too many of them want to be writers for the wrong reasons. They want to be known as writers instead of wanting, needing, to write. Or they go down the wrong paths and do all the wrong things. They're in a hurry. They have no patience. They won't be natural or honest. They seem to equate honesty with cleverness, cuteness, trickery, gimmickry; like the singer who embraces a boa constrictor while performing, they lack the courage to perform without a carnival crutch. There is no substitute for talent; but there has to be patience and courage.

I wouldn't know what to tell them. And I wonder what they're being told all over the country in classes, workshops, and conferences. It's become big business. You can buy stock in it. But what can you tell them, even the talented ones? Writing is a way of life, and I wouldn't know how to make them realize it's not a part-time thing, something you take up and put down when you feel like it. It has to be the center of your life, and not many people can afford that. There are too many other, easier things to do.

Isn't it true that a writer is an amateur as long as he writes about himself, and becomes a professional when he begins to write about other people?

At times Still is slow to give answers. Sometimes he will comment on a remark five minutes after you've made it. I believe this is true when the remark is one that motivates him to test his responses, especially dealing with his attitudes toward writing.

He was in the kitchen and I was in the other room, and we were talking about Janice Holt Giles. He was washing dishes and had to cross the kitchen to place them in a cupboard. He would wash one, then pause in the doorway and talk while he dried it. Once while he was at the dishpan I said I had heard Mrs. Giles say that she considered herself a storyteller and that she had no illusions about her writing. I kept waiting for Still to stop in the doorway with a dripping dish. But he stayed in the corner with the dishpan for several minutes. Then he came to the doorway with only the drying rag in his hands and said:

I can't say that I have any illusions about my writing either. But I think I would have if I had not been published in the Atlantic *and* Yale Review *and* Virginia Quarterly.

In the afternoon on our way to the stock market, we stopped at Littcarr to pick up two friends Still has known for years, John M. Stamper and his uncle Sam Stamper. John M. is a large man of about 45 who talks fast and not always clearly. Part of the time he sits with his mouth open as if listening raptly to profound talk; his chin shifts slightly, and his tongue is poised and quivering as though he is about to speak. Most of the time, though, he is talking and laughing.

Sam is tall, slightly bent, and red-faced. His quiet talk and politeness are a contrast to John M.'s loud voice and rambunctious nature.

When John M. got in the car Still said, *Much of Godey's dialogue* [in "A Ride on the Short Dog"] *came from this man's mouth*. John M. grinned but said nothing.

After a while Still stopped the car and said, *Boys, I've been listening for half an hour and now I've got to stop*. He parked and pulled out his notebook and filled a page.

They talked about the "days" they usually observe. Two of their favorites are "Sapping Day" — when they go into the woods for birch sap — and "Paw-paw Day." A new one to be added this spring is "Mushroom Day."

At the market Still told of a Letcher County woman who, prompted by some distorted mental attitude toward him, taunts him every time they meet, which is usually at the market, by addressing him loudly so that others can hear with such remarks as "Well, if it ain't the great American writer," or by saying to someone near-by, with a hand cupped around her mouth, pretending a confidence, "He's a great big writer."

Of a man standing on the corner as we entered Whitesburg, Still said, *There's something unfinished about him. What is it?*

Sam, mistaking Still's sincere curiosity for fun-making, said, " Now, James, he can't help it. That's the way the Man Above made him."

John M. said, "He could stay in the woods."

The three of them, and sometimes a fourth — Hiram "Shorty" Smith — usually spend Sunday afternoons riding around or visiting people or going to the stock market. And until his death in 1952, John Francis was usually with them. Still mentioned him and they talked about him for an hour. They were still talking about him when we stopped at a restaurant in Whitesburg for coffee. Still said that John was potentially a great man, that he was a born leader, and that they had always felt at loose ends when he was not with them.

Each told of what he had gotten from John's wife as a keepsake. Still got a short pencil. John always carried a stubby, well-sharpened pencil. Although he did little writing, his reason was that "something important might come about and I'd need to jot it down." But Still suspects John carried it because Still at times failed to bring a pencil when they were on trips and would need to take notes. John would always wait for Still to ask if he had a pencil, then he would dig into the chest pocket of his overalls, saying, "I think I just might have one."

After John's burial his wife asked Still if there was anything of John's he would like to have. She asked first, but, as Still later learned from Sam, she knew what he would want, for she had taken the pencil from John's pocket and said, "I 'spect James would like to have that."

While Still was talking Sam reached across the table and picked up the sugar shaker. When he saw it was sugar, he put it down and picked up the salt shaker and dusted salt into his palm and licked it. Then he coughed and said, "Ummmh. That salt's strong," and pulled out his handkerchief and wiped his eyes.

(Back at the house Still said, *If you hadn't been there Sam would really have cried.*)

It may have been the search for graveyards along the highway John M. and I made that led to talk about John Francis. All the way from Hindman to Whitesburg John M. pointed out small graveyards, sometimes a community lot, sometimes only a few stones, or occasionally a single stone that the sun picked out among the grass high on a hillside.

As we neared Littcarr Still said that was the first time they had talked about John in the seven years since his death.

At Littcarr we stopped at a small, clean graveyard and looked at John's grave. Sam said, "Men like John don't die. Not all of him."

April 11–12, 1959

I spent Saturday and Sunday with Still. My main reason for the trip was to examine the clippings of reviews of his books.

Still lived full-time in the house from 1939, when he quit as librarian at Hindman Settlement School, to 1941, when he entered the armed services, and from 1946 to 1951, when he resumed the job of librarian. During the other years he has stayed there only on weekends and during vacations and during the summers.

During the five years after he came out of the service he wrote a lot but published little. He said he doesn't know what was happening to him and that he is still trying to find out. There is a black wooden box in a corner of the house filled with manuscripts that he wrote during the period, but he says they aren't publishable. However, he did publish "School Butter," "A Master Time," and "A Ride on the Short Dog."

John M. Stamper jokingly says that when Still began living at the house full-time in 1939 he went barefoot and unshaven. A neighbor woman who lived above him on Dead Mare Branch said to her friends, "What do you know about that? That man left a good job and just come over here and sot down."

On Sunday morning Still and I went to the upstairs room and looked at old magazines. He went through boxes stacked in a corner that he had not opened for years. They contained manuscripts and correspondence and copies of magazines in which his stories appeared. From one box he took a copy of *Hounds on the Mountain* and said, *This is yours.* He knew I had tried unsuccessfully for years to obtain a copy from used book dealers.

Monroe Amburgey came in the afternoon and saw the book. He picked it up and gently thumbed through it and said, "I didn't know about that book."

During the first year that Still knew Monroe he conducted an experiment: He wrote down practically everything Monroe said. That would be less difficult with Monroe than with most other persons, since he is not an idle talker. He has long periods of quietness, and he talks slowly and uses only the necessary words to express his meaning.

Still said, *He talks the way characters in a story must talk: always to the point, with no wasted words. I learned more about the writing of dialogue from that experiment than I had ever known.*

Monroe doesn't know about the experiment, but he does know that Still in a sense "uses" him, "picks his brain." Monroe has been a farmer, miner, road builder, and carpenter, and he knows about motors and machinery. When Still wants information on a subject familiar to Monroe, he will ask him questions by the hour.

When Monroe was gone Still told me that several years ago he gave Monroe a copy of *River of Earth*, but that neither of them had mentioned the book until that afternoon, when Monroe told Still he had read the book and liked it.

In the afternoon we picked up John M., Sam, and Shorty and went to the stock market. Shorty is a tall quiet man. John M. talks to the wind, Sam talks to the group, but Shorty talks to the individual. He will lean forward and talk in a low confidential voice to the person nearest him.

"Tell about your snake, James," John M. said, punching my shoulder.

You tell him, Still said.

"You tell him," John M. said. "You're the one that lived with it."

So Still told it. The previous summer he came in the house one hot day to find a house snake. He swept it out the door, but during the next week he kept seeing it. It would be coiled in a corner or circled on the floor around a chair leg. At first when he tried to put it out it would begin crawling off. But soon it became friendly, and then it became persistent. It would wrap its body around a table leg and hold on; and when he got it loose it would run to another leg. Or it would run behind the cedar chest or go under the bed. While Still was moving the chest or poking under the bed it would dart to another hiding place. And when he tired of hunting for it, thinking it had crawled out a crack in the wall, he would find it coiled around another chair leg. He usually chased it with a broom, and sometimes it would coil around the broom and he would take the broom outside and lay it down.

He didn't want to kill it, and he knew that as soon as cool weather came it would find a hole. It did. On the first cool night, Still turned out the light and got in bed. He said he didn't pull his feet away, and he didn't throw off the covers. But his entire body moved at once. He had the feeling of moving without effort. He said his entire body lifted from the bed, taking off the sheet and the blanket.

John M. said, "That's called moving."

August 21–29, 1959

I left Jo Lee at the Hindman Hotel and went on to Still's house. He was house cleaning, something he does each summer, spending the greater part of a week at it. He scrubs the walls and floor with hot soapy water and moves everything and dusts it, including each book and magazine. Lausie Amburgey, Monroe's youngest son, was helping him.

He had already cleaned the upper room and had just finished scrubbing the main room and was putting things back in place. Carefully and without hurry he put them back: a string of red peppers on the chimney, a bunch of ginseng near the kitchen door-facing, two dulcimers at the head of the bed, a straw hat in one corner, a brown jug on the hearth, and three carved rabbits on the window sill.

After re-hanging three Van Gogh prints, he opened a box and pulled out a bunch of hair tied with a ribbon. He dangled it between us and studied it for a moment. He has the habit of not saying anything at times when it clearly is his turn to speak. So he dangled the tuft of brown hair. I thought it might have belonged to his brother who died last year. I asked, "From one of your girlfriends?"

He dangled it, his face serious. *No, it's from my old cat that died several years ago.* Then he held up three or four more tufts, each from a cat he has owned.

There were several happenings of the summer to talk about, including the appearance of his story in the *Atlantic*, the week he spent with his relatives in Alabama, the writers' conference at Morehead, and the writers' conference at Berea in connection with the long-range Appalachian study then in progress. "The Run for the Elbertas" had appeared in the July issue, uncut.

I had had a few notes from Still throughout the summer, and one of them was a copy of a letter from Edward Weeks, editor of the *Atlantic*, who wrote him May 22:

> We have all of us been rereading that powerful story of yours which will be in the July issue. We think it is one of the finest narratives we have published in a long, long time, and I take great pleasure in sending you this extra dividend which you deserve in view of its extra length. Thank you again for writing so well, and do please turn our way when next the spirit moves you.

The "extra dividend" was a check for $100. Another note was about John M.:

> Stopped by John M. Stamper's last evening to see the latest White House can of worms opened on TV. The following conversation (e.g., exchange) ensued:
> JOHN: "Did Sid Adams' girl get married?"
> JS: "I didn't know he had a daughter."
> JOHN: "Shore, he's got one."
> JS: "I sort of knew he had a son about high school age."
> JOHN: "Did she get married, Sid Adams' girl?"
> JS: "Didn't I just tell you I don't know a thing about that family?"
> JOHN: "Half the time I don't know what you're talking about."

And two others he sent, shortly after the appearance of the story, he signed "Godey Spurlock," the name of one of the boys in the story. Godey, as well as Mal Dowe, also appears in "A Ride on the Short Dog."

In July I had talked about Still with a friend and let her read the peach story. When she returned to Florida, she read *River of Earth* and sent me the following note:

> Never have I been so greatly moved by a book. It was that he had crept into my soul and captured my own thoughts; this when I was a child. The perfect simplicity of it. Completely lacking in bitterness as a child of seven completely lacks that adult disease. And it is that simplicity that breaks my heart. I do not believe that James Still was born and raised in Alabama. He had to have grown up in the mountains. That he did not is as strange a thing to me as Tolstoy's perfect description of a woman's travail in childbirth. I suppose the true artist is all things—man, woman, a mountain child.

The last sentence gave me a mild shock, for I had recently re-read Still's restrained account of a child's fantasy world in "Mrs. Razor" and experienced a similar response.

Also it was a fitting complement to other thoughts that were in my mind about Still's attitudes toward writing. I had been reading Flaubert's letters, most of them written to Louise Colet and Maxime Du Camp during the four years he was isolated in the country writing *Madame Bovary;* and superimposed upon the image of the Frenchman in his white dressing gown and matching trousers as he labored in his room at Croisset there was the image of Still in sport shirt and overall pants, leaned back in a cane-bottomed chair at his house on Dead Mare Branch, expressing similar attitudes about the discipline, the sacrifice, the objectivity, the dedication that good writing demands. They were the translated words of a Frenchman writing over a hundred years ago that I read, but it was the slow mountain voice of Still that I heard.

> Be regular and ordinary in your life ... so that you can be violent and original in your works.

> What we desire, above all, is to have every author, obscure or famous, in his own idiosyncratic form, in his own characteristic originality, in his own frank and free nature, without timidity or reticence, with his own bitter or sweet savour ... as though he were writing, for himself and in solitude, a work which was never to see the light. We desire the anarchy and the autonomy of art.

> Success seems to me a result, not an end in itself. I have conceived a certain manner of writing and a certain beauty of language which I wish to achieve. When I think that I have gathered the fruit of my efforts I shall not refuse to sell it, and I shall not forbid applause if it is good. If on the other hand when it is gathered no one wants it, that can't be helped.... If a work of art is good, if it is authentic, it will be recognized some time — and if one has to wait for recognition six months or six years or until after one's death, what is the difference?

When Still learned that Jo Lee and I were going to Middlesboro before returning to Lexington, he decided to go with us. Then I would take him back to Hindman and spend the rest of the week there.

Most of the way Still sat sideways, leaning against the door so he could see both Jo and me.

That morning I had read an article in *Writer's Digest* in which a young writer set down his rules for writing successful popular fiction, the kind he had sold to such magazines as *Cosmopolitan* and *Redbook* and that has brought him $25,000 for screen rights to his first novel.

But, as you know, Still said, *I'm not interested in that kind of writing, whether it's done for free or for a fortune. Writing of any kind is so difficult that I don't understand why anyone who can write will take the easy way out by writing formula fiction.*

"For two reasons," I said. "To make money and because they can't write any better."

By its very nature a formula story can hardly be any good. A good story is not one that will fit into a pre-fabricated rack. Formula stories are all alike. A good story writes its own formula.

"What kind of rules do you have?"

Every writer, he said, *has some kind of rules, written or unwritten. I prefer to call them "attitudes." I think there are at least three attitudes I have about writing. First, I think a writer has to choose a subject vital to the characters. The lack of such a subject is the weakness, and in most cases the failure, of stories I have read at the Morehead conferences. And it's the failure of more than a few published stories. Second, a writer has to know his characters. He must live with them and become more familiar with them than he is with real people. As I've said* before, I have to wait until my characters begin talking to me before I can write a story. Actually, the characters have to do their own talking. Then I become a sort of secretary who writes down what they say and do. Third, I think a writer should use simple, clear, natural language. He should not distort the language to get an effect. I don't worry about sentence structure or grammar; they are things that take care of themselves.

Back at the apartment in Lexington the next evening, Still continued with the topic as though there had not been a break of several hours.

After you have a subject and set to work, everything else in your life must revolve around it. It must be nourished by everything that touches you.

It's difficult to get going and it's difficult to get out, but once you've started you're working every day and you're stopping before when you can go on, at the right place. You stop, be sure you know what comes next. When you stop, make a few notes — it's a long way to the bottom of the well; you may have to do some priming next morning.

I've spent many a night unable to sleep well because I couldn't wait till daylight to get up and get back to work. And then I'd sit at the desk cold as a fish.

But no matter. It goes on; and the thing about it is you're pushing, you're working both ways, you're working everywhere in a book. If you write this thing, you realize, Oh, I can't say this unless I go back ... and you go back and find you can't. But it's too good not to say. So you change what you went back to. Then twenty pages later you encounter the same problem with something that violates both earlier passages, but this new something is absolutely vital to the story. Yet, it you omit the two earlier passages you weaken the narrative. It's at times like these that nothing you may have learned from other jugglers will help you. You're on a tightrope a mile above the earth, inching backward into the unknown.

So everything must be relative. The writer's hand must never be shown. A character is expressed by what he does under any given circumstance. Not by saying *the character did so and so,* but by letting it happen. Let the story happen.

I've got all kinds of little tests I run, I've devised myself, after a thing is written, so I can see it. I'll say some of the simple ones. It isn't any secret. Only something I've worked out, simple ones that anybody ought to use. Once a thing is written I can go back in cold blood. At present you can't see it; you're absolutely blind to it. I try to revise it going backward from the last paragraph so I won't get messed up with the narrative itself.

My enemies are the adjectives and adverbs. So I put a circle around the adjectives and a square around the adverbs. Well, I can look at that page across the room and know it has to be revised. I don't have to see the words; I simply see too many circles and squares. Of course, we need adjectives and adverbs, but they better belong there.

My problem is compressing — too tightly, maybe. I think what I do is write it loosely. I want it that way, flexible, so I can make all kinds of changes before I begin to tighten up. It's easier to remove a brick while the cement is still soft. Then

I squeeze it till all the water runs out; then it's too tight, almost telegrammatic. So I have to loosen it up, then tighten. For me this is much of the fun of writing.

Basically, I'd say it's my wish never to use a word in fiction — writing about my kind of people, my characters — that's not in their vocabularies. I don't mean simply in conversation, but in the narrative also. We all know the big words; it's the little ones, you know. There aren't any bad ones. It's a question of a word finding its place.

In "The Run for the Elbertas" now, every word in there is in the vocabularies of the characters except one: "noncommittally." I couldn't do anything about it. I tried. I went through dictionaries; I thought; I played with it. It was either that word or an entire sentence. That was the pivot word: The story turned right on its heel and went the other way, and I could not find another one. I should have held the story longer.

Of course, everybody uses, I reckon, "Stopping by Woods." It's become almost a cliche. Frost was in a dangerous position when he said, "The woods are lovely." That very word "lovely." My father was the only man I've known who could say something is "lovely" and somehow it would be right. It was the Irishman in him, probably. I was always surprised he could do that. But I can't say something is "lovely." You've never heard me say "That's beautiful" either. Nobody's heard me use the word "inspiration," I don't think. I don't use that word because it's one — I'm not throwing it away — it's one of those precious words. You don't know what to do with it. It's too easy to throw it in. If there's a word in the language I would throw away, it's the word "nice."

After dinner Jo Lee asked him about Godey Spurlock and Mal Dowe, two characters in "A Ride on the Short Dog" and "The Run for the Elbertas."

My characters seem to choose their own names, he said. *Recently I gave a character a name I have never liked. Later I tried to change it, but he wouldn't give it up.*

I include only actions I can visualize. I have a miniature screen in my mind on which I project everything before I write it. And I have to hear the characters talking. When they quit talking to me I know something is wrong. In one story I left a character tilted back in a chair for two years because he quit talking to me. I remember his name: Gipson Dabbs. Then one day as I was coming out of the courthouse I heard a voice say, "Lawyers is useless as tits on a boar." For an instant I thought I was both talking to myself and remembering Gipson Dabbs. I finished the story as though I had never left it, but I kept that phrase for "The Run for the Elbertas."

I don't care how much I work at it: until a character speaks to me he's not living, he doesn't take on a life of his own. In a way I have some control, but not much.

You don't "make" a character — I wouldn't know how to "make" one. I have one now I've been working with for years — he's in absolute control; I have no control over him, not anymore. What I do is cut it out, but then I have to put it back.

I mean I have to think it through, write it through, then remove it, then put it back. That's all I can do.

No. I've never used a real person, though some of the people I know remind me of my characters. You can't make up things for real people — I can't. These characters come alive, they just appear sometimes — characters arrive without you needing them or wanting them or realizing you ever heard tell of them.

For example, here are my two characters in the book I'm trying to write. First I had one chapter — I thought. I thought I knew what it was going to be. But it turned out to be three chapters. Here, these two characters are going down the street of a county seat such as mine, and there suddenly standing in the center of the street is somebody I had never thought of, never even knew existed; but there he was, and I knew him instantly. I've known him all his life and mine. But these two characters cannot meet. I wouldn't know what to do. It would just be dynamite. I didn't know what to do, so I just wrote right up to him; and then I couldn't get the other two characters past him. (I hope someday you'll know what I'm talking about.) I just couldn't. I could not because that man standing in the street became a very important character. I couldn't throw him away. He demanded his place in the story. But I didn't know what to do with him; and the character going down the street just couldn't meet him. In the first place, what was he doing there? All of a sudden I realized that I knew all the time — I knew all about him, and nothing good.

Anyway, I think I was getting revenge on a little deputy sheriff I knew there. The way he used to beat people over the head with his stick. Terrible. Anyway, I disliked him. Always did. I think I was getting revenge. The thing about it was he was so ridiculous he was funny. He was really a comical character, and dangerous, too, as it turned out.

In writing a story it's better if you've got a little gripe, perhaps even a score to settle. Desire for vengeance can't be a purpose of writing, but it can be a good motivation for a writer. In the same way a horse shows more energy with a burr under his saddle.

But my character wasn't this man at all. And I just couldn't get my main character past him. So after trying and I couldn't do a thing, I got him on the other side of the street and went on. But when I did that it occurred to me, finally after a few weeks, that my main character knew exactly what to do and what to say. And he was totally in character. And got him past, and that completely changed my next chapter, because a person who was going to be at this particular spot — a lot of people were gathering there — I knew for a long time he would be there — he took over the next chapter, this other character. And it was about time, when I thought of it technically, that the reader had a little rest from my main character. You have to think about that sometimes, you know.

Anyway, it really touched me. And it makes me feel bad to meet this man, the deputy, cause I believed it, you know. And I think the third chapter can stand alone as a piece of reading, and for me is as good a piece of writing as I have done, *and can ever do. But into that went — O, Lord! the people who contributed. Practically everybody I know well contributed to what I'm doing.*

Writing is about people. Once you get away from people you stop doing good writing. The big temptation seems to be to write philosophy and geography. They don't make good fiction. Fiction is drama.

Next day Still and I returned to Knott County. On the way he talked about Yaddo and the Bread Loaf Writers' Conference. I asked if he had met Edith Merrielees at Bread Loaf (I had known her at Stanford).

Yes, she was there the summer I had a fellowship, he said. *She happened to be the first staff member to read the stories I had submitted, and she said, "Don't ever let anybody but editors see your stories." That was encouraging, but I was already publishing and had decided the same thing myself.*

I spent most of Thursday afternoon reading from Still's books. He has an interesting and varied collection, most of the volumes reflecting his interests. Among them are Forbes and May, *Natural History of the Birds of Eastern and North Central North America*; Homer House, *Wild Flowers*; Newcomb, *Astronomy for Everybody*; Wilkinson, *The Flower Encyclopedia and Gardener's Guide*; Nissley, *The Pocket Book of Vegetable Gardening*; Jenkins, *The Complete Book of Roses*; Smart and Ryan, *French Cooking*; Smith, *The Master Book of Poultry and Game*; Whitfield, *German Cooking*; Rombauer, *The Joy of Cooking*; Herzog, *Annapurna*; McGovern, *To Lhasa and Back*; Denman, *Alone to Everest*; Hunt, *Conquest of Everest*; *Mathematics Made Easy*; *Taber's Cyclopedic Medical Dictionary*; Wilkinson, *The Encyclopedia of Fruits, Berries and Nuts and How to Grow Them*; Taylor, *English Riddles from Oral Tradition*; Graves, *The Reader Over Your Shoulder*; Carson, *The Old Country Store*; Sargent, *Manual of Trees of North America*; *A Dictionary of American Usage*. And in addition there are numerous classics and books of poems and short stories, many of them autographed to Still.

I slept in the log house and Still slept in the "Peach House." It is a small rough-board house built with the money he received for "The Run for the Elbertas." He plans to sleep there during hot weather and when he has summer guests.

On Friday night after he had gone to bed I wrote down a list of statements which I labeled "Things I Know and Think I Know About James Still":

1. He believes in taking a stand and defending it.
2. He dislikes cheapness and pretense in any form.
3. He can be ruthless, if necessary, in his efforts to keep people from interfering with his writing.
4. He is outspoken and seldom prefaces a direct question with a softening phrase. Also, he can speak a sentence of two-bladed words when he wants to convey a meaning without alienating the person.
5. There is a hardness about his language that is pleasant. He does not

chatter nor use fuzzy phrases nor weave a pattern of weary details. The talk of the majority of people is the talk of opinions and impressions and emotions, but much of Still's talk is picture-making, and if he is telling an incident he will often imitate the people involved.

6. He likes hats and caps; has several and nearly always wears one.

7. Devotes little time to socializing simply as a means of passing the time for the purpose of being friendly. People whose relationship he cultivates must have something to offer him or must need him.

8. He has a reserve that many people interpret as shyness. (This summer a librarian in Pineville said to me, "He's the shyest man I know of. From what I've heard he seems afraid of people." An echo of an opinion of a mutual acquaintance of ours in Berea: "When I'm talking with him I get the feeling he's fifty miles away.") He seldom goes out of his way to make new friends and does not often initiate conversation with strangers. But he does a lot of talking with people who are his friends and with those in whom he is interested.

9. Above everything else he is an artist — an artist as distinguished from writer or journalist. You can't talk with him long without being aware of his honesty and his dedication as an artist. I suppose he has a certain interest in publishing, money, and popularity as a traditional consequence of writing, but he considers them enemies of the act of writing.

10. He is untouched by the success, artistically and financially, of other writers. (Of Jesse Stuart he said to me, *I'm glad he has done well.*)

11. Most people stumble for years through a number of occupations before they find one congenial to their abilities, but Still knew from as early as he can remember that he wanted to be a writer. And the first time he went to Knott County he must have known out of some inherent wisdom it was the one place where he could best develop into a mature writer.

12. A remark he made this afternoon, *I have remained intact*, sums up a wholeness, a soundness, a contentment, an independence I have been aware of in few other people.

13. There is about him what George Reavy has written of Boris Pasternak, "a spontaneous frankness and often a salutary silence."

14. I feel that the objectivity, the separateness, the perfection of his stories are the result of a certain amorality in his artistic make-up.

15. His method of obtaining a particular bit of information — especially of a personal nature — is not to ask a direct question, which might cause the person to retreat, but to make a remark that will interest or challenge the person.

16. He is fascinated by supermarkets.

After breakfast the next morning I asked, "Aren't there some writers with a philosophy similar to yours and a similar subject matter who have written stories that in some way have influenced your writing?"

No, I don't think so. How could there be? I enjoy and admire what others write, but how could I be influenced by it?

He picked up a copy of the current *Booklist* and said, *Here's the cream of the month's best books. Let me read the titles and see if they would cause you to want to read the books.*

We agreed that most of them were bad, primarily because they echoed other titles, or were meaningless, or were pretentious. We also agreed that a good title is not one that is used simply because it sounds good — as often happens — but is one that encompasses the narrative and at the same time reflects the theme, has levels of meaning, and often may be reflected in the last paragraph.

Still likes colorful titles, yet prefers a mere statement-of-fact title when it is used to emphasize restraint, as in the case of a story that relies heavily on emotion, or when it is used ironically. "Mrs. Razor" is such a title.

He said that titles, like subjects, usually seem to take care of themselves. *I don't choose a subject. It chooses me.*

He often writes a synopsis of a story to unify the material in his mind. Then comes the first draft, which may be an explosion that will carry him through three or four hours of furious writing. After that comes the laborious, day-after-day work of writing individual scenes, of building up the story in blocks, what he has called the movie-camera technique. He said he is amazed by the difference between the crudeness of the first draft and the finished story.

My boiling point is high. It seems that most writers have a low boiling point and can take a simple subject and write all over the landscape. It takes fire to make me boil, and even then I go through a long simmering period. Writing is like cooking. You can study all the recipes in the world and listen to all the chefs, but the only way to cook is to put the skillet on.

A writer must be himself. If he is any good he can't imitate. I don't see how he can be influenced. He has to stay wild. He shouldn't be trained. He's got to stay in the woods. He must be like a cat. No matter how domesticated a cat becomes, it's all on the surface. You can never tame one.

When you have several ways you can go, then the writing is going the way it should. The problem is to choose the best of the several directions.

He said that recently he was writing a "static" paragraph in a story — a paragraph to give the reader needed information — when one of the characters did something unexpectedly, introducing a new direction to the narrative, one that he had not planned but that he now thinks is right. When that happened he heard in his mind the voice of a woman he has not seen for several years who praised "A Ride on the Short Dog." Still said, *I heard her say clearly, "Good Lord!"*

He usually has the last paragraph in mind, and usually writes it first or soon after he begins a story. When he becomes uncertain which direction to take, he writes the next-to-last paragraph. And if more trouble develops, he will write the second from the last paragraph, or perhaps several, each time building backwards.

October 16–18, 1959

I went to Hindman on Friday morning, even though I knew Still would be busy Friday and Saturday. I had planned the trip since last February, for I wanted to be there when the leaves were turning and during molasses-making time.

Early in the week I received this note from Still:

> I want you to come this weekend even though I am tied up Saturday afternoon and night. You could drop around Saturday AM and watch me dig bulbs, and again on Sunday morning.
>
> What I want to do is go home with you Sunday afternoon — or almost home. To the C&O railroad station to crawl on the George Washington for Amherst and the Robert Frost festivities. (Could you go to Amherst with me?) And find out what time the train runs.
>
> I understand Robert Frost himself uses his friends rather rambunctiously in this manner. I'm in good company.
>
> Have you lit eyes on the new Ky. literary map? With what admirable features they have endowed me. Hair full flowing. Slender. Books for background, implying brains. Actually I think it was a mistake.

Because of the dry summer, cane didn't do well. The sorghum making was over, and the Johnson family near Littcarr that makes molasses each year had sold all theirs. So I went searching for molasses. I was talking to Astor Amburgey, a cousin of Monroe's, when someone behind me said, "I know where you can get some."

He was a clean, good-looking man, wearing khaki pants, a dark jacket, and a hat. He had an intelligent, fair face and gave the impression of being direct and especially knowing. His mouth was big and he seemed to smile all over; and his mission that morning seemed to be to show his teeth, for he had a mouthful of white ones perfectly formed, and he showed them all.

"Faris Pigman ought to have some. And if you tell him I sent you he'll let you have some." He told me where to go, and said, "Tell him Mallie Gibson sent you."

When I gave him my name, he said, "I know. James has told me about you. I guess you read the peach story, didn't you? About three years ago he took a trip like that with me. He kept taking notes, and I knew some day he'd write about it. Several things in the story I think he picked up on that trip. But I asked him where he got that 'Fill 'er up to the worm hole.' Remember the boy saying that? He said he was standing at a gas station one day when two boys come up in a flivver, and one of them said it.

"James don't miss a thing. He was with me one day and we come to a steep hillside and I said, 'You'd have to rough lock a chicken up there to get any scratching done.' James went for his notebook. After a minute he said, 'What about that rough lock?'

"My dad used it all the time," he said, "but you hardly ever hear it any more, and thirty years from now it'll be gone."

Before I left he wrote a note for me: "Faris, if you have any molasses, let this man have some. He's a good friend of mine. Mallie Gibson."

When Mal and Still came to the hotel that evening I saw another Mal. Still had told me once that Mal is many persons and that he doubted he had ever seen the same one twice. Mal had spent part of the afternoon in a small truck mine he owns, so he was wearing dirty overall pants, a jumper, and a cap, and there was coal dust on his face. He was not the local promoter I had seen that afternoon, the Chamber of Commerce member giving directions to a tourist. He sat quietly smoking a cigar and did not speak more than half a dozen words.

Still was writing when I got to his house on Sunday morning. He sat in a cane-bottomed chair, and with his heel hooked over a round was using his knee as a desk. I made us a cup of coffee while he finished, then he told me about his meeting Mal shortly after he moved to Dead Mare Branch in 1939. Mal owned a small store, as he still does, and Still went there one dark, muddy night to get some kerosene.

Mal talked and talked, Still said, *and finally I realized he was on fire for me to tell him my name. When he couldn't stand it any longer he asked me. Then he said, "But I thought you had a beard down to here," putting his hand on his chest. That was one of John M.'s stories.*

Mal wouldn't hear of letting Still walk home. He got out his mule and made Still climb up in front of him. Ever since, he has been Still's close, but most elusive, friend.

When I mentioned the time, Still began rushing. We gathered up the gladiola bulbs he had dug the day before, and I washed dishes while he packed a suitcase. In Hindman, where he has a room above the school library, he shaved and bathed. When I went upstairs he was throwing shaving equipment and socks and underclothes into a small bag.

I'll repack it later, he said as he stuffed in a pair of pajamas.

He put on his coat and a gray Stetson hat he had bought that summer in Lexington. He couldn't find the list he had made of things to take, so he began naming those he had packed. *Suit there and one I have on. Do I need another pair of pants? Shoes. Do you think I need a second pair?*

Later, in the car, I asked if he had any rejected stories. He said, *No. That's one of the built-in safety features of having a high boiling point.* Then he qualified it by saying he has a folklore book for children, two poems, and one story that have had one rejection each. The *Atlantic* has seen the poems and the story. They almost accepted one poem and pointed out a weakness in the story which Still realizes resulted from his writing it before the idea matured.

The mind is like a computer, he said. *It picks up all kinds of things and sorts and catalogs them. Then when the right key is punched you get not only what you learned yesterday, but also associated incidents from childhood you have forgotten or never realized you knew. That quality partially accounts for the writer being able to transmit his feelings.*

"But it doesn't account for his being a writer in the first place."

No. Neither does the capacity to feel deeply. Neither do the two in combination. There are other things. Self-training, self-discipline, hard work, patience, need, and the secret — whatever it may be: gift, talent, or maybe just the way the body is put together.

Recently I was going through some old notes and came across a word that switched me onto an idea that came almost full-blown. I have often thought about this material, but it was always in fragments. But the right key brought up incidents that made a complete story. Everything was there.

Coming into Campton brought us to talk about Beulah Roberts Childers, who lived there until recently. (I became acquainted with her in 1940 when she was living in Berea. During the middle Thirties she wrote two fine stories, "Sairy and the Younguns" and "The Sled," which were published in *Story* magazine.) Still wanted to know if she thought of herself as a "Kentucky writer."

There are too many writers, he said, *who want to be known as state writers. I'm not interested in "Kentucky writing" or in being a "Kentucky writer." I might be interested if you said "Appalachian writer." If it's good it's not state writing. It has to be more. I've never seen a state line.*

"There's something that needs saying," I said, "and I think I'm the one to say it. I like Knott County and I enjoy talking with you, and I'll be coming to Hindman quite often. But I don't want you to feel obligated to see me, especially when you have other things to do."

I don't feel obligated to anybody, he said. *And I think we understand each other unusually well.*

I asked what he was doing between the publication of "The Burning of the Waters" in 1956 and "The Run for the Elbertas" in 1959. He said, *Wouldn't you like to know? Well, I would too.*

I was afraid he would cut it off that abruptly. But he added, *Writing is more than putting it down on paper.*

Because we were late, he decided to catch the train at Winchester. We got to the station in time for him to repack his handbag, and when I left him he had the contents spread out from one end of the bench to the other — socks, pajamas, underwear, shaving equipment, and paperback books.

October 24, 1959

I met Still at the bus station in Winchester to take him to Hindman.

The chief reason I think I wanted to go to Amherst, he said while we ate breakfast, *was that Frost was the person who gave me the license to write. I met him in Florida shortly after* Hounds on the Mountain *was published. I met him in the afternoon, then that evening when I went to my room he was sitting there. Imagine the surprise of a beginning writer to walk into his room and find Robert Frost. It's the kind of thing that happens in dreams. We talked for a long time — he did most of it. He talked about the difficulties and the rewards of being a writer and about the need to remain free of pressure and promises and temptations.*

As we left Winchester, Still said: *A beginning writer, even if he can write, can be deceived by grants. The publicity that usually goes with it can puff him up, and he is apt to misjudge the intention of those who give the money. They give for promise, but the young writer too often accepts it for attainment.*

He returned to his fascination with words. *It's interesting what one word can do,* he said. *On the train I read "George's Mother" by Stephen Crane. There was one word that reminded me of a word that I used in a note last week, and that word reminded me of a subject that I collected material on for several years. But I lost interest in the subject and have ignored it for a long time. Now I'm interested again and want to bring it up to date.*

For several miles he hedged around the trip to Amherst; then he said he was glad he went because it is the sort of thing that comes once in a lifetime. *But I'm also glad it's over. I left a character tilted back in a chair, and I'm anxious to get back to him.*

The occasion was the weeklong observance of the bi-centennial anniversary of the founding of Amherst. Most of the town's citizens and numerous outsiders participated in the festivities. The two highlights were the dedication of the Robert Frost Room in Jones Library and an open house at the home of Emily Dickinson. It was Frost, of course, that Still was primarily interested in, but others he met were Louise Bogan, Richard Wilbur, Randall Thompson the composer, and Millicent Todd Bingham and Porter Dickinson, both distant relatives of Emily.

I liked Richard Wilbur very much and wish I could have talked more with him. I thought Louise Bogan was rather ordinary. More so than any of the others. But I saw her slip into a different gear when she learned who published my books. She asked me, and when I told her Viking she said, "Oh, I had forgotten." I felt then she gave me the face she reserves for people she wants to impress.

I did a very natural thing, he said, *which it seems nearly everybody in Amherst heard about but no one had thought of doing. Committees, clubs, and city officials had been working on plans for a long time. They had taken care of everything, they thought. But no one had thought of decorating Emily's grave or of making arrangements for visits to the grave. I went to see her grave and saw* there were no flowers on it. So the next day I gathered some wild flowers and some leaves that had turned and made a bouquet. I was taking it to the grave when Hyde Cox, who had helped with the arrangements and has great admiration for her work, saw me. He looked like he was going to cry. With all their committees and all their planning they had forgotten that one important act. You'd think that was an obvious thing to do. But apparently no one else had thought of it. And for the rest of the time I was there I heard people talking about it.

He said there were so many people taking up Frost's time that he was unable to see much of him. But I had my share of attention, enough to last for a long time. After one of the meetings I was standing on the edge of a group when a Unitarian minister swooped down on me. He was a tremendous man. He was all over me. It was like an eagle trying to land on a ragweed. He had read everything I've published and could name the stories and discuss scenes. It was a peculiar feeling for a stranger to be that familiar with what I've written.

On the way to Amherst Still spent a few hours in Washington and sat in for a while on a session of the Supreme Court. He went primarily to see Justice William O. Douglas. *I couldn't see his feet but I knew they were made of clay.*

Still said he needs to rearrange his schedule so he will have more writing time in the mornings. He gets up at 4:00 am, and after two cups of coffee and a bath he is able to write two or three hours before opening the library. He would like to begin work at 3:00 am and sleep an hour at noon.

"Why don't you go to bed an hour earlier at night?"

Oh, I've got to have that time for reading. I can hardly wait till I reach the room and get to reading. Sometimes I'll have the book open and be reading while I'm taking off my coat.

The solution he said would be to limit his reading until he has made up the time he lost. At the beginning of each month he makes a work chart on a 3" × 5" card, and each day he marks down the amount of time he writes. And if at the end of the month he has not written his scheduled hours, he will work overtime the following month.

As we neared Hindman, some remark reminded him of Mal Gibson, who once asked him, "Who was that woman I saw you with?" A good friend, Still said. "Are you courting?" No, it's just Platonic. "Yeah," Mal said, "and while you was playing Tony you was looking at her legs."

Then he told about the Nashville Chamber of Commerce man who was showing a group of visiting teachers the city's more impressive sights. When they reached the replica of the Parthenon, he said, "This is our prize. It's called the Parthenon. There are only two of them in the world. The other one is in Greece, but ours is in much better condition."

Among the mail waiting for him was a letter from Dayton Kohler and one from Marshall Best, his editor at Viking, in reply to one Still sent him recently telling him, What I'm up to. He read me a section from each. Kohler: "I still think *River of Earth* is one of the most beautifully executed novels I have read."

Best: "'The Run for the Elbertas' is almost unbearably effective in its poignancy. Its effect grows out of the situation rather than out of any power-charged words of yours."

December 19–20, 1959

I spent about four hours with Still and had lunch with him. On the 15th I had this note from him:

> Come up this weekend if it so suits. I'll be free Saturday A.M. and all day Sunday.
> Big happenings here last week; want you to hear it from my own teeth.
> Also want you to read the Marjorie Kinnan Rawlings letters before I pack them off as a gift to the U. of Florida Rawlings collection.

The "big happenings" was that his house had been robbed. Practically everything had been taken except his books, magazines and manuscripts, and his bed, stove, and refrigerator. They took his clothes and typewriter, emptied his refrigerator and took his canned goods, and even took his shaving equipment.

He was practically certain he knew who did it. There was one man who most of his life had stolen from people in Knott County, and he had a reputation as a thief with everyone on Littcarr. So Still swore out a search warrant against him. The Sheriff deputized Still, and with one of his own deputies and the magistrate of that district they went at night to the man's home on Breeding Creek. It was only by accident that a few days previously Still had overheard the man say where he was living.

Still said he smelled his turkey cooking the moment the door was opened. Inside they found two additional men and their wives. And he found most of his possessions—all but the tin-can food. While the Sheriff and his two men stayed in the living room Still gathered up his things.

You'd have seen a James Still you don't know. I called them everything. You dirty dogs. You lazy thieves. You lousy bastards. Too lazy to work. You have to steal for a living. Everybody in this county knows you're thieves. The Sheriff didn't know what to make of me. He had always thought of me as a meek librarian. He probably thought I didn't know what I was saying.

But he was enjoying it. Don't think he wasn't. On the way up there he seemed afraid. He said he wouldn't be going if it was anybody but me. I've decided there were two reasons he didn't want to go. We had learned there were two other men there, one of them dangerous. So the Sheriff was probably afraid of trouble. But I think the real reason was that he thought he wouldn't find anything. He had gone on searches before and found nothing, and he didn't want to go on another wild-goose chase. That can be bad on a sheriff's reputation.

But he was a different man when we left. After he got the prisoners in the car and got started, he said, "Men, I'm going to make a deputy out of Still. I got a bunch of deputies paid to find things, but they always come back empty-handed. This man has a nose. I've got a right to make a deputy out of him any time. That's what I'm going to do."

When Still got out of the car the Sheriff got out and shook hands with him and said, "God bless you."

During the following week the Sheriff could be seen on the courthouse steps telling the story to anyone who would listen. Still said, *I've never seen a more pleased man. I'll probably get him re-elected.*

For the past few weeks Still said he has been going through some old notes and transcribing them. He is finding it stimulating, for the notes bring into focus some things he has been thinking about. One note — a remark he had heard a man make humorously but that revealed a deep feeling he had for his son — has served to make a story out of an incident Still has had in mind for years.

It's been like throwing up a jigsaw puzzle and all the pieces falling into place. But the key piece was always missing. I've been throwing up the pieces for years. The note I found was the gimmick that brought the incident into focus and made a story of it.

But he said it irritated him, for it meant he had to interrupt something he was working on. And he said he especially regrets things like the robbery, for they take away some of the isolation and privacy he needs. (Most of the people in Knott, Letcher, and Perry counties knew of the incident, for accounts of it appeared in the local newspapers and on the radio.) In his mind apparently the robbery is another manifestation of the outside world — the machine and the paved road — that has been changing Knott County, destroying the customs and the colorful language, making it like other places.

Also, he has been depressed by the humorous, almost malicious satisfaction that two or three people in Hindman seem to gain from the robbery. One man, for instance, said to Still, "Why would anybody want to rob a dump like that?" And he wasn't joking, either.

In the afternoon in the school library I read the Marjorie Kinnan Rawlings letters to Still. In one of them, dated July 13, 1939, from Hawthorn, Florida, she told him she thought he was right in dropping a poetry course he had been auditing that summer at a Florida college, for:

> Your lessons, James, are in your Kentucky hills. They are in the waters of Troublesome Creek. They are in the strange minds and destinies of your mountain people. They are most of all in your own innate good taste in writing — and in your own heart, sensitive and raw....
>
> I don't remember whether I told you that Herschel Brickell corroborated my feeling about this. After I had read your poems to him, I asked, "Does this man have anything to learn from anyone else?" He said, "Nothing. His own instinct is perfectly sound. The individual lines are beautiful."
>
> It is only two or three of your poems that I have seen that satisfy me in

every single word and phrase. But I can say the same thing of all the great poets. The meaningless or colorless phrase creeps in with everyone. But you have a gift that, at its best, satisfies and stirs me exactly as does the best of Wordsworth, of Whitman, of Keats and Shelley. I am not afraid to tell you this.

On October 24, 1938, she wrote him:

> I shall be more than glad to say my say in behalf of a Guggenheim. I know no writer in whom I feel more confidence than in you.... I see many of your stories, and I love their quality. You have the real thing.

On April 12, 1942, after Sigrid Undset, the Norwegian Nobel Prize novelist, had been a guest of hers for a week Rawlings wrote:

> I am writing especially to pass on a lovely message that I have for you. It weighs as heavily, undelivered, as any sense of guilt....
> She [Miss Undset] picked up your *Hounds on the Mountain* with keen interest, and said she had read your two other books. She said she was very certain that in time you would be one of our *major* American writers. I gave her the second copy of your poems, which you had signed with just your name, and she was delighted. She was immensely happy to hear that I knew you, and asked me many questions about you and your life. Then she said, "When you write him, *please give him my love.*"

December 29, 1959

On his way from Louisville, where he had been visiting friends, Still spent Tuesday afternoon and evening at the apartment.

In the late Thirties he was at the MacDowell Colony when Katherine Anne Porter and Carson McCullers were there. During a conversation in which Carson disagreed with Katherine Anne, Carson said, "Don't be a child, Katherine Anne." Porter remarked later to Still, "There's something monstrous in every genius." At that time McCullers had published only a couple of short stories.

A result of Still's friendship with McCullers and of his recognition of her talent was that he recommended her for a Guggenheim Fellowship, which she received. The synopsis of the project she submitted became *The Heart Is a Lonely Hunter.*

Still has a story about John M. Stamper he intends to write some day. *I've been thinking about it a long time, but it's not ready yet.*

"How can you be certain you've got a story?"

If I wait long enough I can usually tell. Of course, I'm always working on sections that I think will join together, but I don't begin the real writing until I'm certain. And I do know. There are at least two tests that help me determine if I have a story. One is whether my premise is carried out. And another is whether the characters go through some change.

I've got to live with a story until it's ready to be written. I don't push it. I don't have to, for I know it'll begin pushing me when it's ready. And I do know when it's ready. Then I write a first draft, at one sitting usually, sometimes so fast that words blur into wriggling lines. Then I play around with it until I know it's right, sometimes for years.

I don't know that I have any right to have confidence, but I never for a moment asked myself even once whether I had any talent. That never occurred to me. Anyway, I just wanted to write one poem, then one story, and then another.

Poetry is definitely a disease. And, alas, incurable. And when the time comes, there isn't any use in trying to do anything about it; just go right on into it. But many people say, Why is it you don't write poetry anymore? Well, sometimes I do, but I can't take it. I can't stand it. My nervous system can't stand it. I can't live that life. No, it's too difficult. I'm trying to tell you I can't live like that. I'm just not willing to pay the price.

There's one thing I don't think I ever told anyone that has had an influence on my attitude toward writing. A few days after River of Earth *was published, I saw a copy of it for 25 cents in a used bookstore in Nashville.*

I have no particular urge to publish. I think I would write even if there were no hope of ever having anything published. I was not built with switches marked "To Write" and "Not to Write." There was a time when I got a great lift out of having something published, but not so much anymore. There are some things a man does just for himself. For instance, much of my writing is like my dulcimer playing. It's just for me. Nobody has heard me play the dulcimer, and nobody has read many of the stories I have written. I did them only because they satisfied my urge to write.

I want to say that being able to write is a great privilege, because I can live many lives, not just this one; but I live in a book and go on for years. I'm much more satisfied there than I am in the so-called real life. And during all my years of writing I think I have gotten a few things exactly right. There are some things, you know, that you can catch on paper only once.

It would be enough if I were to write one book of enduring merit, or one good short story. That's more than most writers do. My only concern is that what I write is good.

James Still on His Life and Work: An Interview

Judith Jennings

This interview with James Still was conducted by Judith Jennings at Appalshop in Whitesburg, Kentucky, on August 19, 1991, for reproduction as a spoken piece on the cassette tape Heritage, *released on June Appal Recordings in 1992. This interview is the basis of the spoken piece on the* Heritage *tape. The part of the interview that was edited out from the original taping appears in italics.*

Jennings: Mr. Still, I think you were born in Alabama? Is that right?
Still: Well, yes.

What part and when, are you going to tell?
Well, East Central somewhat, still in the hills. Between the Buckalew Mountains to the south and Talladega Mountains to north. And from our farm, from our highest hill I could see the Talladega Mountains and used to wonder about them as a boy.

What did you wonder about — what it would be like to live there?
Well, to go there, to go anywhere. I spent a great deal of time wanting to travel, to go someplace. It didn't occur to me that someday I would be able to. When I would hear a train in the night, say a whistle blow, I would have a yearning to be on it.

You would born in 1906, is that right?
1906 and that was 85 years ago.

So your parents were farmers?
My father was a vet, and a farmer. A vet meaning a horse doctor, no formal training. Although he did go to Auburn and take a course.

Judith Jennings, "James Still on His Life and Work," *Heritage* (cassette tape), June Appal Recordings, 1992. Transcription by Carol Boggess. Reprinted with permission.

James Still in the garden at a bed and breakfast in Salisbury, England. Photograph by Don Ritchie and Anne Campbell Ritchie. Used with permission.

And your mom?

She read a lot. I'm sure she read all 18 of the Elsie books, a popular book in those days. And then a peddler would come by sometimes selling books.

So you grew up reading a lot of books?

Well, no I didn't, alas. And that might, in the long run, have helped. Because by the time I got to books, I was absolutely starved for them. I had just enough of them to crave books to read. I knew there was a big world out there, and I wanted to know more about it.

I remember the First World War and I was 10 or 11 when it ended. During the war, soldiers used to come to schools and talk to us. But to go back further than that, veterans used to come and talk to us (Confederate) and we would go to the cemetery with little Confederate flags and decorate each grave. I didn't know that we lost the war.

So you had a strong identification as being Southern?

Oh yes. My Grandpa Still as a young man was in the Civil War and was wounded twice. He used to show us the finger that a Yankee bullet nipped off. Also he had a body wound. But my Grandma Lindsey's first husband was killed in the Civil War in North Georgia during the time Sherman was on his way to Atlanta. She married again.

There were Confederate veterans around. They came into school on special days. The Confederate flag was common everywhere and it hadn't been desecrated.

So you came from a big family?

Ten, counting a half brother. He died at the age of 4 with dengue fever at the same time I was having it and almost died.

Did you get special treatment for being the first boy?

No, I always felt independent. Grew up in a happy family. Never an unkind word. Now we lived on a farm (40 acres). In the spring, Papa had somebody to plow it. After then, we children cultivated it. We hoed and chopped and picked. Well, looking back I never thought we ever worked very hard though I remember there were times when I wanted to do something else.

Well, you're a good gardener now. Do you think it goes back to that?

Oh yes, I had a garden by the time I could walk. I had a little garden. I can remember my little garden. Once every summer I used to go every two weeks and spend at Grandpa Still's over at Marcoot. And my uncle Bob and Aunt Molly had a very large family who lived on the farm adjoining and I was mostly with them all that time. I would go every year. I hated to leave my garden and I was gone two weeks and I couldn't wait to get back to see what had happened to it.

My mother was a great gardener. Papa would plow it in the spring and she would never allow us or anybody else in there working it. It was her pleasure, her *joy and she didn't think anybody could do it, do anything right. Now I'm the same way. In my garden I'm a perfectionist. Nobody really pleased me when they tried to help me. Apparently there are ways to do everything right: hoeing, chopping, and pulling the dirt or taking it away or whatever.*

So you are the oldest boy and I heard you say you were small for your size.

I was. In the first grade I was the only child in the room who had to stand on a box to reach the blackboard. And that's the reason I remember that I was smaller than most. In time, I caught up though.

So what kind of school did you go to?

It was a good school for that day. It was the town school, city school of Lafayette. We lived two miles out of town and we walked in. *It was once — the building, a great brick building — it was once called a college. It was a college once, long before my day.* Roomy, with an auditorium. I don't remember a library; it may have had one. Teachers were considered superior to those in the country schools.

And the best teacher I ever had was my first grade teacher. She was a hands-on teacher. She involved you in what you were doing. My first day of school she handed me an ear of corn and she wrote my name on the desk with a piece of chalk. And I was to outline my name with grains of corn. Which I did, many times over. And before that day was over, I knew the shape of my name and I could write it.

She read to us and we acted out these stories. I was Adjidaumo, the squirrel. It has a few lines to speak. We grew corn. Each child had a half egg shell and it had a grain of corn in it, which we grew. And we learned about soils and about plants.

So you feel like you had a pretty good education?

Well, through first grade. I suppose it was average up through 5th grade. In the 5th, a Miss Almond, I remember she used to read to us from the Youth's Companion, *many stories. It was a long discontinued.... It ran for many years. No equivalent now. Maybe* Highlights for Children *but more advanced. Fiction and poems and articles, illustrated. We looked forward to being read to.*

Didn't do any writing in elementary school.

So where did you go to high school?

Well, we moved then. *I was born on Double Branch Farm, just out of Lafayette. The town has now taken it in. From there, after my grandmother died (suddenly and fairly young) we went to live with Grandpa. I barely remember that. Then we moved to the Carlisle Place, lived in a more or less tenant house until we could build one of our own. In the style of the day, large rooms, high ceilings, a hallway, a parlor with a mantle in it. I remember what we called the far room, the room in the back which was where we put extra things. Quilt boxes. There was a bed back there. I liked to sleep back there. We used to gather, and get* a bottle full of bees and get in the bed under the covers and open the bees up. [Laugh] We'd be in danger, enjoyed danger, running around the room. That was the place on rainy days we played.

We lived there. Pretty soon we had screen doors. I remember my sisters were grinding peanuts making peanut butter. We had a Model T Ford. First I remember we had a carriage with fringe on the top. And going some three or four miles to church once a month. I remember my sisters wore dusters over their dresses. We'd get to some woods near the church. We would stop and they would take off their dusters and shake them. My mother wore veils as women did. And women sat in a certain place.

I remember my kin are buried there in rows.

The church was Rock Springs.

My grandparents lived equi-distant on either side. Grandpa Lindsey was a Primitive Baptist elder. And Grandpa Still, we thought he owned the Missionary Baptist Church. He had a special seat. And he was called on to pray often. He was called Uncle William. He was something of a patriarch. So were both of my grandparents. They owned land, large areas of land, both grandpas did.

So you went to the Missionary Baptist Church?

We went to both. They met once a month. We went to both. Though I think my father belonged to the Missionary Baptist Church. I thought of them as two different religions. Some difficulty putting them together even now.

That famous sermon in River of Earth. Does that go back to those days?

Well not entirely. I remember my father. Grandpa Lindsey was just a little askance of the Missionary Baptists. I remember Uncle Ed one time. They had a revival. He was going every day for about a week, and I remember telling this. He came back — called him Eddie Boozer, Papa did. Boozer is a family name. Somebody was named undoubtedly after a Primitive Baptist preacher. It's a real name. It didn't have anything to do with alcohol. I don't think any of my people ever drank alcohol. I never knew if they did. I smoked cigarettes.

Grandpa would say, "Eddie, how many souls did you save today"? Uncle would say, "Ten thousand."

On the other hand, Grandma Lindsey, she really was extraordinary. I think we would call her a brain nowadays. She was very forthright. She would say exactly what came into her head and that was not always something you wanted to hear. They lived a kind of antebellum sort of life. Both sets of grandparents had large homes. Grandpa Lindsey lived in a great house in a great park with oak trees and that sort of thing and there was a chandelier in the parlor. We thought it was grand. Often had lots of visitors, especially at church time. Invite people. In the dining room there was a great table there and I recall the goblets they had, you'd drink out of on special occasions. Also there was a great big fan maybe four or five feet square hanging over the table which was controlled by a little rope which went through a hole in the wall and there was a little colored boy sitting out there pulling that back and forth to keep the flies off the table. This big fan had streamers of newspaper hanging down. I can remember that.

So you'd go there and have Sunday dinner after church?

Well, no I don't know that we did then, but they were, perhaps. I had dozens of cousins, lot of cousins and aunts. I don't remember us having much to do social except our kin folks. We'd get together all these cousins. But in a sense, the Stills and the Lindseys. The Stills were definitely English, rather austere. You might call them a little bit cold. I've noticed that through the years. Very polite, very kindly, but you would never really know anybody Still. You would know there was something you couldn't make out. It was kind of an enigma. I wondered about that. I have a mixture of both. On the other hand, the Lindseys were Scotch Irish, outgoing and giving. Generous on the one hand, frugal too in a certain way. You couldn't go to any of my relatives without coming away with something. You never let anybody come without going away with something.

In the poem that you wrote about those you want in heaven with you, were those these aunts and uncles?

Yea, but there were lots more. Those were just ones that had good lines. [Chuckle]

One of your grandfathers, you said he had so many grandchildren that he couldn't remember their names.

Well, that I'm guessing sort of. I never remember my grandpa ever looking at me. I never remember him speaking to me but he must have. There were so many of us. That's what I really meant. But Grandpa Lindsey talked to us all. And one day Grandpa Lindsey came to visit us, and we all had toothbrushes hanging on nails. Next morning just for a joke Papa said, "Well, Grandpa Lindsey used one of your toothbrushes. I don't know which one it was." So we threw out all and he had to buy more.

So you had a pretty happy childhood family?

Oh yea, I don't remember any traumas.

Did you consider yourself fortunate, or you thought everybody should have that?

I think everybody ought to have had...

I think there is no substitute for a Southern boyhood if they are like mine — now everybody's was not like mine, I'm sure — but I think my first cousins lived the same sort of life. I think they did.

So where did you go to high school?

Well, let's go back. In our home, we had three books. The Bible of course was there. One was The Anatomy of the Horse, which I used to look in but wasn't too much interest to me. The main one was a huge book with one back off called Cyclopedia of Universal Knowledge. It had everything in it like an encyclopedia would today. However, it was more instructive than anything else. It was how to write a business letter, the language of flowers. It had every science, a small chapter devoted to them. There was horticulture, how to prune trees, about 10 languages, about 10 words of each and how to pronounce them. I'm pretty sure I was the only person in the state who knew ten words of Arabic. The poems though were the important ones. They had some of the great poems by Byron, Shelley, Keats, Shakespeare and so on. And I memorized them. And one other book. When I put out a search for it about 20 years ago, I actually got to find one: it was called The Palaces of Sin or The Devil in Society. According to this book, the author (it's an autobiography for the most part)— in the beginning this man inherited about one million dollars. Think how much that would be in the early part of the century. In fact there was a drawing of him going to Washington, D.C., with a valise that said one million. Well, he went to Washington. Being a very rich man he got to know a lot of congressmen and senators and this book was to expose the evil of Washington, D.C. In fact they played cards (which is the devil's work) and they drank gin — I knew about whiskey, but gin, it was terrible to drink gin. And also he went on to tell of some of the bad things, in a nice way. Now when I advertised for that book in the Antiquarian years ago, there were several letters. One from the author and one from a literary agent, surname Fix. It seems that the niece of the senator from Oregon whose name I can't remember at the moment, found this book in her uncle's library after his death. She thought here was this letter which indicated he had deposited $5,000 in the bank to reprint this book for the moral uplift of the country. She wrote to the bank and found there was no money there. There were these return letters, you see. Also she thought the book should be reprinted just for laughs. Here are these letters from this literary agent trying to place the book. It is in very bad shape.

But that made a great impression. I learned something about evil in the world that I didn't know existed. But his evil came to be not my concepts of evil.

Well, what made you decide to go to Lincoln Memorial?

We moved eventually. We went to town for two or three years, and then we moved to a mill town called Shawmut in the Chattahoochee Valley. There's a factory. Still there.

Now my father didn't work in the factory. The factory (Westpoint Manufacturing Company from Boston) owned the town, and people had cows in their backyards and they wanted my father to come down and doctor these cows. He did and we lived in what they called Boss Row, Lanier Avenue — one of the better homes. That's what we were doing there, and I went to Shawmut High School. For two years. It was a brand new high school. There again, we had better teachers than average because they were chosen by the factory people and not the common run of teachers in the county. I worked one summer in the cotton mill. I did it just because I wanted to. Some of the other boys were doing it.... The child labor laws hadn't come along then. And I made band for the spinning machinery. Twisted bands on a machine. Then we moved to Fairfax, near Fairfax — Jarrett Station — and I walked to school. Not too far. And graduated from high school there. In my senior year. I always wanted to go to college.

My father had homesteaded in Texas before I was born, about 1890–91, and two of my sisters were born there and I might have been but my father came back [to Alabama] on a visit and a little sister about ten years old died of scarlet fever, named Nixie. And she asked my mother not to leave her. And my mother would not go back to Texas. Our farm in Texas is now part of Fort Hood, near Killeen. I have many relatives out there, many. But I never went back until — let's see. We went when I was twenty. We visited that farm and relatives or the spot where it had been. And the graves of some relatives are still there at this place. I can see my father pulling up the weeds off the graves. And I was back again as a soldier in San Antonio.

There was really no chance to go to school. This was Depression days. My father was being paid in chickens and hogs and cows and whatever. People didn't have any money. We got along somehow.

I don't remember personally any privation of any sort. I belonged to the Boy Scouts there and became an Eagle Scout. I had to have 21 merit badges for Eagle, but I had more beyond that. But I was a little unhappy with the Boy Scouts. There was too much sitting around. I wanted to camp and get out in the woods. I yearned. That's what I liked about them. We did some of that.

I was the office boy in summer — at the mill. It was a building near the great factory, which is still there. It makes towels. Nowadays, Martex, West Point towels, and many other kinds. And I remember distinctly there was a tool or supply room under the ground. I used to go there, under the weave. Overhead there was a hundred or more, slamming away. The motors were down hanging above my head and when I heard many years later Stravinsky's *Rites [sic] of Spring*, [laugh] I knew I'd heard it before, many times. I heard great music. I was hearing organ music. I was hearing Wagner, the slamming and humming these motors were making.

Then I had a teacher. *One of the teachers left and they hired a teacher through a teacher agency. My teachers were all women except one.* Well, here came a man down from Tennessee, his father was dean of LMC [Lincoln Memorial]. He didn't last long. He was a young fellow. He didn't last long, maybe 2 or 3 months. But during this time, he had a catalog of LMU. And he put it on the desk and said anybody who wants to may look at it. And I took it. And I read in it and saw that people could work their way through school. That summer I earned 60 dollars, and I saved every penny of it and I went. And that's all the money they ever got out of me. And when I left there after graduating, they owed me $75. I worked. I had nothing, literally nothing.

That's a pretty far way to go away from home.

It was quite a way. I was just delighted to go to school. I was kind of bored in high school. Not really that, but — my teachers, alas, didn't know anything much. They were not readers. We just had a little textbook work and that was all, as I remember. So when I went to Lincoln Memorial that was the kind of school I needed where you had personal attention. Only about 800, I believe, students at the time. And rather dedicated teachers, but not scholars as I came to know them. But they, I think, were just about what I needed. They took a personal interest in you.

The first year, I worked in the rock quarry in the afternoon, school in the morning, rock quarry in the afternoon. Everybody worked. Then at night at 9:00 I went to the library, and I was the janitor. I used to lock the door, sweep the floor, empty the waste baskets, rub up the tables; then it belonged to me. I was like a child in a candy store. I didn't know what to read first. It was an overwhelming experience for me to have all these books and magazines. I found a lot of authors for myself. For example, Conrad — no teacher introduced me — and Hardy.

Although I was an English major, I wasn't introduced to any particular ones. I had a double major: history and English. And I took biology which was the best course I ever had. And I was fascinated by that course. I stayed in the summer and took it, took it only because I was working at that school as well to try to get some money to pay my way the next year. We had a very spartan existence there. There was not enough to eat in the dining room for growing students. We ate everything off the table every meal, I remember. But they had a great apple orchard and many walnut trees on that ridge. Lincoln Memorial then owned a great deal of valuable land and beautiful land. And it may be the most beautiful natural campus that I know anywhere. The only one that comes near it and reminds me of it is Hollins College over in Virginia with a great mountain cliff rising over it. Just such a scene at Hollins as well.

That was a good time, a hard time as well. My grades were not good the first year. I was too sleepy. I was too tired after working. But after then I had work that was not too hard. So my grades picked up and I had good ones from then on: As and Bs.

Did you do any writing while you were there?
Yes, I began to write little things. I discovered *The Atlantic Monthly.* At that time it was the most prestigious publication. Still up there, but nowadays it has some rivals. And the school received many missionary barrels full of clothes. They also sent years of issues of magazines. Especially they got the *Atlantics*, all through the teens. I was supposed to check the files and if there was one missing, put it in, then to burn the rest, put them in the furnace. So I saved them and one summer I remember, distinctly, there being no work in the Depression, I spent the summer practically eating those. I read everything, and I decided I wanted to write for *The Atlantic.*

I discovered a magazine called American Speech. *It's a magazine for schol-*

ars. I didn't know it was a scholarly magazine. Didn't know about such things. Well, so I wrote two articles for them and they published them. Then when H.L. Mencken got around to publishing the American Language, he used both those articles. I think I was a sophomore and I was aware of little Sunday school magazines. They give you Sunday school magazines in different grades. And I began to write little things, might get $2 or $1 for these little Sunday school magazines.

My first publication was written in high school but it wasn't published for a year or two. Boys' Life, the Boy Scout magazine. It was an environmental poem. It was called "A Burned Tree Speaks."

Was Jesse Stuart in college?

He was there and I have never been able to account for the fact that I was never in a class with him. It can only be because I was out one year and he was out one year and they were different years. And we didn't have a great variety of courses, so I imagine you just went along taking rather specified courses. I knew him. I didn't run with him. I had my own crowd and he had his.

Was he writing things then?

Yea, he was trying to write things too. We had a professor there named Harry Harrison Kroll, who was writing and published a novel which I never read. I tried it once. And Stuart claims he was a great influence. But not with me. I had two courses with him. One was poetry which amounted to nothing and the other was the teaching of composition. And we did write compositions every day; that's all we did. And he would choose one and read it to the class. I don't remember any criticism of them. I didn't know him really. But I got to know him many years later and liked him very much. He wrote and published about 30 books before he died.

He did one on the Hatfield McCoy feud once. A few years later he published a book which was made into a movie, and a very popular one: Cabin in the Cotton. One day he put out a manuscript of this book. He called it at that time "The Woodpeckers," meaning farmers, i.e. farm workers. He asked if anybody wanted to read it. It was dog-eared. I took it with me but I saw it wasn't very rewarding and I didn't read it. I read a little and took it back. It later came out in book form. I still haven't read it. But he was a very unusual man. Not a gifted teacher. He'd never been to high school. He took a test and went into college. But he had something to give, and I'm not sure what it was.

So, did you join the service after...

Well, I had no work. Nobody had any for that matter. I went around trying to find it. I was on the road — hitch hiking. When I had a little money, I would ride buses maybe. I remember being on a freight train once when there was a number of veterans of World War I going to Washington, the bonus army they called them. I remember that. I remember going into Atlanta. Someone said "police ahead" and we all jumped off that moving train out at College Park. I tried to get work at Sears Roebuck. Signed up at an agency for a job — no nothing. Went up to Rome; tried to get a job in a factory that made stoves. Well, those were rather humbling years in a way but valuable to me because I saw something in the world that I wouldn't have seen at times, what it was really like. I had the ... it appeared then it would never be otherwise.

That was the year I was out. Then I went back to college somehow. Benjamin Duke of the Dukes of Carolina, who gave money for a building at Lincoln Memorial, was ill in the hospital, on his deathbed really. But his wife and daughter came to the dedication. I graduated that year and I entered five literary contests and I won all of them including a gold medal called the Rush Strong medal for an essay called "The Value of Truth," which, thereafter, I called my solid gold liar's license. And this was in their little publication, and Benjamin Duke read it. So he wrote to me and offered to send me through Duke University graduate school, all expenses, and sent money for me to come over there and make preparations. And they did take me; a professor's wife took me. Duke was a building then, and Trinity College was a school. I signed up, was ready even, had my thesis subject picked and approved. But two things were working at once.

There was a man named Guy Loomis, a man about eighty, or maybe just seventy then. And he'd given money over the years to Berea and to various schools, to Lincoln Memorial. And he'd furnished work scholarships, of which I'd had one, and then once he left some money there or sent money there. He'd come down to visit. We'd never see him. He saw we needed clothes, so he left money for, I think, 12 boys to have suits of clothes, and I was one of them. Cost about 12.50 per suit. And I insisted on thanking him, but the librarian said he didn't want any responses. And so I said, may I just send him a letter and thank him? And then when I graduated, I sent him an invitation the same way. He had never been invited. All the people he'd sent to school and he'd never been invited.

And he came down in his limousine Cadillac, with his chauffeur from New York, spent a whole week there, attended class day and all the functions. And when he came out, he said to me, "Would you like to go on to graduate school?" And I said, "Yes." He said, "I'll send you through any school in the South of your choice." And I chose Vanderbilt, although I had this scholarship to Duke. And he said something else important: "I will make it possible, not easy." And it was, just barely possible. So I didn't go to Duke.

Now, he said to me, "I don't want you to go alone. Do you know some student with good grades who'd like to go?" I said "Yea, my roommate." And sight unseen, he gave both of us the same offer. But my roommate wanted to go to the University of North Carolina.

This past Saturday I received a letter from his son saying that he passed away a week ago.

Why did you choose Vandy?

When I went to Duke, as I said, it was a building. And I don't know — I'd heard more about Vanderbilt, or something. I don't really know for sure.

Were the Fugitives there then?

They were there. I didn't know anything about them then. Nobody else knew. But I had John Crowe Ransom and John Donald Wade, both of whom contributed to I'll Take My Stand, *the book they published the year after I was there, after I graduated. They read their chapters to us. Doing something like this in isolation, it's not remembered very well. I just remember they read them. It was my first encounter with scholars, and important ones. Robert Penn Warren was in Oxford at that time. Anyway, the book came out the next year and by that time I was at the University of Illinois. It was a very busy year. For one thing, my tuition was paid, which was high for the day as it is now there. And those things were taken care of. Loomis's secretary took care of that. And he furnished me the room. However the money for food was not enough. So I ate a bowl of cereal in the morning and I paid 35 cents at a boarding house. I was eating one meal a day until Loomis came down at Christmas time on the way to Florida. And he had me come up and have a meal with him in a hotel. It was rainy, drizzling. I didn't have a raincoat and I was a little damp. He said, "Don't you have a raincoat?" I said, "No." He said, "I will buy you one," and I said "Remember, you said you would make it possible, not easy." He didn't buy the coat. But then he said, I think based on that, "Would you like to go to school another year, somewhere else?" Anywhere except New York City, where he lived.*

And then, though, this teacher, the librarian at Lincoln Memorial — it turned out there was a scholarship which she got for me and he (Loomis) paid the rest or some way or another in library science at the U of I. She engineered that. I never thought to be a librarian. But it was something to do. You see. There's no work, so I went on. He made it a little better then.

So you went to Vanderbilt for one year and then to Illinois?

Yes, it took a year to get a Masters. And had a little unusual experience there. I didn't know anybody. And in my American lit class under John Donald Wade, about the first class he said, "I want to give you a little test. No grades will be recorded. I just want to get some idea of what you already know about American literature." So he handed us out a card and we numbered ten on each side, and then he said I've done this every year and nobody ever passes so don't worry about it. So he read one sentence from writings, authors from the Civil War period to that day, and there were Dreiser and whoever was writing in those days. Well, nobody did pass except me, and I made a perfect score. Well, I was nobody that day. Next day, I was famous.

I did my thesis under the Chaucer scholar, Walter Clyde Curry. That was one of the most marvelous and punishing and cruel courses I ever took and most rewarding in the long run.

My thesis I chose was "The Functions of Dreams and Visions in the Middle English Romances," which required that I learn to read Middle English quickly and I had to go through 106 volumes of the Early English Text Society. And I wrote this thesis and I can't believe that I wrote it. It's not bad at all. It was written in blood I assure you, as most theses are.

So then you went to Illinois and became a librarian?

No, I went to Illinois and got a library degree. And there were no jobs. Then I had a spell. There was a biology professor that I had traveled with a good bit and that's how I got around as a young man. He went up to Yale and got a Ph.D. and was teaching biology at Yale and his wife remained librarian at LM. But we would go up there and spend the summer. One summer he had the Yale Table at the Marine Biological Station, so we lived

[end of first side of rough tape]

there all summer and as Mrs. Grannis was interested in antiques, we visited everyone surely in that area. I got to know everybody in the Osborn lab at Yale, and I used to go around and watch these fellows working on doctorates in science at what they were doing because I was very interested in biology, in botany as well. And if I'd had the opportunity I would have followed that field. Before I went to Vanderbilt, I was up at Yale. They made every effort to get me into Yale. I was just going to get a degree from Yale, that is, do the last year or two years or something. The problem was they required four years of Latin and I had only two. Now, no Latin is required. I would say, alas. I regret I didn't have those four years.

Middle English wasn't too difficult if you had had two years of Latin and if you had had five years of French and knew some English and you put it together. There are only about 400 words of original import anyway. It looks like a foreign language to look at, but when you get into it, it's not difficult at all.

Chaucer happens to be the only author that I totally relate to. I feel that I knew him. I sometimes feel that I am Chaucer. And may I say last week I ordered *Canterbury Tales*. My copy got away from me so I ordered one.

So you came down with Hindman as a first job?

The way I came back from the U of I, I stopped at Nashville. There was one of my classmates at Vanderbilt, going to school in religion.

And he was working out at the settlement house. I went to the settlement house and waited for him to come and when he came in, he asked me to come to Knott County with his brother-in-law. He and his wife were going to teach a vacation Bible school. And I did go. He furnished me the train fare. We stayed at the Hindman Settlement School for a week, then it closed. And then we went up on Mill Creek and stayed with a man named Dan Pratt and his wife, and we had about four baseball teams across the county. We walked everywhere, camped and played ball all summer.

Well, it happened that Hindman Settlement needed a librarian so they hired me. I was what they called a "volunteer worker." What I mean is that I was involuntarily a volunteer worker. I would have been delighted to have a salary, but their endowment was in stocks and bonds, and they weren't paying much. And they couldn't pay us, the teachers. They did feed us and house us and for that day and time, a man would have been happy to have that much.

That was in the late 1930s.
I came in '32.

Was it isolated and wild then?
The road, I was told, that came from Hazard to Hindman had just been paved so a car could go over it. There was no bridge in town. There had been one, but it had been washed out.

[pause in tape Still is getting his coffee.]

To cross the creek you stepped on rocks if it was low enough, and sometimes there was a plank there and sometimes there was a jumping pole. And I really had come to the jumping off place.

From Hindman wagon roads served the rest of the county, ruts nearly knee deep some places. And the Settlement School was really a little New England island. The teachers were mostly women; they were mostly graduates of Wellesley (some Smith, Bryn Mawr, Mount Holyoke), well educated young women and highly motivated. The library was surely the best of any secondary school in the state. And I can't imagine any other school in the state of Kentucky having such a staff as this one had. And the facilities we had.

There again the children always worked. There were approximately 100 at any given time. They were there during the school year (not in the summer). There was a dairy there, an enormous garden, woodworking, weaving. Everybody worked. They just scrubbed floors that didn't need scrubbing and raked lawns that didn't need raking. They ran a tight ship, I assure you. They interviewed their students, their parents. They got the best. Well, from the first graduating class one of the students got a doctorate from the Sorbonne. His diploma hangs on the wall of the dining room now. Josiah Combs was his name. Others went to Harvard. Many of the girls went to Wellesley and graduated. They went to Phillips Exeter and places like this. The girls usually, though, were expected to go after they graduated; they went to a finishing school down state, which doesn't exist anymore. Were supposed to learn manners and that sort of thing. There was once a prodigy. I encountered two prodigies there and one near-one. Both were girls. They hardly knew what to do with them really. They just let them help in the grade school. And then they sent them over to me at the library. This girl read 210 books of substance in nine months.

So you were in charge of choosing which books were bought for the library?
Let's put it this way, the library was there; there was no money. We bought no books. Often people sent books, Wellesley people, good books as a rule. In later years, we got so many books we couldn't use and eventually, the county gave us $400 to buy books, just to replace what was needed for the schools.

Did you live at the Hindman Settlement School?

I did. *I lived in the lower room of the boy's dormitory for a while and eventually I lived in a room, the magazine stack room at the library and then the last couple of years, I lived in the house I'm occupying now.*

I stayed. I had nothing, not a dime. I couldn't mail a letter even. And our jobs.

We had those hundred students on our hands seven days a week so just being a teacher, a librarian or whatever your job was was just a part of it. For example, I had those boys on my hands for the weekend, took them on hikes, to the ball park to play. Everybody worked round the clock. It was a very busy time. Study halls in the evening, though I never kept one. Anyhow, all that time, I was reading and thinking about writing but not writing....

I was going to have to do something about money. Some donor offered $15 a month to keep me there. So I stayed that year. The next year there was a little more and the next year, well, a little bit more still.

When I averaged it out, after six years, I had received an average of six cents a day. So as I tell it, I retired, I was so rich. I went over on Dead Mare Branch nine miles over a wagon road and one mile up a creek bed to the Amburgey log house, a structure that was built in 1837. Not a cabin as people call it. A very substantial log house, two stories. It was between the waters of Dead Mare and Wolfpen Creek facing Little Carr Creek, with the mountains rising behind. In June, it was late for planting a garden, but I did plant one and as the frost held off, I had a pretty good garden. I began to visit my neighbors and get to know people and go down to church meetings weekends, once a month rather. And I went to candy pullings sometimes and pie suppers at the school house and helped my neighbors, and they helped me. And I also dried apples and canned stuff for myself and holed up potatoes and cabbages. I got a couple stands of bees and then I ate. My neighbor asked me to come out and eat with him so I ate my evening meal five nights a week with them and sort of became part of the family. So then the war came. And I was drafted and off I went.

Did *River of Earth* come out before?

It did. Published in 1940.

I know that you said people around you didn't know about it, but it made quite a stir in the outside world, didn't it?

Yes, it had reviews, good ones. *Time* magazine called it "a work of art." It was reviewed by the *New York Times Book Review* and *Atlantic* and *New Yorker* and Scribners and places where books get reviewed. And with no exception, the reviews were good.

But before then, before I left Hindman, I had published a book of poems. Viking Press published them and those poems are still in print in another volume called The Wolfpen Poems *along with others written later. Also it had good reviews without any bad ones I know anything about.*

You shared an award with F. Scott Fitzgerald in 1940?
No, the Southern Authors' Award was given to me jointly with Thomas Wolfe. Thomas had died and he's never been recognized. I suppose it was late for him to receive it. They gave it to him and at the dinner of awards in N.Y., his sister, Mabel, received it for him and I got to know her, and there began certain adventures.

That was 1940?
Yea, maybe '41. I think February '41.

Why do you think* River of Earth *was so well received?
I don't know, and I don't know why after 51 years it seems to be going strong and selling a few more copies every year than before. It's been taken up by colleges and universities and nowadays high schools, especially in the Appalachian region, about a dozen states use it. It's used in folklore and in history of the area, as there are no histories. Nobody has ever written any. And this seems to cover a period of time nobody's written about. In fact when it was reprinted about 10 years ago by the University Press of Kentucky, several state history associations reviewed it, explaining, "Although we do not usually review fiction reprints, this tells us something about that region and is a good source of knowledge about southeast Kentucky."

Was* River of Earth *based on a family that you knew?
One summer there at Hindman—no school in summer—I was asked to take the place of a social worker at FERA [Federal Emergency Relief Administration] *for two weeks, but they didn't return so* all summer I was a social worker. I had the southwest area of the whole county. Miles of walking so all summer I walked except one place on Quicksand I used to hire a little horse, a little crippled horse, but mostly I walked, visited families who invited me that wanted help. I would go to their homes and look in their meal barrels and see how many chickens they had and how many eggs they got and look at their gardens and see what the general situation was in the family, and I put this down in composition books.

One day a week we four or five would stay in the office in Hindman and write up our reports, using our notes.

Really out of this came the book. Those composition books are in Morehead, in the so called James Still Room, if anybody wants to look at them. That's really where it came from.

So you really got to know the lifestyle of the people.
Oh yes, and what they said and how they thought, one way and another. None of these characters are real; I never did write about a real person. But in a sense they have a prototype. The little boy who narrates it is undoubtedly a little boy who was at Hindman, William Lee Parks. He was about ten. He came from a fine family over in Letcher County. His father worked for the Kentucky

power company. There were two boys in the family. I used to wonder why they would let such a delightful child be away from home. I knew the family. Anyway, he would ask the housemother for permission to come in and visit me in my room. He would come in and tell me things. I became a kind of a father to him. He treated me like I was his parents. One day I was sitting at the typewriter and he came in and started telling me the time he like to got killed. He had many narrow accidents, like a log rolled over him once. As he told it, I just typed it. And then when the *Courier Journal* had an anniversary 100 years old or 150 or something, and asked me for something I sent this, it's called "I Likta Got Killed." Alas, this boy went on to college; was in the army in Australia, came back and went to medical school at UK and when he was home he was in the car with somebody and had an accident and he was killed. He did die at last, see.

But another child there, whose name was Cotton Miller, was younger still. There are two boys rolled into one. He was a mischievous little boy. They called him Cotton because of his hair, white hair, and he was blue-eyed skinny. He fought somebody everyday. He never got mad, he just fought everyday. He was expelled for something (it was easy to get expelled there) and then I went to the director and pled with her to let him come back. In fact, I told her I would buy his books. So she let him come back and then in about six months he got in some more mischief and she wouldn't let him come back.

And then later that year I heard that somebody killed him.

Wow, so being around children helped you write that from a child's point of view?

I think so. You see, I had story hours at the library and I had every grade and had story hour for the first three grades. We had a children's room with the best of children's books. And I would hold the picture up and tell the story. We'd act out some of these a little, like "Three Pigs." The fourth grade, though, they would just come for library hour, once a week.

Remember, I was there six years, then I went away back in the mountains to live on Dead Mare. Then to the army. Then I came back for three years or so, then I was back in Hindman for seven more. By this time, my brother was in a nursing home and there was nobody to care for him except me. My take-home pay was $114 a month. His drug bills were sometimes more than this. He had worked for a boatworks during the war in New Orleans, he did have some Social Security. So there again I had nothing because, of course, everything was going to take care of him. I'm proud to say that I could do it. So time came I had to make more money.

So I went down to Morehead State University where I taught 10 years, before I left.

In 1940 when you published River of Earth and it was so well received, did you consider leaving the area then?

Never. I have never. Before I went back to the Hindman Settlement this one time I felt I was getting too isolated. I had planned to go out and work in an Indian school in Arizona, but then they asked me to come back to Hindman for a year. I'd promised to come a year, but I stayed on seven. And that's how I happened to go back again.

One more question about River of Earth: **I think one of the most powerful pieces in it is the sermon that Randy Wilson does so well. Is that from your early days of listening?**

I've heard many Old Regular Baptist sermons. I invented it. I think it rings pretty true. It's stood up with time.

Did you ever think about being a preacher?

You know I wouldn't. No. It's not my nature.

When River of Earth *came out, did you hear from other authors and other writers around the country?*

Oh yea, Oh yes.

Katherine Anne Porter?

Well, I had these fellowships. I had the Publisher's Fellowship at Bread Loaf, where I got to know a number of well-known people — for example, Eudora Welty and Carson McCullers and Katherine Anne Porter, and Robert Frost and several others I could name. Then I had a fellowship at MacDowell Colony for a summer. There again I got to know a number of authors as well as composers, writers ... artists rather. And then I had a fellowship at Yaddo at Saratoga Springs, New York, first one in 1939. And altogether I've been there seven fellowships, the last one about five years ago.

Who else was at Yaddo in 1939? Do you remember?

There again, Katherine Anne Porter was there and Eleanor Clark (Mrs. Robert Penn Warren). Eudora Welty came, not in my time, but at a later time. However, she visited Katherine Anne at the time I was there and we spent one evening at what they called the Farm House, which is on the campus or grounds. And she read to us — and this was in 1940, twenty years before the book was published — the last chapter of Ship of Fools. And 20 years later when it was published, I opened it up to see if it had been changed and it was right there. I remember it well. She talked that evening. We listened to her.

[Katherine Anne]* was sort of just beginning, as I was. She talked about two things. One was one of Napoleon's generals that interested her greatly. I think she intended to write about it. Also she intended to write about Cotton and Increase Mather. Now at Vanderbilt in the American lit class, the class wrote together a history of American lit. They divided up the various fields. My chapter — two chapters — was on Cotton and Increase Mather. So when Bread Loaf invited Katherine Anne and me over there to come over and visit — Katherine Anne to lecture

*Here Mr. Still actually said "Eudora" but apparently meant "Katherine Anne."

or read — we went together. Well, you can't get there from Saratoga. That meant we had to ride little buses, change several times during the day to get to Middlebury, Vermont. But we talked. She told me about Cotton and Increase. I was fully ready to discuss with her. That's what we talked about, as I remember.

So when you would go up to Yaddo and come back to Hindman, did it seem like a big difference?

Of course it was. It's a different world. Someone asked Doris Grumbach if there is such a thing as a literary establishment in this country. She says, "There certainly is. I meet them at Yaddo every summer." Granted you have what it takes, it is well that you get to know other people in the field. I would say I got my Guggenheim Fellowship because Katherine Porter told them to give me one. I got two in the end. There's always somebody responsible. The last award of note I received is the Peabody Award given by the American Academy and National Institute of Arts and Letters in New York. And I learned later that Walker Percy was responsible for my receiving it. He insisted that I get it, although the other judges had their own candidates.

Would you consider yourself a writer's writer?

No, I never think of being a writer. I got a lot of interest in things that I think about. I don't even think about writing except when I'm doing it.

When did you start keeping the notebooks?

When I moved over there in 1939, nothing before. I began to put things down in a little notebook. I was very casual about it. I'd go six months and nothing. I really could have had something, actually, if I had thought about it. It's just informed what I might be writing later. And nobody ever saw them, though I mentioned them a number of times to people. Alfred Perrin wrote recently and said, "Well, I began to think those notebooks were just a figment of your imagination, but actually they exist."

So you started keeping those in 1939?

Just off and on through the years. Most of the quotations there are from people passed on. I would say 85 percent of the people have died.

And it was just something that would catch your ear?

Well, something I thought was kind of unique. For example, a man's preaching a sermon. I'd just get one sentence out of it. When he said, "Hell is not a haystack." Sometimes a whole paragraph, or a few lines. Something unexpected. Several of us have written poems, short stories, novels about the mountains. Here the people are speaking for themselves. I'm not adding a word to it. All I did is put quotation marks around it. I tried not to wrestle with dialect because just to write it down, it becomes strange even to the man who's just said it. Dialect bothers me. Idiomatic ways of speech, okay.

So you've written a lot of poems. I mean I appreciate a lot of the poems you've

written since the '50s and '60s. You always wrote poems; your first things were poems. But a lot of the readings you do are poetry. Do you prefer verse?

I don't prefer either. I would write more if I preferred to be a writer. I wrote poems when I could not do it. It keeps bothering me and I write it to get rid of it. And some of the stories bother me and I wrote them and got rid of them.

Do you use the notebooks when you do your poems?

I have never looked in notebooks to write it, fix it in memory. If I need it, it comes forward by itself. I never force myself to write anything. There are times when I couldn't write a note to the milkman. Once in a while I get in a state of free association — that's the best description I can give it — when I can write anything. It just goes. I don't look back. I just type away.

You said you weren't sure there is an Appalachia. One of your quotes I read, you said "If there is an Appalachia." A lot of your poems, especially "Heritage," seem to be very rooted in Appalachia.

Yes they are. The sense of place is very strong there as people have noted. At the writing, I don't think about that. I'm not writing Appalachian stories. I'm just writing something I know or want to tell. I'm a storyteller. I will say the writing of poetry trained me to write prose. I think just speaking of, say, a short story: every sentence should advance that piece of fiction. No static or dead sentence in there. And more than that, it should have almost the value of a line of poetry. It should carry some burden beyond what it's saying. I think a story or poem should be more than the collection of its parts. And the readers have to meet me half way, however. I think every author hopes they will.

The presentation that you've developed with Randy where you do the readings and he does the music is very engaging. Do you try to reach new people with that? How did you start doing that?

We were invited to University of Rome in Italy and I suggested instead of doing something separately that he'd play his own and I'd read, that we make a little show out of it. And we practiced a little bit and we tried it. I don't think it was a success, maybe not too bad at the Institute of American Letters, but since then we've worked on it a little bit and changed the format a little bit and have different pieces to read and he had a few pieces to sing and play until it's evolved to a 55 minute program.

And do you think people would come to that and then get interested in your poems?

I will say this, nowadays I take some of my books with me from the Hindman Settlement School and I notice several occasions people look at the books, but they don't seem to be very much interested. And certainly not buy one. But after the program, they buy them all. The music and the words seem to go together.

Anything else we need to ask about?

Children's books.

Yea, that's right.
    Well, I always sort of planned, wanted to write a children's book. And I remember two little boys who belong to a neighbor over there. They were borrowing things all the time. For example, they were supposed to get a scuttle of coal. Instead of digging it out of the coal bank, they'd come up there and borrow it from me. But they always paid it back eventually. One Sunday, I was in bed reading. It had rained the night before. It was church time. And come a knock on the door and these little boys came in and said, "Mama wants to borrow a gallon of beans." So I get up, put my clothes on, go out and wade, getting wet to the knees, pick a gallon. And then I said to Russell, "You have a garden full of beans over there." He said, "Mama didn't want to get her feet wet." So I picked the beans for them.
    One day they came to borrow something. And I had this Random House Grimm stories, the wicked ones, the ones that weren't bowdlerized, and I read "Little Red Riding Hood" to them. And they listened. And I said, "Next time you come over here I want you to tell it to me." Well, when they did come back two or three months later, one would say something. And one said "Get your old paws off that window." Well, I wish I'd put it down right then but I didn't. From that I intended to write, but I never did. Years later, I was in bed one morning, propped up. It was cold and drizzly. I made a cup of coffee and got back and reached for my clipboard and I was going to try to write that. Instead, the first line of "Jack and the Beanstalk" occurred to me and I wrote it instead. And just two cups of coffee. I wrote it with a Flair pen on a legal pad. Got up then, typed it. Then later I remembered.
    Even before then, though, years ago in the '30s when I had these story hours, the children were interested in riddles. Now these were authentic Appalachian riddles that had come down. Many of them were universal; however, their way of telling it was unique. Sometimes they would bring it from the grandpas or parents, written down. I have some little slips even yet. Sometimes they just knew them. Well, I put them down. And then years later it occurred to me. So I took those and made a book out of them, Way Down Yonder on Troublesome Creek, *and then the next one,* The Wolfpen Rusties. *Then last year the two were put together and made into one. Now it's called* Rusties and Riddles and Gee-Haw Whimmy-Diddles.
    My little nephew has that and he loves it.

What are you writing now? Or are you going to tell? You usually won't tell me.
    I think anybody ... people sometimes ask me, "Well, have you run out of material?" I say I couldn't live long enough to hardly scratch the surface. About every three days, I think of a new book I want to write. I really am somewhat plagued by unwritten things. I have a lot of ideas, but I think it's psychologically bad to even mention something you plan to do specifically or might be doing.

But I know "Those I Want in Heaven with Me" is a fairly new poem.
    It is.

So when something just grabs hold of you, you have to write it; that's when you write it.

Well, I just had the title for two or three years, and one day I came in from a trip into Hindman and just went in to go over to my log house. I was tired, worn out and everything and all of a sudden I knew there was a poem there, but I knew if I didn't put it down, it would never get down. I have written many poems at night in my head that never got printed. So, I went in there under protest and wrote it fast as I could write it, left it on the typewriter and walked out. And when I came back Monday, I saw it and typed it out.

Didn't change it?

I don't know, I must have made a little — I don't know. Usually a thing comes out, that's it, pretty well. Maybe a comma, period change, sometimes a word.

And you're still keeping your notebooks though some have been published now.

Oh, I still do once in a while. You don't hear much any more.

So you think the distinct way of speaking, or colorful way of speaking is fading away.

Well, it's fading, but it's not gone. I hear "druthers" nearly every Saturday. I usually hear something that somebody says somewhere that's worth repeating. But it's always an older person. Now I have been out. After all, I worked at Morehead. I've been down in Louisville and Lexington, and places. I have never put down anything anybody ever said there. It's mostly homogenized.

So you're still putting things down in the notebooks?

I put things down on scrap paper. I'm always doing that. Usually throw them away.

A week or two later when I look at them. They don't make the grade.

What do you think? Anything we've forgotten?

That's all I know, and more too.

Thanks.

James Still: Conversation with a Kentucky Writer

L. ELISABETH BEATTIE

My full name is James Alexander Still, Jr. I was born on a farm very near Lafayette, Alabama, on July 16, 1906. My father was a horse doctor; that is, a veterinarian without formal training. He was also a farmer. Altogether, there were ten of us. There were five girls first and then five boys. After my mother passed on, my father married again and had another boy, so I'm including him as well. I was the first boy that came after the five girls. I think all in our family were welcome. I grew up in what I would call a very happy home. We children, none of us could remember an unkind word spoken between our parents.

We lived in various places. First, we lived at Double Branch Farm, which was, as I said, very near Lafayette, Alabama. I think we left there after about five years, but I remember it very well. After Grandma Still died rather suddenly we went and lived awhile with Grandpa in his place at his big farm — at Marcoot [Alabama]. It's still a place down there. There's little more than a store and a church. My grandparents on my mother's side, though, they were Lindseys. They were Scotch-Irish.

What was your mother's full name?

Her name was Barcelona Anadora, and she was called Lonie. She was born in Georgia, up in horsefly country. When she was maybe fifteen or sixteen they moved to Alabama. Both of my grandpas were from never-the-twain-shall-meet sort of families. My Grandpa Still was a veteran of the Civil War. In fact, he was wounded twice. When I was growing up, the Civil War was sort of yesterday, and I knew several war veterans. They used to come to the school on Confederate Day and talk to us.

My grandfather had rather a large plantation. My grandpa never owned

Beattie, L. Elisabeth, ed. *Conversations with Kentucky Writers*. Lexington: University Press of Kentucky, 1996. Copyright 1996 by the University Press of Kentucky. Reprinted with permission. Original Copy of Interview in the Kentucky Writers Oral History Project, Louie B. Nunn Center for Oral History, University of Kentucky Libraries.

James Still standing by the banner announcing the book signing of *Sporty Creek* at Joseph-Beth Booksellers, Lexington Green, Lexington, Kentucky. Photograph taken October 9, 1999, by Linc. Fisch. Used with permission.

slaves himself, but his parents did, my great-grandparents owned slaves. To think I've come, you know, across this length of time to now. Don't mistake me: I have very liberal ideas, and I concern myself with the civil rights of all people. I'm as good as anybody and better than nobody. I am, however, proud of my southern boyhood, and I don't know of any substitute for it. But I had to leave home. I would have gone to sleep there. I could never have done anything there.

Do you recall a particular age when you felt you wanted to, or needed to, move on?

No, I never thought about that. I just wanted to go to college, which was impossible. There was no precedent in my family, but I intended to go. I didn't know how.

Do you know where that desire came from?

Well, I knew other people who went, and I knew about college. I was a reader.

When did that start? Were you read to as a child before you knew how to read yourself?

I believe I could read before I went to school. My sister, she taught me to read. There was a little book we had on the Eskimo, and I remember that book particularly. I loved that book. They'd read it to me. I knew every word in it. I could recognize those words. They were taking me to school sometimes before I was ever enrolled, and the teacher welcomed these little visitors. In fact, I was told that the teacher asked me why I didn't come more often. I said, "I would, wouldst* Momma would let me."

The best teacher I ever had was the first grade teacher. She was a hands-on teacher. She was the kind of teacher that Foxfire has. I was the smallest person in the class. I was the only child who had to stand on a box to reach the chalkboard. We did things, like the first day of school she handed me an ear of corn and she wrote my name on the desk, and I was to shell off grains and outline my name, which I did, over and over. Very soon that day I could write my name; I knew its shape.

We planted things. We brought eggshells to school, and each one of us had a grain of corn, which he planted, and we learned about growing things. We acted out. I recall *Hiawatha*. We acted *Hiawatha*. I remember I was a squirrel.

I had several teachers in grade school who were average, I would say. One, as I remember, in the fifth grade, read stories to us nearly every day from a magazine that's long discontinued for children.

Then we moved to Lafayette and lived in Judge Norman's house, which was a grand home. It's not there anymore; too bad.

---

*The interview by Laura Lee and the Foxfire students rendered this as "wust," possibly a regionalism.

What was it like?

Well, it was a bit like some of the antebellum homes that are still there in Lafayette, Alabama. You know, with the chandelier, great hall, and roof. I know that it was so big that, although we'd come from a big home, we still didn't have enough furniture to fill it up.

First we lived in another house — it was sort of a compound — adjoining that first house, and we'd play school. We moved back to the farm after being there a while, but there was a mortgage on the farm, and we had to leave it again. We moved into Chattahoochee Valley, which has five or six great cotton mills. In fact, the Lanett Cotton Mill was in that day the largest one, perhaps, in the world.

Then we moved to Shawmut, on Lanier Avenue, Boss Row. In those days, the people lived in the factory homes. Those on Boss Row, where the bosses lived, lived in nicer homes, you know. We lived in one of those.

Was your father working for the factory?

No. My parents wanted to move there because nearly everybody had a cow in their backyards. And anyway, there were a great deal of other animals — horses, mules, and things like that, down there. When we lived up in the county there, of course it was mainly cows, horses, and so on. Little by little my father's practice became a small-animal practice as tractors took over. Also, he looked after dairy cattle. He was appointed by the state as a rabies inspector. That is, every dog had to be inoculated. And, as we lived almost on the Georgia line, and there was a lack of veterinarians, he worked both for the states of Georgia and Alabama for a while. Also, we were very near to Auburn University where he used to go down and take short courses. There they would send up interns and veterinary students to travel with him and go with him in his work, toward the end.

We lived there and then we moved — I don't know why — to Jarrett Station just out-side of Fairfax, still in a line down there. I went to high school there and graduated, and then later I went off to school and I never lived with my family again. My mother died and my father moved out in the country about four miles.

How old were you when she died?

Well, she died in 1935. She was fifty-five years old. Then my father married again, and he married a girl who was the same age as my older sister. Naturally we just resented it, not knowing her, and when we got to know her, we liked her very much. It astonished all of us. She died in childbirth within a couple of years. Several years passed, then my father married still a third time.

Did your mother die from a terminal illness or an accident?

It was a malignancy. I was at the University of Illinois at that time.

So your father married a third time, then? There were not children by that marriage?

Oh, no. He was older then. His wife had a son about seventeen, eighteen. In a way we liked him all right. But I never felt welcome at home again. She somehow felt threatened, by me, especially. And if I went home, she made it unpleasant for me. That was a great source of pain for me for several years, and something I couldn't do anything about.

You were talking about the teachers in elementary school that were so good. Did you have the same experience in high school?
I had only one man teacher, the principal at Shawmut, Alabama, Carl Lappert. He was a good teacher, but he taught to the tune of a hickory stick, as the old saying goes, and all the students were frightened of him. We studied, because we were afraid not to, which is not the best way. I regret to say that I did not have, except for this man ... well, there was a geometry teacher who I'm sure was a good teacher. I mean, she meant well, but I've always been a dumbbell in math. I think she was probably good. But aside from that, I cannot think of a teacher who did anything for me, really, or for anybody else.

Did you have a particular interest in reading or writing at that point?
Not much. I remember in high school I started a novel.

Ambitious, for high school.
I know I had never seen the ocean, but it was a sea story, and I used to write it every night. I was just enjoying doing it, you know. I was living it as I wrote it. When I was somewhere in the grades, I don't know when, I wrote a story on a tablet, which I still have, with a hard pencil. It is now hard to read. Of course, I wrote it on acid-free paper, or it wouldn't exist today. I found it not long ago. It was called "The Gold Nugget." I read that with some difficulty; it was pretty faint. But I could see then that whoever wrote that would be writing again. I only stopped when the paper ran out.

As you read it now, what do you see in that story that was so promising?
I saw my future in it. Everything I was to do and be was right there. I saw it between the lines.

You're talking about style as well as philosophy, content?
I don't know anything about style, because style is me. I have no more idea what my style is than anything. I can't even imagine what my style is. I just write the way I can write. In our home we had three books that I recall. One was the Bible, which I don't know whether people looked in or not. Then there was a book called *The Anatomy of the Horse*. And my father got the *Veterinary Journal*, which I used to try to read, with no success, but there was another book. The back was off of it. It was a big, large book called *Cyclopedia of Universal Knowledge*. It had a little of everything in it you could imagine, and some things you can't. It had some short history of every country, population, size, products, a few things like that of every country. It had social

correspondence, it had business correspondence. It had samples of maybe ten or twenty or twenty-five words of several foreign languages, and how to pronounce them. I'm sure that I was the only person in that state, or child, who knew twenty-five words of Arabic. Then there was a section of poetry — Byron, Shelley, Keats, great poetry — and Shakespeare. I memorized them. It was my first introduction to poetry. I remember Wordsworth.

I recall one day a student brought to school a copy of the *National Geographic*, and I remember he let me borrow it. Here was an article on Alaska, "The Valley of Ten Thousand Smokes." I was fascinated by that. That started me on my journeys around the world, right then. I knew I had to go to Alaska someday. Well, I never did, and it's very low on my priorities now. No matter. And once in a while I might see a copy of the *Geographic*. As you know, we used to have here copies going back to 1897 or '98, when it was founded.

At the Hindman Settlement School?

Yes. I don't know what became of them. But I went to high school in town, in Lafayette. We walked two miles, I believe. My high school had once been a college, one very large building. Unusual for a schoolhouse, in those days. More than that, we didn't have the usual county teachers. It was a city school, so we had better teachers, generally, than there usually would be. In fact, our teachers, like mine, came from somewhere else in the state. They always referred to it as *The* College.

Did you live in the state at all after high school?

I was office boy in the towel mill, Fairfax Towels. There wasn't anything else to do.

This was in Alabama?

In Fairfax, Alabama, where I went to high school.

How long did you work there?

Oh, just that summer. But I was home one summer and couldn't go back to school; I needed the money. They gave me a job and didn't give me anything to do. Nobody pointed out anything. What I did, I learned the styles of towels, numbers, and names, and I found out what was happening, and went and sat down in all the offices and saw what was going on. That's what they wanted me to do. But I knew it wasn't for me. And I couldn't go back to school. I left. It was the Depression, and I couldn't get any job with nobody. I went to Texas. I picked cotton. I rode the rails. I went to Atlanta, Sears and Roebuck. I went through Rome, Georgia, tried to get a job with the ironworks.

On the roads there were people everywhere. How I made it, how I got along, I don't know. The thing about it is, I don't remember, except one time, in which I kind of got downhearted. That was in Rome, Georgia. I remember one time and I remember what I wanted to do about it, but I didn't. Now, don't get me wrong, I'm very optimistic. I'm not self-destructive.

What year did you go to college?
  I went in the fall of '24. I had sixty dollars. I went to Lincoln Memorial University, and that's all the money they ever got out of me. And when I graduated, say five years later — I was out a year — they owed me seventy-five.

How did that happen?
  I worked everything. I had nothing. There was no money, nobody could do anything for me. And that meant work scholarships; everybody worked. It was sort of a Berea situation. I worked in a rock quarry the first year. Eventually, I was a janitor. Had all kinds of jobs. My grades were poor the first year because I was so tired. You went to school in the morning, worked in a rock quarry in the afternoon. At nine o'clock at night in the library I was the janitor, and I swept the library and scrubbed up the tables and emptied the wastebaskets. I was too tired to study. I wanted to sleep.
  But after the first year, when I was out of the rock quarry, my grades picked up. I had a double major, English and history. I stayed an extra year. I graduated in 1929.
  The college had a magazine called the *Lincoln Herald*, which they still have, a college publication in which the doings of the college were recorded, and you'd send it out to donors and people like that, to alumni. Nowadays it's mostly for alumni notice.
  Anyhow, I had a good teacher in classical literature there. I had a wonderful teacher in biology and a good history teacher. Aside from that, it was a lost cause. But I will tell you, I needed that place. You see, my high school training wasn't what it ought to be. I think maybe they were doing remedial work, in a way. But what Lincoln Memorial did for me was the library. I discovered the publishing world, all these magazines, and I discovered, no thanks to any teachers, the writer Thomas Hardy.

So, you spent a lot of time in the library on your own?
  I lived there. I just went mad; I didn't know what to read first. I discovered the *Atlantic Monthly*, and I knew it was a most prestigious publication. I decided I was going to write for it. And while in school there, I reckon my sophomore year, there was a magazine there called *American Speech*. It's a scholarly study of language. Still going. I wrote two articles for them, and I was a sophomore, and they published both. In time, H. L. Mencken wrote his *American Language*, and he used both those articles, and gave me credit. I have a copy of the one volume. James A. Still, you find me in the index.

What were your articles about?
  One was on Christian names in the mountains, the Cumberlands, and then the other was on place names.
  Then I had nothing. Not a dime, nothing. The school was in trouble financially, and we students had a very Spartan living. We ate everything off the table

every day. The school had a marvelous apple orchard, and plenty of walnut trees. They have a great acreage there, or did. It's, to my notion, the most beautiful natural campus in America, and I've seen an awful lot of them. Notice I said natural campus.

What happened after college? What did you do as soon as you were graduated?

I began to write little things for Sunday school magazines, and I'd get two dollars, three dollars. I don't know how many articles there were. Even later, after I came here [Hindman, Kentucky], I wrote things for the Sunday school magazines for adults, because my sister subscribed to them. I wanted her to see something I'd written. I remember I wrote an article about the Hindman Settlement.

Had you grown up going to a particular church that these magazines related to, a particular denomination?

My father's people were Missionary Baptists, attended the Rock Springs Church, where all my people are buried going back in time. The old cemetery. I've got a book that lists all of the graves in the county. There they are, lined up. My mother's people are Primitive Baptists, and they attended a church about a mile beyond. Each met once a month, and we attended both of them. Grandpa Lindsey was an elder in the Primitive Baptist Church.

I went to Sunday school all those years. I can remember the preacher once, in the church at Fairfax, heard that I was going away to college, and before the service he came and sat down beside me and told me to stay at home and do something for my parents. Well, anyway, I did go. Grandpa Lindsey thought I shouldn't be running off, thought I should be working, because that's what children were supposed to do. But before he died, he sent me word he'd changed his mind, I'm glad to say.

So, after college you were writing these articles. Where were you living at the time?

I went to Lincoln Memorial, then I went to Vanderbilt University. Actually, I'd won all these awards. There were six essay awards available, different judges.

At Lincoln Memorial.

Yes. I entered five writing contests and I won all five of them. Well, there was a man who gave work scholarships to students. Also, when he used to visit there—of course, I didn't meet him or anything like that—he noticed we were pretty poorly dressed, so he left money to buy a suit for about a dozen of us. They cost about fifteen dollars then, and somebody measured us up on campus for suits. I went to the librarian who was in charge of this and I told her I wanted to write him a letter and thank him. She said, "He doesn't want any communication." He was a man who gave things to Berea and other places. He was a man about eighty years old, a philanthropist. But I said, "Could I just write him a letter and you send it to him?" "Yes, all right."

Well, he got this letter, so this is probably the first letter he'd ever permitted, and the next time he came down, he got acquainted with me and others he was helping. He had us over at Middlesboro, Kentucky, to a luncheon, kind of got acquainted with us. When I graduated, I sent him an invitation. He had never been invited. He came down and spent the whole week, went to the class day and everything, and then I won all these awards. They dedicated the Duke Hall of Citizenship. Benjamin Duke of Duke Power Company had given the money for this building they still use, a big auditorium and classrooms and so on. He was actually on his deathbed, he was ill, but his wife and daughter came to the dedication. Well, this little magazine I spoke of, *Lincoln Herald,* spoke about my winning all these awards, and he read it, and he wrote them and told them that he would send me through graduate school at Duke University, all expenses paid. He sent two hundred dollars to one teacher to bring me to Duke. So, I went and had my subject already picked out for a thesis, and Duke was just a building. They'd taken over Trinity College, which they still use there.

Those prizes you'd won, were they in English?

They were just for essays. One was the gold medal given in all the colleges in Tennessee called the Rush Strong Medal for Truth, an essay on the value of truth. Solid gold. I always called it my liar's license.

Well, then this man arranged it so I'd have this scholarship. I was going, and then this other fellow said he would send me to graduate school anywhere in the South. I went to Duke, and I wasn't favorably impressed. It was just a building, you know. They hadn't used that new campus. But anyway, I knew about Vanderbilt, so I went to Vanderbilt instead.

And there [at Vanderbilt University] were the members of the Southern literary movement the Fugitives, and this is what happened. I had John Donald Wade in American literature, and the first week or so in the class, we students didn't know each other. We came from California, Yale, all over, all graduates. The Fugitives were our teachers. Wade said he wanted to find out just where we stood in American literature before he started class, so he gave us all a card, and we numbered one through twenty on each, ten on each side. He read one sentence from the writings of authors from the beginning of the Civil War period to that day. No, it went back before that, because they had Emerson and Thoreau and Longfellow and whoever. He told us that he did this every year, and nobody had ever passed it yet, not to be concerned. Nobody did except me, and I made a perfect score. Well, I was totally unknown when I went in that classroom. When I came out, I was famous. It's partly a fluke that I got them all, but that tells you what that library did for me.

So it was your own self-education, you think, as much as anything else that caused you to know so much?

Yes. I was a mad man in that library. I wanted to know. And I do today; I still want to know.

What other Fugitives did you have as professors?

Well, John Crowe Ransom was there. There were others there that I didn't have. Robert Penn Warren was at Oxford at that time. Another one was in Sewanee teaching, I think. He came back and read to us all. But I had those two. You see, they read their chapters from *I'll Take My Stand*, which was published the next fall, to us. If you read them singly, you're not impressed with them.

I did my thesis under Walter Clyde Curry, the Chaucer scholar, who wrote the book called *Chaucer and the Mediaeval Sciences*, which was a textbook for years. I wrote on the function of dreams and visions in the Middle English romances, which meant that I had to learn to read Middle English, which I did. There are a hundred and six volumes of the Early English Text Society I had to peruse. I wrote this thesis and really should have thought about sending it to Freud, who was alive in those days. I wish I had. It was right in his line of thinking.

How much Freud had you read before writing your thesis?

I just knew he existed, that's all. Anyway, we were just learning what psychiatry was. I also made a dream book out of it, too. It's kind of an appendix. I don't know how I came on that subject. But Curry was the first true scholar I ever had, and some people would say he was cruel and demanding. I needed him, let's put it that way

For the discipline of scholarship?

I did. I got it there. Ransom was a great teacher and has been noted; he's in a book called *Ten Great Professors*. But Walter Clyde Curry ... the thing is, Chaucer is the only author that I feel I sort of identify with, to this day.

I graduated then in 1931, and here was this scholarship to the University of Illinois. There were no jobs, so I went there. And this philanthropist, up until then, as I understand it, had never given a scholarship, except a general one, like a work scholarship. He had never given a specific scholarship to a man. He only gave them to girls with the idea that they would be school teachers. But the librarian there got him to give it to me.

I went to the University of Illinois and got a degree in one year, a degree in library science. I never had the slightest desire, inclination, to go for a doctor's degree. I didn't even think about it, ever. My history professor at Vanderbilt, after I had turned in a paper on Gustavus Adolphus, I remember he called me up the day after he read it. He suggested that I come and work on a doctorate in history, and he would be my advisor. But I didn't have the slightest interest in getting my doctor's degree.

At that time, did you think you were going to spend your life as a librarian?

Who knows? I had taken enough courses, thinking I might have to teach school, to qualify to teach school. I had education courses, which, I'm sad to say, were a waste of my time and everybody else's time. They taught methods, no content. Or little content. Illinois, though, was very strenuous.

In what way?
It was never hard, the work, but there was too much of it. A good many students already had master's degrees, you see, and nearly everybody had had some training, had worked in a library.

Was this a second master's [for you]?
No. It was a B.S., and I found it very tedious, cataloging and so on. But I loved reference, I'd have made a good reference librarian.

If I had to go again, I'd probably be a biology student, or a botanist or something. That's a field I never gave up. I'm right into that even now. I'm learning still. I'm still reading and so on. I'm still going at that, because I'm just curious. I have these wonderful conversations here at the Hindman Settlement School with the extension director who lives on campus. He knows so many things I want to know. And I take a magazine called *Science News*. It's a weekly for people like me with very weak backgrounds in chemistry and physics and astrophysics and medicine and behavioral sciences and so on, and it also gives a list of the new books in the fields that you never see anywhere else. So, if you read that over thirty years, you pick up considerable knowledge and awareness of the earth. Everything from the weather to geology, and so on.

All that goes into being a writer.
Well, I always say anything somehow comes to bear on what you're doing. I'm not an educated person. I don't like the word *educated*. That's an arrival, and education is a trip, it's a journey. You never really arrive, you know; you're on your wax.

Education doesn't end when the degree ends.
Yes. And to this day, including last night at midnight. I was reading a history of Sears and Roebuck from the beginning. I once tried to get a job with them. Anyway, but I just had to turn the light out I don't know how many times. Reading wakes me up. I keep four or five books going at a time. I just go from one to the other. They're mostly nonfiction, except these studies I've been doing. One of the French writers, Daudet—I love Daudet, Alphonse Daudet, I just love him. I read him in French first when I was studying French. I had five years of him. I used to read French. But it's gone awful rusty now, and I have to read translations. But he survives translations. As a person, I liked him. Henry James said he knew Daudet and Turgenev, and he kept saying several times in his biography that he loved them both. I know what he meant. He was ideal. He was exactly the kind of person that I would like to be.

What is it about him that attracts you?

There's no way to tell. His little book called *Letters from My Mill*, which overnight made him famous, this was during the era of Napoleon the Third, he wrote a book of poems first and got the attention of the Empress Eugenie. The first part of that is a book called *La Petite Chose*. I noted in 1920 Little, Brown published all of his works in translation. They have disappeared from the earth, almost. I sent out a search for *La Petite Chose*. It's easily available in any library in France, but not in translation. They found one, a copy in the Anderson, Indiana, public library, and it's on its last legs, I assure you. I had to patch it as I read it. It was one of the great reading experiences. I wish I had read it years ago. This was just a year or two ago. The first half of that book is a masterpiece. He wrote it before he went to Paris. The last half he wrote later. It's excellent.

I'll jump ahead a little bit to say the greatest novel ever written by a Kentuckian about Kentucky is *The Time of Man* by Elizabeth Madox Roberts. The first half of that book is a masterpiece. The rest of it is excellent. But that was a slacking off. She wasn't able to sustain it all the way through. No matter. It's a great book. I have a few little quarrels with it.

You see, I think there are two kinds of novels. One is a told story, the author's telling. You know, this man is writing this story. You may just sort of forget it or lose it. He's there at your arm. That's one novel. The ones I like to read are those where there are no authors there; you can imagine it existing in nature. I like to think *River of Earth* is one that exists in nature. James Still is not there and never has been.

Which is why the style, to you, is something that should be irrelevant.

It's not irrelevant; it's itself. You know, I have no idea whether I can look at myself. I don't remember writing much of it. It should be timeless. It doesn't date. Timelessness is what saves it. I wish some publisher would let me choose some books that I think they ought to bring into print again.

What happened after graduate school, then? Where did you go after that?

I came back in June; I stopped in Nashville. There was a student there that I'd gone to school with, Don West. He was in the school of religion; he was going to be a preacher. He was working, still going to school, and he was working at the Settlement House. I went out there and he was not there, but expected. I remember sitting there quite a while and he didn't come, and I remember there was a big clock up there and I thought, "I'm going to wait ten minutes, and if he doesn't come, I'll leave," and he came within that time. Otherwise, I wouldn't be sitting here.

Well, he was coming here to start a vacation Bible school — he and his wife — and he wanted me to come out with him. His brother-in-law was from Rockcastle County, Kentucky, and we were to establish three Boy Scout troops and three baseball teams, which we did. We came and we camped and played all summer long. We had nothing to do with vacation Bible school itself. At the end of that time the librarian here left, and they needed a librarian, so they hired me, but they couldn't pay me anything. They couldn't pay anybody. They had an endowment as now, but it wasn't paying off, and they were having a hard time, feeding the students here and keeping them. So I worked three years with no pay. Then, times had gotten better, but don't ask me what I did in summer. There was no work.

Did you stay here, though?

No. I figured that out. Having nothing, not a dime, after the fourth year, I was going to leave, and some donor offered to give them fifteen dollars a month to pay me, so that I got for nine months, fifteen dollars a month. Then there was the summer with nothing, and then it got a little better, and I was paid a little bit more. But after six years—I averaged it up once—I had averaged six cents a day, for six years. Toward the end of that I began to write little verses and poems. I was not alone here; there were a number of teachers. For the most part, though, the women teachers were from wealthy—mainly, Mount Holyoke, Smith—colleges and other such institutions, and they were generally people who were doing voluntary work. I think I was the only one who wasn't getting anything at all. They did pay the woodworking man some after he was married, they paid the gardener, they paid the workers coming in, the hired people here. They paid partly the principal. But then I had a story or two in the *Atlantic*.

That you wrote while you were living here?

Yes. I started at twenty-six years old, and one day I sat down, I had written some poems, and I sent them to the *Atlantic*. Eventually they took one. After that the editor always looked at my stuff, and then he published about two stories.

So really, you started at the top in publishing.

That's what I intended to do. Back at Lincoln Memorial, in college days, it was a school where they say only missionary barrels came, you know, clothes and things like this. But they also took old books and magazines and back numbers, years of them, and they used to get back numbers of say, the *Atlantic*. I was supposed to check the files for missing numbers, and burn the rest. But I saved them. I have years of the *Atlantic*. I took them home, and I spent the summer reading them. I intended to write for the *Atlantic*. It can be said if I learned the art of conversation, I learned it from the *Atlantic*, from the best writers of America and England of that day. That made all the difference. Anyway, I then published three poems and ten stories over the years. Then Viking published a book of poems from me, called *Hounds on the Mountain*. Beautifully made book. In fact, it won a graphic arts award for bookmaking that year.

What year was that published?

1937. It's a letterpress book. If you ever see it, you can open it; it stays open, you know. Beautiful paper. An edition of seven hundred and fifty copies, none were autographed. After then, they asked, didn't I have a novel? Well, yes, I did, I was writing one. "Well, let us see some of it." I sent them the first section and the last section. I hadn't written the middle. And they sent a contract.

Viking?

Yes. Later, I asked my editor, Marshall Best, who was also at the same time the editor of Elizabeth Madox Roberts, and who was at the same time riding herd on John Steinbeck, but wasn't his direct editor.... Well, I had these marvelous letters from him, as I think anybody writing for him would. At least twice he sent a story back and said he was sorry, there's something about it, you know. They liked it and all like that, but in each case I looked at it, and looked at the ending, made a few minor changes, and sent it back. A story called "The Run for the Elbertas," which is very long, as long as most magazines want to publish, while I was writing it, somehow or other *Esquire* learned that I had this long story, and they wrote and said they would like to look at it, no matter how long it was. But already, at that time, the *Atlantic* accepted it. They sent it back to me and asked me to shorten it. They said if I couldn't, then they would try to do it. Well, what I did, I added some sentences to it. I thought we should know, specifically, how old this boy was, in two, three little lines. So they published it as it was. They couldn't do anything, either. I met, several years ago, the poetry editor of the *Atlantic,* at the University of Kentucky, and he said to me, "We remember the day 'The Run for the Elbertas' arrived at the *Atlantic.*"

They gave me four hundred dollars for that story, which was a lot in those days. Then, when it was set up in galleys, he sent another hundred dollars, saying they liked it even better than when it was submitted. Behind every little story you write, there's something behind it somewhere, the little adventure on my part. I read about all these unhappy authors, you know, struggling. I think the one thing that saved me was, I never had unrealistic expectations. If something came back, well, I already knew where it was going next.

It sounds as though when you started sending out manuscripts, you started with a positive attitude that this was where you were going to send it, it was what would be accepted, and it was.

Listen, anything literate can be published.

I mean published in good places, reputable places. Places that set the standard instead of ignoring it.

Most look at current magazines and so on for that. You know, I look for the classics. People have some idea I just whittled. That isn't the way I work. The way I work, if you call it work, is I play, really. A story takes on a life of its own, after a while. Until that time, you're not getting anywhere with it until it's working on itself. In the meantime, I'm enjoying writing it, playing with it.

I know where I'm going. I don't have a story otherwise, do I? I don't know how I'm going to get there. So, I can write the first paragraph and I play with it a while, and play with it. Type it over and just play. It's like stirring concrete. Ideally, I think every line of prose ought to have the values of a line of poetry. I'm not talking about poetry, actually, but anyway, it should have the longevity, it should have the essence, in every line. Most of my stories start going from the first word. Any single line that impedes that flow should come out, no matter what it is. You drive toward the end.

Some writers think that with prose, especially novels, or with longer prose work, that more irrelevancies can be included because of the space you have to work in. It sounds as though you don't believe that.

Well, with a novel, you've got more elbow room. The novel's a lot more fun to write, because you can knock around and do a lot of things with a novel. Every sentence must belong there, or it shouldn't be there. Just look at the great writers, every one of them. They're going somewhere. Every sentence is advancing, almost unbeknownst to the writer.

You mentioned that you know from the beginning, before you start a story or a novel, what the end is going to be.

Well, I don't know about the ending. I never just say I'm going to write a story or something. It just grows in my head, I just think about it a while. I just keep playing with the idea until it gets imprinted, and I write something down. I say you've got to start somewhere, and I just start right quick and dash off that paragraph, then play with it. If I get stuck, I like to go right to the end then and — this is no method, I want you to know I just do it every time and catch off that last one.

So, the concept you might have at the beginning could change by the time you play with it.

Oh, yes. They're all surprises, every sentence. Every paragraph surprises me, otherwise what fun would it be writing it? When I get through, if I feel I've done something, it's a feeling that I can't get from anywhere else. Even when it's published, usually by the time it's published, I don't feel anything. The book is on its own, nothing to do with me anymore.

It's the creativity that causes the pride and the sense of accomplishment, you're saying?

I like to think of a story in this way, till you touch a nerve somewhere, you know? Make a contact someway. Till I jump myself, almost. No, I just play my way through. If you get stuck on the way, go to the last paragraph and play with it. Eventually, I can get it almost to work anywhere, and I did. Then, of course, when I get to that point, I usually throw it out. Then revisions: I don't know what you are going to revise for; I've already done it. When I get through, I'm through.

So you revise as you write.
   I play with it. I play with it until it comes true, till I believe it myself and the characters are talking to me.

But do you find it difficult to move on in the story until the part that you've already worked on comes true?
   No, I can hardly wait, because in the meantime, another part of my mind is already doing....

So you can focus on several things at once.
   Oh, sure. Everybody does. You are every person in that story, you are simultaneously one person and another. You're in their body-skins. You know everything about them, everything. Every character has no secrets.

Before you start writing do your characters reveal themselves, or do they do so as you write?
   Eventually you know everything about them.

Eventually. So, that could be while you're writing.
   Yes. A story makes itself as it goes. Frost said it very well; with a poem it's like ice in a skillet. It grows on its melting. That's what he said. It's very well stated. Sometimes I've been asked, a student will say, "How do you write a poem?" Well, what can you say? But I finally found the answer to that.

Tell me.
   The first time I related this was in the Humana Building at Louisville. I had never been in that magnificent structure, and there were several of us who were going to do a little talking. They got around to me, and I said, "First, I can't help remarking what an extraordinary room this is. I never would imagine such a wonderful place. I like it in here." I said, "Also, there is only one other structure that's more beautiful than this building, and," I said, "it's my log house back in Knott County." Then I said, "I'm sometimes asked how do you write a poem, and not just by children, either." Well, I found out. Some years ago, Eleanor Clark, who is Mrs. Robert Penn Warren, I knew her. In fact, I knew her before Robert Penn did. Up at Saratoga Springs, New York. She spent a good part of her life in Italy and so on, was very mature, just a marvelous.... Has a book about oysters or something, I can't think of the title. She told me what to do if you were attacked by an octopus, and were all wrapped in these many arms. There is just one thing you can do. What you do is you poke your hand in his mouth and get a handful of something and turn it wrong-side out. And that's how you write a poem. The attack has to be there. You can't escape that that poem has got you there. You've got to do something about it. How can you get rid of it? The subject has to be turned wrong-side out to see the inside of it. A great many poems are written about the tentacles drawing circles. The insides of the octopus is what you're going to write. Anyway, the interior of a poem has to be exposed. That's how you write a poem.

I think that's a great answer. Did you get your first contract with Viking on the strength of your poems in the *Atlantic*?
Yes. And other places—poetry in the *New Republic,* the *Nation*—places like that.

You didn't have an agent?
No, I didn't have an agent for a long time. Agents don't handle people who can't make them money, you know. There wasn't any money with me.

You went directly to Viking with your manuscript, then?
Well, a friend of the founder of Viking connected me with Viking Press.

The first novel of yours that they published was *River of Earth*.
1940.

When did your military service come into play? Was that before this?
After, at the beginning of World War II.

You were drafted, weren't you?
Yes. I knew I was going to be drafted. I was older for a soldier; I was about thirty. The average soldier was about twenty, twenty-one years old, in my outfit. I was the oldest man in my outfit except the colonel, and I wouldn't have been drafted, except for the politics. I didn't have any voters here, you know what I mean, no family here. Parents did everything in the world to keep their boys out of the army, and I had nobody to do this for me. In fact, I didn't want anybody to try.

I was in Florida when the superintendent of schools, a friend here, learned that I was going to be drafted from his brother in-law, and he told me I'd better come back, and I did. But when I got back here, he'd gone over there and talked to his brother-in-law and said, "This man, you know, his age, you shouldn't be drafting this man." He got me off. But when I learned that, I went over there and told him that I didn't want anybody taking my place.

So you wanted to go?
No, I didn't particularly want to go. I didn't want anybody taking my place. He asked me, "You really want to go?" I said, "*Yes,* I do. I don't want anybody taking my place." Well, there was a woman that's sitting in there and she's trying to get her son off. I remember what she said; it's in the book. She said, "Let them that want to go go, and them's that want to stay stay." I remember someone said, "Well, we couldn't fight much of a war if we did that." So I went.

At the time when you were drafted, where were you? You say you were in Florida.
You see, I nearly froze over here. I spent two winters over here and nearly froze in that, so when I sold a story to the *Saturday Evening Post,* I lived off them several years. I just sold them one story a year. After then I went to Florida, and that's what I was doing in Florida.

Then the army all those years, it seems like a blip on the screen now, but I shipped out of here and went to Fort Thomas, and after a week there, we shipped down to San Antonio. There was a train-load of us. It was March, cold. Got off the train in New Orleans, and they took us in trucks into the Duncan Field, which is part of the big field complex, Lackland Air Base. They left us in the street to freeze all night, the rest of the night. I remember how cold it was. Next morning, they came, they called the roll, they called two names of these couple of thousand of us. One was mine and one was another fellow. They told me to report to a certain headquarters, which I did.

We went to the first sergeants of the headquarters squadron. He was an old Irishman, an old retread from World War I. He was a regular soldier; hard-drinking, red-faced, gambling, mean as a snake. He could barely read and write, and he wasn't going to have anybody in there with more education than he had. So, he refused me. He sent me to the main headquarters, where I should have been in the first place.

Well, as soon as I got there, the sergeant-major was an old retread, First World War, and he was going to be discharged, retired, but they had retained him. He'd belonged to the Book-of-the-Month Club, and he knew about me. My book was in the catalog, and he remembered that. He told me to sit there by him and he said, "You're going to have this job someday; see what's going on." I'll never forget that headquarters. All these men were torn from their homes. It was an unhappy place, and there was cursing, language I'd never heard. Nobody ever said anything civil or decent. Sergeant Jacobs, this first staff sergeant-major, had me sitting there by him, and I had contracted from my niece chicken pox. But I didn't tell anybody that I was sick, and I thought I was going to fall off that bench. Another thing was, as a private, I would have to line up in a long line, and it would take a long time for me to get in, get something to eat, and then get back to the office. So what he did, he immediately made me a private first-class, got a stripe so I could be in another line, in another dining room where it couldn't take so long. But in time I wasn't eating lunch, because about everything I ate came up.

I got acquainted with myself. I really didn't know myself till I got in the army. There are things I won't do and nobody's going to push me around. I didn't know that. I wouldn't take anything off anybody.

How many years were you in the army?
Three and a half. I had some unbelievable exploits.

Have you ever written them down?
No.

You think you will?
I don't know. I don't think so.

What happened when you returned from the army, what did you do?

It was rough. It was bad. I came home and I couldn't keep food in my stomach. I'd had malaria twice, almost died once. I'd had the dysentery that kills you. I got it in Ethiopia, in Eritrea, is where I got it. I ate something there I wasn't supposed to eat. And I'll never forget that. Terrible. Anyway, I was just skin and bones, really.

What did you do career-wise when you returned from the war?
What did I do? I didn't do anything for a year. I sat in that door over there by the creek, day by day. I remember I was having trouble keeping food down, and I wasn't going to the Veterans Hospital, so I went to Lexington Clinic. Dr. Kirkpatrick was there. He became a friend. He knew about me; he'd read my things. He talked to me, and then they had about a day to go through everything, heart and everything. When I came back to him he told me that, "There's nothing physically wrong with you; you're just like an old clock, you've been wound up too tight. You're going to have to wind down. How are you spending your days?" So, I told him. He told me, "Whether you want to or not, you get out and go where people are, where things are doing." And I did.

Is there a book that you would like to have written and haven't yet?
No, there isn't. I like the old, great ones.

Jim Wayne Miller has observed that in your poems, novels, and short stories, your characters, he says, "journey out into the world like Jack, get their barrel full, and return gladly home." Are your characters returning to something innately Appalachian, do you think, or do you think most people want to return to their place of origin, wherever that may be?
We're all homing pigeons, you know; I think we all are. And although I live here, and will never live anywhere else, I still feel like homing to a place that doesn't exist anymore, really.

I remember the writer Johnny Cheever saying toward the end of his life—I didn't know him, but I used to see him at Yaddo—he said, on his life, when he was dying, "I want to go home, but I don't know where home is."

The quest, the constant seeking, do you think that's something we all do?
It's seeking, but there is a spot, a place. It's not just the seeking. There was a place, you know. I feel that more as I get older. And I would go. If it was there, I would go. But the trouble is, I go there and I can't bear it for more than two days. Too much nostalgia, it's just too much.

You're talking about a literal place?
Literally, I can't bear it.

Where is that?
In Alabama where I was born. I lived a very different life from this, in a sense, which I wish I could write about.

In your poem, "River of Earth," you speak of "the thing laid open, the hills translated." You've translated the hills as well as or better than anybody, but is there anything about Appalachia that you believe remains untranslatable?

Of course. How do people describe the Great Plains? I have all these books, and everybody's trying it. They never quite make it. Nobody quite makes it. I used to be a Civil War buff. I still occasionally read a book. I mean, I have read on the Civil War, several biographies of Robert E. Lee, but nobody has ever made him come alive to me. He's a paragon. You simply cannot. Nobody's been able to do it for me. The nearest to it was Charles B. Flood's book, *Lee: The Last Years*. He came as near as anybody is ever going to do it, I think, but not quite. When I read Leon Edel's *Henry James*, I feel like I know him now. He became a human being.

I recall reading in the *New York Times* some time ago, there was an actress — I didn't know her name, but I should have known maybe — who was ninety-eight. They gave her a reception at the Waldorf Astoria Hotel, I believe, a small group of the famous actors of this day, and some they talked to a little afterwards and they said, "What would be your advice for, let's say, a young lady who had it in her heart to be an actress, who had come to New York and went to acting school, and really means it?" She said, "Go home. Go home and live a normal life." Your chance of succeeding in this business is practically minuscule, nil.

Would that be your advice to writers?

I would say in the first place, "Don't write. But if you can't help it, maybe, all right, go ahead and do it." I don't find many people willing to work.

Do you think that's a drive that comes from within? Don't you think that writers, real writers, know that that's what they are?

I don't think they have any choice. I understand there are preachers who, in a sense, would rather not be preachers, that they felt called or something. I don't feel called. But I don't know why that answers something that I have a need to do, and why I get something out of it that I can't explain to anybody. I never particularly admired writers. I mean, I knew a lot of them in a way, and I rather liked them and so on, but the lives of writers never interested me, particularly. They always seemed to me so unhappy and tragic, and so far as the world will let me, I'm pretty optimistic. I've been happy with it. I didn't, as I've said, have unrealistic expectations. But maybe I did, I sent work to the *Atlantic*; I started there.

Well, I don't think it's unrealistic if that became a reality. Your writing got published.

But then there are a lot of good surprises in the world. There is something called, I'm sure, networking that anybody ... you can hardly go it alone. Somebody, for example in my case, got two Guggenheims for me. There has to be somebody. But then you've got to have what it takes; otherwise it doesn't do any good. You've got to be ready. Sure, there's something called damn fool luck; apparently I had what the *Atlantic* could use.

Doesn't sound to me like luck: it sounds like you had the talent and you knew what you wanted.

No, it wasn't luck, is what I'm trying to say. It's something. But even so, then what would have happened if I hadn't, some way through this professor who introduced me to the publisher, for example, who asked me if I had a manuscript....

Well, when the American Academy of Arts and Letters gave me the Peabody Award, I learned later that there was a committee of three people and one was a famous southern writer who died recently. He insisted that I get it. I never had any connection with him whatsoever, wouldn't have imagined he had ever read anything of mine. He wouldn't give up. He insisted that I get it, so that finally the others just said okay. They gave it to me. They had their own candidate and were putting him forward. One of the others agreed with him, so I got it.

Is there anything else that you would like to mention about yourself?

No, I think I've said too much already. I believe I've told you more than anybody.

August 2, 1991

Conversations with James Still

Frank Edward Bourne

A long-time admirer of James Still's work, Frank Bourne asked us, not long after Mr. Still's passing in April 2001, whether we would be interested in his journal accounts of two visits with the writer. Of course, we were. Mr. Bourne's remembrances offer us insight into the far-ranging mind of James Still and of readers and journal writers everywhere.

(1986) I have had a literary treat. Last month, while traveling east out of Whitesburg, heading towards Hazard and Jackson on Kentucky Route 15, just past Carr Creek, my eye caught a sign that read, "Hindman Settlement School 11 Miles," and an arrow pointing north, down a side road. I quickly turned. James Still, the poet, had said to me during our brief meeting in Knoxville, when he was there to celebrate the hundredth anniversary of the Lawson McGhee Library, "When you are up my way, drop in."

Upon entering Hindman, a mountain community of maybe 800, I saw the Settlement School, and, next to it, the library, James Still's home base for over fifty years. He is retired now, but he had told me to ask for him at the library, which I did. The librarian phoned the poet for me, and I got on the line. "Mr. Still, do you remember our meeting in Knoxville? Well, here I am." He had just awoken from a nap; could I give him thirty minutes to shower and shave and he would be right down? Of course I could, and I was told to make myself at home.

I browsed about the library while I waited, picking up a book or two. The history section was next to the telephone, and I was surprised as I looked at some of the titles. Out of curiosity, I sought out the biography stacks, then the literature and fiction stacks; and I turned with awe and said to the librarian, who had been so helpful to me, "The library is very current, and the selections are remarkable and interesting." She said, "Mr. Still advises us on what volumes to purchase, and he keeps us up to date."

James Still, poet, short story writer, novelist, and journal writer, is an Alabamian from the Chattahoochee Valley. He graduated from Lincoln Memo-

Bourne, Frank Edward. "Conversations with James Still." *Appalachian Heritage* 30.1 (Winter 2002): 26–32. Reprinted with permission.

rial and Vanderbilt universities during the Great Depression; and then he landed here at the Hindman Settlement School as librarian, with room and board the payment. He is now eighty, looks fifty, and is very agile and sharp. To discriminating readers, Still has always had a unique niche as an artist of prose and poetry, with an acute ear for the ways of the Kentucky mountains, a specialist in feeling for an isolated civilization, its values, nuances, and exaggerations and the useful, colorful language that accompanies it. But to the general public, he has just come into his own in the last twenty years. I suspect some of this popularity has to do with his being for a while a regular commentator over National Public Radio's *All Things Considered*. His books sell well now.

It has become common to observe, and I do not know who first expressed the thought, but it goes something like this, that it is a pleasure to get away from New York's idea of Kentucky mountain people as seen through the saccharine and contrived and maudlin prose of Jesse Stuart, and to get to the basics with James Still. I have a friend here in Knoxville who was raised on Troublesome Creek, and she says emphatically, "Stuart doesn't speak for me. Where does he get that stuff?"

James Still has published two novels, several collections of short stories and two volumes of poetry. His novel, *River of Earth*, is a precious work of art — the story of a poor mountain family during the Depression. His collections of short stories, *On Troublesome Creek, Pattern of a Man*, and *The Run for the Elbertas*, are also about mountain people, yet his themes are universal. His collections of poems, *Hounds on the Mountain* and *Wolfpen Poems*, are popular, too. What is so special about Still, besides his breadth and depth, is his ear for mountain speech, the distinctive mannerisms and expressions: *Silver War* (Civil War), *Torment* (Hell), *white eye* (avoid work), *whet* (small amount), *Crossbar Hotel* (jail), *doughbeater* (wife), *granny-doctor* (midwife), *frog skin* (dollar bill), *jowl* (jaw), and *force put* (necessity). Still's work has been published in *The Atlantic Monthly, Esquire, The Saturday Evening Post* and *The Yale Review*.

James Still has also written stories for children, *The Wolfpen Rusties* and *Jack and the Wonder Beans*, and he is sometimes called to read to school children when it is known he is in an area, which he is most certain to do.

We have been told James Still has been keeping a journal all these years, writing at his work cabin along Wolfpen Creek, setting down impressions of people and the mountains, his thoughts and other vagaries, and that this will be left to the University of Kentucky. A journal in this age? That is a throwback to Thoreau and Emerson, and the avid diarists of the Adams Family. How enviable. Imagine the privilege, self-created of course, of sorting out and putting down one's thoughts, and recording the happenings in the mountains, the redbird on a winter bough, the sound of the creek in springtime, the fresh smell of a plowed field, the singing at a Sunday night meeting, watching neighbors on the next ridge grow up, grow old, and so on.

As promised, James Still showed up, all eighty years of him, bouncing about and looking like a forty-year-old, in a sport shirt and a pair of new blue jeans. The hour was now supper, but Mr. Still explained that the Settlement School dining hall was serving rather bland food this month, to go along with the school's program to help special students who stay there for the summer, learning to read.

"Well," said I, "How far is Hazard?"

"Twenty miles."

"Let's go there, then."

On the trip, I showed Mr. Still my tape machine and my first talking-book, something I was then trying out, what with the forty thousand miles I drive annually. It was plugged into the cigar lighter on the dashboard for power. That started us off, literary-wise. The book was *The Oregon Trail*. He wanted to know who the reader was. I didn't know and played the machine for a few moments. He didn't recognize anyone. Had I read anything by Parkman?

"Oh, I've read them all but this one. I do things backwards, been through all of *France and England in North America*. The book on LaSalle is my favorite in the series."

"Do you remember the chapter where LaSalle paints himself?"

"No, I don't recall. He was arrogant, a man of the world, ambitious and industrious, with tremendous energy."

"Oh yes," replied Mr. Still, "I have my ideas. The University of Pennsylvania Medical School, at one time, decided to officially list diffidence as a mental illness, and described its symptoms. I sent them a copy of the chapter 'LaSalle Paints Himself,' and they wrote me back thanking me, that this was the perfect description of diffidence; and it had never before been pointed out to them."

"I will read it again. [I have; it is amazing]. When I am hiking in the Smokies, I always think of LaSalle and his incredible winter walk from Central Illinois through Indiana and Michigan and across southern Ontario to Lake Erie, and then on by canoe to Montreal, over one thousand miles in sixty-five days, mostly at night, without daring to shoot a gun or light a fire in hostile territory."

We arrived in Hazard and, after some discussion, decided on a pizza. The restaurant we chose was having a special, the large, with as many toppings as wanted, in which we sure did partake. But instead of cola, which went with the deal, we had water.

"I believe Parkman was ill, too," said Mr. Still.

"Well, he had bad eyes, almost blind at times."

"Oh that, too, but I think he was manic-depressive. I've been with two such; I know it well."

(This statement bears out. I have finished listening to *The Oregon Trail*, a personal narrative, and there is much about sickness and headaches. In my opinion, this is the worst of Parkman's books, but the most popularized in the schools.)

"That Associated Press reporter down in Knoxville, what's his name?"

"Torn Eblem."

"Yes, he gave me a nice write-up when I was there, and it was picked up across the country."

"We don't see those things in the Knoxville papers. I have read Eblem's writings in the Sunday Atlanta paper and they are good."

"And James Dickey gave me a nice review in a Los Angeles paper, about my book of poetry. It is sold out — darndest thing I ever saw, a book of poetry sold out."

"It wasn't in New York, was it?"

"No. In the South and West."

"I have often thought about your novel, *River of Earth,* that Northerners wouldn't believe it."

"No?"

"No, I have lived down here twenty-five years now, but I am a Northerner and I know how they think. I believe you."

"Oh, I know that you do. You know, there is a wealthy coal mine operator here in town, and he called me up once to come over and meet a millionaire friend of his, as he wanted to talk to me. When I saw him, he was from a poor West Virginia family, and he said, 'Who told you how I was raised? Now, my mother didn't burn the house down, but everything in your novel is just how I was raised.'"

On a different subject I made the observation, "You know, it is amazing how different the weather is in Tennessee as opposed to Kentucky."

"Different? How do you mean?"

"The springs and falls are longer, and the winter is shorter in Tennessee. And the change occurs right at the state line, on the high ridge. Amazing! Why, you have snow by the first of December, while we rarely see any before New Year's."

"I'm out of Kentucky before any snow; gone to the Yucatan. Been there for the last seven or eight winters."

"You were in Iceland last fall, I've heard, before the Knoxville library gathering."

"Yes, before Reagan and Gorbachev. I am going to England this summer, with a wedding couple, to Devon."

"That was Raleigh's home base."

"Yes, and I have been to Rye, to Henry James' house. He wasn't there, but all his books were on display and the place was just as he left it. I had a delightful meal at a nearby inn. The food in England is usually bad. I have a saying that I never had a bad meal in France, and never a good meal in England. But the dinner at Rye was an exception."

As one can see by now, with trips to the Yucatan, England, France, and Iceland, James Still is widely traveled. The first trip was at the pleasure of the United States Army Air Corps, where he did duty in North Africa during the Second World War.

Since Mr. Still did his graduate work at Vanderbilt, the question had to be asked if he studied under Donald Davidson, or any of the Fugitives? The answer was no, his mentor was Dr. J. D. Wade, who I believe was one of the later Agrarians. This led the conversation down another path.

"I have been to Yaddo three times. That's where I met Eleanor Clark. Later, in Washington, Robert Penn Warren was a little shocked that she made such a fuss over me." Chuckle, chuckle.

Yaddo is an artist colony funded by the late Wall Street financier Spencer Trask and his wife Katrina. It is a place where artists are invited to reside at the mansion for an extended time, with all necessities provided, and where they are free to compose, write, paint, or follow whatever their muse might be. This is in northern New York, on a four-hundred-acre estate overlooking the Saratoga Battlefield.

"Since you were at Yaddo, did you know Flannery O'Connor?"

"No. Do you remember the O'Connor story where the little boy drowns himself seeking the Lord ... in his troubled world wanting to be counted?" ["By the River"] There was a long pause, James Still was thinking. "Or do you remember the story where the woman is gored by a bull?" ["Greenleaf"]

"Oh, yes. She deserved it, tyrannical as she was. I thought it was a good surprise."

"That was sexual."

"I never thought of that, but you are right!"

I then made a comment about the roads: "You know, there is a big change in the roads back here. I remember one time spending innumerable hours just getting back to Pippa Passes, going around those crooked two-lane roads, never knowing when a loaded coal truck might be coming towards you on the next curve, and those houses every now and then that might be perched curbside, between the road, the creek and the mountain. Now there are mountain parkways."

"And billboards."

Hooray for our side! Mark one up for Mr. Still!

"The reason I was journeying to Pippa Passes was because Alice Lloyd College was looking for a vice president for development and the president wanted to see me. Since I had been a developer of dormitories at several universities, I thought I might be just the man for the job. But after all that travelling, it turned out that their idea of a VP for development was one who raised money! So there went my fantasy of becoming a college vice president. They certainly are a little different and strange over there, especially with that faculty set-up, well-paid, houses on a mountain-bound campus, and clubby. I got there in time for the president's faculty tea, wives and all. You wouldn't dare sneeze: the news would be all over the mountain. You are somewhat of a neighbor. What do you know of them?"

"Well, that's why I came back here, to Alice Lloyd College; saw where I didn't understand them and came over here."

So on and on it went. We talked of Carl Sandburg, Edmund Wilson and Ambrose Bierce. We must have chatted for an hour and a half. He ate most of the pizza, and I love the stuff. We drove back to Hindman, where I let him off, and he said the next time I would have to visit his work cabin, which is on Wolfpen Creek.

He enjoyed our talk. Naturally, I did too, and, as can be seen, I jotted a good deal of it down. I found lodgings for the night up on the parkway, but for breakfast, I had to go back down to the drugstore, where the soda fountain, the only restaurant around, served meals — shades of the 1950s. It being Saturday, the town bank was open for the morning, and during weekdays, I noted, the hours were eight to two. *The Troublesome Creek Times,* a four county weekly newspaper, published in Hindman, has "a circulation under one million."

(1997) That was twelve years ago. We soon became Frank and Jim, fellow bookworms. I read somewhere that Jim had said he has read about three hours a day for the last fifty years. I am envious. The Knoxville Dickens Society, which I headed, had finished the fifteen novels of that author, and then we decided to go on, reading such writers as Thackeray, Fielding, and Twain, to name a few. I put Jim's name on the mailing list of our monthly literary newsletter, and he followed along with us. One time when he was in town, our group had started reading Thomas Hardy's *The Return of the Native,* and I commented how prolonged the first chapters are, forever and ever getting to the story, describing the heath, the reddleman and Druid rites. Of course the scene was Dorset, and Jim told of visiting Hardy's two graves, one at Westminster Abbey, where his body lies, the other in Dorset, where, at the author's request, his heart is buried.

For a while, Jim was employed by the University of Kentucky to visit and lecture at various colleges, such as Cumberland, Sue Bennett, or right here in our neighborhood, at Maryville College. His theme was always about writing of the Appalachian heritage. He saw to it that I was called, and after his talk, we had lunch. Afterwards, we traveled to a local grade school, where he read his story *Jack and the Wonder Beans* to a third-grade class, who sat around him on the floor with rapt attention. Later, he would tell me that he collects the writings of Richard Jefferies and W.H. Hudson, nineteenth-century writers. He thinks Jefferies was the finest writer of children's books. He has visited the graves of both in England.

As can be seen, James Still has a penchant for visiting the homes and final resting places of authors. He told me one time that when in Knoxville again he would like to visit the grave of Harry Harrison Kroll — could I locate it? Well, nobody around here seems to have any recollection of such a writer. In going through the clippings at the McClung Room in the Lawson McGhee Library, I found Mr. Kroll's obituary and that he is buried in the cemetery of the Gallaher View Baptist Church, which I visited. Why Mr. Kroll was buried here, no one can tell, but he spent most of his life in West Tennessee. He did teach at Lincoln Memorial University from 1925 to 1928, and that is probably where Jim knew him. Kroll was a prolific writer, and his most famous piece was made into a motion picture, starring Bette Davis, *The Cabin in the Cotton*. His manuscripts and papers are at the University of Memphis, four hundred miles west of here. Unfortunately, Jim has not been back here to visit the site, but I sent photographs. Kroll's life is one of accomplishment, from the cotton patch, with little formal education, to teacher and writer.

I have been to Hindman for Jim's ninetieth birthday celebration. Now I have an invitation to "eat a piece of cake with Mr. Still on his ninety-second birthday, at his cabin on Wolfpen Creek, this July 18." I have yet to see the cabin. Many years ago, a friend let him use it as his work cabin, and when the owner died, it was left to him. There are many pictures of the place: two story, rustic, yard grown with weeds, the perfect place for a library, work table and bed for a writer and reader who desires seclusion. I cannot wait.

II

STILL ON OTHER PEOPLE'S MINDS: MEMOIRS

Obscurity Begins Back Home for Kentucky's James Still

RENA NILES

James Still, Kentucky author, can claim the well-nigh unique distinction of never having had any of his works permanently rejected. True, he has a few rejection slips to show — a very few; and one of these came with a poem he had sent to a very inferior publication, the editors of which returned the contribution — only to see it accepted — and acclaimed — by the editors of *Atlantic Monthly*.

But James Still is not one to boast about his good standing with the press. Indeed, he almost regrets the publishers' willingness to accept all he sends them, and wishes that some stories and poems he submitted in the past had been politely returned.

For James Still is one whose standard of perfection involves far more than success, and the success he has achieved can be explained partly by the care lavished on each poem and story before it ever is allowed to leave his hands. He is not one to throw judgment to the winds and let what so often passes for inspiration have full sway. His style is surely not labored — but its apparent ease is the result of lengthy and hard work.

Still has a profound respect for his medium — the English language; and he chooses to use it as a precision instrument, rather than wield it as a pickaxe.

The facts in the life of James Still are these: He is a serious young man; he lives at Hindman and is librarian of the Hindman Settlement School. He likes library work and hopes to guide people to more intelligent reading.

But behind these facts looms the more significant — and surprising — fact of James Still's relative obscurity. For here is a man who is far better known in the North and East than in his own state, although — along with Jesse Stuart — he represents the best that the younger generation of Kentucky writers has produced.

Like charity, obscurity seems to begin at home. James Still is not as well known in Kentucky as he deserves to be — but in Hindman he is practically

---

Niles, Rena. "Obscurity Begins Back Home for Kentucky's James Still." Louisville *Courier-Journal Magazine*, April 30, 1939. Reprinted with permission.

unknown; unknown as a writer and a poet. To the people of his community he is a hard-working school teacher — it is as a pedagogue that they know and admire him, and James Still would be the last one to want things changed.

Few people suspect him of being a writer — so much the better says James, adding: "It's far healthier for them to think of me only in connection with the job at hand." And, if there be members of the community who, thumbing through the *Saturday Evening Post*, have come across the familiar name of James Still and stopped to read, they have kept their secret to themselves. Indeed, when this wandering reporter, accompanied by a photographer, arrived in Hindman to interview Mr. Still, there was considerable speculation in the community as to the purpose of the visit — the people of Hindman wondered what Jim Still had done to get into the papers.

True, this situation is partly explained by James Still's firm opposition to all forms of publicity. We are pleased to announce that this is the first interview he has ever granted to anyone even remotely connected with a newspaper. At the same time, he has steadfastly refused to speak over the radio, and literary clubs which have solicited his services have come up against an impassible wall.

Speaks Through His Works

This should not lead us to the conclusion that Still has snubbed the press, the radio, the literary clubs. On the contrary, his persistent refusals have been caused by an insurmountable shyness and a patient willingness to let time take its course and bring him either fame — or the lack of it — as destiny ordains.

A fatalist? Not so much that as a man who believes that a writer should speak through his books, a painter through his pictures, a musician through his music — and

James Still, 1939. PA8ZM9:#795, John Jacob Niles Photographic Collection, University of Kentucky. Used with permission.

that this "personal appearance" gag is a dull error. And there are not a few among the literary fraternity to agree with him. We might almost say that the best writers agree with him — but that, too, would be untrue. In the final analysis, an author refuses to appear before his public because public appearances annoy him, just as another accepts similar invitations because public appearances amuse, delight, or otherwise please him.

James Still — though completely identified with the State of Kentucky — was born in the Buckalew Mountains of Northern Alabama, in that mountainous country not unlike the hills of Kentucky where he now lives — except, to quote his own words, that "the earth is redder there, and the valleys broader." In addition to tobacco and corn, James Still's family and neighbors raised cotton — a crop unknown to the Kentucky mountains in these days, though some of the older men and women tell us that they can remember the time when the mountain folk raised, spun and wove their own cotton.

But James Still belongs to Kentucky, if only because of his firm determination that nothing shall force him to leave its hills. One of the most perfect poems in *Hounds on the Mountain*, his volume of collected verse, speaks this determination:

> I shall not leave these prisoning hills
> Though they topple their barren heads to level earth
> And the forests slide uprooted out of the sky.
> Though the water of Troublesome, of Trace Fork,
> Of Sand Lick rise in a single body to glean the valleys,
> To drown lush pennyroyal, to unravel rail fences;
> Though the sun-ball breaks the ridges into dust
> And burns its strength into the blistered rock
> I cannot leave. I cannot go away.
>
> Being of these hills, being one with the fox
> Stealing into the shadows, one with the new-born foal,
> The lumbering ox drawing green beech logs to mill,
> One with the destined feet of man climbing and descending,
> And one with death rising to bloom again, I cannot go.
> Being of these hills I cannot pass beyond.

Was Editor at Seven

It was not till 1932, however, that James Still came to Hindman. He has been there ever since. Before that date, he had spent a not unusual childhood, attending the rural schools near his farm home. His father, a farmer and veterinary, still is living; his nine brothers and sisters all are living, all married, all in Alabama. James, the sixth child and the first boy in the family, is the only one to leave the state, the only one to remain unmarried, the only one to do anything at all outstanding.

At 7 James Still decided to be an editor. A magazine for children entitled *Little Folks* gave him the idea, which he immediately put into practice by making up folders, tied with string, and filled with stories, poems and illustrations—all from the hand of James Still. It was a one-man show, from kivver to kivver. At 8 he decided to become an author, believing that his writings might some day appear in textbooks. This childhood dream came true. Two college textbooks have included short stories of his.

The young editor soon went into the writing of stories on a larger scale than his magazine would allow. One especially he remembers—it ran to the extraordinary length of thirty-odd pages and went by the title of "The Golden Nugget." The subject was a hidden treasure.

Of his other literary efforts James Still retains only the haziest memory, until we come to his sophomore year in high school. The family moved to a new community, and the moving involved a change of school, a change of friends, the plunge into something new and hostile.... It was during this unhappy period that James Still wrote his first novel. He was too young to be a satirist and deride the things he hated. His first novel was a purely escapist affair—the magic key into the world of dreams....

Looking back over the early period of his life, James Still remembers his mother as the person to whom he owes the most. This, in itself, is not unusual. History often has repeated the story of the artist, the poet, the writer who—misunderstood by the rest of his family—secretly was encouraged by the mother. It is a stock situation in literature, even a stock situation in life, and it happened to James Still.

Of all the Still family, she alone read his stories; she alone read the poems when they first were published—and even before they appeared in print. The rest of the family had no time for Jim and his scribblings—even when publishers' checks began to come in. Only when the slick-sheet publications—like *The Saturday Evening Post*—began to take him in did they read stories written by James Still, and even then they thought mighty poorly of their brother's talent. When the news got back to them that publishers were not merely accepting James Still's stories, but were paying for them in three-figure checks, they merely shook their heads and decided that the big city editors must be stark raving mad to pay such fancy prices for Brother James' stuff.

It is indeed ironical that the one person in his family who would have gloried in his success, as she encouraged him in his obscurity, lies buried under Alabama sod—his mother: Lonie Lindsey Still. A simple marble slab marks the grave. She had always wanted a marble slab over her grave; the proceeds from *Hounds on the Mountain* paid for it.

Disappointed at College

From high school in Alabama, James Still went to Lincoln Memorial University at Harrogate, Tennessee. Curiously enough, he was the classmate of another Kentucky poet and writer—Jesse Stuart. The two of them sat in the same English classes—but the similarity ends there. They are different in temperament, different in their approach to life, and even more sharply different in their approach to literature.

James Still was disappointed bitterly in Lincoln Memorial University. Like every young man who goes to college as the faithful go to church, he found that college and culture both start with a "c"—and end their relationship with the first letter. He found that the men who were supposed to initiate him in the study of English literature were as uninspired as they were uninspiring; that they treated poetry as a meathacker treats a round of beef, and that even the immortal Bard of Avon turned to dust in their hands.

Partly out of his reading and partly out of the imagining of his own mind, James Still had fashioned for himself a medieval university ideal—an ideal based on the transference of knowledge through the intimate association of minds; on the one hand, the minds of the professors—learned, wise, inspiring; on the other, the minds of the students—young, uninformed, but eager to learn. To him, as to many others, Hopkins sitting on one end of a log and a student sitting on the other constituted a university.

Instead of all this, he was served with a puzzling assemblage of campus and buildings, teachers, classes, examinations, papers, required course and student-indicated activities—all the rigmarole of high school warmed over and served up in a new dish under a false name.

And, as James Still grew older and went on to other universities, his disillusionment grew greater, and his disappointment in Lincoln Memorial University grew milder—for he found that his Alma Mater was no better and no worse than many another college. He realized that the mistake was his—he had thought education and culture went hand in hand. He was to discover that the Philistines had invaded the halls of learning and substituted degrees for cultural development.

From Lincoln Memorial University, where he received his B.A. degree in 1929, James Still went to Vanderbilt University. This was very much better. Nashville was then, as it is today, the literary capital of the South. Such men as John Crowe Ransom, Edwin Mims and Walter Clyde Curry taught in the English Department, and the inspirational quality of their teaching found immediate response in the young writer. His stay at Vanderbilt was, however, of short duration—he left in 1930, M.A. in hand.

From there to Chicago. Time was closing in on him. It looked as though the big days, the lavish twenties, were over. He had to learn something "practical." He had always loved books and libraries. The librarian's course at the University of Illinois seemed the logical next step.

When he emerged from there, with three diplomas tucked in his vest pocket, the depression had settled down in earnest. James Still — the gentle poet, the doe-eyed dreamer — was not the one to fight the economic chaos of 1931. Stronger, tougher men than he had gone down in the maelstrom — who was he to buck it?

There followed the strange escapist period of his, the wanderjahrung, during which he hoboed over the United States, or over every state east of the Mississippi, and got as far West as Texas and New Mexico. He spent some time in the mountains of North Carolina, and worked at odd jobs — anything that came his way: jobs on railroads, in restaurants, on farms. This lasted nearly two years.

Strange that James Still, the writer, did not draw upon this period of his life for literary material. At least, he has not done so, to date. His unwillingness to exploit his years of wandering cannot be explained away by the fact that he is primarily a poet, and that what passes for high romance — the broad sweeping stuff that novels are made of — leaves him rather cold.

It is simply that the years of wandering, with their adventure and their heart-break, are too close at hand. James Still has not forgotten those years. He is simply awaiting the time when he can write thereof — not dispassionately, perhaps, but philosophically and with a perspective that comes only after the passage of years. It was Wordsworth who said that poetry is made from emotion recollected in tranquility, and we must remember that James Still is primarily a poet.

Could Not Write

He is also one who had to be firmly anchored before he could write. Unlike the French author, Andre Malraux, who wrote what is perhaps his greatest book while in command of the Loyalist Air Force in the late Spanish war, James Still could not write during the difficult year. Tossed upon the storms of life, he could only suffer and look out upon the world with soft, troubled brown eyes — wondering where it all would end.

Coming to Hindman Settlement School as librarian provided the anchorage. He understood the people of the hills. They were like the folks he'd known in Alabama. And they liked the studious young schoolmaster.

He began to write. His stories and poems immediately were accepted. *Story, The New Republic, The Yale Review, Virginia Quarterly Review, The Atlantic Monthly, The Nation* and *The Saturday Evening Post* have brought the talent of James Still to their readers. A book of poems, *Hounds on the Mountain*, was brought out by the Viking Press in New York, and the O. Henry Memorial Collection included stories by James Still in 1937 and in 1938.

Oddly enough, it was "Bat Flight," a story intended for the scholarly *Yale*

Review, that was picked up by *The Saturday Evening Post*. The *Post* readers liked it so well that the April 1 issue of the magazine contained another story by James Still. Two of his stories have been transcribed in Braille, and the list of his accomplishments is far greater than one might expect from a shy young man in his early thirties.

"I Write Because I'm Unhappy When Not Writing" — James Still

Gurney Norman

The layman no doubt wonders just exactly what makes writers write. Mr. James Still, an Alabamian by birth but a Kentuckian by choice and one of Knott County's most prominent sons as a very successful writer, has a broad yet quite inclusive answer to this question:

"I write because I am unhappy when I am not writing," he says. He adds that he can't remember, even as a boy, not feeling a compulsion to write.

Mr. Still, perhaps as much as any individual, has placed Hindman and Troublesome Creek on the map by achieving considerable renown in the United States with his poetry, short stories, and a novel, *River of Earth*. In 1939 he was second only to one of America's most distinguished writers, William Faulkner, when the O. Henry awards for that year's best short stories were passed out, and the next year, *River of Earth* shared first honors with a novel by the late Thomas Wolfe for the Southern Authors' award. His poetry and short stories appear often in such outstanding magazines as the *Atlantic Monthly*, the *Yale Review*, and the *Virginia Quarterly Review*.

Came As College Student

The author came to Hindman one summer several years ago as a college student, and says he knew then this was where he wanted to live. He has never felt himself to be a stranger in the Kentucky mountains, he says; rather, it was almost like coming home when he chose to settle in Knott County.

Mr. Still is a former story writer for a prominent weekly magazine, long

---

Gurney Norman, "I Write Because I'm Unhappy When Not Writing," Hazard *Herald*, October 2, 1958. Reprinted with permission.

recognized as one of the most financially lucrative markets for commercial writers. But after published in this magazine several times, he noticed that his writing tended to become more commercial than serious. He caught himself using little literary tricks to make the story sell. The gift of writing is not something one should misuse, he decided, and now he says he had much rather have a story in the *Atlantic* than the other publication despite the financial differences of the two magazines.

As librarian at Hindman Settlement School, a post he has held for several years, Mr. Still puts in full days to maintaining the high state of efficiency which so clearly characterizes his library. The building is a neat one built of native stone, and books from generous donors pour daily into the library, from which Mr. Still uses his experienced eye to select the best reading for Hindman students.

Author Reads Avidly

Mr. Still is an avid reader himself. Though he reads some fiction, he is especially fond of history and archeology. He recently embarked upon a 38 month program of study in the Shakespearean masterpieces. He plans to spend a month on each of the playwright's works, reading in his spare time, studying them in detail.

Not long ago, Mr. Still bought a 1949 model automobile, the first one he has ever owned. Formerly he got to where he wanted to go by riding with friends or by walking. His home is about a 20 minute drive from the Hindman School, just off the road leading to Litt Carr.

Mr. Still's home-life is reminiscent of the 19th century Concord, Mass., philosopher and poet, Henry Thoreau, though he is far from the recluse that Thoreau fancied himself. Mr. Still lives alone in a neat cabin almost 150 years old, one of the oldest houses in Knott County. He has lived there 19 years. Though small and with a rough floor of wide boards, the cabin has most of the conveniences found in rural homes. The relaxed, happy mood the author displays when he returns to his cabin in the evening is evidence enough that no home could ever compare with this one for Mr. Still.

Does Not Live Completely Alone

When asked if writing compensated for his living alone, he almost scoffed and replied that by no means did he live alone. He explained that he was surrounded by about 800 children every day and that neighbors were in close proximity. Mr. Still's very quiet home, with the large four poster bed and walls lined with books and reproductions of famous Van Gogh paintings, and with the little garden, apple orchard and quaint stone well outside, is enviable.

Mr. Still mentioned the fact that many writers picture themselves as tortured individuals, creating from their pain from existence. He smiled at this and said, "Not me. I enjoy everything I do."

And this quote perhaps as completely as any characterizes a very simple, intelligent man who seems to have found his haven in a Kentucky valley midst the common people he feels so much a part of and of whom he writes so movingly.

"...Some things a man does just for himself": In Regard to Writing, That's the Philosophy of Gifted Kentucky Author-Poet James Still

Joe Creason

James Still is a Kentucky writer and a poet who has been called one of the most skilled hands in the author business today and who, over the last 20 years, has won more literary awards of one kind or another than you could shake a rejection slip at.

Yet, in philosophy, technique and attitude, he bears no resemblance to the typical successful creative writer.

He has never made a literary-club speech, attended an autograph party or submitted to any kind of publicity gimmick in an effort to spur the sale of his three books or dozens of short stories.

He has a trunk bulging with completed short stories which he never has submitted for publication even though editors are standing in line to get anything he writes.

He lives alone in a picture-postcard–type, 150-year-old log cabin on Dead Mare Branch deep in the Knott County mountains and rises at four every morning to begin writing even though he has no particular urge to see his writing published.

He has an almost complete indifference to the price received for a story, exhibiting much greater concern over where his material is published than what it nets.

Joe Creason, "'...Some things a man does just for himself': In Regard to Writing, That's the Philosophy of Gifted Kentucky Author-Poet James Still," Louisville *Courier-Journal Magazine*, February 14, 1960. pp. 7–9. Reprinted with permission.

James Still at the well beside his log house. Courtesy the Hindman Settlement School. Used with permission.

He has declined flattering college teaching offers to remain as supervisor of the Knott County Bookmobile and librarian at Hindman Settlement School, the fine mountain institution where he has been since 1932.

And, as if to underline the fact that he is unusual indeed among authors, Still twice has declined very large literary awards rather than interrupt his routine long enough to go receive them.

Many of these distinctions are explained by Still's own admission that he is a compulsive writer; that he writes because he must — not because it is a shortcut to gold and glory.

It can be said in complete honesty that if it was impossible for him to write, he would lose his reason for being. Writing, in truth, is almost as much a part of his living as breathing out and breathing in.

That is the impression that is bound to overshadow all others in a conversation with James Still. Since his ideas about writing, his approach to the art and his unconcern for certain conventions are so different and fresh, a visit with him is a downright refreshing experience.

It was a cold late–January day when this particular visit came off. After having opened the settlement school library for the day and making one check at a school on the Bookmobile route where the students weren't reading as much as previously, he had gone directly to his log house on Dead Mare Branch.

There, in the main room of the picturesque old house, he talked about many things but especially about writing.

"I have no particular urge to publish — my urge is to write," Still said in his soft-spoken way as he scuffed a shoe across the hand-shaped, square-nail–secured floor. "I think I would write even if there was no hope of ever having anything published.

"There was a time when I got a great uplift out of having something published, but not so much any more. There are some things a man does just for himself and nobody else.

"For instance," he continued, "much of my writing is like my dulcimer playing — it's just for me. Nobody ever has heard me play the dulcimer and nobody ever has read many of the stories I have written."

Still paused and gazed through the window at the snow-mantled ridges through which Dead Mare Branch has chewed its crooked path in rushing down to flow into Little Carr Creek.

"I have written many stories and poems which I never intended to be offered for publication," he said after several seconds. "I did them only because they satisfied my urge to write.

"That, I suppose, explains my not being worried about things being or not being published. If they are good enough, they'll be published, eventually; if they aren't good enough, they shouldn't be printed."

Likewise, that attitude no doubt explains Still's singular unconcern about the price received for his more than 30 published short stories, some of them considered classics, which have appeared in most of the leading slick-paper magazines.

"I'm more interested in where a story is published than in the price it brings," he said. "I've always liked seeing my stories in *The Atlantic Monthly*. I could get more some other place, but *The Atlantic* is a real good magazine and more stories are picked from it for reprint than perhaps any other."

Reprints of Still short stories have appeared in anthologies, pocket books and textbooks. Three have been selected among the best American short stories, and three have been O. Henry Memorial prize stories.

Almost as unusual as Still's left-handed approach to the publishing of stories is his reason for leading what almost amounts to the life of a literary hermit. While there now is an all-weather road within a quarter mile of his place, which is about 8 miles from Hindman, when he settled there in 1939 it wasn't even within sound of the nearest road of any kind. The only way in was up the rock-studded bed of Little Carr Creek.

"But the very day I moved here," he pointed out, "they started a blacktop road from Cody over this way.... They've always pursued me with roads."

Still had been at Hindman seven years before he found the log house on Dead Mare Branch. He came to the school in 1932 after graduating from Lincoln Memorial University and having gotten a master's degree from Vanderbilt and a degree in library science from the University of Illinois.

His first job at Hindman was mainly in recreation, with a little library work in his spare time. He tramped all over the hills organizing Boy Scout troops and baseball teams. The next year, however, he became librarian full time.

Seeing the need for books in the area, he began delivering reading matter to schools and cabins far up the hollows long before Bookmobiles appeared on the scene. In those days, he loaded a box with books, hoisted it on his shoulders and walked his rounds.

Although he became interested in writing when he was a boy of eight back in Alabama, where he was born in 1906, it wasn't until 1936 that his first short story was published in *The Atlantic*. His first book, *Hounds on the Mountain*, a well-received volume of poems, was published by Viking the next year.

"I wasn't satisfied with the place where I was living," Still went on. "Then one day I saw this place and knew it was what I had been looking for all my life — remote, picturesque and quiet."

The place belonged to Jethro Amburgey, a genuine mountain dulcimer maker, but it had been unoccupied for years. When he talked to the owner about living there, they were able to agree on everything except price — Still wanted to pay some rent, Amburgey didn't want to take any. They finally agreed on Still's taking it for the taxes.

"I don't think the neighbors from up the hollows knew what to expect of me," Still laughed. "My being a writer didn't mean a thing to most of them.

"One old gent would stop by almost every afternoon for a spell, and always he would start off by saying the same thing — 'I bet you've blacked many a page this day.'"

When he moved in, Still had no furniture except a cot, and a trunk he used for a writing desk.

"Things have changed since then," he remarked as he glanced about the room and his eyes picked such incongruous items as the chinked-log walls and the fluorescent reading lamp, and the hand-made dulcimer hanging by the window and electric blanket spread across the foot of the bed, the massive creek-stone fireplace and the electric refrigerator in the next room.

"I'm not trying to prove anything by living out here," he insisted. "When that electric blanket there is gone, there will be another.

"When I first moved here, I often didn't have any money and I lived the way I did because I had to. I didn't own a car then and I raised most of my own food just to get by.

"But, most of all, I liked it here, despite the lack of conveniences because it just suited my needs."

Two books — *River of Earth*, a 1940 novel which earned him a share, with Thomas Wolfe, of the Southern Authors' Award for that year, and *On Troublesome Creek*, a collection of short stories in 1941 — were produced along with numerous short stories for *The Atlantic, Colliers, The Saturday Evening Post*, and other leading magazines in the next two years.

"I've been asked how I ever learned to cook, living alone as I do," Still commented. "My answer simply is that I got hungry.

"Actually, for years before and after the war I ate supper with my nearest neighbor, Melvin Amburgey. When the idea came up, I asked him how much he wanted for board and he told me, 'Nothing, I just want you to talk to my children.'"

Talk to the children Still did — and listen, too. His classic short story, "Mrs. Razor," was nothing more than a recitation of the make-believing of Amburgey's youngest daughter, who played a game in which she was married to a fictitious character named "Mr. Razor."

That story, incidentally, has been reprinted dozens of times, including use in a psychiatric textbook in which it appears as an illustration of juvenile fantasy. It also was the first of the three Still works which have been selected among the best American short stories in various years.

Still's selection for O. Henry Memorial prizes came in 1937, 1939, and 1941, the year after he was named Phi Beta Kappa poet by Columbia University, an honor he declined going to New York to receive. Then in 1946, he was awarded the Van Wyck Brooks citation for "gift of style and master of character and scene," another honor he failed to accept in person because he was "too busy at the time."

Last October he was invited to Amherst College to help dedicate the Robert Frost Library, an honor he did accept because of his great regard for Frost and "the encouragement he has given me."

Two Guggenheim Fellowships have been won by Still, the first in 1941, the second in 1946 after he returned from 3½ years of Army service in Africa and the Middle East.

"The same person who went away didn't return from the war," he mused. "I had changed, this hollow had changed, and my neighbors had changed.

"I used to say that the people here always would be the same, but I returned to find many of them saying their children now wouldn't work for anything but money.

"I knew then they had changed."

The immediate postwar period was difficult for Still, a time when he yearned as always to write but when he couldn't seem to get anything down on paper.

"I was mixed up," he said. "I didn't write, I didn't read; I just sat in the door and played the dulcimer. I haven't touched one since.

"The second Guggenheim Fellowship was a lifesaver. It helped me over a difficult time when I was adjusting and getting my bearings."

The stories have poured from Still's typewriter in a steady stream since that time.

But only a comparative few of the lot have gone to fill the requests of publishers. The others have gone into a big attic trunk which by now is bulging with stories, most of which could find a ready market if Still would let them go. Being the stickler for near-perfection that he is, Still often puts what appears to be a completed story away, then comes back months later to make changes.

"When a story comes true, when I can believe it, when everything seems right, then I quit," he explained.

"In reality, I want my characters to do their own talking. All I want to be is just a secretary who puts down what they do and what they say."

Still sees nothing unusual about the fact he gets up before even a light-sleeping rooster to start his work. That simply is the way that is best for him.

"I don't ask myself if I want to get up at 4 A.M.—I know I don't," he said. "But I work best then.

"And, after all, nothing happens unless I'm sitting down to work."

Before Saying Yes: Discovering James Still's "First Sweetheart"

Ann W. Olson

One of James Still's defining poems, signed and framed, hangs on our dining room wall: "Those I Want in Heaven with Me Should There Be Such a Place." I have heard Mr. Still read this poem aloud more than once, and an early version of this same poem appears in the memorial program from his funeral, in 2001.

The two lines from the poem that have always intrigued me are:

> And my first sweetheart, who died at sixteen,
> Before she got around to saying "Yes"

Surely I'm not the only one to have wondered who she was. And what did he actually ask her? What happened to her? And does anyone know this story? Mr. Still was a man who gathered up words and returned them sparingly. By the same token he didn't choose to tell every story he knew. He possessed a natural reserve that kept many of us from directly asking him personal questions.

However, between fortuitous circumstance and natural curiosity, I have uncovered pieces of this bit of his story — only because my last name is the same as Ted Olson's, the editor of Mr. Still's poetry collection, *From the Mountain, From the Valley: New and Collected Poems* (University Press of Kentucky, June 2001).

I had met Ted just once before hearing him being interviewed by Bob Edwards on National Public Radio on the occasion of Mr. Still's death. I was delighted that there was a national tribute, but I had no idea, of course, that because of those five on-air minutes, a story of mine was about to intersect with a glimpse into Mr. Still's past.

Ann W. Olson, "Before Saying Yes: Discovering James Still's First Sweetheart," *The Alumnus* (Lincoln Memorial University), Summer/Fall 2002, pp 13–15. Reprinted with permission.

It turns out a friend in Connecticut, Betty Brown Whitney, also listened to this same NPR piece. When I called her house about six weeks after Mr. Still's death, I had done so only to talk with her husband, Jim, whom I had known in college when I dated his roommate for two years. I had recently uncovered a trove of letters in my attic, including ones from the two of them, and I had wanted tactfully to find out if my former boyfriend was doing all right. I never had a chance to ask.

Instead, since Betty answered the phone, she told me early in our conversation about hearing the Bob Edwards radio interview. She brought it up simply because she wanted to confess that at first she had mistakenly thought Ted was the name of my husband. She had soon remembered, however, that I am married instead to Frank Olson. She and I would never have talked about Mr. Still if Ted Olson and I didn't share the same last name, an uncommon one in Appalachia.

Then I was further surprised to hear her say she had a connection with Mr. Still and, it turns out, with the poem I love so well. As soon as Betty spoke the words "My aunt was Mr. Still's first sweetheart," I switched from a curiosity about my former boyfriend to an all-consuming interest in Mr. Still's college love instead. It thrilled me to realize a mystery could be about to be solved.

Of course I didn't know at first that his sweetheart was from his college days. Betty just told me her aunt's name — Mayme Woodson Brown — and said that she had died in her teens. Over the phone I read her the two lines from Mr. Still's poem, which she had never heard before. She was amazed. We both felt sure that these words were a tribute to her aunt.

In the next few weeks I asked around. Who, if anyone, had information about this woman? From people I knew who knew Mr. Still well, all I came up with were just a few hints here and there of some story somewhere, but certainly nothing close to a sweetheart's name. However, Mayme's family members generously shared memories and memorabilia when I went to Tennessee for visits with them. I felt this story was handed to me, and I had a responsibility to go where it took me with Mr. Still leading the way. He put it out there by writing those lines in his poem.

Mayme was born February 15, 1910, in Campbell County, Tennessee, near Knoxville. She had an older sister, Martha Alice, nicknamed Mattie, and two younger brothers, Thomas Milburn and John Reynolds Woodson. Their mother, Mary Chaney Reynolds, had taught at what was later the Red Bird Mission School, in Clay County, Kentucky. She married Woodson Hodge Brown, a School Board member there who had had to leave school at an early age to work.

The Brown family ended up living just north of La Follette, Tennessee, on Route 63 near the Kentucky border, in the progressive rural community of Well Springs. They were quietly nicknamed "the genius family," and Mayme particularly was known as "the genius." In 1925, she started college when she was 15, attending nearby Lincoln Memorial University in Harrogate. The first year she roomed with her older sister, Mattie, who was also a freshman.

James Still, meanwhile, was born July 16, 1906, making him 3½ years older than Mayme. He had begun his studies at LMU a year before Mayme, on September 26, 1924. In the introduction to *From the Mountain, From the Valley*, Mr. Still explains, "the opportunity to work my way through was the draw [of LMU]." Even so, with college well beyond the means of most people then, he writes that he was often hungry. Perhaps that is why he was not a student at LMU for the '26–'27 academic year; he graduated in June 1929.

I haven't yet heard how the two met. Betty thinks perhaps Mayme tutored him in math at some point, but she isn't sure. Written date requests were common at that time, and Mayme's Memory Book contains a hand-written invitation signed *James Still* that reads "Mayme — May I have a date with you for the 'math picnic'? R.S.V.P."

Mayme completed two years of college before her death on September 6, 1927. Her family is pretty sure she died from typhoid, though some say it was food poisoning. Her death certificate simply states "Collitis [sic]." Her closest brother, called Milburn by the family, was five years younger. He was very ill with the same disease but survived.

Mayme died at home, and she is buried nearby, in the Well Springs Community Cemetery. From something Mr. Still once said to his friend and mine, Lois Combs Weinberg, I gather he didn't realize how sick Mayme was until after she had died. Her obituary in *The Mountain Herald* reports she was ill for a month. It also says, "Mayme was affectionally known on the campus as 'Brownie' because of her small size, her name and her large brown eyes. Her death came as a shock to her many friends and was keenly felt on the campus by students and faculty." The 1928 LMU yearbook has a memorial page dedicated to her.

Mr. Still's poem states she "died at sixteen," but the record shows her dying at age seventeen. Mayme's family, who called her "Little Mayme" or "an angel," grieves her loss to this day. She was clearly a remarkable young woman. Mattie's daughter Mary Ellen told me her mother spoke of Mayme every day. Mattie's other daughter, Alberta, is the family member who has Mayme's Memory Book in her keeping.

Betty told me that Mr. Still regularly put flowers on Mayme's grave and had done so as recently as several years earlier. Betty's Aunt Mattie would tell her of going to the cemetery and finding Mr. Still there, providing an explanation for flowers found other times. Betty was relieved when I told her that Mr. Still never married. She had worried about what a wife would feel about his remembering a former love so faithfully.

I never met Betty's parents. Her father, Mayme's brother Milburn, died in 2000. Just the year before he had taken his grandson, Thomas, and two college friends to visit Mr. Still in Hindman, Kentucky. Betty knows her dad would have loved to talk at length with me about this visit and about his beloved sister.

Even if a curious person like myself were satisfied with the story so far, which I was, next Betty showed me the copy of Mr. Still's *Pattern of a Man & Other Stories* signed the day of that last visit, "For Milburn Brown, brother of my <u>first</u> sweetheart. James Still."

James "Lucky" Still: A Fortunate Man

Carol Boggess

> ... I trust to be understood for imagining the heart of Appalachia to be in the hills of Eastern Kentucky where I have lived and feel at home and where I have exercised as much freedom and peace as the world allows. — James Still

How fortunate a man is to be able to say that he has lived and felt at home in a place where he can exercise "as much freedom and peace as the world allows." Such is the claim that James Still makes in his description of Appalachia as a "somewhat mythical region" (*Wolfpen*, frontpiece). James Still was always comfortable in his own skin, satisfied to be where he was and who he was. His ninety-four years of contentment and good health were surely a sign of his general good fortune. But what about luck — was he a lucky man?

When I first met Mr. Still, I would have said he was no luckier than average. But coming to know him better, I thought perhaps he enjoyed special blessings. After hearing his many stories and reading countless letters and journals, I decided he was definitely lucky. Let me present you with some anecdotal evidence, and you can decide for yourself. Regardless of your conclusion, you will enjoy the stories. Some of them he told me in interviews; others are excerpts from published or personal letters and diaries; several are based on notes that he made for the National Public Radio spots he prepared in the 1980s.

I would not call myself lucky; I have never won the lottery or anything else that I can remember. But I do consider myself fortunate. I have a happy, healthy family, an interesting job, and a home in a beautiful part of the world. One important example of my good fortune is the opportunity I had to know James Still. I was searching for a dissertation topic while a graduate student at the University of Kentucky in the early 1990s. When I heard James Still and Randy Wilson perform on campus, my decision was made. A few months later I found myself interviewing Still in preparation for my study of *River of Earth*. By that time, I knew the book rather well, but I wanted to know more about the man.

Since it was one of my early encounters with Mr. Still, I was prepared with a list of carefully researched questions. At the start, he made an effort to answer a few of them. For example, in his papers at the UK library, I had come across several letters addressed to "Jimmie." I was curious about his relationships with people in his early life, so I began with a simple question: "Were you ever called Jimmie?" His answer was definitive: "Never." He seemed slightly insulted that someone might address him by a nickname. I learned quickly that talking with James Still meant listening. The best questions inspired responses and stories, not answers.

My goal at that time was to discover something about the person he had been at different stages of his life. During that interview he fell into his rhythm when he began talking about his army years. I came away assured that he had never been called "Jimmie" (though, of course, he had) but in the army, he was called "Lucky."

That nickname surprised me. How could a man who was drafted into World War II and who would serve three years and seven months in North Africa consider himself lucky? I presumed that the name was either facetious or that he was a soldier who insisted on finding the silver lining in all wartime

"Still Life with James Still." Mr. Still is standing in front of the shelf located near the rear entrance of the Amburgey-Still log house on Dead Mare Branch, Knott County, Kentucky. Photograph taken October 1980 by Linc. Fisch. Used with permission.

experiences. Later, among his papers, I found some notes he had made in preparing radio shorts for NPR; in them was this story of the origin of his army nickname:

> It [the name Lucky] came from one day refusing to indulge in the mandated calisthenics which included thirty-seven push-ups, plus other punishing activities.
>
> I was having back trouble, and I figured the health of my spine was at stake. When the whistle blew to fall-in, I headed for the showers. And I skipped the exercises thereafter.
>
> Envious hut-mates promptly nicknamed me "Lucky."
> And what happened to me in the way of discipline? Nothing.
> It might not pay to mess with the Personnel Sergeant Major who has control over every soldier's records in the outfit, from lowly private to the colonel [Miscellaneous Still Papers, "Names"].

Still enlisted as a private in the Army Air Force on March 10, 1942; by June he was a corporal; by July a sergeant; finally, when he was honorably discharged in September of 1945, he was a Technical Sergeant Major. The explanation for his rapid rise in rank could have been his maturity; most of the recruits were in their twenties while he was 36 years old, had three college degrees as well as three published books. Still never hesitated to use his brains and experience to work the military system to his benefit. His personnel job brought with it knowledge, and that meant power. In a way, he was his own boss, and he claimed that he was always telling officers what he would and would not do. Certainly he was no ordinary soldier. He never saw action on the battlefield, and he spent little time in basic training because he was always needed at headquarters for some kind of desk work. In that sense, he was lucky.

He was a lucky soldier in another way as well. Still used his time in the army to see the world. Although he had traveled some in the U.S., he had never been outside the country until he boarded the *Acquitania* on September 20, 1942, on his way to Cape Town. He served most of his time on the Gold Coast Colony of Africa (now Ghana), but he grabbed, and sometimes cleverly created, opportunities to travel whenever possible. One December, he made a trip to Palestine and Egypt, writing of the experience to his father in a letter which was published in his hometown newspaper. The following excerpts from this letter show his poetic powers of perception and his appreciation for the chance to experience ancient sites:

Staff Sergeant James Still Tells of Trip to Holy Land

> I walked the Via Dolorosa to Calvary; I entered King Solomon's quarry, a cave under the city, where milk white marble is still mined, as in ancient times; I went to the Mount of Olives, the Garden of Gethsemane; I saw Zion, the Valley of Jehosaphat, Valley of Kedron, Tyropoeon Valley, Mount Moriah, Mount Scopias, and went in and out of the various gates, the Damascus Gate, Golden Gate, Jaffa Gate, Herod Gate, Dung Gate....
>
> On another day I traveled with a group through the Province of Samaria

> to Galilee. We stopped in the Plain of Esdraelon and our guide informed us that in a special sense this plain was the Key to the World. No other place has had so many decisive conflicts....
>
> We drove on to the old Roman city of Tiberius, on the Sea of Galilee. A retired missionary led us to his porch over-hanging the sea and pointed out the places of interest. Somewhere thereabout Jesus walked on the water, and there he fed the five thousand, there were the cliffs before us where the Gadarene swine plunged into the sea, there rose the "Mount of Beatitudes."
> ...
> At the end of seven days, I enplaned for Egypt, and checked in at the casual section of an Army camp in the desert — a camp of tents, sand, more sand, and at night, stars. I spent four days in Cairo, returning to the camp at night, revisited the Pyramids, King Tut's funerary objects and the Old Kingdom and Middle Kingdom relics in the Museum of Egyptian Antiquities... [Cadle Collection].

It was in the army that James Still began to realize his passion for traveling the world, an appetite he indulged many times during the next half century.

One last story of his army luck recounts his return from Cairo to his base camp. In this adventure, which he told me in 1998, he was lucky to survive. You will notice the tone of urgency, fear, and confusion here, so different from the more poetic, documentary feel of the published letter above.

> We were on a C-46, a two-engine plane going down the Nile and all of a sudden one of the motors stalled. And we started falling. You don't have any pressurized cabin and you know it — you think your heart's going to burst. The radio boy came out; then here came the copilot and the pilot. They were white as sheets. They said the radio instructions told them not to turn back.
>
> We went on one hour and 35 minutes before we saw Khartoum airport. There were two runways, and we saw the ambulances running to keep up with us as we came down. We didn't have the power to come around and land on the runway. We just went across. We put blankets over our heads in case of explosion. I was relieved when we saw the ground. I'll never forget. I was sort of proud of myself. I knew I was going to die — and what I thought about. I tried to speak to this lieutenant next to me, he looked so terrible. I tried to speak to him and I couldn't get my mouth open.
>
> I didn't remember a thing about the actual landing. The next thing I knew there was an MP and he was holding me by the arm, feeding me. Then we were sitting in a room. There were five of us. And we didn't have broken bones or anything. They brought us coffee. We couldn't have told you our names. I'd had a concussion. I didn't know where I was. Then they put us in a carrier and took us to the hospital which was a warehouse with cots in it. A British doctor came after a while and he spoke to each of us. He told us not to talk. In the night somebody came in with a flashlight and called my name. Told us to dress. We did. Took us to the airport and we went west and back to the base. And that's all we ever knew [Interview 8/10/98].

From his visits to exotic places and his position of relative power over people, Still left the army to return to his quiet log home on Dead Mare Branch in Knott County, Kentucky. Though physically weakened by repeated bouts of malaria and dysentery and suffering from what we would now call post-traumatic stress, he was alive. That alone meant he was luckier than many of his fellow soldiers. His army nickname did not seem to carry over after his discharge, but his luck remained.

As in his story of surviving the crash, sometimes good luck brings not happiness but protection from disaster. That narrow escape reminds me of another one. Still had his first adventure in seeing the world when he was a soldier, but it certainly was not his last. In 1972 when he was 66 years old, he began visiting Central America. Each of the 14 trips he made there must have held its own thrills and excitement, but the one that stands out occurred in 1977. Here is the description of his miraculous escape, which he wrote in a letter dated March 2, 1977, to his friend Alfred Perrin at Berea:

> A quick word to let you know I escaped without a scratch from the riot [political disturbance following the election of a new president] in San Salvador, El Salvador February 28. I was suddenly caught up in the well-organized mob, pressed to the wall, practically forced to join. I refused. I was either saved by women who shielded me, or by the arrival of the army. Soldiers fired into the crowd. Some were killed, many wounded. I don't know what happened then. All was confusion. Buses were burned by men with gasoline in bottles, cars overturned and set afire. At one point I was pulled through a metal door, the door barred, and huddled there with a group. When we came out all was not over. Somewhere a man appeared at a corner and said, "Come into the American house." I went in and they kept me for 24 hours and fed me 3 meals. Firing was heard all night. By morning the army was in command, I got back to my hotel, grabbed bag, grabbed taxi, and headed for the airport. The greatest danger might have been the wild ride to the airport through soldiers and tanks [Still Collection, Berea College Library].

One last example of a lucky escape is the story he told in a 1997 interview. He was explaining why he was partial to wisteria vines and was thus allowing them to grow on his log house. This incident does not carry the weight of the others, but it illustrates that luck was always protecting him, even on his home turf of Alabama. Just after returning from his service abroad, Still visited Fairfax, Alabama, and went with his brother, William Comer, to visit family.

> They lived about seven miles out in the country in an old Southern home that had a porch all the way around. When I got back from the army, I went out there with my brother to visit [his wife's] grandparents and we sat on one side of this big porch. High porch. There was a pillar that had fallen out from under the house at one time, a concrete rock in a big bush or hedge. Her uncle sat beside me, he was a big man. As we were sitting there talking, the pole gave way and we fell backward. He fell into the bush and that saved him. As I went down, here was that concrete that would have killed me. Here was a wisteria vine and I managed to hook my arm on that and missed the pillar. They had to take him to the hospital. I was okay, but shaken. That's one of the reasons that wisteria is taking over my place [Interview 7/11/97].

James Still often acknowledged the good fortune of his birth place with the declaration: "There is no substitute for a Southern boyhood." He was born into a rural, agrarian culture of the deep South at a time when people remembered better days before the Civil War as well as the tragedy of that war, but lived in a time when they worked hard and valued their families, neighbors, and churches. Young Jim was the sixth child and the first son born to his parents Lonie Lindsey Still and James Alexander Still, Sr. What the Stills lacked in material wealth, they made up for in kin folk. He had "barrels of relatives, dozens of cousins" (qtd. in Miller 231), but his luckiest early influence came from his sisters.

One important day, while hoeing in the fields, the boy listened as his sister Inez began a story that lasted for what seemed like hours. At first he thought the incident she was relating was true but eventually he realized she was making everything up as she went along. That was Still's first lesson in story telling. From that moment, he claimed, "my horizon expanded into the imaginary. I could make my own tales and did. Oral ones" (Still, "A Man Singing" 7). That was not the full extent of his sisters' positive influence. They also taught him to read by reading to him over and over a little book on Eskimos. The listening child memorized the sentences, then began reciting them as the pages turned. This was the very beginning of his lifelong habit of reading. By the time he was in his nineties, he was reading an average of five or six hours a day.

Storytelling and reading were essential activities for the child and later the man. Public performance and, of course, writing were also keys to his development and his future. Even at a young age, the boy enjoyed the attention of an audience. More than seventy years after it happened, Still told of a childhood event that made him momentarily famous. It was his "first public appearance" and featured his favorite teacher, who was also, in this case, his rescuer:

> Every grade had its day to perform in chapel — and Miss Porterfield taught me a verse by Robert Louis Stevenson as my contribution.
> Our class of first graders marched onto the stage, the principal at one end of the platform, the teacher on the other, we children seated between. Proud parents and students made up the audience.
> My turn came.
> I marched and began.
> Hardly had I spoken "birdie with a yellow bill hopped upon a windowstill" [sic] when squeals and squalls of glee broke loose in the audience, followed by general pandemonium.
> The principal jumped to his feet — mystified.
> But Miss Porterfield guessed the cause and dragged me into the wings.
> I was unbuttoned!
> So — I brought down the house on my first recitation [Miscellaneous Still Papers, "First Reading"].

He was fortunate to have Miss Porterfield for a first grade teacher. On the opening day of school, she had taught him how to spell his name by writing it with chalk on his desk then giving him an ear of corn from which he plucked the kernels and used them to outline the letters. Partly because of the good, hands-on start she gave him, the boy went through school loving to read and write. His least favorite subject as he entered high school was algebra. *Elementary Algebra* by Walter Marsh enjoys the distinction of being the only book that James Still ever hated. Fortunately he found an outlet for his frustration and dislike. He wrote a rhyme in the front of the text:

> Walter R. Marsh
> Ain't got no sense by gosh.
> He wrote crazy lines
> For me to work all the time.
> If he were near and could be seen,
> I'd crock him on the bean [Miscellaneous Still Papers, notes].

The summer following that year at Shawmut High School, Still kept a diary. It was 1922 and he was turning sixteen. In later life, he described this diary as self-centered and uninteresting. Granted, the young man is focused on himself—what teenager isn't—but the writings have value because they reveal his perceptive interaction with his Alabama world, a place he would soon leave. The diary also shows that, as with most young writers, spelling was not his highest priority! In this brief entry, he acknowledges that one day can bring luck of different sorts. His summer job was in a general store, where he had spent the night.

> July 22
> Arose at 6.15 and began to clean up. Was reading The Birmingham News and saw an article I had written printed in it. I was so supprized [sic] I like to have fainted. I had won second prize. Good luck! eh! Came home at 7.15. Fell down when I steped [sic] off of the electric car. Skin [sic] up a little. Bad luck! bah! Retired at 8.30 [Miscellaneous Still Papers, Diary].

James Still was certainly grateful for his Alabama childhood and his large Southern family, but he was also fortunate enough to know when to leave home. His memorable statement while visiting a Hindman class led by Jim Wayne Miller in 1994 said it all: "I was born in Alabama, thank God. And thank God I left." After graduating from high school, he attended Lincoln Memorial University in the Cumberland Gap of Tennessee. The move expanded his boundaries and multiplied his experiences. He was very lucky in making friends and attracting supporters. One person he met early was Dare Redmond from Asheville, North Carolina. Here is the story of their meeting as told by Redmond in his autobiography:

> My advisor signed me up for five courses.... I had to drop something, so decided to drop Latin. There was another boy in Latin class named Thad Brown. He decided to drop Latin too. I didn't know him very well, having had only one class session with him. A few days later I met a boy in the hallway whom I thought was Thad Brown.

> "Hello, Thad," I said.
> The boy said, "That's not my name."
> A day or two later I met him on the stairs and said, "Hello, Thad. Are you glad you dropped Latin?"
> He replied, "You called me that before. My name's not Thad."
> A few days later I was in the Cashier's office when the boy I had mistakenly called Thad walked in. We started talking about my calling him Thad. We left the office together, and became close friends. We graduated together and went to the University of Illinois together. His name was James Still, and he is the closest friend I have ever had [Redmond 15].

Their initial meeting may have been based on a lucky incident of mistaken identity, but the friendship they developed was solid and long-lasting. As is evident in their correspondence, Dare and "Jimmie" (as Dare addressed him) remained close for many years.

While at LMU, Still came under the patronage of a generous donor, Guy Loomis, who supported him through his MA at Vanderbilt and a second bachelor's degree at University of Illinois. Loomis continued to pay him a stipend even after he began working at Hindman as a librarian. Loomis and Still maintained their correspondence until the older man died in 1946, at which time Still received a final check for $500 (worth about $5,000 today). Still enjoyed the generosity of patrons and friends throughout his long life, but in 1927 when "Uncle" Guy Loomis informally adopted Still, whom he addressed as Jimmie, the young man's writing career had not yet begun. Surely there was some luck at work in their meeting.

Everyone who knows the writer James Still realizes his permanent connection to Eastern Kentucky, to the mountains of Appalachia. After he had completed three degrees, two of them financed by Loomis, he was searching everywhere for a job, but in 1931 he had no prospects because of the Depression. What led him to Knott County, Kentucky, can be attributed to a combination of luck and personal connections. His friend from LMU, Don West, was conducting a Bible School there during the summer, and West's brother-in-law, Jack Adams, was running a recreational program for Boy Scouts and baseball teams. Still joined them as a volunteer. Although he would not have known it at the time, he was becoming attached to the place that would be his permanent home. In his autobiographical sketch he describes his experience that summer: "We camped and played ball all summer and I became enamored with the forested mountains, the valley and hollows of this backwoods country, and with the independent and forthright folk" (Still, "A Man Singing" 16).

He was lucky to land in Hindman, but he was also lucky that he found work outside the area's main industry—coal mining—because he suffered from claustrophobia. Instead, he worked in a library at Hindman Settlement School, a perfect job for him because it combined books, children, and sometimes the outdoors. He became a walking librarian, spending one day a week taking boxes of books to the remote schools in the county that had no access to a library.

He might have continued with this job indefinitely except that his calling was to write. When in 1939 his friend, Jethro Amburgey, offered him a two-story log house nine miles from Hindman, Still took the offer because it was a place where he could write full time. Later Amburgey deeded the house to his friend for his lifetime. Some years after that Still became an honorary member of the Amburgey family, and, of course, he was always a member of the Hindman Settlement School family.

Although his ties were strongest with eastern Kentucky, James Still eventually became associated with the entire state. And a Kentucky man's luck is often measured by his success with horses. Still's father had been a horse doctor, so the boy would have grown up around animals, but that does not fully explain Still's "horse sense." One of his stories tells of his affinity for Man O'War, perhaps the most famous racehorse of the twentieth century.

> After retirement, Big Red, as he was affectionately called, spent his last days on a bluegrass farm near Lexington, Kentucky. And had swarms of visitors, particularly during the racing season. I visited him twice during his last years. On the first occasion Big Red was grazing on the well-cropped grass in a sizeable barn lot. And as it was the day following the Derby in Louisville, there were many onlookers. We hung over the fence, many of us, trying to attract his attention by whistling, or tempting him with bunches of grass we pulled outside the fence. I held a bunch, waving it. He lifted his head, swung round and surveyed his audience. He chose me, came and ate my grass, declining all others. But before my head could swell an inch or two, I figured it out. I was the only viewer holding a child in his arms [Still Miscellaneous Papers, "Man O'War"].

Perhaps it was the child that made the horse choose him, but I prefer to think that the horse felt the magnetism of the man holding the child, and maybe the grass played a part too, especially if it included a sprig of wisteria.

That time Still was chosen by a winning horse in Kentucky, but another time, he chose the winners in a day at the races in Saratoga, New York. It is a truly lucky man who knows when to bet and when to quit. One day while Still and his close friend, Jim Wayne Miller, were attending the writers' workshop at Yaddo in August of 1983, they decided to go to the races. Still had been to Yaddo five times before and had frequented the races, but this was his first time to bet. Later, Miller wrote up the events of the day and published them in the *Troublesome Creek Times*, but this account was written by Still himself in a letter to Cratis Williams dated August 17, 1983:

> The Saratoga Race Track, the oldest in the country, adjoins the Yaddo estate and some afternoons we walk out to see the last three races of the day. Last Saturday was the 114th running of The Travers, the race that put Man O'War on the map. Betting has no interest for me but "When in Rome ... etc." I put two bucks on a horse I'd never heard of. The Travers, called the "graveyard of champions," led me to pass over the winner of the Belmont who was competing. So I won. Bet on no other race....

> Three days ago I went again to the races with Jim Wayne Miller. I bet on five races, and won in four of them. To Jim this was a sensation. "Cleaned-up" in one of them. Came away with a bank roll of the size to choke a small-enough calf.... Was this a fluke? So I went alone to the track yesterday, bet on five races, and won four! Unbelievable. Not so much money this time as the odds weren't great. But still a bundle. Of a size to choke a still smaller calf. So ends my betting days at the races. I don't expect to return. It becomes a vagary in the life of one Jim Still [Cratis Williams Collection].

We could find other examples of such vagaries or luck in James Still's life. In 1953, for example, he won $10 (would be $75 today) in a Dial Soap Discovery contest. Maybe the amount is insignificant, but Still remembered it. That he could recall such detail and tell such excellent stories up until his death at age 94 also gives evidence of his exceptional good luck in life. Some would say luck is not arbitrary. It does not necessarily come to those who avoid black cats — James Still loved cats of all color — or to those who stay clear of the number 13 — his box number at the Bath post office for years. Luck does not result from hanging horseshoes in the correct position, though for years Still did have a horseshoe above the entrance to his log house. Most likely luck is the result of diligence, preparation, common sense, and courage. Was "Lucky" really or figuratively James Still's middle name? If asked, he might have responded in his characteristic way: "No matter."

Regardless of the role luck played in his life, James Still was a man of good fortune. He was never wealthy, but he lived a rich life; his writings were never best sellers, but they have endured and still bring pleasure and insight to many. He had full use of the land and house he loved. He made strong connections with many families and finally adopted his own; he benefited from the company and support of friends, but he also enjoyed his privacy. Most importantly he shared his performances, his stories, his sense of humor, and his positive spirit with those who knew him. I am grateful that through his writings he continues to share his good fortune with us all.

Works Cited

Miller, Jim Wayne. "Madly to Learn." In *The Fort to the Future: Educating the Children of Kentucky*. Ed. Edwina Doyle, Ruby Layson, and Anne Thompson. Lexington: Kentucky Images, 1987. 230–43.

Redmond, Dare. "The Autobiography of Dare Vincent Redmond." Courtesy of Alan Redmond, Kingsport, TN.

Still, James. Letter to Alfred Perrin. Still Collection: Box 1, Correspondence. Special Collections and Archives, Hutchins Library. Berea College, Berea, KY.

_____. Letter to Cratis Williams. Cratis Dearl Williams Papers No. 102: Box 19 Folder 1D James Still. Belk Library. Appalachian State University, Boone, NC.

_____. "A Man Singing to Himself: An Autobiographical Essay." *From the Mountain,*

From the Valley: New and Collected Poems. Ed. Ted Olson. Lexington: University Press of Kentucky. 2001. 5–24.

_____. Miscellaneous Papers. Personal diary; Rough transcripts or notes for NPR: "First Reading," "The Only Book I Ever Hated," "Man O' War." Papers stored in Hindman, KY. Accessed summer 2002. The materials have now been added to the James Still Collection, Margaret King Library, University of Kentucky, Lexington, KY.

_____. Personal interview. Lexington, KY. 11 July 1997.

_____. Personal interview. Lexington, KY. 10 August 1998.

_____. "Staff Sergeant James Still Tells of Trip to Holy Land." Newspaper clipping in the Dean Cadle Collection. Folder 12. Exact date and title unknown: Probably Dec 1943 or 1944 in *Chattahoochee Valley Times*. Margaret King Library, University of Kentucky, Lexington, KY.

_____. *The Wolfpen Notebooks: A Record of Appalachian Life.* Lexington: University Press of Kentucky, 1991.

Sgt. James Still's Gold Castings

Jack D. Ellis

The James Still Room at Morehead State University holds many of the famed chronicler of Appalachia's manuscripts, photographs, documents, books, poems, and personal memorabilia. At one time among those items were a dozen or more small figurines about 3 or 4 inches tall. They were cast from high grade gold ore in the Ashanti Kingdom of Africa (which today would be located in central Ghana). But needless to say those objects are intrinsically valuable. While those African art objects were housed in the James Still Room at Morehead State University, they were securely locked in a glass display case, and very few people knew of the gold content in the display.

Each of those artistic figurines represented one aspect of the daily life in a small African village. Some were women in colorful head gear cooking over an open fire. Others were children playing nearby. Also, there were men carrying fresh-killed game or making weapons, while others were hunters carrying their spears in a ready position. But it was an extremely valuable display, not just because the figures were made of gold, but because of their value to the art history and culture of that nation.

Of course, the big question everyone asked was "How did a librarian, writer, and teacher from eastern Kentucky come into possession of those small rare art objects from deep in the heart of Africa?" That is a story in itself.

James Still and this writer are both Army Air Corps veterans of World War II. I was also the library director at Morehead State University while he was the writer in residence. Many times we would discuss our similar experiences during that conflict. In the 1970s during the construction of the new Library Tower addition at Morehead State University, it became necessary to move the James Still Room from the first floor to the second floor. Later it was moved to the fifth floor of the tower where it is now located.

As library director, I supervised the move, making sure everything was secure and accessible. Professor Still and I personally unlocked the case and carried the small gold artistic figures from the first floor to the second floor. They were then placed back in a new case and securely locked. It was during that move that James Still told me the following story about how he came into possession of the tiny African art objects.

Many people were not aware that the quiet, scholarly, mild mannered Mr. Still was a crew member on a B-17 bomber stationed in North Africa. He served almost four years in World War II with two and one-half years overseas duty. Much of the time between missions was boring with little to do. However, it was during that time between missions that crew members would gas up their planes and practice flying, navigation, emergency landing and survival training. On one navigational and survival training mission, they flew south into the heart of Africa.

James Still in Army Air Force uniform, 1945. Courtesy the Hindman Settlement School. Used with permission.

There they spotted a large clearing in the jungle and made a simulated crash landing. While on the ground the crew, fully armed, began exploring the terrain to determine how they might best survive in those conditions. It was during that time they came upon a small peaceful village of the Ashanti Tribe in the middle of a jungle.

As GIs were prone to do during World War II, they bartered with the natives for souvenirs. (This writer did the same thing many times in Europe during the World War II. We called it "scrounging.") It was in that way that James Still came into possession of those valuable artistic creations from the Ashanti Kingdom. But that is certainly *not* the end of his story.

Young Sergeant Still shipped his souvenirs home safely. However, after the war ended in 1945, he was able to return home by coming back across the Pacific. Many GIs were able to do that in order to say they had been around the world. When he landed in San Francisco, the first thing the young sergeant and former librarian did was visit the San Francisco Public Library. The first thing he saw as he entered the lobby of the library was a lighted, locked display case flanked by a guard. Upon further examination, James was shocked to see it contained one single gold object from the Ashanti Kingdom of Africa.

After examining the piece he asked the guard if he could see the library director, and James asked the director if that was an art figurine from the Ashanti Kingdom. The director assured him that it was, and that it was a rare and valuable object. Then Sergeant Still said, "I have more than a dozen of these things at home in eastern Kentucky." At first the skeptical director doubted his story, but upon further questioning, he decided that the GI knew what he was talking about. Then he asked Mr. Still if he could visit Hindman, Kentucky, and see the collection for himself. Of course the young sergeant graciously said, "Yes, come anytime."

A few weeks later the San Francisco library director came to the small Hindman Settlement School to examine the tiny original art figurines. He authenticated each piece, cataloged it, photographed it, and registered it at the National Museum of Art. That was done in case they should ever be stolen, so that they could be identified.

James Still, the quiet, modest humble librarian, teacher, author, and African art collector, would later become a giant in the literary world of Appalachia. He was also a professor and writer in residence at Morehead State University until his retirement. Following his retirement, and in honor of the now famous Tuskegee Airmen of World War II, Mr. Still placed those African art objects at Tuskegee Institute in his native Alabama. There they are available for everyone to see and appreciate the art and culture of Africa.

Both Ends of a Walnut Log: The Correspondence of James Still and Jesse Stuart

JAMES M. GIFFORD *and* ERIN KAZEE

In May 1982, Jesse Stuart suffered a stroke that left him comatose for the final twenty months of his life. For most of that time, he was a patient in the Jo-Lin Health Care Facility in Ironton, Ohio, only fifteen miles from his home in W-Hollow. His wife came to see him each day, along with many other caring visitors.

That August, shortly after Stuart's seventy-sixth birthday, his longtime friend James Still visited. "Jesse, this is old Jim. I've come to see you. You look good," he said as he proceeded to reminisce about their shared experiences of almost sixty years. When James Still spoke, Mrs. Stuart remembered, Jesse did not open his eyes, but his eyelids moved. No one knows what's behind the unresponsive veil of the comatose. Perhaps Jesse was taking in all that was said and replaying, in his mind's eye, thousands of images of the man who had been pictured next to him in LMU's 1929 yearbook, *The Railsplitter*.[1]

The lives of these two great Appalachian writers had run a similar, often intersecting course. They were less than a month apart in age: Still was born July 16, 1906, in Lafayette, Alabama; and Jesse was born August 8, 1906, in W-Hollow, Greenup County, Kentucky. Their rural boyhoods eventually brought them both to Lincoln Memorial University, and they graduated together in 1929. In the early 1930s, they attended Vanderbilt University, where Still received an M.A. degree. After earning a degree in library science from the University of Illinois, Still served as a librarian of the Hindman Settlement School in Knott County, Kentucky. Jesse Stuart taught and administrated in schools in the Greenup County area, traveled, lectured, and wrote. Both men received Guggenheim fellowships and numerous honorary degrees. As the years went by, these two mountain poets, who lived only 120 miles apart, rarely saw one another, but they maintained a lifelong friendship through their correspondence.

Page from *The Railsplitter*, Lincoln Memorial University yearbook, featuring photographs of James Still (on left) and Jesse Stuart (on right), 1929. Courtesy the Hindman Settlement School. Used with permission.

They parted "one cold ... morning in the wee small hours" of June 1929. Four years later, after drifting around the country for almost two years, James was back on his farm in Fairfax, Alabama, working, fishing, and "writing a trifle and reading a great deal." Although Still liked small town life, he allowed that it could be "tedious, gossipy, etherizing," and the people "dull, oftentimes insufferable." When the boredom pressed too hard, he "hit the rails and roads for a few days" and returned refreshed with new ideas and enthusiasms.[2]

James' and Jesse's early letters were filled with news of their mutual LMU friends and their post-collegiate lives; they also betrayed budding literary aspirations. The young men encouraged one another and understood that they benefitted from the other's strengths. James wished that he could visit with Jesse, who was "one of the best conversationalists" he had ever known.[3] Jesse, in turn, wrote:

> What are you doing in the way of writing lately, Still? Let me know, I'm interested. I know you are working. That is an advantage you have over me — a harder worker. Keep it up.... James I wish I had you here. This would be a paradise for us. My work is so easy and the children are so worthwhile that I give them all I have and love them so.[4]

A few months later, Jesse wrote again how much he missed his old friend and their robust conversations. He appreciated James for treating their classmate Creola Cambell so well and reported that she "dearly praised the ground [James] stepped on." She had also told Jesse "a few secrets" that he did not tell James when the two boys "were running around together" the previous summer.[5]

The years passed quickly as both men consumed themselves with their careers, their writing, and their youth. "Imagine you have changed considerably," Still mused to Stuart in 1933. "People here say I am 'the same Jimmy' as always. I look older [and] my hair is not as thick as it sometimes-once-was." In the decade after they left LMU, their letters suggested both professional growth and greater personal maturity.[6]

Their letters also reflected their personalities. Stuart's were almost always handwritten in a semi-hieroglyphic style that required a combination of careful analysis and guesswork to decipher. They flowed from his pen like water from an artesian well and often brimmed with emotional commentary on his personal life, as well as his literary efforts. Where Still typically offered a concise report of his life and publications, along with his esteem for his friend's most recent accomplishment, Jesse was given to confess his many loves. "Boy, I'm telling you I'm living my youth," he wrote.[7] He openly detailed his romances with Elizabeth Hale, Marion Ives, Charlotte Salmon, anonymous Italian and French women, and eventually the woman he married, Naomi Deane Norris. "All of my life, James Still, I've been in love," he insisted.[8]

Never reluctant to share his opinions on almost any subject, Jesse frankly advised James to let his hair grow longer to cover his prominent ears; but he complimented his friend for "the finest looking brown eyes I've ever seen." He also lauded Still's great intellect, saying, "You should be proud of yourself."[9]

James Still's letters were overall more formal and often typewritten; they were more polished, more considered, and less personal. When he did eschew the typewriter, his missives were still neat and well thought out. Jesse complimented him, saying, "If I had a handwriting like yours, I would never type a letter."[10]

The two men were both concerned with image — Jesse because he was often in the public eye, and James because of a meticulous and naturally formal nature. In their letters, however, an openness crept into their discussions. Jesse, usually saturated with external swagger and bravado, shared his self-doubt. "I often think how far I am behind you but I'm just waiting like a strong man does to finish a race," he ruminated just months after finishing his undergraduate career.[11] Almost a decade later, he was still unsure of his future: "You know, Jimmie, I'm liable to never do anything worthwhile, and again I'm liable to shoot the moon."[12] Similarly, Still, normally decorous and reserved, occasionally allowed himself a more impassioned discourse with Jesse.[13]

From their youth onward, they consoled one another on writer's block and near misses with the publishing industry. "Boy if we lose, let us be good losers," Jesse pressed.[14] They continually reassured one another of their formidable talents, even well after timorous youth had passed. In the early 1950s, James expressed some doubt about his popularity, and Jesse comforted him, "You are wrong when you say people, not many, have read your books. I know better."[15]

Their early publication careers also ran parallel courses. Between 1934 and 1941, Stuart published five major books: *Man with a Bull-Tongue Plow* (poetry, 1934); *Head O' W-Hollow* (stories, 1936); *Beyond Dark Hills* (autobiography, 1938); *Trees of Heaven* (novel, 1940); and *Men of the Mountains* (stories, 1941). During that same period, Still published *Hounds on the Mountain* (poems, 1937); *River of Earth* (a novel that is considered an American classic, 1940); and *On Troublesome Creek* (stories, 1941). They also published stories and poems in major American periodicals. Not surprisingly, their shared success bred some antagonistic feelings in Jesse, whose agent told him in 1937: "Now that James Still is coming into some prominence, maybe the magazines will feel that they can't give space to so much Kentucky material. But we shall see."[16]

Despite this warning, their writing careers began in concert, rather than competition. During their undergraduate years, Jesse and James were part of an informal group of writers that also included Roland Carter, Louise McCamey, Winnie Palmer, Edith Jones, and several others. They met in Avery Hall for a session of free-spirited discussions with their spontaneous mentor, Professor Harry Harrison Kroll. "Once we were together time had no meaning for us," remembered Kroll. "We'd read, talk, discuss, argue." Appreciation, amateur criticism, and support were the coins of exchange.[17]

The Still-Stuart letters bespoke their zeal for writing and ambitions to publish. Jesse suggested a "contract" that they only write after they placed something in a "reputable magazine," but of course they relapsed frequently and wrote to one another regardless.[18] As they began to publish more prolifically, they continued to offer congratulations, or to send clippings from magazine or newspaper articles.[19] They also discussed their various work duties.

In the summer of 1932, Still had worked for the Congregational Board in Knott County, Kentucky, and he had enjoyed his brief stay in the eastern Kentucky mountains. In May 1933, he was back home in Alabama and looking for work. He had a Kentucky high school teaching certificate and hoped to get a job in a Kentucky school or library. "If you suspect a school needing such a person," he wrote to Jesse, "I would appreciate the tip off."[20]

Three months later, Still was "positively oozing satisfaction from every pore," because he had accepted the position of librarian at the Hindman Settlement School. He left Fairfax, Alabama, on August 26, because the school year commenced on September 4, and there was "work to be done before school opens." Now that they were both employed, they postponed a hiking trip they had planned to North Carolina. Jesse invited James to visit him at his home, and James invited Jesse to visit Hindman and Knott County.[21]

By 1934, Stuart and Still had settled into the routine of their Kentucky jobs, but there was nothing routine about Jesse's life. *Man with a Bull-Tongue Plow* was published that year, and James Still sent a letter of sincere felicitations, asking for an autograph "at first opportunity." Jesse received so much press that Still began a clipping file of "blurbs, criticisms and mention of the book" at the Hindman Settlement School library. He nominated Stuart's book for the Pulitzer Prize in poetry, and Jesse was deeply grateful, although he thought he had no chance of winning. It mattered more to Jesse that Still, who was honest and had high standards, felt the book warranted such acclaim. "You are the type of man," he wrote, "who would not send in the name of a book you did not think deserving regardless if your own brother wrote it." Jesse added that he was thrilled for Still's own poetic successes: "It looks to me like you are on top of the world. I feel proud that you are doing what you are a-doing."[22]

A pall settled over James Still's life that autumn when his youngest brother fell ill with dengue fever and eventually died from it. He spent a week at home and was unable to write for the rest of year.[23] Nonetheless, he and Jesse kept corresponding with words of advice and support. Mr. Still commented that the reviews of Jesse's books in *Nation* and *New Republic* "were constructive and should be of some future use," but *Time* and *Writer* "took a dirty crack at you." James was "immensely proud" of Jesse and offered to share his clipping file.[24] "You must remember this, James Still," Jesse responded, "life is before us now and we are young. We have the fire in us now and it is time to flame and fight. Tomorrow—the embers and ashes."[25] Always eager to see his old friend, James ended his last correspondence of 1934 hoping to "arrange a meeting" with Jesse in Ashland or Cincinnati over the Christmas holidays.[26]

By 1935, Jesse was enjoying national recognition in the wake of the publication of *Man with a Bull-Tongue Plow*. James, keen to learn of his friend's achievements, had been using the *Reader's Guide* to keep up with Jesse's rapid succession of recent publications. "The way you are forging ahead pleases me," Still wrote. "In a few years I expect you to be as established poetically as the democratic party appears to be established politically." That winter, Still spent a morning in the Cabell County Public Library in Huntington, West Virginia, "reading [Jesse's] publications for the past three years.... Most of them [he] had heard about but never before had a chance to see." Still promised a follow-up letter with more detailed comments.[27]

The same themes continued in their 1936 letters.[28] They often lamented how many years had gone by without seeing one another, despite their close proximity. Jesse declared it a "shame" and reminded his long-serving pen-pal that he was "as welcome as the flowers in April."[29] Still remarked that Stuart's letters were "dynamite. Sometimes I think you have a dual personality. Jesse

Stuart the letter writer never seems like Jesse Stuart the poet."[30] Years before, Jesse had recognized a similar dichotomy in James: "I see you in one strategy of life a mere child—in another I see you strong." Still, he said, could be shy, but was also a natural leader and a hard worker, for which Jesse commended and envied him.[31]

Their ongoing correspondence almost always mentioned their former LMU classmate Don West, whose revolutionary path had long diverged from their own. In 1936, Still shared with Stuart an excerpt from an article Don had written for a New York newspaper. In it, Don spent seven to eight hundred words rehashing a recent conversation he had with James Taylor Adams, in which they

> got off into a discussion on mountain literature and Southern writers. We agreed that John Fox, Jr., had always taken sides with the coal operators in his novels. Jesse Stuart was egotistically sentimental, and smitten with nostalgia for digging up old ghosts of ancestors. James Still, in his pathetically hungry desire to clutch fame to his bosom, was clawing star dust in his own eyes—all hiding the realism, the misery, the struggle that seethes all around them.

Far from being offended, Still found it to be an "interesting commentary since it came from Don"; he enjoyed Don's explosive prose. The letter was signed

> All best wishes,
> Your friend, and Don's friend,
> James Still.[32]

Later that year, during a lecture at a Kentucky college, West accused Still of "[tending] to idealize and idolize" and of being entrenched in "the old romantic approach." "I don't mind these things being said," Still conceded reasonably. "It is just that I don't think Don should bother to discuss my writing one way or the other in public. His idea, I think, is to make it sound as small and worthless as possible."[33]

James Still was somewhat amused by Don West's observations, but Jesse Stuart was infuriated. On January 30, 1936, he responded to Still with a one-page "closely-typed" letter salted with anger, vulgarity, and profanity. He certainly did not agree with Don's assessment of their place in mountain literature. Jesse had a collection of short stories coming out in March. "See if it's sentimental. See. Have Don to see. Yes. Don's got to change his mind about a hell of a lot of things." His fury with Don West thoroughly and colorfully articulated, Jesse commented on a poem that James Still had recently published in *The Atlantic Monthly*. "I feel it," he said. "I could see what you saw in your words. It's damn excellent poetry, James.... I say this without sentimentality too. Your poetry is well done and marching, marching. It is well-informed—clean, strong! I wish Don were doing half as well."[34]

Jesse pronounced Don a failure as a teacher, preacher, poet, and labor organizer. "He couldn't get action enough from the church and the schoolroom. He wanted fame—crazy—ambitious as hell for it. Big boy! Head of the parade!" Don's poetry, said Stuart, was "sentimental mush," and his efforts in labor organizing resulted from "the sweat and blood of other men's labors."[35]

And, as was often the case when Jesse built up some emotional steam, he exploded in an indirect physical challenge. "Hell, I'm not afraid of Don West.... Don't think I can't fight back and two ways," and he reminded Still of how he had dispatched Henry Willis, his knife-wielding assailant in the LMU cafeteria kitchen. He was prepared to fight physically or with words. "When I see Don I've got a lot to have out with him.... You ought to be around."[36] West visited Stuart a year later and James Still was "curious as hell" about their meeting. "Did you cuss each other to pieces, or, somehow, was everything alright?"[37]

"It's hell to write you a letter," Still observed. "What I need is to be sitting on one end of a walnut log with you at the other end balancing your side of the conversation." He concluded his letter with sentiments that should pass between all true friends: "I rejoice in your success. I am glad for you."[38] At the end of 1936, he expressed another familiar refrain: "Why can't we get together some time for a long talk. ... after January 1st I can get over to Lexington some weekend.... Jesse, I'm mighty proud of all you've done—and in so short a time."[39]

In February 1937, Still consoled Stuart because he had "barely missed getting one of the Book-of-the-Month Club Awards." Still also complimented him on his radio interview over NBC in December 1936. "Though the static was pretty bad on [his] battery set," Still reported that Jesse's voice "was clear as a bell on January morning." "Had I been in your place," he confided, "I'd have been scared speechless." He added praise for Stuart's poem "Sonnets for Summer" in *Harper's*. "I still like your poetry better than your short stories. Can't help it, Jesse. Don't stop writing poetry. There's something so fresh, so honest-to-God about your poems. You are the only poet who can make me hear corn stalks rustling in the wind."[40]

That April, James Still, dutiful librarian, was clipping through a pile of newspapers when he stumbled across a headline about Jesse Stuart's Guggenheim Fellowship. "Of all the good things that have happened to you during the past few years," Still wrote, "this has pleased me most. I am happy that this honor has come to you." Always eager to see his old friend, Still also reported that he would be in Louisville for the annual meeting of the Kentucky Education Association (KEA), and invited Jesse to visit or to call him.[41]

Jesse did not get to attend the KEA convention that year. He did write back, though. "Think, Jimmie—I get to go to Scotland! I can hardly wait.... Not even a book acceptance has meant so much to me, [because] my people came from Scotland." He also reminded "Jimmie" that he missed him: "I'd give ten dollars to see you—shake your hand and talk with you."[42]

"Well, Jess, where will you be this summer? Abroad," James echoed back a month later. "Wish I could talk with you before you go away. In the last picture I saw of you, you looked as big as one side of a meat house, and strong as a bull." He planned to be in Ashland on Saturday, May 29, 1937, and hoped to chart a visit to W-Hollow. Excited to talk about Jesse's forthcoming book, James wrote, "I'm expecting *Beyond Dark Hills* to have a good sale. Have had an order in for a first edition about 2 months now."[43]

Normally easy-going and unflappable, Still became furious over a letter he received from Jesse in May 1937. In his vitriolic reply, he demanded:

> Where in the hell did West get the idea I voted for Browder? It's a [profanity deleted] lie! Hell no—I didn't vote Browder or any other Red. I voted for Franklin D. Roosevelt, and I don't give a [profanity deleted] who knows it. By God if your letter doesn't read like you believed him. Surely to hell you know me better than that. West spoke against me, he wrote me up for an ambitious fool in the communist paper, and now he says I *voted* communist last election. Hell, Jesse, what next?
>
> Mad as the devil,
Jimmy.

Use postal card enclosed to tell me you got this letter. I want to be sure.[44]

Such rifts in their friendship were rare and short-lived. Jesse corresponded with James while he was in Scotland; and for the remainder of the decade, they continued to follow and applaud one another. Upon the publication of *Beyond Dark Hills*, James sent Jesse a brief postcard: "1939 is yours! Best wishes, James Still."[45]

Jesse married in October 1939, and James came across "the good news in *Time*" two months later. He was "mightily pleased" and sent congratulations to Jesse and a "warm greeting" to his wife, whom he hoped to meet some day.[46] Meanwhile, Jesse promoted Still to his publishers and colleagues. "I believe in you," he said. "I shall stand by you. Glad to have you for my friend. You do excellent poetry and good prose."[47]

Their correspondence became erratic, but "in spite of silence," James kept abreast of Jesse's progress. "You are a one-man folk movement," he declared. "I am filled with admiration for your literary energy, spontaneity, talent." And then he offered flattering commentary on *A Ride with Huey the Engineer*, which he had recently re-read. "It's a damn good story. No other author in America could have written that one."[48]

Still concluded his last letter of the decade by announcing that he had taken a leave of absence from Hindman Settlement School and that he was not sure he'd return. "Politics over there rottener than a coop of dead buzzards."[49] This was another concern he shared with Stuart, who had recently been "exiled" from teaching in Greenup County due, among other things, to the school district's politics.

During the 1930s, the good spirit of the Stuart-Still correspondence did not suffer from their increasing time restraints. But Jesse had a competitive side that often turned spiteful. In 1940, for example, he had suggested to LMU president Stewart McClelland that Still had been critical of LMU's forthcoming speaker Carl Sandburg. McClelland apparently saw the duplicity in Jesse's efforts and solved the conflict by having Jesse preside over the meeting and James introduce Sandburg. "That will avoid any embarrassment. If I judge Sandburg correctly, he doesn't give a 'tinker's tap' about criticism anyway."[50] Just weeks prior to this incident, however, Jesse had written Still, "Let's renew our old friendship."[51]

By the early 1940s, distinct differences in Stuart's and Still's approach to writing had begun to drive a professional wedge between them. Jesse wrote like a man whose hair was on fire and showed little interest in revision and editing. James Still's standard was perfection, and he lavished great care on each poem and story before he sent it out for publication. Critics said that Still used the English language like a precision instrument, the type of praise rarely accorded Jesse. James, however, refused to cultivate literary comparisons between himself and his former classmate, and steadfastly avoided newspaper interviews, radio interviews, and speeches to literary clubs. He was a shy and truly modest man who believed that his record of accomplishment would speak for itself. Stuart found this philosophy ridiculous and self-defeating. Nevertheless, they did not cease to "rejoice" in each other's success. Still published a short story in the *Saturday Evening Post*, to which Jesse responded:

> "I Love My Rooster" is the best short story you have ever written and one of the finest stories in the American language. Don't let anybody tell you differently. I never saw so many angles in a short story and so fully developed as in that story.[52]

Both men had established themselves as successful writers before they entered military service in World War II. Stuart was eager to serve, and he joined the Navy. He did boot-training at Great Lakes Naval Training Station, where he was made a seaman 2nd class. He was later commissioned Lt. in the United States Naval Reserve and served in a writer's unit during the war. In the strange and inconsistent way that often characterizes military duty assignments, the belligerent and pugnacious Stuart, a strapping 200-pounder with much fighting experience, manned a desk in Washington, D.C., from 1944 to 1945. Still, much smaller and a true gentleman, was the oldest man drafted from Knott County and served with the Army in North Africa. Throughout the war, Jesse sent brief letters to James, updating him on news of mutual friends and inquiring of his health and safety.[53]

During the late 1920s and throughout the 1930s, the Stuart-Still friendship had been forged in the fires of shared difficulties and mutual ambitions. By the 1940s, it was apparent to both of them that they had less in common. They were almost polar opposites in personality, philosophy, and precision; and, not surprisingly, the years ahead brought a gradual change in their relationship. They remained cordial, but the avid bond of their youth was replaced by mature respect and distance.

After World War II, Stuart continued to publish at a frenetic pace. James Still, however, observed that upon his return to civilian life, he sat "for months ... in the door of [his] log house and could not arouse interest in things [he] had done before." He eventually began to write again, but his pace was slower, more deliberate — all in all, less enthusiastic. He had become a "changed man" after the war.[54] Jesse suffered the same postwar malaise, complaining in 1946 that he didn't have any book coming out or any ideas. Despite these doldrums, Jesse once again offered James an invitation for a visit and promised that he and Deane would "be glad to see you, glad to ... talk, laugh."[55]

Their busy lives took them in opposite directions, but they kept in touch. James took the liberty of submitting an essay Jesse had written, "What America Means to Me," for the Freedom Award. Jesse wrote back, thanking him profusely and assuring him, "It would never have happened if it had not been for you."[56] Jesse returned the favor a few years later, recommending James Still's work to *Good Reading*, a book "used in many of the nation's finest colleges and universities."[57]

In 1952, while lecturing at Morehead State University, Jesse spied his friend and former classmate in the audience. He had not seen James Still for twenty-three years! Later that evening they ate together at the president's home and had a pleasant reunion. "When I first saw you ... I couldn't quite believe it was you," Jesse said. "You looked very much the same, only a little taller. But your eyes were your give away. They didn't sparkle; they shone brilliantly." He encouraged James to accept President Spain's offer of employment at Morehead State because he felt that Still would relate well to a student body that came from eastern Kentucky. "These are your people," Jesse said. "No one knows them better than you."[58]

As the '50s and '60s passed, their correspondence became more impersonal. It was clear that they could no longer chat freely, balancing at the ends of a walnut log, although Jesse had admonished after their meeting at Morehead, "Twenty-three years must not pass again before we see each other.... You have and have always had an invitation to visit us."[59]

A tension grew up between them, perhaps the result of professional rivalry and the sting of a bygone friendship. Some of this disquiet was expressed when Jesse became angry after a "reliable source" told him that James Still had said, "Jesse can't write a good sentence." To that, he responded:

> You asked me about James Still and our relationship. Yes, I went to Lincoln Memorial University.... I went to school there with him three years. We graduated in the small class and Still and Stuart are on the same page in that old annual. He went his way at LMU and I went mine. He had his friends at LMU and I had mine.... I thought of him as being a very odd person, never too friendly and a little distant. I tried for all the literary prizes that LMU offered

and never won any. Still won these. But when papers in a literary contest were sent to Duke University to be judged ... I got first prizes in poetry, short story, and my article was taken for a short story and I got second prize on it.... I had no contact with James Still while at Vanderbilt.... I doubt that James Still has ever corresponded with anyone more than a postcard.... There is, perhaps, a reason why James Still likes seclusion and found it in the mountains of Kentucky.[60]

Jesse knew some of his statements were not true. They *did* have mutual friends at LMU and both were part of Harry Harrison Kroll's informal writers' group. Kroll's informal writers' group. Beyond sharing their writing with one another, they also took "little exploration trip[s]" together. "On at least one occasion, they spent too long ambling through the brush of Poor Valley and could not get out before nightfall; they had to stay "all night on the hard floor of an old shed."[61] James Still wrote Jesse Stuart dozens of kind and plauditory letters over more than fifty years. And Jesse knew Still had taken professional stands for him, once resigning from *Mountain Life and Work* over a review of Stuart's book *Foretaste of Glory*.[62] Moreover, Jesse himself frequently reminded James of how "amazingly similar" they were in their politics and views of literary trends, "writing and writers."[63] So Jesse's remarks are somewhat baffling in light of his personal communications with Still during this same period.

Since Stuart and Still rarely saw one another, it is not surprising that their relationship cooled; but each maintained a genuine concern for the other's welfare, regardless of whatever image they projected to the outside world. In 1954, Jesse invited James to their Lincoln Memorial University class reunion.[64] Two years later, he asked him, "Write me something. Tell me something about yourself," and inquired as to James' opinions of various current affairs.[65] Throughout the decade and the rest of their lives, they swapped books and reading suggestions.[66] Jesse, a much more public figure, was always pressed for time and often did not have the opportunity to read as voraciously as James. He relished Still's thoughtful opinions and recommendations. They also sent copies of their own works. As late as 1975, Jesse gladly, but "unexpectedly," received an autographed copy of one of Still's books.[67]

As Jesse Stuart and James Still grew in professional stature, many scholars and journalists wrote about them; their perspectives on one another proved valuable. Dr. Hensley Woodbridge maintained a comprehensive bibliography of Jesse Stuart. In 1960, Stuart asked Still to write a reminiscence of their "days and associations at LMU ... for a cold factual bibliography." Jesse asked no one else to provide this information, because he wanted to acknowledge the bond of "students who struggled together." Their creative writing professor, Harry Harrison Kroll, had written an article for Dr. Woodbridge, but it was, according to Jesse, sensational and "sloppy." He trusted James to be tactful and honest.[68]

They continued to try to see one another when their schedules permitted. James spoke at a writers' conference at Morehead State during the summer of

1956, and Jesse suggested they get together.[69] Later that year, he complimented James on a story in *Kentucky Writing*.[70] In 1957, Still had his students make illustrations of Jesse's junior book *A Penny's Worth of Character* and sent them to the author. Jesse was touched. He wrote back:

> You tell them I think these are very fine indeed — and so does my wife who teaches Second Grade.... I have gone over each drawing and I have not found any two that are even similar.
> So I have enjoyed this very positive work by these very young Kentuckians.... Thank you and your pupils many, many times.[71]

He also had his students send Jesse a get-well card after a heart attack in the mid–1960s. For his part, Jesse nominated James for an honorary degree from their alma mater, Lincoln Memorial University, especially endorsing him for *River of Earth*. Jesse was unable to attend the commencement exercises, but he wrote an effulgent letter: "You can go home again! You went back home to LMU! Congratulations to you! It's wonderful! And congratulations!"[72]

Such kind words were not always consistent with what Jesse said about James in his correspondence and conversations with others. Jesse Stuart was a man given to extremes of hostility and generosity. He was often thoughtless or unkind and treated the majority of his friends and associates in this mercurial fashion. But if he spoke ill of James, it did not mean he was being insincere when he wrote to his friend: "By-hell, [my wife and I] like you! You know I mean this! You're the real McCoy.... We love you, Jimmy!"[73]

By this same token, James Still was mild-mannered and not inclined to combat or even debate Jesse's cruel remarks. He adhered to a high standard of conduct and did not react to his friend's puerile behavior. Surely, he was affected by Jesse's comments, but he took them in graceful stride.

Despite their longstanding camaraderie and efforts to remain in touch, Jesse rarely visited James at the Hindman Settlement School and never got to know "that part of the country."[74] They spent a lifetime of correspondence regretting their estrangement, but Jesse asserted that he appreciated having James for a classmate and a friend.[75] While Still never expressed any animus toward Jesse and unhesitatingly championed his friend's "generous spirit," he chose not to read Jesse's prose: he did not want it to affect his writing style, which was more idiomatic and less dialectic.[76] Several years after Jesse died, James Still visited Mrs. Stuart at her home in W-Hollow. She thought that Mr. Still was a "real gentleman" and regretted that his friendship with Jesse had been "strained" in later years.[77]

In May 1993, Mr. Still donated his correspondence from Jesse Stuart to the Appalachian Collection at Morehead State University, where it was placed alongside archival material donated by Mrs. Stuart. Two young men pictured next to one another in their 1929 college yearbook were reunited in the Camden-Carroll Library, where the Jesse Stuart Room neighbors the James Still Room.[78]

Notes

1. Quoted in H. Edward Richardson, *Jesse: The Biography of an American Writer—Jesse Hilton Stuart* (New York: McGraw-Hill, 1984), 465.
2. James Still to Jesse Stuart, May 21, 1933.
3. *Ibid.*
4. Jesse Stuart to James Still, October 7, 1929.
5. Stuart to Still, January 6, 1930.
6. Still to Stuart, May 21, 1933.
7. Stuart to Still, May 24, 1933.
8. Stuart to Still, September 8, 1937.
9. Stuart to Still, May 24, 1933.
10. Stuart to Still, June 5, 1956.
11. Stuart to Still, September 20, 1929.
12. Stuart to Still, February 11, 1937.
13. See, for example, Still to Stuart, May 8, 1937.
14. Stuart to Still, January 6, 1930.
15. Stuart to Still, July 26, 1952.
16. Marion Ives to Jesse Stuart, November 20, 1937.
17. Harry Harrison Kroll, "Jesse Stuart: The Student I Remember," March 2, 1963, JSF Archive material.
18. Stuart to Still, October 7, 1929.
19. See, for example, Still to "Jessie" Stuart, February 27, 1933.
20. Still to Stuart, May 21, 1933.
21. Still to Stuart, August 23, 1933.
22. Still to Stuart, postmarked October 31, 1934; Still to Stuart, postmarked January 21, 1935; Stuart to Still, January 28, 1935.
23. Still to Stuart, December 7, 1934.
24. *Ibid.*
25. Stuart to Still, December 12, 1934.
26. Still to Stuart, December 7, 1934.
27. Still to Stuart, postmarked January 21, 1935; Still to Stuart, postmarked November 30, 1935.
28. See, for example, Still to Stuart, June 15, 1936.
29. Stuart to Still, October 16, 1936.
30. Still to Stuart, January 14, 1936.
31. Stuart to Still, September 20, 1929.
32. Still to Stuart, January 27, 1936.
33. Still to Stuart, December 11, 1936.
34. Still to Stuart, January 27, 1936.
35. Still to Stuart, December 11, 1936.
36. Stuart to Still, January 30, 1936.
37. *Ibid.*
38. *Ibid.*
39. Still to Stuart, May 4, 1937.
40 Still to Stuart, January 14, 1936.
41. Still to Stuart, December 11, 1936.
42. Still to Stuart, postmarked February 5, 1937.
43. Still to Stuart, April 6, 1937.
44. Stuart to Still, April 7, 1937.
45. Still to Stuart, May 4, 1937.

46. Still to Stuart, May 8, 1937.
47. Still to Stuart, postmarked December 21, 1938.
48. Still to Stuart, December 30, 1939.
49. Stuart to Still, letter undated but probably written in 1935.
50. Still to Stuart, December 30, 1939.
51. *Ibid.*
52. Stewart McClelland to Jesse Stuart, April 10, 1940.
53. Stuart to Still, January 3, 1940.
54. Stuart to Still, June 4, 1940.
55. See, for example, Stuart to Still, January 8, 1944. Telephone interview with Mr. Mike Mullins, Director of the Hindman Settlement School and long-time friend of James Still, May 27, 2007.
56. Silas House, "Remembering James Still," *Arts Across Kentucky* (Winter 2001), 11–12.
57. Stuart to Still, March 5, 1952.
58. Stuart to Still, October 28, 1959.
59. Stuart to Still, July 26, 1952.
60. *Ibid.*
61. Quoted in H.R. Stoneback, "Roberts, Still, Stuart & Warren," *Kentucky Humanities* (2001, No. 1 &2), 30.
62. Stuart to Still, July 26, 1952.
63. See, for example, Stuart to Still, July 26, 1952, and Stuart to Still, March 8, 1956.
64. Stuart to Still, April 26, 1954.
65. Stuart to Still, March 28, 1956.
66. See, for example, Stuart to Still, May 28, 1956; Stuart to Still, June 16, 1956; and Stuart to Still, November 8, 1956.
67. Stuart to Still, October 18, 1975.
68. Stuart to Still, April 7, 1960; Stuart to Still, April 22, 1960.
69. Stuart to Still, June 16, 1956; Stuart to Still, July 16, 1956.
70. Stuart to Still, October 9, 1956.
71. Stuart to Still, April 27, 1957.
72. Jesse Stuart to Frank Welch, January 7, 1975; Stuart to Still, June 18, 1974.
73. Stuart to Still, October 11, 1975.
74. Stuart to Still, October 31, 1975; Stuart to Still, May 30, 1958.
75. Stuart to Still, September 20, 1977.
76. James Still to James M. Gifford, November 13, 1991; a personal visit with Mr. Still at his home, probably in the early 1980s.
77. Interview with Naomi Deane Stuart at her home in W-Hollow, 1986.
78. James Still to James M. Gifford, May 21, 1993.

Why Does Knott County Send the Largest Ratio of Graduates to College?

Jesse Stuart

The most interesting recent news item to parents and teachers reported Knott County leading all (Kentucky) counties last year in percentage of high school graduates going to college.

Kentucky has 120 counties and yet, Knott County, with 356 square miles of rugged terrain and more than 20,000 inhabitants, sent 52 percent of her high school students to college last year. Running Knott County a close second with 51 percent was Fayette County, in the heart of the Bluegrass and home of this state's educational center. The state's average was 31 percent.

What Can Be the Reason for Knott County's Leading the State?

In this part of Kentucky, level fertile acres are scarcer than hen's teeth. There is little, if any, industry; cities, towns and villages are below average economically, and yet, a present generation of young Americans from this rugged land certainly are not submarginal in the head. They will stand up and be counted not only in Kentucky's but in America's future. There must be wise parents and good teachers in Knott County.

Maybe James Still, novelist, short story writer, poet and teacher, has been influential. He has been in Knott County many years. Being a classmate of Still at Lincoln Memorial University and at Vanderbilt University, I know he is a builder of youth.

Stuart, Jesse. "Why Does Knott County Send the Largest Ratio of Graduates to College?" Louisville *Courier-Journal*, August 14, 1957. Reprinted with permission.

I've heard that Congressman Carl Perkins's sister, who is a teacher there, remains unsurpassed. Then, too, let us not forget that Perkins himself is a forceful member of the House Committee on Education and has made a fight to improve education in the United States and in Kentucky.

Then isn't it true that the first Bookmobile in the state of Kentucky was operated in Knott County long before Harry Schacter, Mary Bingham, Georgia Blazer and Company put them in every county in the state?

Where this Knott County Bookmobile couldn't operate, didn't Jimmie Still carry books on his back? How much of this basic foundation of education can be accredited to Hindman Settlement School, which has inspired youth to go to Caney, Berea, Union, Eastern, Lindsey Wilson and Lincoln Memorial?

The Bluegrass area is filled with the finest colleges of the land. So is Louisville. Counties of Western Kentucky have excellent farm land and outstanding high schools and colleges. Why couldn't one of these counties have sent the highest number to college?

The Answer?

Maybe I have the answer to this, maybe I haven't. Being a hillman myself, I know these upland folk quite well.

They either are or they aren't.

This state should know them in athletics—football and especially basketball. Last year, when a headline said Lafayette of Lexington had ended mountain rule, I heard a coach say that headline would bring mountain rule back to the state tournament.

For a county to lead the state in sending its high school graduates to college is a greater achievement than winning a state basketball championship. This is the most important achievement of secondary schools I have read. Compared to other states, Kentucky has a low percentage of her high school graduates going to college.

If all the counties in this state could match Knott County, then Kentucky would not be one of the very low states on America's educational totem pole. Articles such as appeared in *The Chicago Tribune*, about east Kentucky's mountain counties, would not be written. If written, they would be in reverse.

I receive many requests to answer these. I couldn't. I found too much truth in these articles because I was back on the firing line teaching!

But how far will Chicago's city schools, for example, surpass Knott County, one of the poorest counties, economically, of this state? Knott County is reaching a high batting average for any Kentucky county, especially one of eastern Kentucky's upland counties!

Why are these young Knott Countians people of determination and integrity? Why are they young Americans with dreams? Why are they in some respects keeping pace with, perhaps forging ahead of the progress of young people from other areas? If they were making big money, they probably (at least many of them) would prefer to leave school, own cars.

Maybe roads are narrow and winding in Knott County where I read the families were the largest in this nation. Let them be large! They are producing good, industrious future leaders of America. I read where someone suggested pensions for these large families! No, thank you! Why?

Have you ever taught school? If you have, have you taught young people from large families? For the most part, they are an unselfish group. They've had the first lesson in American democracy: how to get along with others.

Give and Take

They wear each other's clothes, learn to give and take and, above all, they know what it is to scratch for themselves. If you don't believe learning to do for themselves is valuable, check with your teachers and others who are holding key positions today, they were the ones who had the struggle.

Ask James Still how he liked the rock crusher at Lincoln Memorial. Ask Congressman Carl Perkins what inward drive compelled him to go to Caney College and how much money he had? Ask his sister, a fine teacher, if she had to struggle. Ask others in Knott County.

Let me end this with a story. Once in a poor family in this state, a youth was born. He was born in circumstances close akin to many youths' in Knott County. He, too, had a lust for knowledge but there were not any schools for him in his day. He was self-educated.

He was born on poor soil in Kentucky. He later lived on infertile acres of Indiana and the poorest land in Illinois. When an emergency arose, he was not a man of wealth but he had integrity and fortitude. Who has ever come out of America to surpass Abraham Lincoln in world greatness?

Personal Memories of James Still and Jesse Stuart: These Noted Writers Had a Great Effect on a Young Knott Countian

WILLIAM HENRY YOUNG

In schools across the United States there are numerous young folk growing into manhood and womanhood without having that first moment of pride in themselves and their social, cultural, and hereditary backgrounds. There was a time when I wasn't proud of who I was and where I came from. I didn't understand what my section of our country had to offer myself and others of my generation.

It was Jesse Stuart, whom I came to know, first through his books and later as a person, who led me to a keen sense of pride in my background as an eastern Kentuckian.

It was another fellow Southerner who added to the intensity of that pride: James Still.

Those of us who have read the books of Jesse Stuart, especially *The Thread that Runs So True*, remember that Stuart was a student at Lincoln Memorial University at Harrogate, Tennessee. The same years that Stuart attended LMU, James Still, destined to spend his long life in the tiny village of Hindman, the county seat of Knott County, was a student at LMU.

It was the year of my seventh grade that I came to know James Still, a native of Lafayette, Alabama, as "the man with the books." One of those first books he handed me at the Upper Lotts Creek Elementary School on the head

William Henry Young, "Personal Memories of Jesse Stuart and James Still: These Noted Writers Had a Great Effect on a Young Knott Countian," *The Kentucky Explorer*, November 2001, pp 12–14. Reprinted with permission.

of Lotts Creek was Stuart's book of poetry, *Man with a Bull-Tongue Plow*. I had told Mr. Still that I liked poetry.

I had seen Mr. Still, as most folks in our county referred to him, on court days in Hindman. He was a small, quiet man, who flowed endlessly through the court day crowd. It was with this same quietness that he told me it was a book about our mountains and was written by one of his friends. That book led me to a life of reading and learning about who I am, where I came from, and what my existence could become "if."

This "if" had bothered me for some time. At the age of three I had gone to live in a children's home in Tiffin, Ohio. I am certain that separation was traumatic. At that young age, time soothed any feelings I had when I left my mother's home.

When I was nine I returned to our home on the head of Young Fork of Lotts Creek. I left a sheltered environment, which I shared with five or six hundred children. In one day I left this shelter for an isolated log home my grandfather had built, when he first married in the late 1870s. The nearest neighbor my age lived more than a mile away. When school began that autumn, my northern Ohio accent immediately said, "Here is an outsider." The initiation began, and often it wasn't pleasant.

We all encounter elements of conflict wherever we happen to be. Conflict is part and parcel of our everyday lives. It can become unbearable for many of us, enough so that we deny our heritage.

Until the day that James Still handed me the first of Jesse Stuart's books I would read, I was an unhappy and unwilling member of one of our country's richest heritages: Southern mountain culture. James Still, who carried a book for me, along with other books, to our isolated school started me on a journey which I live to this day. It is a journey of thought, reading, and writing about my land and its people.

Mr. Still was a librarian and operated our county's first bookmobile. Before the bookmobile, he used an old Jeep. Where the Jeep couldn't go, his feet went. The day I personally came to know him, he had walked a mile or two with a feedsack full of books on his back.

Conflict became unbearable for me. I dropped out of school and left my mother's home; but in the end, as all escapists before me have learned, "We cannot run away from ourselves."

I wouldn't admit to anyone that I had come from the head of a hollow in tiny Knott County, Kentucky. I understood then, as I do now, that this denial of my heritage was a denial of who I was and am. The message that Stuart and Still were leaving for my and future generations hadn't hit its mark with me in 1951.

As a student at Carr Creek High School during the winter semester of 1951, I learned that Mr. Still lived in a log home across from one of my kinsmen at the mouth of Dead Mare Branch, not too far from the high school. I went to talk poetry with him, for I had obtained a copy of *Man with a Bull-Tongue Plow* from the library in Hazard and was anxious to talk about it and how it affected me. The natural cadences of Stuart's poetry, its content, and the cadences of the very life I lived had made me a lover of poetry.

I remembered that Mr. Still had referred to Jesse Stuart as his friend. This was the reason I had gone to visit him on Dead Mare Branch. On that spring evening, I learned that Mr. Still had written poetry. He let me spend an evening reading his book, *On Troublesome Creek*. One of my teachers, Jethro Amburgey, loaned me his copy of Still's *Hounds on the Mountain*.

In the two months left to me as a full-time resident of Knott County, I spent several evenings at the log cabin on Dead Mare Branch. Mr. Still was a conversationalist of the first order and seemed to be pleased with my interest in Kentucky literature.

It was through James Still that I met Jesse Stuart. They both had been invited to attend the Bread Loaf Writers' Conference the year I was released from the Army. I had bought my first car, and Mr. Still allowed (in his verbiage) I might want to meet Jesse Stuart; if so, I could take him over to Greenup, Kentucky. I was game for the trip and a pleasant visit with the two men became one of my treasured memories.

In *Man with a Bull-Tongue Plow* and in all of his stories, novels, and poetry, Stuart exposed his mountain heritage. It has been said that few pieces of real estate in all literary history have been written about in as much detail and intensity as Stuart wrote about his land. His books expose his people to the sunlight of reality. They think and act, save and kill, love and hate. He exposes the good and bad, the comic and the tragic, the acceptable and the unacceptable traits of his people, my people.

The credible and ridiculous exist side by side. For the absent mountaineer, he taught us to laugh at ourselves when we are ridiculous, to accept our weaknesses and our strengths, and burst with pride at our achievements. I have never denied my heritage since the time I read and laughed my way through his delightful novel, *Taps for Private Tussie*.

It wasn't until many years later that I had the opportunity to read James Still's novel, *River of Earth*. It was from that novel that I came to understand the folk of my own county.

Why had my mother chosen to send her two youngest children so far away from our home of Lotts Creek?

For my sister and me, the 1930s and early 1940s were not a time of depression. We didn't know there was such an awful social/economic situation outside the grounds of Tiffin, Ohio, Junior Home. We were well fed, well clothed, well educated, and in general, extremely well cared for. His novel, *River of Earth*, is about what families in Eastern Kentucky did and can endure in a depression. To this day, I am thankful for the insight of this novel.

As an English teacher, I came across one of Still's short stories, "A Ride on the Short Dog," in an anthology of American Literature. In that story a passenger tells one of a pair of unruly twins that if he doesn't behave he would have the man on Lotts Creek have horns grow on his head.

My grandfather was known to many as "Boggart John Young." Many supernatural stories were attributed to him. I once asked Mr. Still if he was referring to my grandfather in this story. He "allowed" that he was. He told me that he had known my grandfather through Jethro Amburgey's brother, Lemuel, who had married my first cousin, Ocea Combs.

Jesse Stuart once told me, "Don't tell me a story or a kernel of a story if you wish to attribute it to yourself. When you tell me, it becomes a thing that imagination turns into mine."

He was a listener, a talker; a big, gregarious man. James Still was a small man, a quiet observer who listened to us as we traded horses and mules, swapped guns and knives, visited with friends and relatives, and told our wild tales of court day in that long ago time I lived through as a boy. He was one of many persons who showed me another way to live my life.

For me, Jesse Stuart and James Still were catalysts who turned a runaway from his heritage into a proud son of his Kentucky mountains.

Jesse Hilton Stuart died in 1984; James Still died this year [2001] and lived to be an aged icon of Appalachian literature.

Yet, Jesse and James live on in my memory and in the minds of others who have been touched by their lives and creations.

Green Peppers and a Straw Hat

Jan Walters Cook

At Tuesday's lunch, Mr. James Still pulled out a ladder-back chair and sat down by ME in the dining room. ME, eating at the same table with our guru! My gosh, what would I say? What could I say? Nearly dumbstruck, I managed a "hello." Mr. Still nodded in acknowledgment a "hello" as kitchen helpers placed food before him as if he were royalty. With our elbows nearly touching, we crumbled cornbread into our soup beans in silence.

On that hot humid sweltering dog day in August, Mr. Still brought forth a shiny green pepper, not a bell, but a long, funnel-shaped one. Fascinated, I watched as he lifted it from his shirt pocket and laid it on the oil-cloth table beside his plate. From the corners of my eyes, I stole glances as he cut off bits of his pepper and ate them between spoonfuls of soup beans.

I come from a large mountain family that yattered on and on while eating. Silence around the table denoted sickness or guilt or some such. Anyway, I felt pressured to say something because I could stand the silence no more. I asked my simple question, "Is that the hot kind?" Honestly, Mr. Still's expression had failed to register any changes when he took a bite. To add to the situation of no air conditioning, the overhead fans whirled above us, driving the heat of the nearby kitchen around us too. Yet no beads of perspiration arose on Mr. Still's forehead. More silence. Oh boy.

Finally a reply, "Yes, I eat one every day from my garden."

Hallelujah, I was saved.

His garden! There it was. The curtains parted. I had gardened most of my life, and all of a sudden we were off, discussing vegetables, flowers, weeds and seeds. He told me he had turned to gardening as a solace when he returned from duty after World War II. He munched his pepper as if it bordered on sweetness. Someone brought him a piece of cake. He ate on. Gardening had seen him through those difficult times he told me. Gardening has seen me through tough ones as well....

Jan Walters Cook, "Green Peppers and a Straw Hat," *Crossing Troublesome: 25 Years of the Appalachian Writers Workshop*, ed. by Leatha Kendrick and George Ella Lyon, Wind Publications, 2002. n.p. Reprinted with permission.

When he returned home, he couldn't write or do anything. He was in an awful state. "I just sat in my doorway and did nothing for a year."

What I gleaned from all this was that notable writers were human beings just like myself. Knowing Mr. Still had not written for a year gave me reassurance and comfort because I too went for periods without writing. Sitting in my "doorway" like Mr. Still, I can always meditate. I know I will write when the right time presents itself.

I miss seeing Mr. Still come into the dining room holding his straw hat behind him. I miss his deep voice around the dining table at Hindman where I know for sure something happened to me. He and others gave me the courage to be a writer.

Travels with Mr. Still: In Search of Richard Jefferies

Judith Jennings

I first met James Still in the mid–1980s, when I worked at the Kentucky Humanities Council and he was a member of the Board. I was in my 30s and Mr. Still was in his 70s. He didn't talk much during the board meetings, but after the meetings, he would talk a lot about his life and friends in eastern Kentucky. My mama was from eastern Kentucky and I taught for a while at Union College in Barbourville, so I had many of the same friends that he did: Mike Mullins, Jim Wayne Miller, and Gurney Norman, to name a few.

Once you got to know Mr. Still, you could see that he was a man of many paradoxes. He loved his home on Wolfpen, but he loved to travel, too. In the late 1970s (and before and after), Mr. Still traveled a lot with Jim Wayne Miller. Jim Wayne used to laugh and shake his head and say he would write down all the stories about their travels after Mr. Still was gone. Nobody thought that Jim Wayne would go before Mr. Still.

Mr. Still liked to enter all kinds of contests, and he was always winning prizes. If he had a new radio or television, he would tell you he won it as a prize. I was never really sure if he was telling the truth or just joshing, but I do know he entered the contests.

I like to travel, too, and by the 1980s I had lived in England for two one-year periods. I went for one year when I was in graduate school at the University of Kentucky and was doing the research for my dissertation. I went again in 1981 after my mother died. I ended up living in London again for nearly a year that time.

When I got back, I went to work at the Kentucky Humanities Council and met Mr. Still. After I had known Mr. Still for about three years, I told him I was going to the International Oral History Meeting at Oxford. Mr. Still asked me if he could go, too. He just called me at home one day and asked if he could come along. I am not quite sure why I said okay. Of course, I was intrigued by the idea of spending that much time with such a great writer, but I was a little worried, too, because of his sometimes quirky ways.

Anyhow, I said okay, and after that one trip there was no stopping him. He would just say, "Well, where are we going next time?" We made four or five trips in all. I have many friends in England, so I would always want to go there. But he wanted to go to France and Italy, so we went there, too.

I went to work for Appalshop from 1987 till 1991, and Mr. Still and I went to the Appalachian Festival in Rome during that time. His friend George Alexander went, too. Gurney Norman was there, and Alessandro Portelli was in charge of the festival. After the festival was over, Mr. Still and I went to Florence and Pisa. We spent one whole day in the Uffizi Gallery in Florence on that trip.

I left Appalshop in 1991 and moved to Louisville. Mr. Still and I didn't travel together anymore after that. I don't think he made any more transatlantic flights after our last trip to England. He was in his 80s by then and getting more creaky and cranky sometimes. I am not quite sure why I ever started making those trips with Mr. Still, but I sure treasure those memories now.

Over the course of several years in the late 1980s and early 1990s, I traveled to England, Italy, and France with Mr. Still. (Even so, I still cannot reconcile myself to calling him James, much less Jim.) Our first trip was to England. Mr. Still and I, along with Anne Campbell Ritchie and her husband Don, participated in an international oral history conference at St. John's College, Oxford.

After the conference was over, Mr. Still told me he wanted to visit the home of Richard Jefferies. I had never heard of Richard Jefferies and didn't have any earthly idea where his home might be. Mr. Still said he thought it was in Swindon. Swindon is a medium-sized railroad town, not too far from Oxford.

On a bright Sunday morning, we drove from Oxford to Swindon. Mr. Still said Richard Jefferies lived on a farm, perhaps one of the very farms we were driving past just then. I was concentrating on staying in the left lane. I wondered how we would know Richard Jefferies' farm if we did drive right past it.

When we got to Swindon, I went to the city center to look for an information office. It was closed. We drove around Swindon for awhile on the off chance that we might just stumble upon Richard Jefferies' house. We didn't. I enquired in two petrol stations and one grocery store. No one I asked had ever heard of Richard Jefferies, and they didn't know where his house was.

I found a city park and stopped. I suggested that Mr. Still wait for me while I looked for lunch and directions to the Richard Jefferies house. Since it was Sunday morning, few food places were open. I finally found a family-owned shop and bought some sandwiches. They had never heard of Richard Jefferies.

When I returned to the park, Mr. Still was nowhere to be found. I walked round and round the park and finally spotted Mr. Still on a side street. He was sitting in a yard next to a severely disabled young man in a wheel-

James Still at St. John's College, Oxford, England. Anne Campbell Ritchie is in the center, Judith Jennings is to the right. Photograph by Don Ritchie and Anne Campbell Ritchie. Used with permission.

chair. Mr. Still was admiring two cats the young man had with him in his wheelchair.

I gave Mr. Still his lunch and told him I couldn't find anyone who knew anything about Richard Jefferies. Mr. Still wondered how I could have a Ph.D. in British History and have never heard of Richard Jefferies. We ate our sandwiches and left Swindon.

Later, Mr. Still was invited to participate in the Appalachian Festival in Rome, Italy, and I went, too. Crossing the busy streets of Rome with him presented a major challenge at first. Mr. Still would stand on the curb, waiting for the cars to stop. The cars never do stop in Rome.

After a few days, I got so I would take his arm, and the two of us would wade out into the traffic. I was pretty sure the cars wouldn't hit an older man like him. After that trip, Mr. Still sent me yellow roses and said he never would have gotten across the streets without me.

On another trip, Mr. Still wanted to go to Verdun in eastern France to see the sites of the World War I battlefields there. Mr. Still had read extensively about the trench warfare and military history of the Great War. So Mr. Still and his British friend George Alexander and I took the ferry from Dover to Calais and began driving east.

We drove past charming villages and fertile fields and then — unexpectedly to me — we began to see the cemeteries. The soldiers were buried where they fell. Canadians, Australians, New Zealanders, British and Americans buried in Army and Air Force regimental cemeteries. We stopped at each cemetery we could and signed the visitors' book.

Touring the battlefield sites in Verdun was more death and destruction than I could take in one day. George and Mr. Still explored the bunkers and peered into the trenches and walked around the building full of the bones of the unidentified dead. I wandered through the forest and found the site of one of those charming villages which had been pounded into oblivion during the war. The places where the streets and houses had been were marked by ropes and signs.

Before we left the battlefield that day, Mr. Still said he would like to drive around the perimeter in the car. It was about 4:00 in the afternoon on a warm summer day when I turned the car into the road around the battlefield area. Mr. Still soon asked me to stop so he could examine a site where he knew some particular maneuvers had taken place.

While Mr. Still examined the site, I drifted around the edges of the deep woods that surround the battlefield now, thinking how different it must have been then. After about 15 minutes, I returned to the spot where I had left Mr. Still but found only George looking around in bewilderment. "He was here five minutes ago, and now I can't find him," he said. "Where could he have gone?" I asked George, as if he knew but wasn't telling me.

George and I searched the battlefield site for nearly two hours. I kept running back to the car thinking that Mr. Still might be waiting for us there. Finally, near 6:00, as the dusk was gathering (no daylight savings time in France), I saw Mr. Still walking toward us.

Mr. Still explained, completely unapologetically, that he had found a foxhole and had crawled into it to see what it would feel like to have been a soldier. He lay down in the foxhole and stared up at the summer sky, thinking about all the history he had read about the battles at Verdun. And then he fell asleep for nearly two hours. Refreshed after his nap, he asked me if it wasn't time for us to be looking for some place to eat dinner.

My last trip with Mr. Still was to England again. This time we were driving from Castle Howard in Yorkshire to Budleigh Salterton in Devon. As we drove southwest from Yorkshire, Mr. Still asked if we could return to Swindon and look again for the Richard Jefferies house.

This time I made sure we arrived at the city information center when it was open. Yes, they knew all about Richard Jefferies and his home. It was just outside of town on what is now a very busy road. Just go to the big round-about, I couldn't miss it.

Circling a busy British round-about is not the best way for an American driver to look for a tourist spot. I went round once, twice, three times. Neither Mr. Still nor I saw anything that looked remotely like the Richard Jefferies house.

Finally, in desperation, I pulled the car off the road (the left side of the road, of course). I began to walk around the circular road. Sure enough. A small sign on a nondescript gate read: "Entrance to Coate Farm, home of Richard Jefferies."

Richard Jefferies was born at Coate Farm on November 6, 1848. He became, as the guide-book said, "one of England's best known nature writers." Jefferies died in 1887, at age 37, so his list of published works is not long: *Bevis: The Story of a Boy*, a series of letters to the London *Times* in 1872, and a few essays like "The Gatekeeper at Home" and "Round About a Great Estate."

That day I learned that Jefferies wrote what has been described as one "astonishing book," *The Story of My Heart*, in which he tried to explain his vision of nature and life. His nature writings, the guide-book told me, "reveal an intense absorption in such details as would escape a casual rambler, the ascent of a caterpillar upon an almost invisible thread, a speckled trout immobile in the shadow of a bridge, the subtle differences in colouring in a tuft of grass." His writing became a nineteenth century standard for close examination of nature. One critic coined the phrase, "as minutely observed as Richard Jefferies describing a hedgerow."

So Jefferies was a nature writer, but he was more than that, too. He was a visionary who saw eternity in the sunshine of a country lane. In *The Story of My Heart*, he wrote: "It is eternity now. I am in the midst of it. It is about me in the sunshine."

Sometimes I think about sunshine differently since that day Mr. Still and I finally found the home of Richard Jefferies. I think of the sunshine on a creek bank and a silver minnow leaping for air. A little boy riding his pony, not far but far enough at the time. George Alexander and I scurrying across the battlefield at dusk. Two travelers, going round and round, looking for Richard Jefferies.

Still Writing After All These Years: An Author Who Began His Career Nearly a Half Century Ago in Hindman, Kentucky, Is Being Rediscovered and Honored

SHIRLEY WILLIAMS

In 1932 a writer and Renaissance man named James Still went to Kentucky's Knott County from his native Alabama, via Lincoln Memorial University (where he and Jesse Stuart were classmates), Vanderbilt and the University of Illinois.

In Knott County he worked, at first for little or no pay, as a librarian at the Hindman Settlement School; and always, he worked at the writer's trade, rising as early as 4 a.m. to pursue his craft.

He still lives and writes in Knott County, almost half a century later — and the man and his work are undergoing something of a rediscovery.

During his first years in Kentucky, Still began to produce some of the finest writing that has come out of the Appalachian area; fine enough to induce poet Robert Frost to wander into the *Yale Review* office every so often and ask, "When are you going to have another story by James Still?"

His work gained national recognition quickly. His first short story was published in *The Atlantic Monthly* in 1936. A book of poems, *Hounds on the Mountain*, was published in 1937. He won the O. Henry Memorial Prize for a short story in 1939. His first novel, *River of Earth*, appeared in 1940 and shared, with Thomas Wolfe's *You Can't Go Home Again*, the Southern Authors' Award

This article originally appeared in the *Louisville Courier-Journal* magazine section on July 9, 1978, pp. 23–31. Reprinted with permission.

that year. A collection of short stories, *On Troublesome Creek*, came out in 1941. In 1947 he won the American Academy of Arts and Letters and the National Institute of Arts and Letters award. His work was included in the *Best American Short Stories* collections in 1946, 1950 and 1952. He was the recipient of two Guggenheim fellowships (1941 and 1946) and fellowships at three writers' colonies: Yaddo, Bread Loaf, and MacDowell.

But until about four years ago Still feels he was virtually unknown (or at least, unread) in his own adopted state.

Now recognition is coming his way from across the Bluegrass. He is frequently invited to read on college campuses; he conducted both a reading from his works and a seminar at Bellarmine College in Louisville this spring. He has been discovered by graduate students, and he and his writing are becoming the basis for master's theses and doctoral dissertations (three thus far). This spring also brought the publication of a James Still issue of *Kentucky Poetry Review*.

In May Still was given a special Weatherford Award at Berea College for the body of his work: an award that goes each year to publications that "best illuminate the problems, personalities and unique qualities of the Appalachian South." Three days later he received an honorary doctor of letters degree from Morehead State University, where he was once writer-in-residence and where the Camden Library has housed, since 1961, the James Still Room which contains some of his manuscripts. He also holds honorary degrees from Lincoln Memorial (1974) and Berea College (1973).

In May, the University of Wyoming's Archive of Contemporary History asked him to consider placing his papers with them, writing that "We, of course, know of your outstanding accomplishments as a novelist."

And last month the University Press of Kentucky reissued *River of Earth*, long considered a classic, in a quality paperback. Out of print since a 1968 Popular Library paperback edition, it is sure to find its way onto the reading lists of many an English course and Appalachian studies program.

When *River of Earth* was published in 1940, *Time* magazine called it a "work of art," saying that "among other good qualities," Still had an invaluable attribute as a writer, "a sense of what is fitting, in the best meaning of the word."

Two years ago Gnomon Press in Frankfort published a collection of Still's short stories, *Pattern of a Man*, and last year Putnam's published *Jack and the Wonder Beans* (a retelling of "Jack and the Beanstalk") and *Sporty Creek*, which were classified as children's books. But Still says he is not a writer of children's books. He is simply a writer and many other things as well: poet, teacher, gardener. His collections of wild and domestic plants and herbs vie for space in his garden and his yard; he has every known variety of violet. He studies insects and has an avid interest in primitive civilizations.

Although he may not have been widely known, James Still the writer has not been totally unsung in Kentucky. *The Courier-Journal's* library has a sizable file of clippings. He was one of the late columnist Joe Creason's favorite people, and more than once Creason referred to him as a gifted Kentucky mountain writer-poet "as unusual as your only child." As recently as 1974 Creason wrote of Still's fourth book, *Way Down Yonder on Troublesome Creek*, a collection of Appalachian riddles and "rusties," that "in it, as in his other works, one can all but feel the gentle wit and humor of the mountain people Jim Still has come to know so well and love after being 40 years among them."

A lengthy 1939 "Kentucky Profiles" piece in *The Courier-Journal* by Rena Niles observed that Still "can claim the well-nigh unique distinction of never having had any of his works permanently rejected." Much of what Mrs. Niles wrote about Still and his work then still applies. For he has continued to write of a specific period of time in a specific setting and has made them undeniably his own.

Mrs. Niles has seen him occasionally since the interview. "I cannot say that we have kept in close touch; I wish we had," she said. "He's a rather shy, reticent person. His writing hasn't changed. He hasn't changed as much as most people would have in 40 years. And I think one reason is that he lives very much the way he did then. He came right back to Dead Mare Branch and put down roots and stayed. It seems to me that James Still has literally stood still."

And in a protective sense he has. Still avoids reading the works of other writers who deal with the Appalachian area, to avoid anything that might overlap or affect his own work.

Alfred Perrin of Berea, a retired executive who is a book collector and financially backs the Weatherford Awards, has been Still's friend for the past 10 years. "He told me one time," Perrin recalled recently, "that as far as his writing is concerned he is interested in only a certain period of years that begin about the crash year of '29 and go through to 1940 or something like that. He said, 'As far as I'm concerned, this block of time is the only thing that I'm ever going to write about. People ask me about writing about strip mining and all that. It hurts me too much, what's going on. But it just isn't in my time block.'

"He has chosen a particular period of time and all of his material, of course, sort of fits in. So many things happened in that period. Of course, he says that he feels that he has to guard — and it's important for him to guard — his essence, not to dissipate. In a way, I think that's right. He is a person who has guarded himself pretty well, really. He has always said to me that a writer should stand on his work and not his personal relationships or the fact that he attends the cocktail parties that the publishers put on."

But, Perrin thinks that Still has mellowed. "He enjoys being contrary, you know. I write him fairly regularly. He's just starved for companionship and books. And he's a man that has preserved a wonderful sense of curiosity at his age. He's interested in so many things, like mountain climbing and the Yucatan; things he is interested in and works at. So many people as they get older they sort of shrink up into smaller and smaller pieces."

James Still's stories have been used in textbook anthologies after they initially appeared in various major magazines in this country. But things were a little different in the '30s and '40s than they are now in publishing, and Still likes to talk about that period.

"I never intended to repeat myself, though writing about the same region. I never wanted to write the same story again. You notice how different they are, one from the other? But there are so many stories you can't come to the end of them. We haven't scratched the surface.

"And here [writing about Kentucky] there are three of us, if you want to include me with Jesse Stuart and Harriette Simpson Arnow. We are all at least 65. And I simply don't know of any writers coming along right now who are being published generally like we were in *The Atlantic, Yale Review,* that sort of thing.

"Those places that used to make reputations don't do it anymore. It would be a good thing to be in *The Atlantic* nowadays, sure, but it doesn't have the prestige it used to have. One story in *The Atlantic* would almost certainly turn up in a textbook back then. Every story—they published 10 of mine, and several poems—every one of those turned up in a textbook, some a number of times, and would not have, I think, except they were in *The Atlantic*."

Still has spent much of his life working around young people, and his love for children surfaces frequently in his conversation. "Well, I used to take children to the hospital in Louisville and sort of look after them until they were released. One child had epilepsy. I took him every three months."

Years ago, he got a child to pull a dangling tooth by offering him candy. The word spread, and soon children throughout the county were bringing their baby teeth to Still to be ransomed with candy bars. Now he carries in his car a little plastic box of baby teeth. The money he received from the Weatherford Award has been invested and will go toward the education of a child.

He was librarian at Hindman Settlement School from 1932–39 and 1951–61, and is still associated with the school. Mike Mullins, the director, considers him its writer-in-residence.

Driving around with Still is a lesson in how well he knows his region. "Morehead's big basketball player lives right here," he would say. A little farther on, "This man just had a stroke, and they had to close the store." And still farther along, "These houses are real grand inside on this side."

His fascination with language soon surfaced. "Now we get over to Betty Troublesome. Did I tell you how I think it got named? As you know, all the waters here go down into Troublesome and eventually get to the Kentucky River down around Haddix or Jackson. Well, back in colonial days we had a lamp called the betty lamp. It was merely a little whale oil lamp. Well, that word betty, it came from the Anglo-Saxon. It's bettnig, which means oil — b-e-t-t-n-i-g.

"These streams, as you know, get low and there would be scummy oil on top. And there's one man said, 'when I was a boy, we'd burn the waters of the creek in the summer, it was so thick with oil.' That's where I got my title, 'The Burning of the Waters' [one of his short stories]. Well, I think this little stream here was one of them that got very oily scum, and I think they were calling it Oily Troublesome — Bettnig Troublesome. I'm guessing because there has been no Betty — nobody has a recollection of any Betty. The only other speculation is that maybe it was a Pettit, somebody named Pettit, a corruption of Pettit."

Still has always had a reputation for shyness, but once he opens up his speech flows with a rollicking Southern rhythm. At 71, he is slightly overweight and covers his baldness with a hat most of the time when he is outdoors. He has been known to hold a grudge. There is mischief in his brown eyes, and he assumes the attitude that nothing bothers him — if he can't do anything about it, he dismisses it. It ain't necessarily so.

He is contradictory, it sometimes seems, on purpose. He throws out an idea to get a response. Loyal Jones of the Appalachian Center at Berea College says that if Still thinks you've got his number, he will deliberately do something to convince you that you're wrong, and Jones recalls introducing him once as a careful craftsman. "When Jim got up to speak, everything he said indicated that the words just flowed from his pen and were never revised."

An example of how careful a craftsman he is is a story called "The Run for the Elbertas." *The Atlantic Monthly* accepted it, but an editor wanted it shortened. Instead, Still added a few sentences. The editor then tried cutting the story and found he could not, so perfectly did each sentence lead into the next. It was published intact.

But back to Still's Knott County tour.

"Right down there is Where the Calf Went Mad. It's a hollow but they strip-mined up there and it's completely destroyed. I went up to see what happened to it. That's on the right. And then below there is Turkey Hen. Then on the left is Dead Man's Branch. They call it Mad Calf, naturally, where the calf went mad. Though I heard it first as Where the Calf Went Mad. I heard it. I like that better. Now this, of course, is our Betty Troublesome. Now we're coming into the federal district [government land]. See, that's Turkey Hen right there. This is Dead Man. They never solved the mystery. This man and woman, they're supposed to have killed a boy, threw his body out right up there."

And later: "This is my land, right here, and on up the creek." Still's half-cabin once belonged to his friend, the late Jethro Amburgey, a well-known dulcimer maker. Jethro and his twin brother, Monroe, had inherited the building, and they divided it in half. Monroe tore down his part and used it to build a barn elsewhere. When Jethro died, he left the use of the cabin and the land surrounding it to James Still for the rest of his life.

"Well, around the curve there now, there was a man who used to come about twice a month, and he would bring a little suitcase movie machine with those old silent movies. And they would walk down and gather there in a storehouse, and some of the boys would get up in the shelves there, and they would just lay in the shelves just like mummies in the catacombs. All around the boys in the shelves stretched out, and down below we have planks to sit on, and boxes, and would look at these silent movies and they were really old ones too. I saw people you've probably never heard of way back yonder.

"You probably know that was Litt Carr [a fork of Carr Creek] right there. And there's a cemetery on the hill. Or was. Look! They haul two ways. Coal comes in this way, and coal comes out, and coal comes out of my hollow and goes over the hill, and it comes out of the hollow and goes this way. It's going in all directions. You see where they turn the curve and lose coal? You'll have your windshield smashed if you don't watch.

"If you go up this hollow and cross the mountain you come back on my branch. This is Red Fox. Now in *River of Earth* they had a letter, you know, and it was the Red Fox post office, but the post office had moved — it's been moved a number of times — and they didn't know where it was, but they heard they had a letter and they set out to find that letter. Now you go up this road and go over into the head of Wolfpen. It's a coal haul road now."

Still has had quite a catalog of famous friends, writers he met in the '40s. He knew Carson McCullers and wrote one of the recommendations when she applied for a Guggenheim Fellowship to write *Member of the Wedding*. "She got it!" he recalled with a grin, then commented: "I didn't think too much of 'Reflections in a Golden Eye.' I think more of it now — after all, I was young."

Katherine Anne Porter was a good friend and correspondent. "I got to know her very well indeed," Still explained, and described with enthusiasm one of her letters to him that he considers "as good as any short story she ever wrote." He recalled her anger, after signing a contract to "go out to Colorado State University and spend about a month or so to teach." She received a letter from the university president "saying that he had forgotten to mention that they had a law, a sedition law, out there, and that she must sign a paper saying that she was not a Communist. Well, she felt insulted that anybody would even say this to her. And she showed me the letter and her reply, and it's a classic answer, several pages." He heard her read the last chapter of *Ship of Fools* in 1940, years before the novel was published.

To Still, Robert Frost was the kind of friend who belied the many stories about his arrogance. After *River of Earth* was published, Still ran into Frost in Key West, Florida, at a roller-skating rink. And, Still recalls, Frost, with a twinkle in his eye, told him: "I did not sit up half the night last night reading *River of Earth*." "So I knew then he had read it," Still said, smiling at the memory.

He corresponded with Marjorie Kinnan Rawlings (author of *The Yearling*) about gardening, and she reviewed his *On Troublesome Creek* for *The Chicago Daily News* in 1941. She wrote, in part, that James Still "is one of the most delightful and satisfying exponents" of good and creative writing. "James Still would write, and write well and beautifully, in whatever milieu he found himself," she continued. "He is not dependent on any chance quaintness for his writing, for its source is within his own heart and humor, his own love and knowledge of human beings. The Chaucerian archaisms of Kentucky mountain life are only incidental to his art."

He exchanged letters with Martha Foley, editor of *Best American Short Stories*, and in 1976 he received a fan letter from her for one of his children's books. She wrote: "I love *The Wolfpen Rusties*. I knew a little boy once who would have reveled in it. He was my son."

Another friend was poet Delmore Schwartz, whom Still described as "a great big shaggy dog of a man. Big fellow. And pleasant. I don't know any word except 'sweet' to say his nature." After reading his novel, Schwartz wrote to Still, "*River of Earth* is a symphony."

In a foreword to the new edition of *River of Earth* Dean Cadle, a North Carolina college librarian, makes an interesting point. "Published within a year of each other by the same publisher, *River of Earth* and *The Grapes of Wrath* are the only books chronicling the demoralizing Depression years that have continued to gain readers in more affluent ones. The major difference between them is that Steinbeck's story deals with a calamity that has struck America only once in its lifetime, while Still is writing of the struggles that have plagued the mountain people since the country was settled.

"...More than 20 years before the region was labeled a 'poverty pocket' and prior to the surprised reactions of experts and government officials to the problems of destitution, as though they had encountered some recent wonder, James Still had presented the heartbreaking account of what it means for a human being to live out his life hungry and cold. His is not a socio-economist's collection of figures, causes, and possible cures, but the dramatized plight of human beings accepting poverty without accusations or judgments or rantings against outside institutions."

A bachelor, James Still shares his 170-year-old cabin on Dead Mare Branch with a cat and her three kittens but shares the house he uses at the settlement school with only his books and a fascinating collection of miniature sculpture, Ashanti counterweights for gold that he acquired during a 2½-year stint (mostly in Africa) in the Air Force as a technical sergeant during World War II.

"They [the counterweights] were in the markets then," Still recalled, "on the ground, and I bought a few. And then they disappeared [from the market], and I learned that they had come originally from the Ashanti Kingdom. So I got a pass up there, and when I inquired found it was taboo to sell them. Each family had its own set, and no two are alike. I bought them after midnight: The taboo was off between 12 and 1. I went into the village, into the grass huts, and they were high (in price) by this time." Still has about 36 of the weights. "There are two or three that I think are truly works of art," he said.

World War II began a restless period for him, but he has not regretted the experience. "Oh, I was drafted," he said. "I didn't want to volunteer. And also,

I had an out. I had high blood pressure and an operation recently at Johns Hopkins—the doctor told me if I didn't want to go there would be a medical out, and I said, 'No, I want to go.' So I did and never regretted it. But I did not want to volunteer. I'm afraid, with a war going, volunteering doesn't mean anything.

"I didn't write anything for at least two years. Then I thought I would try. I had in mind three stories. One of these was 'Mrs. Razor,' which came out in *The Atlantic*. When I got back, I had a whole year when I could not settle down, could not fit in. I just made a garden out of habit. I had trouble—I had had malaria twice, and dysentery. I was having trouble with food, keeping down meals, no matter what I ate. I finally went down to the Lexington Clinic, and they found nothing wrong. One doctor said I was like an old clock that had been wound up too tight and needed to run down, and nobody could do it for me. And he asked, 'What are you doing with yourself these days?' And I said, 'Well, I get up in the morning, and I like to sit in the door, and I don't do anything.' 'Well,' he said, 'you start going places. Go where people are.'"

Still's father was a veterinarian in Alabama, and Still is one of 10 children.

"I asked my father once how far in school he went," Still said, laughing, "and he said he went as far as Baker in the speller, but that was kind of a joke. He was an educated man; he educated himself. He read and was quite a liberal for that day and influenced me greatly. Well, we all think we have the most wonderful parents in the world, but I really believe I did. I lived in a happy home. I don't have any traumatic experiences in my childhood, and I loved my parents, and I don't have any hang-ups. We were not effusive about it, but we cared for each other.

"Well, in our home we had a book that was called *The Cyclopedia of Human Knowledge*. It had no backs, as I recall, and it may not have all been there. But that was my schoolbook. I read everything in it. I'm probably the only person surely in my county who could speak 50 words of Arabic at 11. But that book probably did more for me than any of the schools I went to. It started me on a lot of subjects. I knew how to prune trees; even the language of flowers, I remember.

"I was the first person on my mother's side of the family to ever graduate from high school, but my father's sisters, except one, were all schoolteachers.

"On my father's side there were Missionary Baptists, and on my mother's side Primitive Baptists. And we go back—my Grandpa Still was in the Civil War. He got a finger shot off, which we used to be interested in."

His interest in primitive peoples began with a book on Alaska one of his sisters brought home from school. "She read it to me many times," he recalled, "before I could read. I believe that started it. I read everything I could get on artic explorations as I got older. And then the Antarctic. But then Tibet interested me and then Australia, the aborigines. And Tierra del Fuego, anything with primitive people." This interest has led him, for the past seven years, to spend a part of each winter researching the Mayan civilization in Central America. He has visited Mexico, Guatemala, Honduras and El Salvador.

Last year, in San Salvador, he found himself stranded in the middle of a minor revolution. Opposition forces staged a protest rally over an election apparently rigged by the military government. The army fired on them, killing "100 people or more," according to newspaper reports.

"I saw the bleeding bodies stacked," Still recalled sadly, vividly, embellishing his memories with sweeping gestures as he talked beside a gnarled flowering crab-apple tree in his yard. "They would just nonchalantly pick them up and stack them, and some may have been alive. I don't know. I didn't know how to think about it, and you can't imagine what was going through my head. I was two people. I was watching myself react and was astonished at who I was. It was disbelief. I couldn't believe it. I thought, this is something Graham Greene writes about in some of his novels; this couldn't be happening to me. I had every chance of being killed."

Despite his experiences last year, Still went back to Central America this past winter, a trip that was delayed because of the heavy January snow. In April he was home again, in time to see his violets bloom.

Because of his age, Still feels an understandable pressure about time. There are so many things he wants to write. Through the years he has kept notebooks or journals—18 of them — records of things he thinks should be preserved: speech patterns, stories. Now he feels that there will never be time to do it all. He has continued to produce, to publish, but not in quantity. Perhaps Tennessee novelist Wilma Dykeman expressed it best earlier this year, writing in *The Knoxville News Sentinel*:

"If publishers priced their volumes by worth of content rather than cost of paper and labor of printing few of us could afford to know the riches of Keats or Mark Twain or Dylan Thomas. I was reminded again of 'small is beautiful' when I discovered James Still's latest book, *Jack and the Wonder Beans*. James Still is the excellent Kentucky writer who distills Appalachian language, beliefs and customs into authentic stories and novels that reveal the region's uniqueness with dignity and humor....

"With his ear for rhythms, for turns of speech, James Still proves again that quality not quantity determines ultimate worth."

Writing About James Still: "Be ye in the world, but not of the world"

HERB E. SMITH

That statement was so familiar to me when I was attending the First Baptist Church of Whitesburg that I thought it was in the Bible. After searching the internet this morning I found a website that says that it isn't in the Bible. I wonder if the website is right. I wish James Still was alive so that we could talk about his remembrances about that statement. Mr. Still might describe a time when he was growing up in Alabama, or maybe a certain preacher. Mr. Still loved to examine a statement or phrase, or even a single word. For example, if it isn't from the King James Version of the Bible, how did the "ye" get into that quote? Do you hear people saying "ye" much anymore? Sometimes it can be used in place of "your," as in "Where's ye hammer?" Other times only "your" will do. If you are pointing to a hammer and asking, you can say, "Is that *your* hammer?" Never, "Is that *ye* hammer?" We would spend hours knocking around such thoughts.

The first time I met James Still he arrived at the log house where my wife, Elizabeth Barret, and I had moved. He was with a mutual friend, Terry Cornett. Elizabeth and I were living in a house built by my great-great-grandfather along the headwaters of Kingdom Come Creek. The house was about 10 miles from Whitesburg, where Elizabeth and I were Appalshop filmmakers, making documentaries about the Appalachian region. Mr. Still seemed to be struck by the romance of what we were doing. The house was known as the John Fox, Jr., House because the author of *The Little Shepherd of Kingdom Come* probably stayed there when he was writing the novel. Mr. Still said, "If I were living here on Kingdom Come Creek, I would write a new version of that book." I didn't know what to say. It was almost like a challenge. I thought he was saying that if we were going to live in that old log house then we had another job to do. I had read John Fox Jr.'s book, but the idea of writing a new version of

"Still Life." View of a shelf near the rear entrance of the Amburgey-Still log house on Dead Mare Branch, Knott County, Kentucky. The rusted washtub was acquired by James Still and John Stephenson from the movie set for *Coal Miner's Daughter*, which depicts the homeplace of Loretta Lynn in Butcher Holler. Photograph taken October 1980 by Linc. Fisch. Used with permission.

it seemed a little outrageous. I was 23 years old and had written nothing for publication. I can't remember how I answered, but I remember the challenge.

Let's think about James Still as a real Thoreau, a person who took to the woods in a truer and deeper way than what Thoreau attempted. Mr. Still told me that he visited Walden Pond, but was disappointed with Thoreau's experiment. Mr. Still said that Thoreau didn't get so far away that he couldn't hear his mother's dinner bell. I think Mr. Still saw himself as being a type of writer that Thoreau experimented with being. In choosing to be hundreds of miles away from his family, Mr. Still chose to take a position that was almost like a monk. I think Mr. Still would like that image, especially for the years between moving to Hindman, Kentucky, and World War II. But let's not stay with the monk image, even for his younger years. He wasn't as separate from the local people as a monk would be. As he was writing poems and his novel *River of Earth* (published 1940), he was fully immersed in the life of the community.

That shifts the image. Let's think of James Still as a folklorist. Now he's not in the woods, but documenting the folk culture of Knott and surrounding counties. He had done graduate work at Vanderbilt University and had a master's degree in library science, but it was the Depression and jobs were scarce. By becoming the librarian at Hindman Settlement School, he entered the world of non-profit organizations working to "improve" the area. In addition to educating mountain children, Hindman Settlement School was a stopping-off place for song collectors. Knott County became known for the ballads that survived in its roadless hollows. Mr. Still thought his journals might be his most valuable work because they document the speech and folkways in Knott County before radios and other modernizing influences were widely available.

Let's hold onto that, but go back to his early years in Alabama. Mr. Still said he remembered when he first saw running water. He was shocked that it was possible to turn a handle and have water come out. He said he was even more surprised when he encountered hot and cold running water. After all, electricity was rare in rural Alabama. Mr. Still was not from a well-to-do family in the northeast. In the 1930s, he ended up in the mountains of eastern Kentucky, but he was different from the Wellesley graduates who were running Hindman Settlement School. In many ways, he was more like the people he was documenting than is obvious.

James Still was a complex person. Even in his writing, all but a small amount of him is below the surface. It's one of the wonderful qualities of his work. In the fall of 1976, Elizabeth and I were looking for a different house than the Kingdom Come Creek house. Mr. Still arranged for us to rent the house across Dead Mare Branch from the log house and garden where Mr. Still raised vegetables and spent the weekends. We were neighbors for three and a half years. Although he was the age of my grandparents (Elizabeth and I were 24 and Mr. Still 70 in 1976), we enjoyed one of the most interesting series of conversations I have ever experienced. Almost every night at dusk, after we had finished what gardening we were doing, we talked. We discussed a wide range of topics. He was a daily advisor, but it wasn't a one-way conversation. For example, I had gotten a copy of *I'll Take My Stand,* the 1930 book by the Vanderbilt "Agrarians." I remember saying, "The corporations are just paper tigers. They only have power if we agree to give it to them." To which Mr. Still replied, "The corporations are pretty powerful." He had a firm grasp on the obvious, even when I thought it sounded interesting or fun to try out some of the book's ideas.

One of the best things Mr. Still freely gave us was his approach to living in the mountains and being an artist. That word, artist, is an unusual one. To some degree, it's a very presumptive position to take because it's saying that we are somewhat separate from the life of our community. An artist doesn't have to live like everyone else nor have the same set of expectations. When Elizabeth and I moved back to the Whitesburg area in the spring of 1980, Mr. Still said, "You've abandoned me." I think all three of us missed the free flow of ideas. Yet, as close as we got to be, I must say that I think of him more as a mystery, not to be solved, but to be left unsolved. It is best to leave our image of him complex.

The way he lived and continued to write is a case study for artists, especially those of us who choose to live and work in the Appalachian coalfields. He was very careful with his expenses. Do you know the saying: "It's not how much you make. It's how much you spend"? Mr. Still kept his expenses lower than his income. Few people who claim to be artists do that.

He was in the world but not of the world. He took pride in his ability to float between the world of poets and artists on the one hand and the world of regular mountain people on the other. On the one hand, artists must have some distance in order to observe, analyze, and portray a place. On the other, artists want to be full members of their communities, as he wrote, "one with the fox." We want to be like the trees in his poem, "Wolfpen Creek." The poem ends with four words: "root deep, grow tall." Yet, although we artists want to be as solid and strong as those trees, we have a more precarious position. Mr. Still showed us how to keep our balance as we walk on a narrow footlog bridging two worlds.

A Memoir of James Still

Jonathan Greene

Some think of James Still as an avuncular, kindly figure who helped young Appalachian writers. But he had his thornier side and at times prided himself for not reading any other Appalachian writers at all, as if reading them might compromise his purity, show he had been influenced by others in the area. One of his refrains was about the writer Jesse Stuart, who like Still had attended both Lincoln Memorial University and Vanderbilt: "Jesse reads me, but I don't read him."

I was friends with James Still for over 25 years. During our friendship there was one rocky period. Mike Mullins, director of the Hindman Settlement School, let me know Still had gotten over this, but it was unusual for him to ever patch up a friendship gone awry.

I first knew of Still through Carolyn Hammer. The presence of Victor and Carolyn Hammer was one of the main reasons I moved to Lexington, Kentucky, in the fall of 1966. They were both fine press printers and at the time I was very interested in their endeavors. Carolyn was the main mover in a group enterprise called the Anvil Press which had reprinted Still's early book of poems, *Hounds on the Mountain*, in 1965 on a handpress at the home of Anne and Wayne Williams. At some point during the winter of 1966 there was what was perhaps a belated publication party at their house, and Still was to be present. Wayne was head of medical illustration for the University of Kentucky Medical Center, a position he left soon after for a similar one at Duke. I had just moved to town and even though it was a short walk to the party, I did not go and thus my meeting with Still was another nine years off.

I must have met Still in 1975 through the poet William Witherup. I had recently quit my job at the university press and was teaching in the Poets-in-the-Schools program. Bill Witherup arrived from the West Coast to teach in the same program and he was headquartered and housed at the Hindman Settlement School for the year, teaching poetry in various schools in the neighborhood. He and Still hit it off and became friends. Bill insisted I meet Still and praised his writings. When I traveled to Hindman to meet him, Still was mostly an overlooked writer known mainly for writing some books for children. I remember an article in the Lexington paper that mentioned a trunk full of manuscripts. In the end, this turned out not to be true.

I remember taking out his classic 1940 novel *River of Earth* as well as *On Troublesome Creek* from the University of Kentucky library and reading them on a vacation in the Bahamas. It was an eye-opener. I immediately set out to ask Still if Gnomon could publish his work. I had started Gnomon Press in 1965, dedicated to producing quality literary and photographic books in handsome trade editions. The book of stories Still wanted to do became the Gnomon edition of *Pattern of a Man*, published in 1976. This ended the drought of 35 years during which he had had no new book of adult fiction. The last had been his previous book of stories, *On Troublesome Creek*, published in 1941. Before I published *Pattern*, Still was a "difficult," intense man who said often that he did not know one neighbor or anyone in Knott County who had read his fiction and poetry. One could see he was hurt by this, even bitter, though he issued disclaimers that he did not mind. He was shy but yearned for friendship and discussion of good books and writers.

Our scheme was to publish first the stories and then a reprint of *River of Earth*. His one public champion in print was Dean Cadle, who wrote an article about Still that was published in *The Yale Review*. With Still I met Cadle in Whitesburg. Dean said, "I did not know you had a beard." My rejoinder: "I did not know you were bald." *Pattern of a Man* was dedicated to Cadle and his wife. I heard that this friendship had gone sour later on when Cadle published things in *Appalachian Journal* that Still considered private, a transgression that left a bitter taste.

Still reworked his stories for the Gnomon book. I liked the way the stories started *in medias res*, in the middle of things, without lengthy prologue and setting the scene. They gave a sense of life in the mountains with unique characters and often a sense of humor.

During this early time of our friendship I remember having lunch with Still in a restaurant on the outskirts of Whitesburg. He noticed a widow of a close friend of his and went up to speak to her at her table. She did not recognize him or remember his name. Still was visibly shaken. As if he were a ghost from the past, invisible.

This incident reminded me of the epigraph for *Pattern of a Man* from *The House by the Medlar Tree* by Giovanni Verga: In those days everybody knew everybody else, and knew what he was doing, and what his father and grandfather had done before him, and you even knew what everybody ate; and when you saw somebody passing, you knew where he was going, and families didn't scatter all over the place, and people didn't go away to die in the poor-house. What I think Still was trying to say by using this quote was that when he moved to the mountains of eastern Kentucky there was a close-knit community akin to what Verga was writing about in Italy, but that those times were gone.

The publication of *Pattern of a Man and Other Stories* reawakened interest in James Still's work. He later inscribed a copy of his *The Wolfpen Notebooks:* "For Jonathan Greene, who with *Pattern of a Man,* rousted me out of the wilderness." Before the publication of *Pattern,* with the exception of a few writers such as Wilma Dykeman and Gurney Norman, Still had been largely forgotten by the literary world that had praised him in the 1940s.

Pattern changed that. At the time of the publication of *Pattern,* I took over distribution of the languishing Anvil Press edition of *Hounds on the Mountain,* and it sold out quickly. *Pattern* received good reviews and notices. I now pressed Still to let me go forward and reprint *River of Earth,* but the university press which previously had rejected the idea of reprinting the novel now reversed its position and Still acceded to their change of heart. But he wanted me to design the novel's reprint, and I did so. Later reprints changed the size of the book, the paper of text and cover, the color of the cover illustration, all in ways neither of us liked.

Our falling out came about when I heard the university press was then planning to reprint *On Troublesome Creek.* I first heard this from our mutual friend Joyce Hancock and then later on the same trip to the mountains from Still himself. I wrote a formal letter stating my objections to this reprint since some of the stories were in *Pattern* and this reprint would be violating the terms of our contract. In addition, a number of other stories were included in *Sporty Creek,* recently published as a juvenile novel. From yet another mutual friend, who was also his closest neighbor at that time, I heard that Still was mad because although we were friends, I had written him this formal letter stating the case. But I thought that it was just such circumstances that called for a formal, objective letter. In the end the university press dropped its plans for the reprint and chose to do a volume of previously uncollected stories, *The Run for the Elbertas,* in 1980.

For a while there was silence between Still and myself. And at times avoidance. Once he started to come into the Cozy Corner Bookstore in Whitesburg to show owner Josephine Richardson some certificate of honor that had just been framed. Seeing me, he turned quickly and retreated from the bookstore's front door. But in the end our friendship returned, perhaps because I never acknowledged that it had ended. He participated in Gnomon's 25th anniversary celebration at the University of Kentucky Library and in its 30th anniversary gathering at the Kentucky Book Fair with a party afterwards at our farm. Some years earlier the shy Still had visited our farm and spent the night in my wife's studio loft, which meant climbing a steep ladder to bed down for the night.

Ironically, years later he would take me aside and complain about the university press, how books promised for one season were often delayed to another and other complaints. I could do nothing but shrug. And ten years after the publication of *Pattern,* I was again involved with a James Still book project, designing and handling production for his collection of poems, *The Wolfpen Poems,* for Berea College Press, a project spearheaded by my friends John Stephenson (then president of the college) and Loyal Jones (then director of the Appalachian Center program there).

In his later years Still was no longer the neglected author, but now was in his heyday, going around giving talks to classes, receiving awards, reading from his work with musical interludes by Randy Wilson, and participating in various documentaries about his life and writings. Students wrote dissertations on his work. At lunch once at the Appalachian Writers Workshop at the Hindman Settlement School I allowed how I liked coming to the mountains to discover unknown writers like James Still. All there thought I was 100 percent tongue-in-cheek, whereas I was only so in part. That writer who complained about having no readers in Knott County had disappeared, and a locally famous one had taken his place.

In Remembrance of James Still

LINC. FISCH

When I moved to Kentucky in 1973, I was acquainted with the works of several writers who called the Commonwealth their home, but not with those of James Still. Perhaps that was to be expected. Mr. Still was not a man who promoted himself very much. Following the acclaim of *River of Earth* and his early poems, he became well known in the country's literary circles, but such attention rarely reached the general reading public or even his home-place neighbors at the headwaters of Troublesome Creek. He was enough out of public view that some people erroneously referred to him as a recluse and a hermit.

In the 1970s, several forces converged to bring Mr. Still's work to a much wider audience than before. Jonathan Greene's Gnomon Press published a new collection of Still's short stories, *Pattern of a Man*. The University Press of Kentucky came out with a paperback edition of *River of Earth*. The *Louisville Courier-Journal* published a two-page feature article by Shirley Williams on Still and his work.

During that time, I unexpectedly became involved in the efforts to enhance Mr. Still's public recognition. While serving as president of the University of Kentucky's chapter of the scholastic honorary organization Phi Beta Kappa, I was engaged in trying to bring a designated Phi Beta Kappa visiting scholar to the campus. Scheduling proved to be a problem, so I began to explore possibilities for inviting someone without national sponsorship. I turned to my neighbor John Stephenson, at that time the university's dean of undergraduate studies, for suggestions on how we might finance such a visit.

John showed me the Williams article and reported that he had been wanting to bring Mr. Still to the campus; he invited Phi Beta Kappa to co-sponsor the visit. I quickly agreed, and in the fall Mr. Still spent two weeks in Lexington during which he appeared in several English classes, spoke to the Fayette County School librarians, met with a group of elementary school student library assistants, and concluded his visit with the Phi Beta Kappa lecture.

I believe this visit to the university was the initial instance of his serving as a visiting scholar at colleges and universities over the following twenty-some years. The visit also established a continuing relationship with the University of Kentucky. Eventually that university awarded him an honorary degree, provided for his papers to be deposited in the university archives, awarded him a medallion from the university libraries, and named in his honor scholarships for teachers enrolled in an Appalachia-based training program.

In 1999, the Lexington Singers commissioned Jay Flippin to compose choral settings of three of Mr. Still's poems and to arrange six others for tenor soloist.

On the evening of Mr. Still's Phi Beta Kappa presentation at the university, he and members of the chapter gathered for a potluck supper. Near the end of that occasion, I stood and somewhat unobtrusively began a procedure that the Phi Beta Kappa members recognized as the ceremony of initiation into the society. My wife had been watching Mr. Still and observed that he seemed to note a change in the atmosphere and character of the occasion but that it took a minute or so before he realized that my remarks were directed toward him — indeed, as a surprise to him that evening we inducted him as the first honorary member of the chapter.

Afterward, Mr. Still declared the recognition to be the finest honor he ever received. He also told me in private that he felt he owed a debt to Phi Beta Kappa. In 1940, Columbia University invited him to be its Phi Beta Kappa poet of the year. That designation would require him to appear at a banquet on the campus and present a poem written for the occasion. Mr. Still declined the invitation because he "didn't have a suit of clothes to wear." Robert Lowell became his replacement.

Still's visit to Lexington also marked the beginning of a nearly thirty-year friendship between the two of us. Often when he came to Lexington on business or for a book signing, we got together for a chat or for dinner. Whenever I traveled near Knott County, I'd stop to visit with him. A few times I journeyed to Hindman just to keep in touch with him.

On one of the Hindman visits, John Stephenson and I spent a couple of hours with Mr. Still at the Settlement School Library. Mr. Still leafed through several file drawers and shared some items with John and me. But more often than not, he would study a scrap of paper, chuckle, and say, "You wouldn't be interested in this," and then return it to the file. John and I were never able to deduce the nature of the items he screened from our sight. On that occasion, I also responded to a request by Mike Nichols, at that time head of the Appalachian college project, to take some photographs of Mr. Still "with his hat off"— most existing photographs of Still showed him wearing one of his many distinctive hats. (Some of my photos of Still appear in this collection.)

One memorable weekend during an extremely dry fall, Stephenson, Gurney Norman, and I drove up to Hindman, in part on a mission to gather information that might qualify Still's log house for listing in the National

Register of Historical Sites. We also responded to Mr. Still's concerns that t he bushes that crowded the house represented a fire hazard. The afternoon of our arrival, the Richardsons from Appalshop stopped by Dead Mare Branch, and we stretched a section of beef ribeye so they could join us for dinner. That evening, Gurney chose to accept the Richardsons' invitation for overnight accommodations in Whitesburg, and Mr. Still returned to his house in Hindman. John and I chose the rustic option: We hauled a couple of old mattresses out of the loft and bedded down for the night in front of the oil heater.

During that visit we learned that the log house, as such, was not as historic as we had thought. When the elder Amburgeys died in the 1930s, the family homestead, which sat down the slope and closer to Wolfpen Creek, was divided between sons Woodrow and Jethro. Woodrow reconstructed his portion into a barn on the south side of Dead Mare Branch (it is now almost completely deteriorated). Jethro, the famous dulcimer maker, used his portion to build the house, which eventually was deeded to Mr. Still. A date, 1937, was scratched into cement by the fireplace, apparently to indicate when the reconstruction took place. We were unable to glean any information on when the original homestead was built; the date 1837 has been mentioned in a couple of places (once by Mr. Still), but that may be an erroneous date confused with the 1937 reconstruction.

Gurney, John, and I spent the greater part of the next day chopping honeysuckle and other invasive shrubs from near the house. Ever after, Mr. Still delighted in claiming the distinction of having three Ph.D.s clearing brush from around his place.

Over the years, I've been able to gain a few insights into Mr. Still's approach to writing. On a number of occasions I've heard him disdain the designation of "poet" or "writer." "I'm just a storyteller," he would say. That he was, and his command of language made him a very good one.

He was also an avid collector of phrases, ideas, and incidents that often found their way into his stories. He constantly jotted notes on scraps of paper and later transcribed them into notebooks. The 23 notebooks were deposited in the University of Kentucky library several years ago, but they have been accessible to the general public only recently.

One can get an idea of the contents of these journals from Still's *Wolfpen Notebooks*. For that publication, Mr. Still selected items from his files and sent them to the students at the Foxfire school in Rabun, Georgia. The students then selected a subset that comprised the primary contents of the book. It's my impression that they were inclined to select the more humorous entries.

Still told me that once he put words to paper he did very little revising, and I've found no evidence in his archived papers to contradict this. He said that the essential part of his composition was mentally turning ideas and phrases over and over in his mind. He committed them to paper primarily to relieve the pressure and to clear his head.

I know of one instance when this process did not produce a result entirely to his liking. In signing a copy of *Wolfpen Poems* for me in November 1986, he wrote:

> For
>
> Linc Fisch,
> Good friend,
> Of mine,
> Of the blossom,
> Of the earth —
> A few of
> them
> people.
>
> James Still

He studied it for a long moment, frowned, and then handed the book back to me, saying, "Here, see what you can make of this...." I'm still pondering on it.

At one time Tawny Acker Hogg and I were considering a publication on Mr. Still. In conversations with us, he told us that his poems "are not just made; they just occur to me and I am really riding herd on them, that's all. I am just ... censoring them as they go down.... I could never just sit down and write something. I can't do it.... I often get in a state of free association — that's the nearest I can come to it and write anything then. I just write 'em; they may not be any good, but you know it just pours out. Then there are times I couldn't write a note to the milkman."

Still was once asked if he had been inspired by Emily Dickinson, whom he greatly admired. He replied, "I wasn't inspired by anybody. I don't have inspirations. Inspirations are usually less than a minute and none of them survives over ten minutes, and it takes longer than that to do anything, you know."

He continued, "As long as I'm writing something, I'm happy. I get a little bit absent-minded.... I am living in a world by myself; I don't know other people exist — except for my comfort and convenience."

Once while Still was at Yaddo, former Yale professor Aleksis Rannit "said that I was a biological writer, that I didn't learn to write, I was born to it. 'We spend all this time in school learning to do these things, but you were born to this.'"

Rannit was one of three writers I've discovered who penned poems to James Still. In 1983, he wrote:

> I hear your tiny
> Cyprinoid fish struggling in the
> Gravelly dying stream,
> And singing praise to the river of word.

> The streaming mountain
> Of the word is
> High,
> And there I see you, Jim,
> Swimming uphill
> Towards the low-voiced
> Ground waters—
> Beyond the mountain.

Kentucky writer George Ella Lyon put it this way in her tribute "For James Still":

> You heard hills speak:
> Gathering stones
> Pressed every leaf
> Dried the heartwood.
>
> Now
> Saved and polished   they shine
> Pieced and quilted   they hold heat
> Tongue and grooved they fit.
>
> We can go home.

In 1989, Margaret Holmes praised Mr. Still in her "The Weaver of Words":

> Your loom of words never idle lies
>   You're the Master craftsman — STILL!
> Threads woven from your magic skein of words—
>   life's joys and sorrows rolled
>   into a ball
> A glowing tapestry creates, with verbal skill.
>
> The colors of your years' experiences are there —
>   the vibrant yellow spring you knew
> When green ideas matured and slowly ripened
>   into rapturous verse.
> The grey of solitude — the birth-pangs of creative thoughts
>   which you could share
>   with few.
>
> Your poet's inner eye, the moments past can recollect,
>   or see beyond this time or place
> And can translate the vision into vivid images
>   that startle with a new
>   awareness.
> How privileged am I to have this sample of the weaver's art
>   you've given
>   with such grace.

Mr. Still was held in esteem by many of his literary colleagues (some of whose comments are included in this volume). Wilma Dykeman and Marjorie

Kinnan Rawlings praised him in their reviews of his books. William Rose Benét endorsed him with a book jacket blurb.

Wendell Berry has said that "James Still is the master of the short story — one who in execution is virtually flawless, in touch and ear so nearly perfect that the difference does not matter.... Still's work claims our interest ... because of his superb storytelling, the richness and subtlety of his understanding of character and his extraordinary clarity of feeling.... We will continue to read [his stories], and to want to read them because they were written by a surpassing artist.... Still is never a collector or researcher — not a sociologist or a folklorist or an anthropologist."

Chris Offutt declares that "even before we met, James Still was my master. Though fifty-two years separated us, we were linked by the great river of literature."

In an afterword to the 65-copy King Library Press limited edition of *River of Earth: The Poem and Other Poems* (1983), John Stephenson wrote, "James Still's life represents a lengthy voyage down a river which is small in its geographic measurements but infinite in the depth and variety of human experience encountered there. On his journey down this river he has stopped often to watch and listen, record & report. His is the journey of the artist-naturalist who enjoys his feelings of wonder about it all. He stops to watch closely the small things which others pass by. He sees the relation-ship of the part to the whole and does not sacrifice detail for generality. He makes notes and sometimes, later, fashions them carefully into story and verse."

Later, Stephenson succinctly characterized Still by saying, "He turns words into windows."

Historian Raymond Betts, who served on the Kentucky Humanities Council with Still, said, "James Still is a man of good measure. In mind and spirit he fits well what he does.... In appearance, in tone of voice, in humor, in general disposition, he is as close to what he writes as any person can be. The word that describes this condition best is a sturdy one: authentic."

At Vanderbilt, Still fell under the influence of the Agrarians (John Crowe Ransom, Donald Davidson, Andrew Lytle, Allen Tate, and others), who read their chapters for the forthcoming *I'll Take My Stand* in the classes he had with them. Still was not considered part of the Nashville Agrarian group, though in many ways he was more qualified than most of them (except for Lytle) to bear the agrarian designation.

James Still had a scientific bent, as well as a literary bent. For a number of years, he tried to develop hybrid wild violets and strawberries, and I also suspect that he experimented with crossbreeding daffodils. He took trips to Central America in several of his later winters in order to study the Mayan civilization. His fascination with mountains and mountain climbing was reflected in a wide shelf of books on these subjects. On several occasions he told me, "I just have to know."

Still commented frequently that he usually spent at least four hours a day reading — often arising early in the morning to do so. "But I don't spend much time reading newspapers," he once told me: "They don't spend much time writing them."

Although Mr. Still didn't have direct access to a research library, he exercised interlibrary loan privileges extensively to obtain literature and resources that he needed. Once when I dropped in on him when he was laid up with a broken toe, I found him sitting up in bed surrounded by six books, all opened to material that he had been working on.

Mr. Still was publishing new works into his nineties, and he expressed pride that virtually everything he had ever published was still in print.

The question naturally arises: Is there material by James Still that is not yet published? The answer is a definite "Yes," although the amount is not known. Most of the short poems he wrote for Christmas and years' ends have not appeared in print. Some of the notes he jotted on postcards to friends while he was traveling are poetic in nature, but they are scattered and no attempt seems to have been made to systematically gather and study them.

My guess is that there are a few longer poems buried somewhere among his papers. The humorous letters and reports on the shenanigans of his notorious prankster "Godey Spurlock," often written while he was traveling with Jim Wayne Miller, appeared in the *Troublesome Creek Times* but have not been generally available.

I know of one longer work by Mr. Still that may yet see publication. One evening, Tawny Hogg and I were visiting with Mr. Still at the log house on Dead Mare. The conversation shifted to Mr. Still's describing a journey that he and a brother took one summer to Texas in the hope of finding work in the cotton fields. They finally settled in with a couple whose young daughter had recently died. As time went on, the couple began to treat Still as though he was their child.

Finally, Mr. Still reached down to an attaché case next to his rocker and pulled out a handful of file folders. "There it is," he said. "Each of these folders is a chapter. I've written it all out in longhand, but I've never even re-read it." (That's another example of his getting a story out of his head by writing it.) The material is being preserved at the Hindman Settlement School, with the intent that at least some of it will eventually be published.

Others who have heard "The Texas Story" have wondered if it's true or fictional. My personal opinion, based on Still's comments, is that it's largely autobiographical, even though distinguishing reality from imagination is often difficult.

Late one Friday afternoon as I was driving home from work, I tuned in to National Public Radio's *All Things Considered* program. To my surprise, I heard Mr. Still's distinctive voice giving his recipe for hush puppies. This turned out to be one of a series of about thirty three-to-five-minute pieces by Mr. Still that went on to air periodically on NPR stations. Kentuckians Noah Adams and Bob Edwards, who were on the NPR staff, probably instigated the series. Most of the pieces were taped in advance at Appalshop, and others were live interviews. Often they featured poems such as "Spring on Troublesome Creek," "Early Whippoorwill," and "Leap, Minnows, Leap." Some were simply stories that Mr. Still related to listeners; few have been published.

Stories, stories, stories...

— About the marriage of his neighbor Mal Gibson's daughter to Broadway producer David Merrick (Merrick's fourth attempt at domesticity). Merrick subsequently invited his new father-in-law to New York, but Gibson was terrified of getting lost in the Big City. He convinced Still to accompany him, and Jim delighted in telling ever after of their celebrity status of just walking up to box offices at 7:45 P.M. and getting choice complimentary seats for any Merrick production that was running.

— About waiting to change trains in Jackson (Breathitt County), Kentucky, in 1941 while on a trip to Florida to visit Marjorie Kinnan Rawlings. A commotion broke out across the street and Mr. Still rushed out and witnessed the point-blank shooting of the sheriff. He commented on this in the letter he had been writing to *Time* magazine, making reference to "Bloody Breathitt." The letter was published in the next issue of *Time*, causing Mr. Still to be especially inconspicuous when passing through Jackson on the return trip.

— About his being on a small plane with the reigning Miss America. Upon stopping at a small town in Georgia, passengers were asked to step aside to allow Miss America to deplane in order to receive the greetings of the welcoming crowd. For some reason, she balked at the last moment, and finally Mr. Still was allowed to step out. The disappointed town mayor nevertheless presented flowers and the town key to Mr. Still, to the accompaniment of a band and the applause of the assembled citizens. This tale about "standing in for Miss America" was a favorite among the NPR audiences when it was aired.

During Still's first stay at the writers' and artists' retreat at the MacDowell Colony, he was paying his participant's obligation to have tea with Mrs. McDowell. By mistake, he entered at the rear door of her house, and the kitchen staff ushered him to the hallway leading to her study. A few steps down the hall he slipped on a throw rug on the highly polished floor. Mrs. MacDowell rushed to help him, and urged him to not be embarrassed. She told him that she had once stumbled on the grand stairway of the Paris Opera House. Her dignity was restored, she said, by a handsome military officer who helped her to her feet and then presented his arm to assist her into the opera hall — and she discovered that was being escorted by none other than Archduke Franz Ferdinand of Austria.

Stories, many stories. Mr. Still was indeed a superb storyteller, often turning obscure events into captivating narratives, and he delighted in telling them to all who would listen.

Mr. Still and musician Randy Wilson developed what Jim liked to call "a dog and pony show." The program sometimes ran to more than 30 minutes and consisted of narrative interspersed with poems and traditional mountain music. The two of them made presentations of it at the Smithsonian Institution, an Appalachian Festival in Italy, a number of colleges and universities, and in other venues. Appalshop produced an audiotape of one version of it.

Mr. Still continued his activity as a visiting scholar on campuses into his eighties. Much of the remuneration he received was devoted to the educational support of Teresa Bradley (now Teresa L. Perry Reynolds). He eventually looked upon her as his daughter and he delighted in serving as surrogate grandfather to her children Jake and Kaila.

Still was always generous with his time, whether visiting with those who came to see him in Hindman or chatting with persons for whom he was signing books in Lexington. One spring, Lou Rice, a friend of mine from Ann Arbor, Michigan, came to Kentucky to revisit Alice Lloyd College, where he had consulted some years before. He invited me to accompany him to Knott County and I suggested that we arrange to meet Mr. Still for lunch. That worked out, and Mr. Still proposed that we then drive to Whitesburg to preview the short film that Appalshop had just produced from one of Gurney Norman's short stories. Following that, Mr. Still suggested that we visit Verna Mae Slone on Caney Creek. We spent a couple of hours with her, chatting about her quilts and viewing the log house she was restoring and furnishing with items from her family home. She described how whenever she needed more money for that project, she would sell a quilt to the Settlement School, where a collection of her handiwork was displayed in the main hall. ("But quilts shouldn't be hung on a wall," Verna Mae wryly told us. "They should be slept under with someone you love.")

Lou's teenaged daughters Claire and Kathy accompanied him on his Kentucky visit, in lieu of a spring-break trip to Florida, and he later reported that they spent most of the return trip to Ann Arbor talking about Mr. Still and what they had learned from him. Whenever I saw the girls in later years, they inquired about him and asked me to give him their regards. Now, many years later, they still speak warmly of their experience with him. That's what I consider enduring education!

James Still's influence is still with us in various ways. I frequently note references to his work or his philosophy in newspapers. Just last week, an op-ed column on stewardship of resources by Pikeville attorney Larry Webster in the *Lexington Herald-Leader* mentioned, "James Still talked about somebody's feet being destined for a certain place."

Perhaps the most popular of Still's recent poems is "Those I Want In

Heaven with Me Should There Be Such a Place." It appeals to readers with its warm humor and nostalgia — until one is brought up short by the five lines following Aunt Carrie's comment,

> Too bad you're not good-looking
> Like your daddy.

Then, in the original version published as a broadside by the Hindman Settlement School and also in the *Appalachian Journal*, it takes a somber turn with

> And my first love, who died at sixteen,
> Before she got around to saying Yes,
> And the one to whom I gave my heart, wholly, unconditionally,
> And there was no return,
> Perhaps there, maybe then.

To my knowledge, Mr. Still did little to clarify these lines, and perhaps few people sought clarification — certainly not I. But in our conversations over the years, I gradually gleaned that the "first love" was a fellow student at Lincoln Memorial University whom Still helped with her studies. They became quite close. At the end of her first college year, she invited him to her home place, not far from the campus, to meet her family. Later in the summer, she became ill and died, leaving Still devastated. An indication of how dear the family held him can be inferred from the fact that several of them visited him in Hindman years later.

Mr. Still revealed even less about the second young lady to whom he was attracted. She came to Hindman and became a ward of the Settlement School, as a number of students did in those days. Still recognized the ethical implications of allowing a relationship between student and teacher to develop, and he took pains to not let it happen. She graduated from the school, married, and had a son. Jim mentioned visiting her grave after her death some years later.

In some subsequent reprintings of the "Heaven" poem, Jim deleted the five lines reproduced above. Perhaps the final decision on his wavering on the matter is indicated by the version that appears in *From the Mountain, From the Valley*, in which lines 17–18 are retained, but lines 19–21 are omitted.

This may be another situation that revealed Mr. Still's guarded stance with regard to certain information, as John Stephenson and I learned that afternoon at the library when we were viewing material from Jim's files.

The last time I drove up to Hindman to visit Mr. Still, it was daffodil season. I chose the time deliberately so that he and I could go out to the log house to view the blossoms of the sixty-some varieties that he had cultivated. But he wasn't up to it that day, so I went out to the log house by myself and found the daffodils in full bloom, row after row of them. I scrounged around for some containers and filled them with branch water from Dead Mare and well over a hundred blossoms. I took them back to Mr. Still in his house in town, overlooking Troublesome Creek. Upon seeing them, his eyes opened wide and sparkled. He borrowed a line from one of his poems and pronounced them "a worldly wonder."

Less than a year later, a multitude of James Still's friends gathered on Troublesome to bid him a last farewell. At one point in the ceremonies, I looked down and saw violets blooming at my feet. Then, just before his casket was locked and lowered into the hillside grave overlooking the Settlement School campus, an impulse struck me and I asked an attendant to slip two blossoms into the casket. He did. It just seemed like the appropriate thing to do for this dear "friend of mine, of the blossom, of the earth" (to return the compliment he once paid me).

Remembrances, many remembrances. My life has been greatly enriched by knowing James Still. Though he has moved on to another world with those he hoped to have with him, his enduring unseen presence fortunately remains with us in this world whenever we open our hearts to his memory and turn the pages of his writing to relive the beauty of his words.

Terrain of the Heart

Lee Smith

Although I don't usually write autobiographical fiction, my main character in a recent short story sounded suspiciously like the girl I used to be: "More than anything else in the world, I wanted to be a writer. I didn't want to learn to write, of course. I just wanted to be a writer, and I often pictured myself poised at the foggy edge of a cliff someplace in the south of France, wearing a cape, drawing furiously on a long cigarette, hollow-cheeked and haunted. I had been romantically dedicated to the grand idea of 'being a writer' ever since I could remember."

I started telling stories as soon as I could talk — true stories, and made-up stories, too. My father was fond of saying that I would climb a tree to tell a lie rather than stand on the ground to tell the truth. In fact, in the mountains of southwestern Virginia where I grew up, a lie was often called a story, and well do I remember being shaken until my teeth rattled with the stern admonition, "Don't you tell me no story, now!"

But I couldn't help it. I was already hooked on stories and as soon as I could write, I started writing them down.

I wrote my first book on my mother's stationery when I was 9. It featured as two main characters my two favorite people at that time: Adlai Stevenson and Jane Russell. The plot was that they went west together in a covered wagon, and once there they became — inexplicably — Mormons. Even at that age, I was fixed upon glamour and flight, two themes I returned to again through high school, fueled by my voracious reading. My book choices proceeded alphabetically: the B's, for instance, included Hamilton Basso, the Brontes.... At St. Catherine's School in Richmond, during my last two years of high school, I was gently but firmly guided toward the classics, but my own fiction remained relentlessly sensational.

At Hollins College, I wrote about stewardesses living in Hawaii, about evil twins, executives, alternative universes. I ignored my teachers' instructions to

Lee Smith, "Terrain of the Heart," The Raleigh *News & Observer*, October 10, 1993. Reprinted with permission.

James Still signing a book for a reader at Joseph-Beth Booksellers, Lexington Green, Lexington, Kentucky. Photograph taken October 9, 1999. Photograph by Linc. Fisch. Used with permission.

write what you know. I didn't know what they meant. I didn't know what I knew. I certainly didn't intend to write anything about Grundy, Virginia.

But then Louis Rubin, my teacher, had us read the stories of Eudora Welty, and a light went on in my head. I abandoned my stewardesses, setting my feet on more familiar ground, telling simpler stories about childhood; though I was never able, somehow, to set the stories in those mountains I came from.

This never happened until I encountered James Still — all by myself, perusing the S's in the Hollins College library.

Here I found the beautiful and heartbreaking novel *River of Earth*, a kind of Appalachian *Grapes of Wrath* chronicling the Baldridge family's desperate struggle to survive when the mines close and the crops fail, familiar occurrences in Appalachian life. Theirs is a constant odyssey, always looking for something better, someplace better — a better job, a better place to live, a promised land. As the mother says, "Forever moving, yon and back, setting down nowhere for good and all, searching for God knows what.... Where are we expecting to draw up to?"

At the end of the novel, I was astonished to read that the family was heading for — of all places—"Grundy."

> "I was born to dig coal," Father said. "Somewheres they's a mine working. ... I been hearing of a new mine farther than the head o' Kentucky River, on yon side Pound Gap. Grundy, its name is."

I read this passage over and over. I simply could not believe that Grundy was in a novel! In print! Published! Then I finished reading *River of Earth* and burst into tears. Never had I been so moved by a book. In fact it didn't seem like a book at all. *River of Earth* was as real to me as the chair I sat on, as the hollers I'd grown up among.

Suddenly, lots of the things of my life occurred to me for the first time as stories: my mother and my aunts sitting on the porch talking endlessly about whether one of them had colitis or not; Hardware Breeding, who married his wife, Beulah, four times; how my uncle Curt taught my daddy to drink good liquor; how I got saved at the tent revival; John Hardin's hanging in the courthouse square; how Petey Chaney rode the flood....

I started to write these stories down. Twenty-five years later, I'm still at it. And it's a funny thing: Though I have spent most of my working life in universities, though I live in Chapel Hill and eat pasta and drive a Toyota, the stories which present themselves to me as worth the telling are most often those somehow connected to that place and those people. The mountains which used to imprison me have become my chosen stalking ground.

This is the place where James Still lives yet, in an old log house on a little eastern Kentucky farm between Wolfpen Creek and Dead Mare Branch. Still was born in Alabama in 1906; went to Lincoln Memorial University in Cumberland Gap, Tennessee, and then to Vanderbilt; and came to Knott County, Kentucky, in 1932 to "keep school" at the forks of Troublesome Creek.

After six years, as he likes to tell it, he "retired" and turned to reading and writing full time. As one of his neighbors said, "He's left a good job and come over in here and sot down."

Last summer he told me he had read an average of three hours a day, every day, for over 50 years. His poetry and fiction have been widely published and praised; his *Wolfpen Notebooks* came out in 1991 from the University Press of Kentucky.

In the preface to that fine collection of sayings and notes he has made over all these years, Still says:

> Appalachia is that somewhat mythical region with no known borders. If such an area exists in terms of geography, such a domain as has shaped the lives and endeavors of men and women from pioneer days to the present and given them an independence and an outlook and a vision such as is often attributed to them, I trust to be understood for imagining the heart of Appalachia to be in the hills of eastern Kentucky where I have lived and feel at home and where I have exercised as much freedom and peace as the world allows.

This is an enviable life, to live in the terrain of one's heart. Most writers don't — can't — do this. Most of us are always searching, through our work and in our lives: for meaning, for love, for home.

Writing is about these things. And as writers, we cannot choose our truest material. But sometimes we are lucky enough to find it.

Remembering James Still

SILAS HOUSE

With the April 28 [2001] death of James Still at the age of 94, a collective grief washed over readers across the nation. However, the mourning was quickly turned into a celebration of Still's remarkable life and career. People like Mr. Still, as he was respectfully called by generations, are immortal. His languid words and strong character will never die.

"He legitimized Appalachian literature," says Mike Mullins, director of the Hindman Settlement School and a close friend of Still. The author of the classic novel *River of Earth*, countless poems, and such children's books as *Jack and the Wonder Beans*, Still had humble beginnings and lived a humble life.

One of Kentucky's most famous and beloved citizens was actually born in the rough hill country of Alabama in 1906. While working on his bachelor's degree at Lincoln Memorial University, Mr. Still worked as a janitor in the school's library, where he claimed that he "read everything I could get my hands on." He went on to earn degrees from Vanderbilt and the University of Illinois.

After graduating, he found his way to the Hindman Settlement School, where he worked as a librarian, and money was tight. According to Mr. Still's own calculations, he spent a six-year period at the school during which he made only 6 cents a day. He moved to a house on Wolfpen Creek, where he has 31 acres, three broken chairs, a small table, an army cot, and two stacked steamer trunks supporting a portable typewriter. Still once said he knew instantly that he "had found a home."

The Writer

In that now-famous cabin on Wolfpen, Still started writing creatively when he was 26 years old. He found inspiration in the landscape and wrote *River of Earth*, which is often compared to Steinbeck's *Grapes of Wrath* and was

Silas House. "Remembering James Still." *Arts Across Kentucky*. Winter 2001, pp. 10–13. Reprinted with permission.

acclaimed by critics throughout the United States upon its publication. The magazines that published Still's work during this time were a writer's dream; his work saw the light of day in such publications as *The Atlantic, Esquire, The Saturday Evening Post,* and *Yale Review.* In that writing, he inspired generations of writers.

"His writing showed me that I could write about my home," novelist Lee Smith says. "When I finished *River of Earth,* I was just stunned. I could hardly believe its beauty. And I couldn't believe that someone had written about the mountains I knew. It just killed me."

"When I discovered that rich imagery and psalmlike rhythms of his poems—which he always referred to as verse, never poetry—they wandered into my memory like Bible verses," says Marianne Worthington, an avid reader of Appalachian literature and an editor at *Now and Then* magazine. "His way of capturing human drama was astonishing."

Shortly after the 1940 success of *River of Earth,* Mr. Still was drafted into the army and served for over three years, mostly in Africa. He came home a changed man. He once said that when he returned from war, "for months I sat in the door of my log house and could not arouse interest in things I had done before." Slowly, he began to return to normalcy and kept on writing, although he never achieved the prolific production he maintained during the 1930s.

Still continued to publish throughout the 1960s, and the mid–1970s saw the appearance of two books, *Way Down Yonder on Troublesome Creek* and *The Wolfpen Rusties,* released by Putnam, but Still's work went largely unnoticed—and mostly forgotten—until 1976, when Jonathan Greene of Gnomon Books published his short-story collection, *Pattern of a Man.* The book instantly caught on with readers, and his work was rediscovered, leading to a well-received reissue of *River of Earth* by the University Press of Kentucky and another story collection, *The Run for the Elbertas.*

By 1995, Still's work had regained such popularity that he was named Kentucky's poet laureate. He spent his later years traveling around the state doing book signings. At the time of his death, the University Press of Kentucky was just about to release his collected poems, *From the Mountain, From the Valley,* edited by Ted Olson. Several book signings had already been set up but were replaced by tribute ceremonies held at the bookstores upon the book's release. Still also spent a lot of his time visiting schools and reading to children. "There was nothing he loved better than to place a book in the hands of a child," says Mullins.

The Man

Although he acquired the reputation of a hermit, living up on Wolfpen Creek, Still was actually a world traveler. He made annual trips to Europe, often visiting World War II battlegrounds, and frequently made trips to Central America, as he was fascinated by Mayan culture. He once made a trip to El Salvador only to find himself in an uprising that was actually the beginning of the country's civil war. Two hundred people were killed in the crowd as Still was pinned against a wall, the only American in sight.

"I think the most misunderstood thing about Mr. Still was the idea that he was a loner. He wasn't," says Sam Linkous, who is editing Still's memoirs. Linkous visited with Mr. Still almost every day. "He was very interested in people and human interaction. He was consumed by the world around him, both close-up and far off. He had so many ideas, about botany and books and human interaction. Mr. Still's humanity always amazed me," says Mullins. "He had an exact sense of fairness, of right and wrong."

Still was a great liberal and often spoke of the government's responsibility to take care of its people. He was appalled by racism and often spoke out in favor of the separation between church and state. He had a great fondness for children and took in many children, calling them "the children of my heart." He grew so attached to one child, in fact, that he eventually adopted her. Teresa Perry Bradley (now Teresa L. Perry Reynolds) was five years old when her own father died, and Still became a surrogate parent to her. After her mother passed away, Still adopted Bradley when she was 32, so he could have an heir.

"He was more than just a writer," says Smith. "He was a man with strong beliefs, and I think people held him in awe for that, as well as for his writing."

The Legacy

James Still will be remembered for many things. Above all, he will be remembered for his writing. But for those who knew him, for those who sat stunned in the audience after he read from his poem "Those I Want in Heaven with Me Should There Be Such a Place," for those who attended his huge birthday celebrations every year at the Settlement School, for those people, Still will be remembered for his humanity, for his ongoing discovery. Once, when a struggling writer asked Still for advice on becoming a writer, Still replied without missing a beat, "Discover something new every day." And it was that belief that led Still to lead a long and happy life.

"I think what I respect most about Mr. Still is that he lived his life just the way he wanted to," says Linkous. "He was an artist who used his art to live the kind of life he wanted to live, to do the things that made him happy."

Still's legacy, according to Mullins, is one of discipline. "He set a standard for writers and for people. He was straightforward and honest. Men like him are impossible to duplicate. And his writing—he could say so much in so few words. He was constantly observing the world."

At Mr. Still's funeral, the word "celebration" came up over and over. Speakers such as Wilma Dykeman, Lee Smith, Gurney Norman, and Loyal Jones spoke of Still and shared his stories. After Still's military burial at the Hindman Settlement School, where he will remain as what poet Jane Hicks calls "the guardian of Troublesome Creek," everyone gathered in the shadow of the mountain bearing Still's burial plot to break bread together. Throughout the crowd, people heaped plates full of food and sat down to share in each other's fellowship. It was a scene that Still would have appreciated: people coming together, asking questions of one another, giving long, drawn out answers. They were learning things about one another, discovering things about themselves.

There was a sense of loss in the dining hall, but more than that, there was a sense of celebration, of memorial. The word "immortal" came up a lot, and people referred to what James Still often said when asked about his thoughts on death: "Death is as natural as sleep," he would say, quoting Benjamin Franklin. "We will arise refreshed in the morning."

Remarks at James Still's Funeral (May 1, 2001)

LOYAL JONES

Being a friend of James Still wasn't easy. He examined every thing you said, and he denied every characterization you tried to lay on him. I once introduced him as a modest man, and he made this observation about an aspect of modesty and humility that had largely escaped both St. Paul and John Calvin: that modesty connotes something to be modest about.

I found and read *River of Earth, Hounds on the Mountain* and *On Troublesome Creek* while I was a college student at Berea, a good while ago. I remember James when he was not at all comfortable with the public. When I invited him to read poems at a Council of the Southern Mountains meeting, he said he didn't do that sort of thing. He was wily, always doubling back on his own track, "slick as a dogwood hoe handle," as one writer put it. He wanted you to know that he was erudite, a reader of the *Atlantic Monthly* and Kenneth Roberts and such, but that he was also "the man in the bushes," who was "smart but had country wrote all over him." We who loved him knew that he was his own best character.

Some saw him as reclusive, but being the recluse took up only a portion of his time. He needed human contact and conversation, and he loved children and being around them. I treasure a Sunday long ago when he called early to invite Nancy and me and our daughters, then eight and ten, to lunch at his house on Wolfpen. I remember Danish ham and green beans from his garden, and a gallon of almonds that he had ordered from California. Susan lay in his hammock to read, and Carol Elizabeth played with his cats. He approved of both.

He was a good poet, seeing things differently from most of us. He made art out of the speech of ordinary people, and he saw strength and purpose in their lives. He watched beleaguered people leave the mountains for better opportunity, and he knew those who chose to stay. Who else would have written of them in this way, so fitting to Kentucky:

"Journey Beyond the Hills"

The wind-drawn manes
And supple knees of the stallions fly the gate
Of hills to smooth meadows beyond the mountain wall;
And the strong mares drink in quivering haste
From the limestone waters, turning their anxious heads
Toward greener shores of grass, toward clattering passings
Of the fleet and proud.

                    Down the mountain lanes,
Down the heavy-hipped ridges stricken and unforested,
They have gone with the streams unhalted and draining
The narrow valleys of the flesh of earth.

O slow the hand and fleet the hoof upon the mountainside
Where men within their prisoning hills have stayed.
Swift are their hearts upon this journey never made.

    I note that James's fellow poet Albert Stewart lay here in this room on April 4, not quite a month ago. James and Albert admired each other's work, but they didn't always get along, as we say. But James, in poor health, was here to pay tribute. He lingered to say this to me, "Our egos got in the way of our long friendship. It happened a long time ago, and it couldn't be helped." There was more that he left unsaid, but his generosity required this much. Indeed, James and Albert were two of a kind — as much their own persons as it is possible to be in this world, and they lived lives on their terms. We are fortunate that they survived into this century to remind us of the value of art, of honesty and integrity, and the need for some such people to be different from the rest of us.

His Side of the Mountains: The Enduring Legacy of Southern Poet James Still

An Interview with Editor Ted Olson

JEFF BIGGERS

In spring 2001, only a few weeks before his final collection of poems was to be released by the University Press of Kentucky, poet, novelist, and essayist James Still died quietly in his adopted mountains of eastern Kentucky at the age of 94. One year later, his enduring legacy as one of the great treasures of Appalachian literature continues to stagger up the Cumberland valleys, whisper on the Blue Ridge mountain fogs, and profoundly influence a new generation of Appalachian and southern writers. On a national level, however, Still's numerous volumes of poetry and prose, including his acclaimed novel *River of Earth*— unquestionably one of the most important American novels dealing with the 1930s— regretfully remain overlooked, like ginseng in the forest, yet to be discovered.

Appalachia has experienced a flourishing of writing over the past decade. It's a fertile and wildly diverse terrain of cultures and traditions that has been cultivated over the past century by a legion of mostly unknown writers; one of their missions has been to provide a glimpse of truth and understanding of one of the most maligned and sullied regions in the States. Tucked back in the hollows of Knott County, Kentucky, though equally adept at traveling "the white highways," no one had a more important role than James Still. With its unabashed lyricism, Still's work chronicled his transcendence among the mountaineers, their cultures, struggles, and land. For more than five decades his log cabin on Wolfpen Creek became a literary shrine for untold waves of writers. He declared in "I Shall Go Singing":

Jeff Biggers, "His Side of the Mountains: The Enduring Legacy of Southern Poet James Still," *The Bloomsbury Review*, July/August 2002, pp 17-18. Reprinted with permission.

> *Until the leaf of my face withers,*
> *Until my veins are blue as flying geese,*
> *And the mossed shingles of my voice clatter*
> *In winter wind, I shall be young and have my say.*
> *I shall have my say and sing my songs,*
> *I shall give words to rain and tongues to stones,*
> *And the child in me shall speak his turn,*
> *And the old, old man rattle his bones.*
> *Until my blood purples like castor bean stalks,*
> *I shall go singing, my words like hawks.*

Still was not alone; Appalachians Jesse Stuart, Don West, and Harriette Simpson Arnow, among several others, also enjoyed fleeting moments of national acclaim and attention for their various writings in the 1930s and 1940s, even though they continued to publish in regional and university presses well into the latter part of the century. The quiet, abiding, hard work of these writers served as streambeds of access for future generations. In a poem also titled "River of Earth," Still spoke of the "flowing script for those who come upon this place":

> *But there are those who learn what is told here*
> *By convolutions of earth, by time, by winds,*
> *The water's wearings and minute shapings of man.*
> *They have struck pages with the large print of knowledge,*
> *The thing laid open, the hills translated.*
> *He least can know of this.*

As their literary offspring, novelists such as Silas House, Chris Offutt, Denise Giardina, Lee Smith, Robert Morgan, and Gurney Norman, and poets Judy Jordan, Ron Rash, George Scarbrough, and Ted Olson, among many others, have been producing some of the best poetry and prose in the country today. Still would have called it a reckoning on Troublesome Creek.

Ted Olson, poet and chronicler of Appalachian life and music, author of *Blue Ridge Folklife*, and editor of the music section of *The Encyclopedia of Appalachia*, worked with Still in editing his last collection of poetry, *From the Mountain, From the Valley*. *The Bloomsbury Review* caught up with Olson last spring for a look back at Still's life and work.

The Bloomsbury Review: Would you describe your first meetings with James Still, and your first impressions of his cabin surroundings tucked along Wolfpen Creek?

Ted Olson: I first met Mr. Still in 1990, when I was a graduate student at the University of Kentucky. He had traveled to Lexington from his home in Hindman, Kentucky, to attend a special event marking the 50th anniversary of the publication of his great novel, *River of Earth*. I had read that novel upon the recommendation of a professor at UK, though I confess I had never heard of James Still before moving to Kentucky in 1988. I liked his fiction right away for its vivid evocations of life in Appalachia, yet I was particularly drawn to his poetry, which I read in a collection of Still's entitled *The Wolfpen Poems*.

That day in 1990, a large audience was moved by the spectacle of actors and musicians portraying scenes from *River of Earth*. It was one of those literary wingdings attended by virtually "everybody who was anybody" in Kentucky letters. The ceremonies that day also included a book-signing event, to which many people brought copies of *River of Earth* for Mr. Still to sign. I was the only one in sight to have brought, instead, a copy of *The Wolfpen Poems*. In my own shy case — not being particularly fond of book signings and their emphasis on mercantilism — that book was my excuse to meet Mr. Still, whose Thoreauvian persona — he lived in an old log house, far from the nearest town — appealed to me. When my turn in the queue came, Mr. Still took my book without really looking up — he seemed shy too, or at least uncomfortable with all the attention — and uttered quietly, "Ah, my verses." Others were waiting, so after he had signed my book and handed it back to me, I said "Thank you" and headed home.

Since Mr. Still was in his mid–80s then, I didn't expect I'd ever see him again. In 1991 I moved to Mississippi to continue my education. In 1995 I wrote and published a scholarly article comparing his *River of Earth* with a far better-known but not necessarily superior depression era novel, Steinbeck's *Grapes of Wrath*. That article apparently caught the attention of a number of people in Appalachian literary circles, including Mr. Still.

In 1998, having accepted a teaching job at a small college in eastern Kentucky not far from Hindman, I learned that Mr. Still was alive and well. That summer I taught Appalachian literature for my college's Upward Bound program. I asked the students to read *River of Earth* as an assigned reading, and they greatly enjoyed it. They wondered if we might invite Mr. Still to our campus to discuss his book. When I phoned him, he accepted the offer without hesitation, confiding that he appreciated the article I had written about his novel. The Upward Bound students — progeny of the same hill-born people he had celebrated in his writings many decades before — found Mr. Still fascinating and reassuring. He was one of them.

And yet he wasn't originally one of them — he was from east-central Alabama, having moved to Hindman in the early 1930s. But his writings reflected his respect for his new neighbors in eastern Kentucky. Mr. Still was not a literary exile, like a number of noted authors from his generation. He was at home everywhere he went, and he traveled frequently. He simply liked eastern Kentucky better than anywhere else, so he kept returning there — much of the time residing in his log house by Wolfpen Creek, at other times living in Hindman.

I first visited Mr. Still at his log house on his 92nd birthday, in July 1998. His longtime employer, the Hindman Settlement School, marked his birthday that year with a public gathering on Mr. Still's lawn at Wolfpen Creek. I recall that the vegetation around the cabin was quite lush that day and yielded a chorus of insects and birds.

I left Mr. Still's home that afternoon thinking to myself, "What an inspiring — what a peaceful — place in which to live and write." Yet Mr. Still didn't technically "own" the log house (in which he had written much of *River of Earth* and many short stories and poems), as a friend of his in the late 1930s had granted him "lifetime rights" for use of the property. What the family of that friend will do with this literary landmark remains to be seen. The last time I was there on the banks of Wolfpen Creek — the morning of Mr. Still's funeral last spring — I noticed that some mobile homes had sprung up not far from the log house.

While Still was still known for his sense of place and rootedness in Kentucky, he was actually quite a world traveler. How do you think his military service abroad and his frequent travels to Central and South American and beyond affected his work?

Mr. Still loved to travel, both within the U.S. and in various other countries. And he was quite proud of his military service during World War II, which took him to Africa and the Middle East. Yet, he told me that the experience of being in a war zone upset his equilibrium, distracting him from his writing. During the 1930s he had rivaled many better-known American writers in terms of literary productivity. The war nearly silenced Mr. Still's literary voice. In his four years of military service he completed just two short stories and one poem: After his return to Kentucky and for the rest of his life, Mr. Still wrote only sporadically. Of course, writing was just one facet of his life; he increasingly spent his time on the other activities important to him. He was always an avid reader on many topics, and one topic of particular interest was Central America. Mr. Still spent many winters there in various countries, exploring and informally studying their cultural history. Yet, his muse must have remained in Kentucky, as he wrote little while on his postwar travels— other than delightful letters and postcards to his friends and loved ones back home.

Wendell Berry once wrote that Still, off the main track of the literary world, became a nearly perfect writer. Do you think he remains relatively unknown to a national readership due to this regional isolation and a certain refusal to mingle among the literati?

Mr. Still is often heralded in Appalachian literary circles as "the Dean of Appalachian Literature," in part for his own literary output and in part for his self-chosen role as a mentor to younger writers from that region. Yet, beyond Appalachia he remains not as well-known as his works merit. Few other American authors have produced oeuvres as memorably yet accurately expressive of their chosen places. Of course, Faulkner and Welty are household names outside of Mississippi; why, then, is James Still's work discussed primarily in

Kentucky and Appalachia and not elsewhere? Well, during the late 1930s and early 1940s, Mr. Still *was* read and appreciated widely, as his first published poems and short stories appeared nationally in many leading literary periodicals. His award-winning 1940 novel, *River of Earth*, was praised by literary critics nationally, and he considered as friends some of the most acclaimed American authors of his generation. Yet, Mr. Still's national reputation slowly faded during the postwar period, the result of several factors: his markedly reduced literary productivity; his choice to remain in eastern Kentucky rather than to gravitate to a literary center such as New York City; and the American reading public's increasing interest in literature that reflected urban and suburban, rather than rural, experience. Mr. Still continued to write, albeit at a much slower pace, during these lean years. Then, in the mid–1970s, his work was rediscovered by participants in the Appalachian Studies movement, eventually leading to the re-publication of virtually all his writings by regional presses. Because his writing identified universalities in regional particularities, and because he had a considerable gift for expressing himself in simple yet eloquent Appalachian English, Mr. Still's work will no doubt interest future readers outside the boundaries of Kentucky and Appalachia.

Still went to great lengths to chronicle the people of Knott County with respect. You once noted that "he resisted preconceived notions; he simply wished to observe that natural and cultural life around him and to reflect upon that world in his writing." In this respect, what type of relationship did Still have with James Dickey, author of *Deliverance*, and other southern writers, in presenting Appalachia to the outside world?

Mr. Still carefully read a lot of authors from different generations, and he counted as friends and correspondents a number of the better-known writers of "serious" literature in 20th-century American literature, including James Dickey. Although often dubbed "the Dean of Appalachian Literature," Mr. Still was uninterested in certain "Appalachian" writing. He had an aversion to writings that rehashed stereotyped notions about the region — whether positive or negative — that were in essence merely 19th-century "local color" writings in modern dress. He preferred writings crafted to the highest literary standards that offered empathetic yet realistic treatments of life in the Appalachian region. Mr. Still identified most, I think, with the larger southern literary renaissance. For instance, he told me that he admired Dickey for his intellectual imagination and his verbal exploration — though I'm sure Mr. Still was appalled by some of the more slanderous representations of Appalachian people in Dickey's novel *Deliverance*.

Was the process of selecting poems from Still's nearly seven decades of work an arduous or enjoyable task? Did you ever feel as if you and/or Still were leaving out or ignoring some critical poems due to space limitations, or, as you once wrote in one of your poems, "on that well-lit road, I choose the wrong route"?

When Mr. Still, the folks at the University Press of Kentucky, and I decided to go ahead with a new volume of his poetry, he was opting for a "selected poems" book — he said he couldn't relate to some of his early poems anymore. I persuaded him that his fans would appreciate the chance to read all his poems, even the formative ones. And that has been the case: Many people who have read *From the Mountain, From the Valley* have communicated to me the titles of their favorite poems, and in numerous cases those are the same ones that Mr. Still did not want to include in the book! *From the Mountain, From the Valley* incorporated every poem that Mr. Still completed during his lifetime (other than a few verses intended expressly for children — those verses were published in various of his children's books). For someone who wrote for seven decades, he did not write many poems. By comparison, numerous other poets every few years publish volumes that are as long as Mr. Still's career-spanning book. He would probably have responded to such an observation by saying wryly that he didn't have much time to write; he had too much living to do. Fortunately, when he did compose a poem, he did so quite memorably!

Author Jim Wayne Miller once wondered, paraphrasing a Katherine Anne Porter review, if Still's fiction was an extension of the experiences that gave rise to his poems. Do you think Still's poetry was unfairly overshadowed or suffered from the success of his fiction, such as *River of Earth*?

James Dickey, in a 1980s letter, stated that he was surprised to learn that James Still also wrote poetry — suggesting that until relatively recently, the literary world thought of Mr. Still primarily as a fiction writer, even though he had initially attracted national attention for his poetry. What might well have contributed to this situation was the fact that upon its publication by Viking Press in 1937, Mr. Still's first published book, the poetry volume *Hounds on the Mountain*, received mixed critical reviews. Meanwhile he was winning major national literary awards for his short stories, which were appearing in leading periodicals. He also needed to make a living, and short stories were more profitable than poems, then as now. Whatever the reasons, after 1937, Mr. Still turned increasingly from poetry to fiction as his primary mode of literary expression. The critical embrace of his 1940 novel, *River of Earth*, further encouraged readers to think of him primarily as a fiction writer. In actuality, Mr. Still's poetry and his fiction were both drawn from the same well — his experience of living in rural Knott County, Kentucky, during the last seven decades of the 20th century.

One of Still's beautiful poems declares, "I shall go singing, my words like hawks." At the age of 94, was he concerned much with the enduring power of his literary legacy, especially within the Appalachian South?

Mr. Still told me that he was surprised by the continued interest in *River of Earth*, and that he attributed the consistently strong sales of that novel to its frequent use in the classroom. In 1998, when I invited him to speak in my classroom, he said rather matter-of-factly that everything he had written was in print "except for a few poems." After some research, I learned that more than a few poems were then unavailable. In late 1999, to address the need that he himself had identified, I wrote Mr. Still a letter offering to help him put together a complete collection of his poems. He agreed to the project immediately, and he eventually participated in nearly every phase of the book's production. Unfortunately, he passed away just weeks before the book was published.

Now, virtually everything he ever wrote—certainly everything he ever completed—is in print. And while Mr. Still was not a particularly prolific author, he left us an oeuvre unequaled in Appalachian literature. Although born and raised elsewhere (and although he might well have become a fine writer elsewhere), Mr. Still will likely forever be associated with the mountains and valleys of eastern Kentucky. His literary voice was powerful (and will remain relevant) because it was, and still is, the voice of a place and its people.

Finally, as a poet and a chronicler of Appalachian life yourself, do you see the experience of editing Still's work as having an impact on your future projects?

An obstacle to writing effectively about Appalachia is the fact that stereotyped notions of the region — whether positive or negative — haunt the American collective unconscious. Appalachia is not a homogeneous place with a monolithic culture, as the American media often portrays. Rather, the region is composed of several geographically distinct sub-regions, each of which boasts different natural and cultural histories. As I discussed in my 1998 book, *Blue Ridge Folklife*, the largely agricultural Blue Ridge fostered a different way of life from that found in, say, the coalfields of the Cumberlands where Mr. Still lived and wrote.

Even people who were born and raised in Appalachia believe modern myths about the region. When I first moved to Appalachia in the late 1970s, I encountered within the academic Appalachian Studies movement a belief that, to accurately characterize Appalachia, "native" voices are more valid than "non-native" voices. Mr. Still's oeuvre suggests that that is not necessarily true. He was not a "native" of the region (considering most boundary definitions of "Appalachia"), yet all his writings reveal a keen awareness of the subtle interplay between culture and nature in his adopted patch of Appalachia. Editing his lifework in poetry—a collection featuring some of the finest poems ever written about Appalachia—convinced me that the most essential attribute of effective "regional" writing is not pedigree but sensitivity.

Reflections on Pappy Still

Teresa L. Perry Reynolds

Good afternoon. It is a privilege to be a meager substitute for the gentleman honored and often referred to as the "Dean of Appalachian Literature."

He once remarked to me that a man shouldn't live to be more than 75 years old — longer than that and he's a burden to everyone and himself. We were blessed that wasn't in the Good Lord's game plan. He only gained notoriety after age 80.

One afternoon at the hospital, he awakened and began to give directions. There were people to call, mail to get out, things to be accomplished, and places to go. There were specifics. He was a man of small words with vast meaning, but a man of precision.

There were certain boxes in the work room going only to the University of Kentucky. Every piece must be touched, read. There were several boxes. There were letters, notes, newspaper clippings, paper clips, scraps of paper, rubber bands, scribbles on hotel note pads, cards, notes on restaurant napkins, gum wrappers, phone numbers, addresses, directions to places with hand-drawn maps, spiders and dead mosquitoes. All important in their own respect.

Those 36 (or so) boxes made their journey from his town house on the campus of the Hindman Settlement School, to my home, and finally to the King Library on the UK campus, just as he wanted. I'm told the collection now measures a vast 60 cubic feet.

Those people who peruse these materials, whether for educational research or pleasure, might find correspondence from Elizabeth Madox Roberts, Marjorie Kinnan Rawlings, or Robert Frost. Or one might find a note from Pappy's neighbor and well-known dulcimer maker, Jethro Amburgey, as an invitation to Sunday dinner. Or, maybe you, yourself, could be found within the boxes.

There is correspondence from Delmore Schwartz, Kenny Rogers, Senator Bill Bradley, and Robert Penn Warren. And, if you're lucky, you might find priceless letters such as from Miss Cleopatra Mathis.

Margaret I. King Library, University of Kentucky, Lexington, Kentucky. Remarks Presented at the Dedication of the James Still Papers, 21 October 2007.

September 13, 1984

Dear James Still,

I tried to find you the night before you left Yaddo, but couldn't. Apparently, you did your laundry after I did mine that evening, and could have taken my black leotard, which I had inadvertently left in the dryer. If you do have it, I would really appreciate it if you would mail it to me. It's cotton and therefore hard for me to replace. Thanks for your trouble.

I hope your return to real life has gone well.

Sincerely,
Cleopatra Mathis

And then, the reply:

September 17, 1984

Dear Cleopatra:

Ye Gods! (Both Greek and Roman)
Under no circumstances will I consider returning the beautiful leotards I purloined from the Yaddo laundry the night of September 4, 1984. How unconsciousably, ungenerous, and inhospitable of you to ask! <u>Finders keepers.</u> They are now thumb-tacked spread-eagle to my bedroom wall where the old goat in me can rejoice at first morning light. And at nap time. Bedtime.

Sorry, dear girl. After all of my seventy-eight years it took a pair of <u>black</u> (ah, black) leotards (cotton, as you say) to bring out the larceny & carnality which were in my soul & loins all along.

Truly
Godey Spurlock
(alias James Still)

P.S. Surely I jest. And so do I. It was the Mark Twain in me. No madam, I never encountered your leotards the evening I dried my pajamas in the basement of Pine Garde. They are probably still there along with the orphan socks usually lying about. Ask Rosemary.

There are letters from family. There is evidence of trips to Iceland, the battlefields of Verdun, London, and the Mayan ruins. There are letters from his Army days, from wintering in Florida, donations to charitable organizations, and frequently, sweepstakes winnings. He was lucky enough to win first prize in a sweepstakes: an all-expense paid trip for two to New York City. I begged, I pleaded, I was usually successful. Not this time. He informed me that my college education was more imperative than a silly old trip to New York. "Who would want to go there anyway?" So, he asked the company if he could get the money instead of the trip. The $5,000.00 check was in the mail.

These papers reflect mainly a private, yet amicable man; a simple, but complex, humble and generous, gentle man. His ways were quiet and loving. However, there might be some present with some tales to the contrary, or maybe I should have said variable experiences.

A few of my tales follow:

1. We (my Mama, Pappy Still, and I) were in my home watching the evening news. When the telephone unexpectedly rang, he picked it up, and said, "Don't you know the news is on?" and slammed it down.

2. From one of his many writer-in-residence jaunts, he brought this sign from Grant Lee Hall:

> ATTENTION GRANT LEE RESIDENTS
> A Famous Author:
> James Still
> will be staying here from 4–6 to 4–16. Please be courteous!

3. On another jaunt, he was to check in at the Holiday Inn in Cincinnati, Ohio. When he arrived on a cold, dark afternoon, he said that it was snowing so hard, it was snowing up! He parked, retrieved his suitcase from the trunk, and went to check in. The gentleman behind the desk asked if he could help.

"Yes," Pappy said, "I have a reservation."

"You do?"

"Yes."

"What's your name?"

"James Still."

The gentleman rose and went to a filing cabinet and rifled through the folders.

"You have a reservation?"

"Yes."

"What was your name again?"

"James Still."

The gentleman turned back to the filing cabinet. Pappy Still waited patiently at the desk. "Are you sure?'

"I'm certain."

"Sir, do you know where you are?"

"Of course, I have a reservation at this Holiday Inn in Cincinnati."

"Sir, you are not at the Holiday Inn. You are at the Cincinnati Police Department."

4. Upon orienting a new physician, Pappy quietly informed the doctor that while it was nice to meet him and engage his services, the good doctor should be aware that Pappy had already outlived seven doctors and two dentists and it may not look too good for him.

5. He once recounted that Lexington socialite Anita Madden told him that only intelligent people had knots on their heads. Then, in the back of her long, black limousine, she proceeded to check his intelligence.

To recount personal stories, at risk, I shall continue. My last Christmas gift was Chanel No. 5 because it was classy, independent; all his magazines said so. One morning, I completed my toilette with a couple of generous spritzes of this classy fragrance and went to Pappy's for breakfast. His meal—buttered toast (made only in the oven and with Land-O-Lakes unsalted butter), two bales of hay (Shredded Wheat), boiled Folger's coffee (with Sweet 'N Low and half and half), and, the kicker, boiled custard with a shot of Maker's Mark—was promptly and elegantly delivered to his bedside. He was sitting on the edge of the bed, in blue Land's End pajamas, with reading glasses and *Courier-Journal* in hand. I kissed him, as always, on the top of the head with a cheerful, "Good morning!"

"What am I smelling?" He asked.

"Breakfast!" I replied.

"No, your fragrance," he said.

"Chanel No. 5," I proudly proclaimed.

"Humph, smells like hot grease."

There was always advice. Like, after pruning, watering, and harvesting habanera peppers, he informed me that it might be best to wash my hands before going to the john next time. Don't use words that you can't spell. Men with hair on their faces might be lazy. While driving, don't eat or use a cell phone because attention should be elsewhere. Never talk to the banker when he's working with your money. And, remember, everyone on the highway, except you, is an idiot.

Among further recollections that crowd my mind are these: Sam and Peggy Linkous' dogs would often go in his kitchen and look in on Pappy. One time he saved Edith Orick from sure and sudden death due to a chicken bone lodged in her throat. During a trip to France, Judi Jennings frantically searched the Verdun battlefield for him, only to find him sound asleep in one of the trenches. And his talking of Molly Bundy's cleaning off her "loaded up" table when company was coming.

I can be sustained with the first verse found in his Sunday school book, dated June 1907. "Cast thy burden upon the Lord, and He shall sustain thee.... He giveth power to the faint" (Psalms 55:22).

I continue to be lost without him ... searching, absent, black, and I am still selfish. Everything, everyone reminds me of him. I can't buy a box of Shredded Wheat again. Buttermilk makes me cry. I still refuse to move the Maker's Mark and cassettes of thunderstorms from the dashboard of his car. His Army dog tags travel with me. I heard that he loved me maybe twice. I didn't need to hear it more. I knew it; I felt it. I absorbed it. I continue to bask in it.

I demonstrated my affection and duty daily. I visited at least three times a day to prepare meals, bring mail, feed the cats, and change sheets. The hospital called me at 2:00 A.M. because he wanted me to brush his teeth. He was not an easy man to please. Some present can attest to this. His freshly laundered shirts had to be promptly ironed, then folded. Further advice was, clean the lint trap in the dryer after each use. Coffee must be boiled. Creamed corn should be mixed with fried green onions. These were the way to do things ... the right way ... his way. I am fortunate that I could do these things for him.

He might call for me to come and hand him a book, one book, out of a wall of 785 books. "Hand me that book."

"Which book?"

"The one I'm pointing to. Right there."

Be aware it was often hard to find him in the bed due to his need to have a book handy. Therefore, the books were many.

Here are some excerpts from his personal journal of a trip south:

> March 11. Back in Florida, at Helen's, I suddenly recalled it was Mama's birthday—Feb. 22nd. Her one hundredth twelfth.
>
> Photographed the sun rising from my window in the Lerida Mission Hotel—the moment of human sacrifice during the day of the Mayan priesthood.
>
> To bus station early afternoon, stuffed ourselves on the vehicle for Progresso. Fare .50 (equivalent). Taxi fare quoted $24.00.
>
> Rented suite in Tropical Suites, facing the beach. John and Sam have loaded the ice box with beer. My room #13.

I share the poem that came to my attention unexpectedly the day of his passing. It appears in *From the Mountain, From the Valley*.

> **I Shall Go Singing**
>
> Until the leaf of my face withers,
> Until my veins are blue as flying geese,
> And the mossed shingles of my voice clatter
> In winter wind, I shall be young and have my say.
> I shall have my say and sing my songs,
> I shall give words to rain and tongues to stones,
> And the child in me shall speak his turn,
> And the old, old man rattle his bones.
> Until my blood purples like castor bean stalks,
> I shall go singing, my words like hawks.

Here is a letter from dear friends to Pappy:

> December 1990
>
> Whenever there is a stillness in the woods and the leaves stop their rattling, and the whole force of the forest stands clean before me I know what you've been talking and writing about all this time. It is about love and hope and solitude, and the beauty of human beings making their way here. It is mostly about love.
>
> Nancy Adams & Jack Spadaro
> Hamlin, West Virginia

Of gatherings, he maintained three points:

> When it starts, it's the right time.
> Whoever comes are the right people.
> When it's over, it's over.

I sincerely thank the King Library, Bill Marshall, and all involved with the transportation, clean up, division, restoration, and archiving of his precious printed materials. Yet another task completed.

Finally, there exists an unpublished James Still manuscript, a precious insight to his boyhood time spent in Texas. It is a pleasure to join with Pappy's literary advisors Bill Weinberg, Lee Smith, and Bill Marshall, to announce that this work is progressing toward publication under the editorship of Silas House. It is extraordinary!

Thank you for being here today.

On the Occasion of James Still's 100th Birthday

HAL CROWTHER

Hal Crowther, a syndicated columnist, essayist, and critic, delivered these remarks at the memorial celebration in honor of James Still's birthday on the campus of Hindman Settlement School on August 2, 2006.

When I first met James Still 20-some years ago, it would have been a great surprise to me, and to him, to learn that I'd be asked to speak on the occasion of his 100th birthday. But for me the greater surprise is that he's not over there rocking and listening to me. If anyone I ever knew seemed as permanent and indestructible as a granite boulder, it was Mr. Still. Of course, there's the possibility that he IS sitting over there—those of you who read Lee Smith's novel *Oral History* remember the last scene, the empty—apparently empty—rocking chair on the porch, rocking and rocking. In my spookiest moments, I've considered that Lee might have the supernatural connections to make that empty chair rock right now, if she chose to, but I don't want to put her on the spot. I remember a few years ago when some of the writers here at Hindman were trying to levitate each other, so I suspect this is an audience sympathetic to the paranormal. If any personality ever haunted a place entirely, before and after the formality of his death, it was Mr. Still at Hindman.

In case you don't own my book *Gather at the River*, I'm compelled to boast that the first blurb on the back of the dust jacket was written by James Still. The second one is from Dolly Parton. And both of these classic Appalachian originals can be found inside. The book includes the essay on Mr. Still that I wrote when he died. On this occasion I'd like to expand on a point I made in that eulogy, where I took issue with something he said to Ted Olson, who edited his collected poems. "My poems don't have much resonance today," Still said, because they describe "a traditional kind of community that hardly exists today."

Hal Crowther, "On the Occasion of James Still's 100th Birthday," *Appalachian Journal*, Winter 2007, pp 186–90. Reprinted with permission.

James Still talking to a group at a book signing, Black Swan Bookstore, Woodland Triangle, Lexington, Kentucky. Photograph taken ca. 1998 by Linc. Fisch. Used with permission.

In the same vein, he once referred to his wonderful stories as "a social diagram of a folk society such as hardly exists today." He was willing to concede, in Olson's words, "that his chosen place had changed and that his time had passed."

James Still's conviction — without regrets or apologies — that he was a creature of another time and place is a conviction that many of us have come to share, many of us who are much, much younger than he was when he came to this conclusion. I'm only a few months older than the trail-bike-riding President of the United States, but the world of small towns, small farms, and small businesses that produced me has been all but buried under strip malls, Wal-Marts, agribusiness, and suburban sprawl. My wife's home town of Grundy, Virginia, has been literally inundated — drowned by the Army Corps of Engineers — and soon to be replaced by a Wal-Mart on a hill. My children are hard-wired to dozens of electronic devices that bewilder and depress me. The typewriter, the tool of my trade that was for 30 years as central to my identity as a mason's trowel or a butcher's cleaver, is to the best of my knowledge no longer manufactured on this planet.

Newspapers and magazines, which provided me with an honorable living, have degraded themselves almost to the level of the TV shows that are killing them, yet they're still losing money, and marked for extinction by wise investors. *The New York Times* is downsizing itself, literally — to a smaller broadsheet to save money on newsprint — and *The Wall Street Journal* has announced that it will sell display ads on its front page. When I attended the national magazine awards a couple of years ago, every magazine that won an award — in other words, every one that publishes journalism admired by its peers — was a publication that loses money. Literature, which I studied in college and have spent decades trying to criticize conscientiously, has become peripheral or irrelevant to commercial publishing.

Worst of all, just about everything I thought I'd learned for sure in the past 50 years — what was right and wrong, true and false, decent and indecent, rational or irrational, honorable or reprehensible — is contradicted flatly, daily, by the current government of the country where I live and vote and pay taxes. Sometimes I feel like a ghost myself, come back to haunt the places where no one would recognize me or anything I embraced or believed. I feel like Rip Van Winkle.

Some of you may empathize. But relevant to the point I'm pursuing is that many of you, perhaps most of you here, are writers. It was one of the great virtues shared by James Still and Wendell Berry, two of Kentucky's most consequential writers during the past half century, that they refused to genuflect, refused to bend their knees to the spirit of the day. Their lack of enthusiasm — in Berry's case, active scorn — for the urbanized, high-tech, high-decibel, wired beehive life of the late 20th and early 21st centuries set an example no serious writer can afford to ignore. Obsolescence was not a thing they feared. They could see, like anyone who stops to reflect, that America is cursed with a popular culture where obsolescence is deliberate and automatic, where the cultural flavor of the week, the day, the hour reigns for such a brief moment that its memory is self-erasing. This society of planned obsolescence is driven by advertising, mass media, celebrity and obsessive over-consumption; if the personality, diversion, or gadget of the moment presented any lasting value, people might not want to let go of it and buy the next thing. The spectacularly popular TV show *American Idol*, which on one occasion attracted a higher voter turnout than the nation's midterm elections, is the last word in pop-culture efficiency because it churns out instant, disposable, interchangeable celebrities at a pace determined by market demand.

My personal hero of the moment, or at least the man who produced the line I've been quoting most often, is a Hemingway; not Ernest the writer, but his son Patrick, the retired big game hunter, who told a reporter, "I don't know what they're going to say about me when I die, but I'll say this much for myself: I'm not a fan, and I'm not a consumer." An epitaph every one of us should covet.

The only writers who prosper in a system ruled by frantic turnover and maximized profit margins are the unscrupulous opportunists of the bestseller list, the human word processors (often teams now, instead of individuals) who scramble to keep up with the publisher's relentless demand for PRODUCT. If they're successful enough, the pressure can become so overwhelming that plagiarism is irresistible. The noxious TV personality Ann Coulter, who publishes crude raw-meat propaganda for the neo-fascist trade, was recently caught red-handed filching a paragraph — word for word — from a newspaper in Portland, Maine, of all places. Dan Brown, of *The Da Vinci Code*, twice sued unsuccessfully for plagiarizing other authors, also stands accused of stealing from a master's thesis. Not long ago, this affluent pair of poachers stood side by side at the top of *The New York Times* bestseller lists.

The literary establishment of 2006 is as different from the one James Still first courted as Wolfpen Creek was different from a gated community on Hilton Head. It was smaller back then, friendlier, more collegial, and more open to cross-pollination, a place where an urban Jewish intellectual like Delmore Schwartz might review James Still's *River of Earth* enthusiastically. It was also, without conscious pretension, much more serious about "Literature" with a capital "L."

Times have changed, as Still, in his old age, so cheerfully conceded. Today, whether you're a literary genius or a willing assembly-line opportunist, the chance that you will get rich or even earn a good living from your writing alone is about the same — and about the same as your chance winning the lottery. Judged by the career of an Ernest Hemingway, whose books earned him fame, wealth, and an enviable place in the literary canon, virtually everyone writing today is doomed to fail. When a writer used to say that selling well was incompatible with writing well, sometimes that was sour grapes; now it's gospel. Americans don't read much anymore, and the books they purchase are not the best ones. Whether your work is commercially published, self-published, or unpublished, no knowledgeable person will assume that any selection on the basis of merit has taken place. How often do you read a review on the coveted book page of *The New York Times*— some gross celebrity memoir or ridiculous pop-culture ripoff, and of course, the reviewer hates it and excoriates it — and you ask yourself, "Why did they review it, then?" And the answer is that it was published by one of the conglomerate publishers that buy the ads that keep *The New York Times* book pages in print.

Writers face the same choice they've always faced — to write for the market or write from the heart. But the grim state of the market has made the choice much simpler, it seems to me. You have almost nothing to lose. Appalachian literature and most of what New York calls "regional" literature has been patronized and treated as if it were obsolete for a very long time now. You could attempt to write for the fashion of the hour and vanish along with it, reaching for a brass ring that's essentially a mirage. Or you can do what every writing teacher preaches like an evangelist, and write what you actually know — write what's in front of your nose. Like James Still, you can be a faithful witness to your time and place. It may sound pompous to declare that you're writing for posterity — for the ages, you might hear a poet say — but the alternative is writing for Madison Avenue, for the German Shysters who own

Random House, for a consumer mass market with a 30-second attention span. For a writer, seriousness—faithfulness—is the pursuit of delayed or even posthumous gratification. Some day in the future readers and scholars—if such creatures still exist—will want to know what James Still wrote about his "folk society," this small world of his that evolved over a period of centuries, with organic links to many earlier centuries. Faithful witnesses are rare; inspired ones like Still are priceless. The current bestsellers and their authors will be naturally or deliberately forgotten, because the worlds they depicted had no roots, no links, no echoes.

"Write what you know" is a sterile discipline if malls, TV shows, gadgets, and chat rooms are the only things you know. It's not impossible that great literature will be written from the strip-mall parking lots, though it's unlikely that I'll read it. Books, good books, may be the only escape from the blind alley of this poisoned and devastated popular culture that's trying to eat our children and grandchildren. In these times, think of writing well as responsibility, rather than a career. Ignore the beehive and all its buzz. Bear witness. Write at the highest, most committed level of which you're capable, and leave the rest, as they say, to a higher power. Art is the fortunate, never inevitable, result of trying passionately to understand the world as you encounter it and to communicate what you find there. Where art occurs, nothing is obsolete, in the final reckoning, except insincerity, mendacity, and sloth. Arguing with Mr. Still's suggestion that his work was out of date, I wrote, "No 'true' story, crafted by a writer of genius, ever becomes archaic. *Moby-Dick* is no less powerful because summer celebrities have replaced Nantucket whalers. *War and Peace* loses nothing because Pierre's lost society of aristocrats lies buried under centuries of social upheaval and disaster."

But then I found a much better quotation, strangely enough in a newspaper in Maine, in an obituary for a wild-looking blacksmith sculptor killed in a motorcycle accident last summer. On the deceased biker's website, the reporter found this line from Ralph Waldo Emerson, one that might apply equally well to the individual and to the words he leaves behind: "Nothing is ever wholly lost. That which is excellent remains forever a part of this universe."

Index

Acquitania 207
Adams, Jack 83, 166, 212
Adams, James Taylor 224
Adams, John 177
Adams, Nancy 296
Adams, Noah 272
Adolphus, Gustavus 164
The Adventures of Huckleberry Finn 94
The Adventures of Tom Sawyer 95
Africa 5, 34, 180, 199, 206, 217, 218, 254, 280, 288
Agrarians 180, 260, 270
Alabama 1, 5, 13, 14, 15, 21, 26, 47, 59, 81, 106, 115, 116, 133, 155, 158, 173, 176, 187, 188, 189, 190, 192, 209, 211, 218, 222, 248, 255, 259, 278, 279, 287
Alaska 160
Alice Lloyd College 180–181, 273
"All Their Ways Are Dark" 6, 100
"All Things Considered" 177, 271, 272
Allen, James Lane 13
Amburgey, Astor 124
Amburgey, Jethro 29, 75, 84, 85, 104, 106, 198, 213, 238, 239, 252, 267, 292
Amburgey, Jim 76, 85
Amburgey, Lausie 115
Amburgey, Lemuel 239
Amburgey, Melvin 85, 199
Amburgey, Monroe 109, 110, 114, 124, 252
Ambergey, Woodrow 85, 267
American Academy of Arts and Letters 8, 23, 175, 249
American Idol 300
American Language 38, 161
American literature 5, 150, 163, 239, 289
The American Short Story 97
American Speech 38, 62, 141, 161
Amherst College 6, 124, 127, 128, 199
Andersonville, Georgia 18
Anglo-Egyptian Sudan 96
Annapurna 96, 101
Antarctica 255
Anvil Press 261, 263
Appalachia 3, 5, 8, 24, 26, 33, 36, 40, 87, 88, 89, 152, 174, 205, 248, 256, 257, 278, 285, 287, 288, 289, 290, 291

Appalachian Book of the Year Award 8
Appalachian culture 3, 9, 181, 256
Appalachian dialect 4, 39–40, 151, 177
Appalachian Festival in Rome 243, 245, 273
Appalachian Journal 1, 262, 274
Appalachian literature 1, 2, 4, 26, 27, 68, 126, 152, 218, 239, 279, 280, 287, 288, 291, 301
An Appalachian Mother Goose 8
Appalachian region 1, 2, 9, 104
Appalachian Regional Commission 26
Appalachian stereotypes *see* hillbilly stereotypes
Appalachian Studies 1, 2, 3, 8, 249, 289, 291
Appalachian Writers Association 8
Appalachian Writers Workshop 264
Appalshop 133, 243, 257, 267, 273
Appleby, Green 19
Arabic (language) 46, 139, 255
Archive of Contemporary History 249
"Are You Up There, Bad Jack?" 55
Army Corps of Engineers 299
Arnett, Willard 104
Arnow, Harriette Simpson 13, 24, 251, 286
The Art Spirit 103
Ashanti Kingdom 216, 217, 254
Asheville, North Carolina 211
Ashland, Kentucky 223, 226
Atlanta, Georgia 20, 49, 78, 82, 135, 142, 160
Atlanta *Constitution* 21
The Atlantic Monthly 5, 6, 28, 39, 49, 55–56, 62, 81, 82, 93, 94, 99, 100, 101, 105, 108, 112, 115, 125, 141, 147, 161, 167, 168, 171, 174, 175, 177, 185, 190, 192, 197, 198, 224, 248, 251, 252, 255, 280, 283
Auburn University 15, 133
Aunt Enore 16
Aunt Fanny 16
Australia 51, 71, 95, 149, 255

Balzac, Honoré de 20, 46, 47
Barret, Elizabeth 257, 259
Barrow, Joe 59
Basso, Hamilton 276
"Bat Flight" 190–191
Belize 24, 51, 95

303

Index

Bellarmine College 14, 249
Bellow, Saul 44, 53
Benét, Stephen Vincent 6
Benét, William Rose 6
Berea, Kentucky 53, 122, 209, 250
Berea College 60, 61, 68, 71, 115, 143, 161, 162, 234, 249, 252, 264, 283
Berea College Press 104, 264
Berry, Wendell 37, 56, 270, 288, 300
Berry College 20
Berryville, Virginia 14, 78
Best, Marshall 25, 128–129, 168
Best American Short Stories 6, 249, 254
Betts, Raymond 270
Bevis: The Story of a Boy 246
Beyond Dark Hills 222, 226
Bible 18, 44, 80, 138, 159, 257, 280, 295
Bierce, Ambrose 181
Bingham, Mary 234
Bingham, Millicent Todd 127
"Birdie with a Yellow Bill" 18
Birmingham, Alabama 20
Birmingham News 20, 211
Bishop, Elizabeth 54
Blazer, Georgia 234
Blue Ridge 285, 291
Blue Ridge Folklife 286, 291
Bogan, Louise 127
Boggess, Carol 2
"The Bonny Blue Flag" 18
Booklist 123
Book-of-the-Month Club 172, 225
Books 7
The Boston Evening Transcript 6
Boys' Life 20, 142
Bradley, Senator Bill 292
Bradley, Theresa *see* Reynolds, Theresa
Bread Loaf Writers' Conference 7, 60, 121, 150, 238, 249
Breathitt County, Kentucky 272
Brickell, Herschel 130
Brontë Sisters 276
Brooks, Cleanth 2
Brooks, Van Wyck 199
Brown, Dan 301
Brown, John Reynolds Woodson 202
Brown, Mattie 203
Brown, Mayme Woodson 202, 203
Brown, Thad 211–212
Brown, Thomas Milburn 202, 203, 204
Brown, Woodson Hodge 202
Bryan, William Jennings 19
Bryn Mawr College 146
Bundy, Molly 295
"A Burned Tree Speaks" 20, 142
"The Burning of the Waters" 126, 252
Byron, George Gordon Lord 139, 160

Cabell County Public Library 223
Cabin in the Cotton 182
Cadle, Dean 1, 2, 8, 33, 34, 254, 262
Calais, France 245
Calvin, John 283
Camden-Carroll Library 230
Campbell, Creola 221
Campbell County, Tennessee 202
Caney College 234
Canterbury Tales 145
Cape Town, South Africa 207
Carr Creek 176
Carter, Roland 222
Caudill, Harry 36
Central America 24, 50, 51, 53, 63, 72, 95, 209, 256, 270, 286, 288
Chambers County, Alabama 5, 14, 15, 16, 18, 20, 21
Champaign-Urbana, Illinois 5, 61
Chattahoochee River 15, 20
Chattahoochee Valley 20, 59, 139, 158, 176
Chaucer, Geoffrey 87, 144, 145, 164, 254
Chaucer and the Mediaeval Sciences 164
Chautauqua 19
Cheever, John 173
Chekhov, Anton 24
Chicago *Daily News* 253
Chicago *Tribune* 234
"Child of the Hills" 82
Children's literature 26, 152–153
The Christian Science Monitor 7
Cincinnati, Ohio 88, 223, 294
Civil War 16, 18, 20, 50, 71, 78, 135, 144, 155, 163, 174, 210, 255
Civilian Conservation Corps 83
Clark, Eleanor 54, 150, 170, 180
Clay County, Kentucky 202
Cleopatra 19
Coal Miner's Daughter 76
Coleridge, Samuel Taylor 90
Colliers 198
Colorado State University 253
Columbia University 23, 199, 266
Combs, Josiah 146
Combs, Ocea 239
Conrad, Joseph 81, 141
Cornett, Terry 257
Cosmopolitan 117
Costa Rica 53, 95
Coulter, Ann 301
Council of the Southern Mountains 283
Country Gentleman 46
Cox, Hyde 128
Crane, Stephen 127
Creason, Joe 249–250
Crowther, Hal 2, 5
Crum, Claude Lafie 2
Cumberland Gap 14, 20, 78, 211, 278
Cumberland Gap, Tennessee 81
Cumberland Mountains 21, 161, 285, 291
Cumberland Plateau 4, 5
Cumberland University 181

Curry, Walter Clyde 144, 164, 189
The Cyclopedia of Universal Knowledge 18, 44, 80, 138, 159

Daddy Long Legs 19
Damon and Pythias 19
"Dance on Pushback" 77
Daudet, Alphonse 165–166
Davidson, Donald 180, 270
The Da Vinci Code 301
Davis, Bette 182
Dead Mare Branch 28, 29, 75, 77, 84, 102, 104, 114, 116, 125, 147, 149, 195, 196, 197, 208, 237, 238, 250, 254, 259, 267, 271, 275, 278
"The Dean of Appalachian Literature" 2, 5, 288, 289, 292
Deliverance 289
Depression Era *see* Great Depression
Detroit, Michigan 59, 88
Dialect *see* Appalachian dialect
Dickey, James 179, 289, 290
Dickinson, Emily 90, 127, 268
Dickinson, Porter 127
The Dollmaker 24
Double Branch Farm 15, 78, 136, 155
Douglas, William O. 128
Dover, England 245, 246
Dowe, Mal 41, 116, 119
"Dreams" 6
Dreiser, Theodore 144
Duke, Benjamin 61, 143, 163
Duke University 61, 143, 163, 228, 261
Duncan Field 172
Dykeman, Wilma 24, 256, 263, 269, 282

Early English Text Society 144, 164
"Early Whippoorwill" 272
Eastern Kentucky University 234
Edel, Leon 174
Edman, Irwin 1
Edwards, Bob 201, 202, 272
Egypt 208
El Salvador 24, 34, 51, 95, 209, 256, 281
Elizabethans 87
Emerson, Ralph Waldo 163, 177, 302
The Encyclopedia of Appalachia 286
England 134, 167, 179, 180, 242, 243, 245, 246, 293
English ancestry 14, 138
Eritrea 173
Eskimo 95, 157, 210
Esquire 6, 56, 76, 168, 177, 280
Ethiopia 173
Europe 280

Fairfax, Alabama 19, 47, 81, 140, 160, 162, 209, 220, 222
Fairfax High School 20, 81
Fairfax Towels 160

Farm and Fireside 79
Farrell, James T. 68
Father Goriot 20, 46
Faulkner, William 70, 103, 107, 108, 192, 288
Fayette County, Kentucky 233
Federal Emergency Relief Administration 30, 148
Fielding, Henry 181
Finnegans Wake 25
Fisch, Linc. 268
Fitzgerald, F. Scott 148
Flaubert, Gustave 116
Fletcher, John Gould 7
Flippin, Jay 266
Flood, Charles B. 174
Florence, Italy 243
Florida 16, 50, 62, 88, 127, 130, 144, 171, 272, 293
Foley, Martha 254
Foretaste of Glory 229
Fort Hood 15, 78, 140
Fort Thomas 172
Fox, John, Jr. 3, 13, 257
Foxfire 40, 86, 157, 267
France 179, 180, 243, 245, 246, 276
France and England in North America 178
Francis, Robert 7, 60
Frankfort, Kentucky 8, 105, 106, 108, 249
Franklin, Benjamin 282
Franklin, Georgia 78
Frederick County, Virginia 59
Freedom Award 228
French writers 165
Freud, Sigmund 164
From the Mountain, From the Valley: New and Collected Poems 6, 201, 203, 274, 280, 286, 290, 296
Frontier and Midland 101
Frost, Robert 6, 7, 34, 54, 71, 119, 124, 127, 150, 199, 253, 292
The Fugitives 144, 163, 180
"The Function of Dreams and Visions in the Middle English Romances" 144

Gather at the River 298
"George's Mother" 127
Georgia 14, 15, 18, 59, 70, 77, 82, 158, 272
Georgia Tri-Weekly Constitution 79
Gibson, Mal 85, 124, 125, 272
Giles, Janice Holt 111
Gnomon Press 8, 249, 262, 263, 265, 280
Gogol, Nikolai 24
Gold, William Jay 7
"The Golden Nugget" 80, 159, 188
Gorbachev, Mikhail 179
Graham, Barney 32, 83
Granberry, Edwin 100, 101
Grand Tetons 96
The Grapes of Wrath 76, 254, 277, 279, 287

Index

Great Depression 3, 4, 5, 28, 31, 32, 56, 74, 81, 85, 140, 160, 177, 212, 254, 259
Great Lakes Naval Training Station 227
Great Plains 174
Green, Paul 7
Greene, Graham 256
Greene, Jonathan 2, 263, 265, 280
Greenup County, Kentucky 219, 226, 238
Gregorian chants 75
Grey, Zane 35, 46
Grover, Edwin 100, 101
Grumbach, Doris 151
Grundy, Virginia 277, 278, 299
Guatemala 24, 51, 95, 256
Guggenheim Fellowships 7, 60, 131, 151, 199, 219, 225, 249, 253

Hale, Elizabeth 221
Hammer, Carolyn 261
Hancock, Joyce 263
Hardy, Thomas 81, 141, 161, 181
Harlan County, Kentucky 32, 53
Harper's 225
Harrogate, Tennessee 5, 14, 20, 189, 203, 236
Harvard University 88, 146
Hatfield-McCoy feud 142
Hawaii 276
Hawthorne, Nathaniel 81
Hazard, Kentucky 86, 92, 146, 176, 178, 238
Head o' W-Hollow 222
Heard County, Georgia 26
The Heart Is a Lonely Hunter 60, 131
Heflin, "Cotton Tom" 19
Hemingway, Ernest 70, 300, 301
Hemingway, Patrick 300
Henri, Robert 103
"Heritage" (poem) 69, 71, 152, 187
Heritage (cassette) 133
Herzog, Maurice 96
Hiawatha 157
Hicks, Jane 282
Higgs, Robert J. 27
"High Field" 68
Highlights for Children 136
Hillbilly stereotype 4, 9, 87, 88, 291
Hillfolk 28
Hilton Head, South Carolina 301
Himalayas 51, 71, 96
Hindman, Kentucky 5, 21, 28, 58, 73, 75, 98, 103, 107, 109, 113, 117, 124, 126, 127, 146, 148, 162, 176, 181, 186, 187, 192, 197, 223, 236, 237, 259, 266, 273, 274, 286
Hindman Settlement School 4, 5, 8, 28, 31, 49, 58, 61, 62, 71, 74, 75, 83, 84, 87, 91, 98, 104, 106, 113, 125, 145, 146, 148, 149, 152, 160, 162, 165, 167, 176, 177, 178, 182, 185, 190, 193, 196, 212, 218, 219, 222, 223, 226, 230, 241, 248, 251, 259, 261, 264, 266, 273, 274, 275, 279, 282, 287, 292, 298

Hindman Settlement School Writers' Workshop 240
Hogg, Tawny Acker 268, 271
Hollins College 141, 276, 277
Holmes, Margaret 269
Holy Land 207
Honduras 24, 95, 256
Hooper, Johnson Jones 20
Horticulture 29
Hounds on the Mountain 6, 28, 50, 93, 94, 100, 108, 109, 114, 127, 131, 167–168, 177, 187, 188, 190, 198, 222, 238, 248, 261, 263, 283, 290
House, Silas 2, 286, 297
The House by the Medlar Tree 262
House of the Sparrow 39
Hoyle, Edmond 46
Hudson, W. H. 181
Hull, Helen 103
Huntington, West Virginia 223
Hutchison, Percy 1

"I Love My Rooster" 227
"I Shall Go Singing" 285–286, 290, 296
Iceland 179, 180, 293
I'll Take My Stand 144, 260, 270
Illinois 235
"In the Mountains" 13
Indiana 88, 235
Institute of American Letters 152
International Oral History meeting 242
Ironton, Ohio 219
Irwin, "Puss" 19, 59
Italy 170, 243
Ives, Marion 221

"Jack and the Beanstalk" 26, 153, 249
Jack and the Wonder Beans 8, 26, 177, 181, 249, 256, 279
Jackson, Kentucky 103, 176, 272
Jackson, Stonewall 18
James, Henry 165, 174
James Still: Critical Essays on the Dean of Appalachian Literature 1, 2
James Still Room 30, 68, 148
Jarrett Station, Alabama 20, 81, 140, 158
Jefferies, Richard 181, 243, 245, 246, 247
Jennings, Judi 295
"Job's Tears" 101
Johns Hopkins University 255
Jones, Carol Elizabeth 283
Jones, Edith 222
Jones, Loyal 2, 36, 264, 282
Jones, Nancy 283
Jones, Susan 283
Jonesville, Virginia 58, 78
Jordan, Judy 286
"Journey Beyond the Hills" 284
Joyce, James 25, 35
Judge Norman house 19, 157
June Appal Recordings 133

Index

The Kaiser, the Beast of Berlin 19
Kantor, MacKinlay 18
KayZee, Kentucky 86
Keats, John 46, 131, 139, 160, 256
Kentucky 1, 3, 4, 5, 8, 13, 14, 21, 30, 49, 50, 56, 57, 61, 73, 98, 111, 126, 130, 146, 148, 166, 177, 179, 185, 187, 192, 194, 195, 212, 213, 216, 218, 222, 224, 228, 233, 234, 235, 238, 248, 251, 254, 256, 262, 265, 278, 279, 285, 286, 288, 289, 291, 300
Kentucky Arts Council's Milner Award 8
Kentucky Book Fair 263
Kentucky Education Association 225
Kentucky Educational Television 63, 69
Kentucky Historical Commission 29
Kentucky Humanities Council 242, 270
Kentucky Poetry Review 249
Kentucky River 85
Kentucky Writing 229
Key West, Florida 253
King, Joe 88
King Library Press 270
Kingdom Come Creek 257
Knott County, Kentucky 3, 4, 5, 13, 21, 23, 26, 29, 30, 32, 49, 53, 83, 101, 121, 126, 129, 130, 145, 170, 192, 193, 195, 196, 208, 212, 219, 222, 223, 227, 233, 234, 235, 238, 248, 252, 259, 262, 264, 266, 273, 278, 285, 289, 290
Knoxville, Tennessee 176, 177, 179, 181, 202
Knoxville Dickens Society 181
Knoxville *News-Sentinel* 256
Kohler, Dayton 8, 128
Kroll, Harry Harrison 36, 38, 39, 47–48, 142, 181, 182, 222, 229
Ku Klux Klan 19
"Kubla Khan" 91

Lackland Air Base 172
Lafayette, Alabama 15, 16, 17, 19, 21, 78, 136, 155, 157, 158, 160, 219, 236
LaFollette, Tennessee 202
Lanett Cotton Mill 158
Lappert, Carl 159
La Salle 178
Latin (language) 211
Lawson McGhee Library 176, 182
"Leap, Minnows, Leap" 272
Lee, Laura 77
Lee, Robert E. 174
Lee County, Virginia 78
Lee: The Last Years 174
Letcher County, Kentucky 29, 112, 130, 148
Letters from My Mill 166
Lexington, Kentucky 8, 51, 105, 107, 108, 117, 118, 125, 154, 213, 261, 266, 273, 286
Lexington *Herald-Leader* 273
Lexington Singers 266
Library of Congress 83, 97
Life on the Mississippi 40

Lincoln, Abraham 235
Lincoln Herald 161, 163
Lincoln Memorial University 5, 14, 20, 38, 47, 48, 49, 55, 60, 61, 81, 82, 83, 139, 140–141, 143, 144, 161, 162, 167, 176, 182, 189, 197, 203, 211, 212, 219, 220, 221, 227, 228, 229, 230, 233, 234, 236, 248, 249, 261, 274, 278, 279
Lindsey, Carrie Jackson 14, 78, 137
Lindsey, James Benjamin Franklin 14, 137, 138, 162
Lindsey Wilson College 234
Linkous, Peggy 295
Linkous, Sam 281, 295
Littcarr, Kentucky 85, 103, 110, 113, 193
Little Carr Creek 28, 75, 76, 84, 85, 102, 147, 197, 253
Little Folks 188
"Little Red Riding Hood" 153
The Little Shepherd of the Kingdom Come 257
Little Women 95
"local color" writing 3, 289
log house 29, 84, 181, 182, 267, 279, 283, 287
Longfellow, Henry Wadsworth 163
Look Homeward, Angel 107
Loomis, Guy 61, 83, 143, 144, 163, 212
"Lorena" 18
Louis, Joe (Barrow) 16, 19, 59
Louisville *Courier-Journal* 149, 249, 250, 265, 295
Louisville, Kentucky 14, 51, 105, 131, 154, 170, 234, 243, 249, 251
Louisville Public Library 107
Lowell, Robert 266
Lyon, George Ella 269
Lytle, Andrew 270

MacDowell Colony 7, 97, 131, 150, 249, 272
Madame Bovary 116
Madden, Anita 294
The Made Thing 91
Mademoiselle 110
Malamud, Bernard 109
Malraux, Andre 190
Man O' War 213
"Man O' War" (poem) 54
"A Man Singing to Himself" (essay) 4
Man with a Bull-Tongue Plow 222, 223, 237, 238
Manning, Ambrose 27
Marcoot, Alabama 16, 135
Marjorie Peabody Award of the American Academy & Institute of Arts and Letters 8
Marshall, Bill 297
Maryville College 181
Mason, Bobbie Ann 66
"A Master Time" 113
Mather, Cotton 150–151
Mather, Increase 150–151
Mathis, Cleopatra 292–293

Matterhorn 96
Mayan civilization 24, 51, 72, 95, 270, 293
Mayan culture 8, 52, 71, 281
Mayking, Kentucky 86
McCamey, Louise 222
McClelland, Stewart 227
McCullers, Carson 7, 59, 60, 70, 131, 150, 253
McLendon, Clyde 17
McRoberts, Kentucky 85
A Member of the Wedding 60, 253
Men of the Mountains 222
Mencken, H. L. 38, 62, 161
Merrielees, Edith 121
Mexico 24, 51, 95, 256
Mexico City 51
Middle East 5, 199, 288
Middle English (language) 144, 145, 164
Middlebury, Vermont 151
Middlesborough, Kentucky 117, 163
Miller, Cotton 149
Miller, Jim Wayne 2, 61, 173, 211, 213, 214, 242, 271, 290
Millstone, Kentucky 86
Mims, Edwin 189
Miner, Ward 107
Missionary Baptists 137, 162
Mississippi 287, 288
Missouri 58
Mobile, Alabama 20
Moby-Dick 302
Montgomery, Alabama 78
Morehead, Kentucky 5
Morehead State University 2, 5, 8, 30, 39, 56, 68, 107, 108, 115, 148, 149, 154, 216, 218, 228, 229, 230, 249, 251
Morgan, Robert 286
Mormons 276
Mount Holyoke College 146, 167
The Mountain Herald 203
Mountain Life and Work 104, 229
mountaineering 8, 96
Mousie, Kentucky 86
"Mrs. Razor" 27, 71, 116, 123, 199, 255
Mullins, Jasper 89
Mullins, Mike 75, 242, 251, 261, 279, 280, 281
Murfree, Mary Noailles (Charles Egbert Craddock) 3

Nashville Chamber of Commerce 128
Nashville, Tennessee 5, 32, 61, 83, 132, 145, 166, 189
The Nation 28, 30, 56, 62, 171, 190, 223
National Public Radio 54, 177, 201–202, 207, 271
National Register of Historical Sites 267
"The Nest" 73, 91, 92
New Farm 37
New Mexico 190
New Orleans 16, 78, 149, 172

The New Republic 6, 28, 30, 56, 171, 190, 223
New York City 82, 107, 143, 144, 148, 177, 190, 272, 289, 293, 301
The New York Herald Tribune 7
The New York Times 30, 107, 174, 299, 301
The New York Times Book Review 1, 147
The New Yorker 62, 147
Newsweek 52, 58
Nichols, Mike 266
Nile River 208
Niles, Rena 250
Nixon, Suzie 75
Norman, Gurney 2, 27, 242, 263, 266, 267, 273, 282, 286
North Carolina 190, 223
Now and Then 280

O. Henry Memorial Prize Stories 6, 38, 100, 101, 190, 192, 197, 199, 248
Oates, Joyce Carol 66
O'Connor, Flannery 180
"Ode to the Confederate Dead" 90
Offutt, Chris 270, 286
"Old Black Joe" 19
Old Regular Baptists 40, 85, 150
Old Southwest humor 20
Olson, Frank 202
Olson, Ted 201, 202, 280, 286–291, 298, 299
"On Defeated Creek" 38, 100, 101
"On the Passing of My Brother Alfred" 21
On Troublesome Creek 6, 7, 101, 177, 198, 222, 238, 249, 253, 262, 263, 283
Oral History 298
The Oregon Trail 95, 178
Organic Farming 37
Orick, Edith 295
Oxford University 242
"Ozymandias" 19

The Palaces of Sin, or the Devil in Society 18, 44, 80, 139
Palmer, Winnie 222
Paris Opera House 272
Paris Review 50, 57
Parks, William Lee 148–149
Parton, Dolly 298
Pasternak, Boris 122
Pattern of a Man and Other Stories 6, 8, 38, 40, 177, 204, 249, 262, 263, 265, 280
"Pattern of a Writer: Attitudes of James Still" 1
Peabody Award of the American Academy and National Institute of Arts and Letters 151, 175
Peden, William 97
A Penny's Worth of Character 229
Percy, Walker 151
Perkins, Carl (Congressman) 234, 235
Perrin, Alfred 53, 151, 209, 250
Perry County, Kentucky 32, 130

Peterborough, New Hampshire 7
Petersburg, Virginia 78
La Petite Chose 166
Phi Beta Kappa 23, 199, 265, 266
Phillips Exeter 146
Pigeon Roost Creek 16
Pigman, Faris 124
Pike County, Kentucky 53
Pikeville, Kentucky 273
Pineville, Kentucky 122
Pippa Passes, Kentucky 180
Poet Laureate of Kentucky 8, 280
Poetry (periodical) 6, 28
Polynesia 95
Popular Library 249
Portelli, Alessandro 243
Porter, Katherine Anne 7, 50, 53, 54, 60, 103, 110, 131, 150, 253, 290
Porterfield, Miss 17, 18, 79, 210
Portland, Maine 301
Pound, Ezra 91
Pratt, Dan 145
Precious Bane 93
Primitive Baptists 137, 162, 255
Putnam and Sons 249, 280

Rabun County, Georgia 73, 267
The Railsplitter 219
Random House 302
Rannit, Aleksis 268
Ransom, John Crowe 144, 164, 189, 270
Rash, Ron 286
Rawlings, Marjorie Kinnan 6, 70, 129, 130–131, 253, 269–270, 272, 292
Reader's Guide 223
Reagan, Ronald 179
Reavy, George 122
Red Bird Mission School 202
Redbook 117
Red Fox, Kentucky 253
Redmond, Dare 211–212
regional writing 70
The Return of the Native 181
Revolutionary War 14, 59, 78
Reynolds, Mary Chaney 202
Reynolds, Theresa 273, 281
Rice, Anne 66
Rice, Lou 273
Richardson, Josephine 263
Richmond, Virginia 276
"A Ride on the Short Dog" 39, 41, 112, 113, 116, 119, 123, 238–239
"A Ride with Huey the Engineer" 226
Ripton, Vermont 7
Ritchie, Anne Campbell 243
Ritchie, Don 243
Rite of Spring 140
River of Earth (novel) 5, 6, 7, 8, 20, 24, 25, 27, 28, 29–30, 32, 33, 34, 36, 39, 40, 41, 42, 49, 50, 59, 62, 65, 69, 71, 76, 84, 94, 100, 103, 107, 114, 116, 128, 132, 137, 147, 148, 149, 150, 166, 171, 174, 177, 179, 192, 198, 205, 222, 230, 238, 248, 249, 253, 254, 259, 262, 263, 265, 277, 278, 279, 280, 283, 285, 286, 287, 288, 289, 290, 301
"River of Earth" (poem) 286
River of Earth: The Poem and Other Poems 6, 270
River of Words 2
Robert Frost Room 6
Roberts, Elizabeth Madox 13, 24, 34, 54, 93, 166, 168, 292
Roberts, Kenneth 283
Robinson Crusoe 95
Rockcastle County, Kentucky 166
Rogers, Kenny 75, 292
Rollins College 100
Rome, Georgia 20, 49, 82, 143, 160
Roosevelt, Franklin D. 226
"Rose of Alabama" 18
Rowan County, Kentucky 86
Rubin, Louis 277
"The Run for the Elbertas" (short story) 33, 41, 65, 92–93, 99, 105, 115, 119, 121, 126, 129, 168, 252
The Run for the Elbertas (short story collection) 6, 8, 177, 263, 280
Rush Strong Medal for Truth 36, 83, 143, 163
Russell, Jane 276
Russian writers 24
Rusties and Riddles and Gee-Haw Whimmy-Diddles 153

Sahara 96
St. John's College, Oxford 243
St. Paul 283
"Sairy and the Younguns" 126
Salmon, Charlotte 221
San Antonio, Texas 140, 172
San Francisco, California 217
San Francisco *Chronicle* 1
San Francisco Public Library 217
San Salvador 34, 209, 256
Sandburg, Carl 101, 181, 227
Saratoga Springs, New York 7, 150, 151, 170, 180, 213
Saroyan, William 103
The Saturday Evening Post 5, 49, 50, 56, 62, 110, 171, 177, 186, 190, 191, 198, 227, 280
Saturday Review of Literature 6
Saturday Review Treasury 103
Scandinavian writers 24
Scarbrough, George 286
Schaeter, Harry 234
"School Butter" 113
Schubert, Franz 75
Schwartz, Delmore 6, 254, 292, 301
Science News 71, 165
Scotch-Irish ancestry 14, 59, 138
Scotland 225

"The Scrape" 35, 38, 100, 101, 105
Scribner's 147
Sears Roebuck 142, 160, 165
The Sewanee Review 28, 56
Sewanee University (University of the South) 164
Shakespeare, William 35, 36, 107, 139, 160, 189, 193
Shawmut, Alabama 20, 46, 80, 81, 139, 158, 159, 211
Shelley, Percy B. 46, 131, 139, 160
Sherman, William Tecumseh 18, 78, 135
Ship of Fools 150, 253
Singer, Isaac Bashevis 64
"The Sled" 126
Slone, Verna Mae 273
Smith, Al 63
Smith, Bern 85
Smith, Herb. E. 2
Smith, Hiram "Shorty" 112, 114
Smith, Lee 2, 280, 281, 282, 286, 297, 298, 299
Smith College 83, 146, 167
Smithsonian Institute 273
Social Forces 27–28
"Sonnets for Summer" 225
South America 288
South Atlantic Modern Language Association 8
South Carolina 33
South Sea Islands 51
Southern Authors' Award 6, 107, 148, 192, 198, 248
Southern Cultivator 79
Southern Fiction Writer Award 8
Southern Literary Messenger 6
Southern literature 26
Spanish Civil War 190
Spadaro, Jack 296
Sporty Creek: A Novel About an Appalachian Boyhood 8, 20, 25, 40, 41, 65, 66, 156, 249, 263
"Spring on Troublesome Creek" 272
Spurlock, Godey 41, 91, 112, 116, 119, 271, 293
Stamper, John M. 112, 113, 114, 116, 125, 131
Stamper, Sam 112, 113, 114
Stanford University 111
Steinbeck, John 103, 168, 254, 279, 287
Stephenson, John 64, 264, 265, 266, 267, 270, 274
Stevenson, Adlai 276
Stevenson, Robert Louis 18, 80, 210
Stewart, Albert 284
Still, Alfred Taylor 15, 21, 58, 78
Still, Annie McLendon 14, 78, 155
Still, Don 15, 16
Still, Elloree 15, 16, 80
Still, Inez 15, 16, 17, 79, 210
Still, James Alexander 14, 15, 16, 17, 46, 79, 133, 135, 138, 155, 158, 210

Still, Lois 15
Still, Lonie Lindsey 14, 15, 16, 17, 59, 78, 79, 135, 155, 158, 188, 210
Still, Nixie 15
Still, Tom Watson 15, 16
Still, William Comer 15, 16, 209
"The Stir-Off" 104
"Stopping by Woods on a Snowy Evening" 119
Story 126, 190
Stravinsky, Igor 140
Stuart, Jesse 8, 13, 38, 39, 60, 82, 110, 122, 177, 185, 189, 219–232, 236–239, 248, 251, 261, 286
Stuart, Naomi Deane Norris 221
Sue Bennett College 181
Suggs, Simon 20
Swindon, England 243

Talladega Mountains 16, 133
Taps for Private Tussie 238
Tate, Allen 90, 270
Taylor, Archer 27
Ten Great Professors 164
Tennessee 32, 47, 60, 95, 140, 179, 182, 202
Texas 4, 14, 15, 49, 78, 82, 140, 190, 271
Thackeray, William Makepeace 181
Thomas, Dylan 256
Thomas, Riar 41
Thomas, "Uncle Ed" 84
Thompson, Randall 127
Thoreau, Henry David 29, 163, 177, 193, 259, 287
"Those I Want in Heaven with Me Should There Be Such a Place" 6, 21, 153, 201, 273, 274, 281
The Thread that Runs So True 236
"The Three Little Pigs" 94
Tibet 71, 96, 255
Tierra del Fuego 95, 255
Tiffin, Ohio 237, 238
Time (periodical) 6, 103, 147, 223, 226, 249, 272
The Time of Man 24, 93, 166
Trask, Katrina 180
Trask, Spencer 180
Treasure Island 20, 46, 80, 95
Trees of Heaven 222
"Trip to Czardis" 100
Trojan War 108
Troublesome Creek 30, 31, 77, 83, 91, 130, 177, 192, 265, 275, 278, 282
The Troublesome Creek Times 181, 213, 271
Turgenev, Ivan 24, 165
Turner, Marie 103
Tuscaloosa, Alabama 20
Tuskegee Airmen 218
Tuskegee Institute 218
Twain, Mark 24, 40, 94, 181, 256, 293

Uffizi Gallery 243
Uncle Jolly 20, 36, 41, 42–43, 65
Undset, Sigrid 131
Union College 234, 242
Unitarians 128
United States Army Air Force 62, 97, 149, 180, 199, 207, 216, 238, 254, 288, 293
University of California 163
University of Cincinnati 72
University of Florida 13
University of Illinois 5, 47, 49, 61, 83, 144, 145, 158, 164, 165, 189, 197, 212, 219, 248, 279
University of Kentucky 2, 28, 37, 56, 57, 68, 70, 71, 149, 168, 177, 181, 205, 206, 242, 261, 262, 263, 265, 266, 267, 286, 292
University of Memphis 182
University of North Carolina 61, 143
University of Pennsylvania Medical School 178
University of Rome 152
University of the Sorbonne 146
University of Wyoming 249
University Press of Kentucky 8, 68, 148, 201, 249, 263, 265, 278, 280, 285, 290
Upward Bound 287

Vance, Wash 86
Vanderbilt University 5, 32, 38, 47, 48, 49, 60, 61, 83, 143–144, 145, 150, 162, 163, 164, 177, 180, 189, 197, 212, 219, 228, 233, 248, 259, 261, 270, 278, 279
Van Gogh, Vincent 104, 115, 194
Van Winkle, Rip 300
Vassar College 83
Verdun, Battle of 245, 246, 295
Verga, Giovanni 262
Veterinary Journal 159
Viking Press 5, 25, 28, 49, 84, 93–94, 127, 128, 147, 171, 190, 198, 290
Virginia 14, 78, 141, 276
Virginia Quarterly Review 5, 28, 62, 112, 190, 192
Volk, Darren 75

W-Hollow 219, 226, 230
Wade, John Donald 144, 163, 180
Wal-Mart 299
Walden Pond 259
"Walking the King's Highway" 15
The Wall Street Journal 300
War and Peace 302
Warren, Robert Penn 13, 50, 53, 109, 144, 150, 164, 170, 180, 292
Washington, D.C. 44, 82, 139, 142, 227
Way Down Yonder on Troublesome Creek: Appalachian Riddles and Rusties 8, 40, 153, 250, 280
Wayne, John 66
Weatherford Award 249, 250, 251

Webb, Mary 93
Webster, Jean 19
Webster, Larry 273
Weeks, Edward 39, 82, 93, 115
Weinberg, Bill 297
Weinberg, Lois Combs 203
Well Springs 202
Wellesley College 83, 146, 259
Welty, Eudora 60, 150, 277, 288
West, Connie 83
West, Don 38, 39, 49, 60, 61, 82, 83, 145, 166, 212, 224, 225, 226, 286
West, Robert 2
West Virginia 179
Westminster Abbey 181
Westpoint Manufacturing Company 139
Whitesburg, Kentucky 69, 112, 113, 133, 257, 260, 262, 263, 273
Whitman, Walt 81, 131
Whitney, Betty Brown 202, 203, 204
Wigginton, Eliot 75
Wilbur, Richard 127
Wilder, Tennessee 32, 83
Williams, Anne 261
Williams, Cratis 36, 213
Williams, Shirley 265
Williams, Wayne 261
Willis, Henry 225
Wilson, Edmund 81
Wilson, Peter 1
Wilson, Randy 150, 152, 205, 264, 273
Wilson, Woodrow 18
Winchester, Kentucky 127
Wind Publications 2
Winter Park, Florida 100, 101
Wisconsin 88
Witherup, William 261
Wolfe, Thomas 6, 70, 107, 192, 198, 248
Wolfpen Creek 5, 7, 28, 75, 84, 85, 104, 147, 177, 181, 182, 242, 253, 267, 278, 279, 280, 283, 285, 287, 288, 301
"Wolfpen Creek" (poem) 260
The Wolfpen Notebooks: A Record of Appalachian Life 8, 77, 263, 267, 278
The Wolfpen Poems 6, 147, 177, 264, 268, 287
The Wolfpen Rusties: Appalachian Riddles and Gee-Haw Whimmy-Diddles 8, 40, 153, 177, 254, 280
Woodbridge, Hensley 229
Wordsworth, William 131, 160, 190
The World of Psychoanalysis 27
The World of William Faulkner 107
World War I 19, 20, 135, 142, 172, 245, 246, 293, 295
World War II 5, 7, 15, 24, 34, 62, 88, 96, 107, 171, 180, 206, 216, 217, 218, 227, 228, 240, 254, 259, 281, 288
The World Within: The Creative Mind Dealing with Psychiatric Materials 27
Worthington, Marianne 280

The Writer 223
Writers at Work 50
The Writer's Book 103
Writer's Digest 117

Yaddo 7, 44, 54, 60, 121, 150, 151, 173, 180, 213, 249, 293
The Yale Review 8, 28, 33, 56, 62, 65, 112, 145, 177, 190–191, 192, 248, 251, 262, 280

Yale University 163, 268
The Yearling 253
Yenni, Julia 39
Yorkshire, England 246
You Can't Go Home Again 6, 107, 248
Youth's Companion 80, 136
Yucatan 51, 95, 179

www.ingramcontent.com/pod-product-compliance
Lightning Source LLC
Chambersburg PA
CBHW051209300426
44116CB00006B/488